Why Public Service Matters

Why Public Service Matters

Public Managers, Public Policy, and Democracy

Robert F. Durant

palgrave
macmillan

First published in 2014 by
PALGRAVE MACMILLAN®
in the United States—a division of St. Martin's Press LLC,
175 Fifth Avenue, New York, NY 10010.

Where this book is distributed in the UK, Europe and the rest of the world,
this is by Palgrave Macmillan, a division of Macmillan Publishers Limited,
registered in England, company number 785998, of Houndmills,
Basingstoke, Hampshire RG21 6XS.

Palgrave Macmillan is the global academic imprint of the above companies
and has companies and representatives throughout the world.

Palgrave® and Macmillan® are registered trademarks in the United States,
the United Kingdom, Europe and other countries.

ISBN 978-0-230-34149-4   ISBN 978-1-137-06957-3 (eBook)
DOI 10.1057/9781137069573

Library of Congress Cataloging-in-Publication Data

Durant, Robert F., 1949–
    Why public service matters : public managers, public policy, and
democracy / Robert F. Durant.
        pages cm
    Includes bibliographical references and index.

        1. Civil service—United States. 2. Public administration—United
    States. I. Title.

JK692.D87 2014
351.73—dc23   2014012093

A catalogue record of the book is available from the British Library.

Design by Newgen Knowledge Works (P) Ltd., Chennai, India.

First edition: October 2014

10 9 8 7 6 5 4 3 2 1

This book is dedicated to past, present, and future members of the career civil service, their teachers, and the leaders among them.

Good and able Men [and women] had better govern than be gover'd, since 'tis possible, indeed highly probable, that if the able and good withdraw themselves from Society, the venal and ignorant will succeed.

—Judge John Tyler

Contents

Illustrations

Preface

When I arrived in Knoxville in 1977 to enroll in the Master of Public Administration program at the University of Tennessee, I was fortunate to meet many persons who had vivid memories of the Tennessee Valley Authority's (TVA) origins, aims, and early accomplishments. Some had even come from afar to the Tennessee Valley in the 1930s to join TVA, having heard the "call of public service" in the midst of the Great Depression. Their aim was to be part of Roosevelt's "New Deal" vision to improve the life chances of people in this then-flood-ravaged, disease-prone, and economically disadvantaged area of the country.

No doubt, many were motivated partially by the availability of employment in an era of job scarcity. But many also expressed a poignant desire to be involved in something larger than themselves—a sense of common purpose enunciated by a president in a wheelchair who was trying to lift a region—and nation—from its economic, social, and political knees. My conversations with several who had answered that call also emphasized a "citizen-centric" view of being a public manager. TVA's first board chairman, David Lilienthal, famously called this a commitment to "grassroots democracy." Part of that commitment for the civil servants at TVA, I was told, meant being careful not to alienate local citizens. One of my first professors, Robert Avery, once told a personnel class I was taking that this meant not insulting the local population with displays of wealth that might be alienating to them, including not going overboard with the size of the house in which one lived or the car one drove.

Subsequent scholarship on TVA's aims and approaches has demonstrated how that spirit changed in negative ways during the ensuing decades. What was lost, researchers claimed, was both the public interest-oriented regional conservation mission of the agency and its heralded citizen-centric focus. By the time I was writing my dissertation on TVA's travails as one of the nation's worst environmental polluters (which later became my first book, *When Government Regulates Itself: EPA, TVA, and Pollution Control in the 1970s*), the agency was reviled by many Tennessee Valley residents as an unresponsive, aloof, and arrogant "power company" that had gone astray. Today, this sense of citizen estrangement and the erosion of support for TVA are partly responsible for a significant contraction of TVA's workforce. In fact, one of its fabled twin-tower headquarters buildings in Knoxville that once was full of TVA employees is now leased to private occupants.

By the eve of the twenty-first century in America, disillusionment with TVA's mission and management philosophy was hardly unique. Ascendant as well was a commensurate erosion of public support for government generally, as well as for public agencies and the career civil servants who worked in them. What Herbert Kaufman in the 1980s called a "raging pandemic" of discontent had begun in the 1970s in the wake of the Vietnam War and the Watergate crimes of the Nixon administration.[1] However, it was also the product of a sustained assault on government "bureaucrats" by elected officials—including presidential candidates and incumbents of that office—and commentators from all wings of the political spectrum. They were portrayed, on the one hand, as incompetent, lazy, and self-interested Caspar Milquetoasts and, on the other, as ingenious Machiavellians bent on feathering their personal and agency nests at the expense of the public interest.

As you are no doubt aware, the decibel levels of this raging pandemic are more high-pitched than ever in the twenty-first century. Although the Great Depression of the 1930s sparked government activism to cope with, if not counter, market failures, recent events such as the terrorist attacks of September 11, 2001, and the Great Recession of 2007–09 have spawned upticks in approval ratings that quickly dissipated in today's 24-hour (or less) news cycles. Moreover, the antigovernment rhetoric, coarseness of political debate, embrace of libertarianism by many in the millennial generation, and allure of isolationism to a war-weary public seem to have sidelined any sense of common purpose. Indeed, doubt about the capacity of government, its institutions, and its civil servants to meet policy challenges abounds in the United States, and talk of America's decline as a world leader is common. The botched 2013 launch of the Patient Protection and Affordable Care Act of 2010 only helped aggravate this discontent.

It was against this leitmotif of policy challenges, national malaise, and bureaucracy-bashing that I decided to write *Why Public Service Matters*. I hope the book helps to convey to you as a potential, new, current, or returning university student contemplating a career as a public manager the same sense of import, purpose, and nobility of a career as a civil servant that animated those former TVA employees I met nearly four decades ago. I also hope that you leave its reading with a fuller appreciation for the critical role that public managers have played and must continue to play if America is ever to reach its full promise as a democratic republic. And I hope you finish the book more excited about a career in public service than you were when you first thumbed its pages.

Why Public Service Matters, however, is no paean to the unerring virtue of public agencies and the career civil servants working within them on the public's business. As you will see, their shortcomings are not glossed over, many of which have fueled opposition to activist government and the flames of citizen estrangement from it. Also eschewed is a romanticized version of how easy it will be to meet today's and tomorrow's public service challenges, choices, and opportunities.

Chronicled instead is how today's policy challenges require public servants to be even more talented and rooted in democratic constitutional values than their predecessors. This, as they are pressed to *reconceptualize* agency purposes to fit these new challenges better, *reconnect* with an estranged public while doing so, *redefine* administrative rationality to heighten their effectiveness, *reengage* existing resources and find new sources of revenue, *recapitalize* personnel assets, and *revitalize* a sense of common purpose infused with democratic constitutional values. A commitment to democratic constitutionalism means nurturing those aspects of American government and politics that have democratized the original constitutional design of a democratic republic.[2]

Nor does *Why Public Service Matters* leave you with only a list of challenges, choices, and opportunities to ponder. It starts from the premise that falling short not only jeopardizes the instrumental goals of government to make a positive difference in the lives of citizens, but it also puts at risk the sense of government legitimacy upon which our democratic republic depends. Thus, the book offers suggestions for dealing with the realpolitik of adapting agencies to new policy challenges in the domestic, international, and "intermestic" policy arenas without losing sight of the unique role they play in a democratic republic. As such, it is relentlessly historical, strategic, and normative in content, tone, and aim.

Why Public Service Matters also differs in several ways from many otherwise excellent introductions to the field of public administration. For starters, it explicitly links policy with administration. Thus, the book seeks to redress an unfortunate distinction made in the founding years of the study and practice of public administration in the early twentieth century. As Camilla Stivers argues, too often "means eclipsed policy ends, or came to be seen as [the] ends" of the profession.[3] Many introductions to the field today do not explicitly embrace that distinction but implicitly do the same by decoupling administrative means from policy ends. In doing so, they unintentionally can make prosaic what is an incomparably meaningful, intrinsically rewarding, and exciting profession.

Why Public Service Matters also differs from a variety of introductions to public administration by offering a concise, digestible, and accessible overview of the public service "forest" before, during, and after you encounter the "trees" of your coursework. To these ends, it is written in a conversational tone that seeks to engage the reader better in the narrative story being told. With the noblest of intentions, a tendency exists in most introductions to cram every last detail of the many subfields of public administration into a single book. No newcomer to the field can digest all this in a semester. Besides, individual courses will later offer in-depth views of those subfields. With this in mind, this book instead gives a sense for why the program you choose requires the courses it does, how and why the seemingly disparate coursework you take reflects a coherent whole, and how the subject matter in various subfields of the profession is adjusting to calls for change.

In addition, *Why Public Service Matters* is among a very limited set of introductions to our field that offers you a consistent overarching framework for analyzing it. It is called a "6R" framework, because it reflects the six pressures on public agencies to adapt to today's public policy challenges noted earlier (reconceptualizing purpose, reconnecting with citizens, redefining administrative rationality, reengaging resources, recapitalizing personnel assets, and revitalizing common purpose infused with democratic constitutional values). This framework will show you in uncommon ways how these pressures—both domestic and international—are affecting six critical tasks that public managers must perform today: aligning strategy with structure, shooting the political rapids, informing policy decisions, linking people to public purposes, stewarding a nation's treasure, and networking in the shadow of hierarchy. In the process, rather than have you drill deeply into individual subfields in a stovepiped fashion (one at a time), this book will mix topics in ways that show you how these subfields must be integrated in practice. Seasoned readers of the book accustomed to particular public administration topics being discussed in traditional subfield "stovepipes" will thus need patience!

Finally, although *Why Public Service Matters* discusses how all three sectors—public, private, and nonprofit—play major roles in governance in America, it is written for persons contemplating, entering, or considering becoming a public manager and leader in the career civil service at any level of government. To be sure, public service can be performed by members of private and nonprofit organizations, especially in today's net-worked state. Indeed, the critical role of managers in these cross-sectoral networks will be emphasized throughout. However, with the graying of the baby-boom generation and public agencies' increasing competition for the best and the brightest, a focus on the unique contributions that one can make in a career as a public manager is what is most needed today. Nor will this focus shortchange you academically if, for example, you are contemplating a career in the nonprofit or private sectors. Your career may, after all, take you to multiple sectors. Short of that, to be successful as a government contractor or nonprofit grantee, you must understand why public agencies act as they do, the forces to which they are trying to adapt, and the remedial avenues open to them.

Any book of this kind incurs a number of debts. I wish to thank Editor Brian O'Connor at Palgrave Macmillan for his patience, encouragement, and suggestions as this project got bogged down in my unexpected administrative duties as interim chair of the Department of Public Administration and Policy in the School of Public Affairs at American University. Thanks as well to Susannah Ali, Karen Baehler, Dan Fiorino, Patrick Malone, Ed Stazyk, and David Pitts of American University, as well as Ed Kellough of the University of Georgia, Rosemary O'Leary of the University of Kansas, and William West of Texas A&M University, for their extremely helpful comments on an earlier draft. Any remaining errors or misinterpretations, of course, are mine alone. Special thanks as always to my wife, Jennifer, for her careful editing of the manuscript as it shrank to manageable proportions and her tireless support in assuring me that I really could finish this project when I seriously doubted it. Finally, thanks to all the career civil servants—past, present, and future—who have kept the ship of state at all levels of government in better shape than we deserve under trying circumstances, anti-government rhetoric, and personal sacrifice. It is to these heroes, the leaders among them, and those who have taught them that I dedicate this book.

RFD
Washington, DC

CHAPTER 1

Engaging the Call to Public Service

This is both an exciting and challenging time for you to be thinking about starting, continuing, or returning to a career as a public manager. Our very idea of what public managers in the career civil service do as public servants, how they do it, whom they do it with, and what knowledge, skills, and values they need to be successful has undergone profound change. What has *not* changed, however, are the core values that citizens in a democracy expect from their public servants, including efficiency, effectiveness, representativeness, responsiveness, accountability, equity, constitutional rights, and due process.[1] The rub is that we are still trying as a field to discern how best to meet the challenges, choices, and opportunities that these changes occasion without jeopardizing those core values of a democratic republic.

Since you are reading this book, you have already either embraced the idea of public service or want to see what it means to embrace such a commitment as a public manager at any level of government in the United States.[2] Thus, one aim of this book is to help you see the myriad connections between what you will do as a public manager and the ability of the United States to address its most challenging public policy problems in the twenty-first century. A second goal is to help you gain a sense for the exciting challenges, choices, and opportunities that await you as a career civil servant in our democratic republic. A third aim is to give you a realistic sense for the challenges and implications for our democracy of making these adaptations and, thus, to show you why public management today requires the recruitment and retention of persons with unprecedented talent and a special calling to public service. As Peter Drucker writes, "One does not 'manage' people. The task is to *lead* people" (emphasis added).[3] Finally, in an era of citizen estrangement from government, this book aims to alert you to the role public managers must play if our commitment to democracy in America is to wax rather than wane in the twenty-first century.

Our journey begins in this chapter with a review of how beliefs about the nature, the skills, and the best way to pursue a calling to public service have evolved since the nation's founding. Introduced in the process will be a variety of topics, issues, and dynamics that we will cover in greater detail later in this book. You will leave the chapter appreciating how the definition of public service in government agencies has evolved in the United States. Also clear to you will be how our changing definition of who qualifies for public service, what training or education they require, and for what purposes they labor cannot be separated from the socioeconomic, political, and cultural environment of the day. With this as historical context, we will turn to the substance and logic of six major challenges facing public managers today and how these challenges will be front and center for you during your career. We will conclude by previewing the remainder of the book.

So You Want to Help Run a Constitution?

Our review of the evolution of the concept of public service in the United States has to begin with the nation's unique political culture. Some politicians and pundits today call this uniqueness "American exceptionalism," and they use the term inaccurately to mean that the United States has a kind of moral superiority over other nations, that it is immune from challenges faced by other nations, or that the nation is predestined for greatness. These are *not* the meanings attached to it here. Rather, our reference is to a set of values that Americans hold dear—at least rhetorically—and that have been translated into the relatively unique political system you will operate in as a public manager. These values include a preference for limited government, individualism, states' rights, equality of opportunity, and markets. These—and, most especially, limited government—are reflected in the Madisonian system of separation of powers, checks and balances, and federalism.[4] Thus, when thinking about how changes have occurred in the definition of public service, its purposes, who does it, and how one prepares for it, you must think in terms of three pivotal eras that also had to come to terms with this cultural and institutional legacy: after a so-called "era of gentlemen," these are the patronage state era, the administrative state era, and the networked state era.[5] In the patronage state, public service jobs were viewed as mundane and, thus, ripe for rewarding campaign supporters. In the administrative state, civil service positions were viewed as too important to leave to patronage and, thus, best filled on a merit basis. In the networked state, the authority for decision making has been diffused to a variety of public, private, and nonprofit organizations but with the government still first among equals and held accountable for results.

Toward the Patronage State: Beyond the Era of Gentlemen

If you were considering a public service career during the founding era of this nation, you might have either been advantaged or disadvantaged by your economic, racial, or gender status in society. Ascendant for the federal government was a belief that only the best and the brightest could discern *and* administer the affairs of the new nation in order to create a national—rather than state-based—sense of identity. Public service was thus a calling or vocation for "gentlemen," or as Washington put it, for people of "fit character"— namely, the well-heeled, educated, and connected white male gentry. Politics, however, did play into appointments to the extent that regional representation was deemed prudent for gaining allegiance to the new national government.

No greater exemplar of a public servant exists than Cincinnatus, the reluctant, simple, and virtuous Roman citizen who left home and hearth several times to serve his country before always voluntarily relinquishing power. And what power was envisioned during the presidencies of Federalists George Washington and John Adams! Each embraced the necessity of what Alexander Hamilton called "energy in the executive" in opposition to the fear held by anti-Federalists of the concentration of power in the executive and national government. In state and local governments, in contrast, Americans' fears of centralized power largely meant neutering the administrative capacities of chief executives, such as governors and mayors. Idolized in American imaginations were New England town meetings where citizens debated and addressed the issues of the day. Yet, here again, the class, gender, and racial biases of the day limited public service to white, property-owning males. In fact, the sense of entitlement held by the landed gentry produced an informal system of incumbents passing on their positions at death to their eldest sons! So, depending on your family tree, the odds of you successfully pursuing a public service career were either flush or minimal.

Launched in reaction to these biases, perceptions of elitism and government excesses by the Federalists in (among other things) the Alien and Sedition Acts during the Adams administration, and related scandals was a more egalitarian (albeit still white male-dominated) and prosaic view of public service. But this move toward what is called the "spoils" or "patronage" system would not be institutionalized until the inauguration of Andrew Jackson in 1829. To be sure, party considerations played a role earlier. Following Adams—who pursued a partisan-focused, upper-class appointment process favoring Federalists—President Thomas Jefferson found his "gentlemen of fit character" almost exclusively among fellow anti-Federalist Republicans.

All this changed, you will learn, when a largely uneducated and poorer "frontier" constituency in the newly settled states west of the Appalachian Mountains catapulted Jackson to the presidency. Reflecting the interests of his political base, Jackson argued that an upper-class-based public service with de facto "property rights" to jobs was not only intolerable in a democracy but also reduced the responsiveness of government to the general public. For Jackson, what your coursework will call "rotation-in-office" was necessary to correct this situation and "democratize" the public service. Put most bluntly by Democratic senator William Marcy at the time, rotation-in-office meant "to the victors of elections go the spoils" of appointing their supporters to government jobs. Out went the "rascals" of the defeated party in government and in came appointees of the victorious.

Jackson argued that "no one man has any more intrinsic right to official station than another."[6] Nor was an upper-class bias in staffing these positions necessary, because public service jobs *admit of being made*, so plain and simple that men of intelligence may readily qualify themselves" for the performance of the roughly 20,000 positions available.[7] Often, the "admit of being made" phrase was left out of Jackson's statement by patronage critics. In reality, he justified his position in a fundamental principle of bureaucracy that you will learn in your coursework—the "division of labor"—arguing that rotation would help diminish any negative side effects on government operations: "Labor was to be divided, tasks defined, jobs simplified."[8] "In this system, individuals could be placed or replaced [after an election] without upsetting the integrity of the whole."[9] Animated by this principle, Jackson removed over 250 persons of the opposite party from office during his two presidential terms, more than all his predecessors combined.

Begun in this fashion, the spoils system accelerated in the ensuing years. This occurred as the Whig Party—staunch opponents of patronage until 1840—discovered the virtues of spoils once its own candidates captured the White House! Under presidents James Buchanan and Abraham Lincoln, for example, roughly 53,000 positions were available by the end of the Civil War, while approximately 131,000 positions were available for patronage appointments by the time of President James Garfield's assassination in 1881.[10]

As Theodore Lowi points out, this trivialization of public service produced a "patron-age state" bent on promoting a "commercial republic."[11] The latter aggressively promoted economic development through government funding of internal improvements, subsidies, contracts, tariff protections on imported goods, public land disposals, and patents to encourage innovation. If that meant helping one's friends, allies, and political patrons first to government largesse or jobs in what Daniel Carpenter calls a "clerical state," what harm was there?[12] So, were you seeking a public service career in the federal government, your allegiance to the party in power and implicit (but, hopefully, not enthusiastic!) tolerance of their mischief would determine your fate.

Nor, however, were patronage jobs limited to the federal government. No scholar has ever afforded a more evocative summary of this era in state and local government than that written by Pulitzer Prize–winning novelist William Kennedy. In his novel *Roscoe*, fictional Albany, New York, party machine leader Felix Conway indoctrinates his son and heir Roscoe in the finery of the city's real-life, patronage-based machine known as Tammany Hall:

> How do you get the money, boy? If you run 'em for office and they win, you charge 'em a year's wages. Keep taxes low, but if you raise 'em, call it something else. The city can't do without vice, so pinch the pimps and milk the madams. Anybody that sells the flesh, tax 'em. If anybody wants city business, thirty percent back to us. Maintain the streets and sewers, but don't overdo it...Keep the cops happy and let 'em have a piece of the pie. A small piece...When in doubt, appoint another judge, and pay him enough so he don't need to shake down the lawyers...Control the district attorney and *never let him go*; for he controls the grand juries...Make friends with millionaires and give 'em what they need. Open an insurance company and make sure anybody doing city business buys a nice policy...Give your friends jobs, but at a price, and make new friends every day...anybody on our payroll pays us dues, three percent of the yearly salary [what were called "political assessments"], which is nice. But if they're on that new civil service and won't pay and you can't fire 'em, transfer 'em to the dump.[13]

Indeed, this view of "public service" stretched across levels of government. Federal agencies—such as the Agriculture Department, the Interior Department, the Postal Service, and the Treasury Department—became satrapies of state and local political machines and members of Congress throughout the Gilded Age of the late nineteenth century. With public land, custom house, and other financial corruption scandals rife and attributable to machine politics, however, harbingers of successful proposals for civil service reform came from President Rutherford B. Hayes during the 1870s and after the election of Garfield in 1880.

Hayes appointed Carl Schurz, a reform advocate, to head the Interior Department, where he instituted a merit system for hiring. Garfield was a compromise candidate nominated on the 39th ballot of the Republican Party convention and elected with only the reluctant support of the so-called "Stalwarts" of his party who—like New York state party boss and US senator Roscoe Conkling—supported the spoils system. Upon taking office, he felt that the time consumed in meeting individually with patronage seekers diverted him from governing. From 10:30 am to 1:30 pm each day, he met in the White House with office seekers who one administration official characterized as "beasts at feeding time" and who Garfield said "would take my very brains, flesh, and blood if they could."[14] Alas, in 1881, it might have been you standing in these lines or in lines at the departments of State or Justice trying to persuade overwhelmed officials of your fealty to the party in power!

After initially trying to compromise with Conkling, and owing his support to civil service reformers known as "half breeds" in his party, Garfield refused to fill the New York Customs House with the senator's appointees. Indeed, he did so as his vice president—Chester Arthur—who had once been appointed by Conkling to serve as collector of this custom house, worked actively with Stalwarts in their party against his reform efforts! Asked Garfield, "Shall the principal port of entry in which more than 90% of all our customs duties are collected be under the direct control of the Administration or under the local control of a factional Senator?"[15] Calling his bluff and hoping to force Garfield's hand, Conkling resigned from the Senate, thinking that the New York State Legislature would quickly reinstate him. He was mistaken, and his career ended in humiliation.

Meanwhile, a growing number of civil service reform associations were created at the state and local levels of government, associations that confederated into the National Civil Service Reform League in 1881, the year of Garfield's assassination. Building on public outrage over the assassination carried out by a disgruntled and mentally disturbed office-seeker named Charles Guiteau, Garfield's two-month-long illness and painful death from botched medical care united Americans in ways not thought possible after the Civil War. Moreover, unlike Lincoln's assassination, Garfield's death was directly attributed in popular minds to political corruption, and they "turned their wrath on the spoils system" to ensure that such a tragedy would not happen again.[16] Some in the national media went so far as to link Conkling and Vice President Arthur to Guiteau as co-conspirators, an unfounded allegation. Regardless, the *Nation* wrote that the assassination "seems to have acted on public opinion very like a spark on a powder-magazine."[17]

Premised on the idea that replacing patronage employees with more qualified people on the basis of competitive exams was needed to reform government, Dorman Eaton's arguments and proposals successfully led reformers to petition Congress to enact the Civil Service Act of 1883 (known as the Pendleton Act after its sponsor). Eaton became the first chairman of the Civil Service Commission (CSC) created by the law to administer the federal merit system. The CSC was a three-person bipartisan commission, with commissioners appointed by the president and approved by the Senate. Clothed with rulemaking and investigative powers, the CSC was, among other things, to ensure that workers were hired on the basis of merit determined through competitive exams, did not suffer political assessments, and were protected against arbitrary political actions. It would not be until 1912 and the passage of the Lloyd-La Follette Act that arbitrary dismissals were legally prohibited. Still, by the mid-1930s, the CSC expanded its monitoring and examination functions by centralizing critical personnel functions such as classifying positions and efficiency ratings, developments that were not superseded for nearly a century until the enactment of the Civil Service Reform Act in 1978.

Although strong emotional and compelling managerial reasons propelled the move toward a merit-based civil service system (dismissingly characterized by machine politicians as the "snivel service"), you should appreciate that success also was made possible through several additional political factors. For starters, reformers wanted to cripple the political parties, because the spoils system was largely responsive to lower-class ethnic voters. The latter, of course, were the base of urban political machines. Moreover, diminished in the process would be the likelihood of socialist and anarchist political parties gaining strength in America, developments feared by upper-class and upper-middle-class voters.[18]

At the same time, with the nation dependent on customs taxes collected at their ports, corruption and incompetence were hindering tax revenues and international commerce spawned by the industrial revolution of this era. In turn, the captains of industry realized that if party funding for political campaigns was lessened, politicians would turn to them for financing—and thus increase business influence over government decisions. Relatedly, Republican congressional losses in the 1882 elections led the Stalwarts to support the bill in order to head off spoils appointments should a Democrat be elected president in 1884.

Finally, by then, President Chester Arthur not only supported passage of the law, but he called for civil service reform in his first address as president. Why the shift? Certainly, the preceding factors played a role. But Arthur, who was openly regarded in the press as unfit to be president, was by all accounts moved to tears and fear by Garfield's death. Moreover, his courage to change direction was buttressed by a series of 23 unsolicited letters he received from a 32-year-old invalid woman named Julia Sand. Sparking his attention initially was a letter that acknowledged how his resignation was demanded by many: "If there is a spark of true nobility in you, now is the occasion to let it shine. Faith in your better nature forces me to write to you—but not to beg you to resign. Do what is more difficult & more brave. Reform!"[19]

You should also understand that these powerful political forces notwithstanding, only about 10 percent (approximately 15,000) of the federal workforce was covered initially by the act, a fact that caused some civil service reformers not to support the bill, believing it was too tepid to make a difference. Still, this percentage increased gradually to nearly 50 percent (approximately 86,000) of available federal positions by 1897 and to 70 percent by the end of World War I,[20] largely through presidents "blanketing in" their appointees into the civil service—that is, extending coverage to them—by means of executive orders so their successors could not replace these workers.[21] Nor, were you in the federal public service, would you have had merit protection against partisan removal until an executive order issued by President William McKinley in 1897 that was later codified into law in 1912.[22] Moreover, you still could have engaged in political campaigns for your favorite candidates—such that party mischief regarding your career might still exist—until Congress passed the Hatch Act in 1939. But even here, the act was propelled by political considerations: conservatives feared that employees of New Deal agencies—and especially those given jobs in the Works Progress Administration during the Depression—would work in political campaigns for Roosevelt democrats.

Likewise, at the subnational level, whether you were a patronage or merit appointee depended on the state or locality in which you worked. With exceptions such as Massachusetts and New York, most states did not follow the federal merit system lead in 1883. And once they began creating civil service systems, patronage proved resilient in states such as Illinois, Missouri, and New Jersey. For example, in Chicago and other cities, "temporary workers" were hired who were classified as such for decades!

Toward the Administrative State and Bureaucratic Administration

You will also learn during your coursework, however, that the most significant and successful counteroffensive against the patronage state occurred between 1890 and 1920.

At that time, a motley coalition of small business, agrarian, anti-vice, suffragette, anti-immigrant (or nativist), urban professional, and social reformers coalesced into what is known as the "progressive reform movement." Derisively called "morning glories" (with its negative connotations of effeminacy) who would "wilt in the noonday sun" by political machine leaders, they were joined by men from well-to-do backgrounds—such as Senator Henry Cabot Lodge of Massachusetts and future president Theodore Roosevelt—who jumped into elected politics with more than civil service reform on their minds.

On a moral level, progressives believed—as did the Founding Fathers and civil service reformers—that political parties were detrimental to society, were corrupt, and had to be drained of their power. Quite pragmatically, they also were alarmed that urban political machines teeming with immigrants left them legislative minorities, and this disadvantage had to be overcome. Roosevelt characterized part of the task confronting progressives as one of demonstrating to the recently arrived southern European immigrants in overcrowded urban areas that they need not put up with the corruption of the political machines in order to get the jobs and services they needed. But civil service reform was not enough. Progressives also called for nonpartisan elections, direct primaries, citizen referenda, and secret balloting.

Another part of their agenda with the most relevance for understanding the development of our field was administrative reform. And the essence of those reforms was a focus on bureaucratic administration rather than democratic administration. Bureaucratic administration emphasizes a policy-challenged public in need of and passively accepting bureaucratic guidance, whereas democratic administration envisions an educable public capable of meaningful participation in policy deliberations and with experts having no overriding claim to dominating that process.[23] What is more, and as we shall see, this early propensity to favor bureaucratic administration has continued to dominate administrative reform prescriptions in our field ever since.

The Path to Bureaucratic Administration. In 1887, Woodrow Wilson wrote that what was needed was a science of public administration.[24] Arguing that European autocracies understood that effective service delivery was critical to maintaining their power, Wilson wrote that time had long passed for the United States to do the same. Failing to do these things, Wilson claimed, would place the United States at an economic and military disadvantage internationally. The Madisonian system of checks and balances, separation of powers, and federalism needed a boost of executive-led economy and efficiency if the United States was to emulate, if not surpass, its more administratively and legislatively efficient competitors.

But could a democracy adopt administrative principles from autocratic governments without losing its democratic soul? Not to worry, said Wilson, because elected officials set policy while administrative experts staffing new government agencies merely carry it out. This is known as the "politics–administration dichotomy." In one of the most famous phrases in public administration history, Wilson wrote: "If I see a murderous fellow sharpening a knife cleverly, I can borrow his way of sharpening the knife without borrowing his probable intention to commit murder with it."[25] In reformers' eyes, the "knives" of a science of administration could ameliorate the new problems facing governments in a rapidly urbanizing, industrializing, and Manifest Destiny-animated nation. Competence that was politically neutral was now essential.

Given the national scale and negative externalities of the newly emergent industrial economy they faced in the United States, the early progressives also claimed that a national democracy was the only way to ensure the civic life of Americans.[26] This, in turn, meant fundamentally shifting the balance of policy-making power from state and local governments to the federal government and circumventing corrupt, fractionated, and dilatory legislatures by shifting power to an energetic executive branch staffed with public interest-oriented experts wielding the measurement tools of the scientific method to identify problems and solve them.[27]

Thus, progressives joined the nation's founders in offering a more ennobling vision of public service. Unlike political machines, experts in government bureaucracies would see above crass political interests. There was no Democratic, Republican, socialist, or anarchistic way to build a road, treat a child with tuberculosis, or provide police and sanitation services; there were only scientifically informed, professional, and objective ways to do these things—many of which you will be exposed to in your coursework today. From this calculus of "neutral competence," public managers would discern a public interest.

There were, of course, dissenters to these prescriptions as the years passed, even among progressives themselves. The first, dubbed the "forgotten progressives" and led by Herbert Hoover, was a movement known as "associationalism" that offered a reform path quite different from other progressives.[28] Like them, and better steeped in American exceptionalist values, associationalists believed in applying the scientific method as a means for increasing industrial and government efficiency and, hence, the pivotal role that experts in the professions could play in reducing the social tensions of the day. However, associationalists feared the centralizing tendencies of the dominant wing of the progressive movement, worrying they could lead to state socialism and stymie individualism. But they were equally worried that continued emphasis on laissez-faire economics that disdained government intervention in markets was dangerous as well and jeopardized the nation's survival as a democracy.

Thus, the associationalist prescription involved trained experts in federal government agencies still collecting social science and economic data, but they would not make policy on these subjects. Instead, they would hold conferences on topics such as unemployment, crime, and child labor abuses. Associationalists believed that the notoriety of these national conferences would catalyze voluntary associations of businesspersons, nongovernmental organizations, citizens, and state and local government actors that would develop and implement policies to address the problems their research identified. The associationalist movement, however, failed to carry the day in public administration circles, despite it becoming the preferred approach to governance during the 1920s under Hoover's leadership as secretary of commerce during the Warren G. Harding and Calvin Coolidge presidencies.

This now-largely forgotten rift notwithstanding, all progressive reformers' dreams during this era were not without ethnic, class, and gender biases related to who could and should be civil servants. For starters, being a professional expert meant you had to be educated, which meant only those with the means to gain that education were eligible. Moreover, claiming that administrators merely carried out policies that elected officials enacted while shifting real policy-making power to the professional bureaucracy maintained a fiction that disadvantaged populations were still in control because they voted. You need to appreciate, though, that progressives held what your professors may call a "social evolutionary" view of immigration. Over time, immigrants would acquire the tools of education and citizenship by participating in local government and through the work of local civic associations. But, in the interim, the national administrative apparatus had to be sheltered from their influence.

Likewise, on the racial front, one of the leading progressive advocates of reform and a person considered the father of the self-conscious study of public administration—the aforementioned Woodrow Wilson—was a product of his southern heritage. He "defended segregation and disenfranchisement as the result of sad experience during Reconstruction when political power was held by Negroes, whom he saw as 'ignorant and unfitted by education for the most usual and constant duties of citizenship'...In private Wilson seemed even less liberal, referring several times to blacks as 'an ignorant and inferior race.'"[29]

Wilson also opposed antilynching laws to combat a rising tide of these atrocities, did little to assuage race riots victimizing blacks between 1917 and 1919, and continued segregation in federal offices.[30] In fairness, he did appoint some blacks to federal positions (to his then-southern-dominated Democratic Party's consternation) and signed a bill that included an affordable housing program benefiting blacks in the District of Columbia.[31] Still, it did not help that, in the White House in 1915, he showed D. W. Griffith's incendiary, pro-Klu Klux Klan (KKK) movie *Birth of a Nation*.

Not all progressives, of course, shared these beliefs or defended Wilson's actions. Wilson was excoriated by some progressives, saying his actions led to the revival of the KKK after its decimation by President Ulysses S. Grant in the 1870s. Likewise, many sided with Republican Theodore Roosevelt's position when he was criticized for supporting and giving jobs to blacks in the then-racist South; met in the White House with the most notable black activist of his day, Booker T. Washington; ended racial segregation in schools as New York's governor; and then championed its abolition in schools when in the White House. But it was the early 1890s and 1900s, and racial tolerance was hardly a linchpin of democracy during that era that progressives championed widely. Indeed, it is frequently noted that Roosevelt never invited Washington back to the White House and that he dismissed African American soldiers from the military when they were accused unfairly of going on a shooting spree in Brownsville, Texas. He was also "less respectful" of black aspirations after his reelection when he no longer needed their votes, and recent research shows that he tolerated his second wife Edith's use of racial slurs in the Roosevelt household and in her correspondence.[32]

Finally, the role of gender in definitions of public service cannot be gainsaid. Interestingly, progressives such as Roosevelt and Wilson were sympathetic to women's suffrage—Wilson, after an initial reluctance, supported (for political reasons) the Nineteenth Amendment to the US Constitution ratified by the US Congress in 1920. Still, until the enactment of the Nineteenth Amendment commenced a slow changing of attitudes, the dominant view of the role of women in public service was confined to civic and voluntary associations—what we today would call nonprofit or nongovernmental organizations—dealing with maternal issues of "home and hearth." A woman's primary duty was "republican motherhood": women upheld "moral values in the home and prepar[ed] their *sons* [emphasis added] to practice citizenship."[33]

Thus, a second split among early progressives emerged—largely, but not totally, based along gender lines—that involved bureaucratic versus democratic administration and that has been compellingly described by Camilla Stivers.[34] Were you an activist woman in that era, according to Stivers, you might have shared the impulse stressing social justice and even joined a movement led by "settlement women." Animated by a new "social gospel," women such as Jane Addams started or worked in settlement houses that provided social services, moral education, citizen empowerment, and civic education to new immigrants in the inner cities.

The other reform impulse in the early progressive movement was associated with the so-called "bureau men"—largely operating in a burgeoning "bureau of municipal research" (BMR) movement. Proponents sought to bring business principles to government in order to eliminate corruption by making it work more efficiently, effectively, and economically. Ultimately this bureau men's focus prevailed and many of the settlement women—with their proclivity for democratic administration—moved on to create the field of social work. This meant that public administration was on its way to being seen as harnessing science, engineering, technology, and the new social sciences to identify and solve the nation's problems, to eliminate waste and inefficiency in government, and to promote modernization.[35]

Administrative reformers would do so, however, without an equal emphasis on developing citizenship or civic engagement in the policy process, despite occasional initiatives to do so (e.g., in the Great Society programs of the 1960s and, more recently, in a so-called "New Governance" movement). Granted, as Charles Goodsell argues, a variety of institutional techniques to involve the public directly in agency activities have been tried, including "advisory groups, citizen boards, town meetings, neighborhood meetings, community workshops, community scorecards, focus groups, planning forums, citizen policy panels, agenda-formation exercises, citizen coordinating councils, and volunteer activities."[36] Likewise, techniques such as alternative dispute resolution, the federal Administrative Procedure Act of 1946 with accompanying state administrative procedure acts, and regulatory negotiations have also been tried. But as subsequent chapters in this book will review, although sometimes effective, these efforts often meet the letter of the laws requiring or allowing them but not their spirit.[37] As such, they are too often conducted in a perfunctory and less-than-timely manner to have meaningful impact. They also create opaque administrative processes that require policy and procedural expertise mustered only by well-organized interests, and they are approached reluctantly by agency participants more comfortable with informing citizens regarding policy than gaining their input.

Training for Bureaucratic Administration. This focus on bureaucratic administration, of course, required professional training during the Progressive Era. But of what was it to consist and who would offer it? Not everyone believed that narrow technical training in the principles of administration was sufficient for public servants. For instance, Woodrow Wilson repeatedly warned that science had not "freed us from ourselves" and that education for the public service, such as at his beloved Princeton University, had to be a "school of duty" where *young men* (consistent again with his times) acquired a sense of "righteousness in this world" and "salvation in the next."[38] As we will soon cover, however, some even today worry that technical concerns in public administration—what we will refer to as "instrumental" values focused on matching administrative means to policy ends—have ever since overwhelmed more ethical, democratic, and normative ones grounded in constitutional values—to the detriment of public service education.

Putting this aside for now, though, if you were alive in this era, interested in public service, and had the "right" race, gender, and socioeconomic background, you might have been attracted to this important instrumental, skill-based view of public service training. Clearly, something had to be done to stop corruption, out-of-control spending, and technical incompetence in government. Perhaps not unlike yourself or some of your classmates today, you most likely would have already been trained in a profession such as engineering or public health when you began study in public administration. Indeed, most "students" in this era were either working in government agencies or seeking to ply their professional skills within them.

What would have differed from today during the first 15 years of the twentieth century, however, was that you would *not* have been seeking to hone your public service skills in a university setting. The first, and only, graduate school addressing public administration during this era was established at the University of Michigan in 1914. Offered jointly with the university's engineering department, it focused exclusively on municipal administration and, especially, public works administration. Instead, you would likely have already been working in government and have enrolled in the so-called "training schools," the first of which was the Training School for Public Service. This school was launched in 1911 and then formally affiliated with the New York Bureau of Municipal Research in 1922 to create the National Institute of Public Administration (NIPA). The first in the BMR movement noted earlier, this training school focused on making urban administration more businesslike.

Had you attended the NIPA, you would have received knowledge of government institutions, research skills, and a sense for how the "science" of administration could improve public programs.[39] Likewise, you might have witnessed a burgeoning number of municipal associations getting involved in the educational process, such as the International City Managers Association, the Municipal Finance Officers Association, and the American Public Works Association. All were trumpeting the value of analysis in solving public problems and either promoting or providing training programs. By the late 1920s, you would have seen many of these associations linking arms to create the Public Administration Clearing House and the "1313" public administration center in Chicago, respectively. What is more, you would likely have read many of the reports that these associations produced, as they became the "textbooks" of the day.

As you may experience today in only some courses, most of your training school experience would have been totally comprised of work on specific government projects. In most of these projects, you would have been sent into agencies to do the work. As time passed, you would have chosen from a selected course menu of "majors" as well that included topics such as public accounting, police and fire administration, purchasing and supplies, civil service, and ethics, plus "minor" subjects such as statistics, graphics methods, and publicity. And in many of these programs, you would have done apprenticeships.

Over the 1920s and 1930s, however, you were likely to begin having more options to weigh for beginning or furthering your public service education. You might have considered pursuing your studies at one of the 30 to 40 universities grounded in Progressive Era principles that began offering courses and perhaps degrees in public administration (Michigan and Syracuse University).[40] Moreover, during World War I, the legitimacy of social science methodology and what it might offer to public servants soared and began to affect course contents in these programs.[41] Indeed, you might be surprised to learn that you might have attended what is known today as Brookings—the Washington, DC-based think tank known previously as the Brookings Institution—for training programs in public administration premised on these social science methods, and especially on economics.

To be sure, the quality and scope of university instruction was uneven, and some only offered courses rather than programs.[42] What is more, many of these pioneers later dropped their public administration programs (e.g., the University of Chicago, Stanford University, and the University of Illinois-Urbana). But if you had been admitted to schools such as the Maxwell School of Citizenship and Public Affairs at Syracuse University (to which a large portion of the Training School for Public Service was later transferred), Columbia University (to which the National Institute of Public Administration was later affiliated between 1931 and 1942), the University of Chicago, or the University of Southern California (the first total professional school in public administration), your thirst for gaining knowledge for use in public agencies might have been quenched.

Moreover, by the early 1930s, your aim for a college-based public service education grounded in progressive principles would have been advanced appreciably by a dozen or so universities offering training programs and creating research bureaus as adjuncts to their programs. These included the University of Iowa, the University of Cincinnati, and the University of Wisconsin. These bureaus—some of which were later combined with schools or institutes of public administration—construed their missions as providing applied graduate education, doing basic and applied administrative research, and affording management assistance grounded in Progressive Era principles to local and state governments.

Alternatively, during that decade, you might have entered the Harvard Graduate School of Business, a school grounded partially in associationalist-based progressive principles at the time.[43] Social science methodology was again the Archimedean point of leverage in their search for administrative and social order amid the chaos of the Great Depression. The curriculum you would have studied was infused with a belief, however, in a business-led rather than government-led system of governance. Their view was that a technocratic elite spanning the public and private sectors should lead society—a private-public partnership capable of "bridging" the imperative of expertise with democracy while avoiding socialism and laissez-faire extremes.

Social Inequity and Bureaucratic Administration. Regardless of where you might want to pursue your education during this era, however, were you an African American, a woman, physically challenged, or openly gay, public service education and jobs were still largely closed to you. For instance, were you an African American or woman seeking federal government employment during the New Deal, your chances were largely limited to being a member of FDR's Federal Council of Negro Affairs—known informally as Roosevelt's "Black Cabinet." Refusing to speak out against lynching laws in the South lest he lose Southern Democrat support for his New Deal initiatives, Roosevelt also created 45 administrative and leadership positions for middle-class black men and women in federal agencies. Notable among those serving were the legendary Mary McLeod Bethune, who directed the Negro Division of the National Youth Administration (NYA), and Robert C. Weaver, who served as an aid to Secretary of the Interior Harold Ickes.

More likely, if you were black, you might have been fortunate to either work in or have had younger members of your family or friends among the 300,000 blacks employed by Bethune's NYA. But, even then, the chances that you would have relatives or friends receiving aid and jobs were higher if they lived outside the South, where local NYA boards were dominated by racist whites. Were you able to obtain employment at the NYA itself, however, you would have been part of an administration that helped to create a new generation of educated middle and upper-class blacks. The NYA targeted—that is, established covert racial quotas for distributing—over $600,000 of undergraduate and graduate student aid for over 4,000 black men and women. And in each of these instances, you would have been part of FDR's ultimately successful but "quiet" project of pursuing minority jobs and funding that eventually began the realignment of blacks from the Republican Party to the Democratic Party that you see today.

The Disintegration of Administrative Orthodoxy. The rub for *anyone* thinking about a public service career and wanting to get an education in public administration by the late 1930s was that the field would—within a decade—come apart. At issue was what the field was, what its values should be, and, thus, what should be taught to students in public administration programs. In the process, the principles of bureaucratic admin- istration that had been the cornerstone of your education in preparing for a career in public service were declared inadequate to the task, variously, as promoting too narrow a set of values, as based on experiential rather than scientific evidence, and as incapable of offering advice in other than US settings.

This all began in the late 1940s, as a number of scholars who had served in govern- ment and who otherwise saw government activism as a necessity worried that demo- cratic values might well become marginalized, if not displaced entirely. They feared that professional specialists intent on making government work effectively at the lowest possible cost were—in training and practice—losing sight of democratic values such as responsiveness, representativeness, equity, equality, due process, and constitutional rights. Famously, a scholar you are likely to hear a great deal about in your coursework— Dwight Waldo—argued that the real question confronting public servants was "efficient for what?"[44]

Explained Waldo, the "descriptive or objective notion of efficiency is valid and useful, but only within a framework of consciously held values."[45] He called for public servants trained to possess a "knowledge of the place of the public service in its relationship with basic economic and social forces and some realization of the potentialities of govern- ment as a means for meeting human needs."[46] In your program today, you will definitely confront aspects of Waldo's legacy whenever you take courses in ethics and values, pub- lic administration and democracy, bureaucratic politics, or the legal context of public administration or management.

Around the same time as Waldo's classic, other scholars such as Robert Dahl began critiquing the US-centric conceptualization of the field.[47] They argued that the principles of administration emphasized in most educational and training pro- grams could not be "principles" unless they were universal in application. However, Dahl argued that different national, political, social, and economic contexts across nations made universal principles impossible. Still, and spawned first by the Vietnam War, efforts to do so sparked an interest in comparative administration of which you might have taken advantage at the time. Yet, again, a focus on instrumental- ism prevailed. As conceived by nongovernmental philanthropic organizations such as the Ford Foundation and the World Bank; by professionals at the US Agency for International Development; and by university programs at Harvard, MIT, and the University of California-Berkeley, the focus soon became one of advancing national planning for economic development.[48]

Another devastating critique of public administration education and practice in the late 1940s was launched for a different reason by Herbert Simon.[49] Were you taking classes then, you would have read—and will be exposed to today—his claim that the principles of administration and their focus on government structures were not worth your time. The principles, he argued, were "proverbs" with no scientific grounding. The most profitable focus of public administration research, training, and education, he claimed, was on decision making in organizations. Moreover, contrary to Waldo's argument, Simon said that efficiency was not only the primary value to be pursued by agencies, but it was inherently separable from other values. Public service—and educational preparation for it—thus consisted of applying sophisticated decision-making techniques to finding what your coursework will call the "one best way" within a bureaucracy to meet the goals set by others.

Not so, responded critics such as Norton Long.[50] Like Waldo and Dahl, he ridiculed the idea that one could separate either facts from values or policy from administration. For Long, values were inseparable components of policy choices. Moreover, it was impossible to separate politics from administration. Anyone doing so misunderstood the practical reality that the "staff work on which well-conceived public policy making must depend can scarcely be supplied elsewhere [e.g., in legislatures] than in the great government departments."[51]

Long also added to Waldo's and Dahl's insights that agencies having the wherewithal to inform policy successfully had to understand, acquire, and protect power in order to do so—and would, in turn, gain power whenever they did. Long wrote evocatively, "There is no more forlorn spectacle in the administrative world than an agency and a program possessed of statutory life, armed with executive orders, sustained in the courts, yet stricken with paralysis and deprived of power."[52] It was not efficient budgets and operations but the "budgeting of power" that matters most in public agencies.

The Administrative State Marches On. These critiques notwithstanding, the early progressives' instrumentalist vision of training and education grew even further over the next four decades. This, as World Wars I and II, the Depression, the New Deal of the 1930s, and the Great Society of the 1960s spawned legions of government agencies at the federal government level bent on solving societies' problems. In the process, the blanketing in of federal positions into the federal civil service system since the Roosevelt years meant that, by 1960, the position you held in the federal government might now be protected by merit principles. Indeed, the high point of civil service coverage—86.4 percent of all federal employees—occurred in that year.[53]

Opportunities for merit system-protected public service employment—and the technique-based civil service exams that gained you entry to public service—also blossomed during this era at the state and local levels of government. As mentioned, however, coverage varied across those jurisdictions. Consistent with American exceptionalist values, activist federal policies were pursued "atop the foundation of federalism" wherein "state and local governments...remained active, influential, innovative, and indispensable."[54] This not only created ever more complex webs of intergovernmental networks across different policy areas. It also produced a sizable expansion of university-based public administration programs to meet the demand for skilled public managers, with most programs you might have applied to at the time housed in government or political science departments.

Driving all this was a profound shift in public philosophy. Indeed, so profound was the change initiated by the New Deal in the 1930s and amplified by the Great Society programs of the 1960s that Theodore Lowi considered them the founding of the "Second Republic of the United States."[55] He said this because government's role was expanded dramatically to a focus on redistributing resources (taking from one broad class of recipients and giving to another) and regulating largely bad economic behavior (e.g., monopolistic price fixing, stock fraud, and price gouging).

The Second Republic received a further boost during the 1960s and 1970s by what legal scholars refer to as the "new social regulation."[56] Whereas economic regulation both promoted and regulated particular industries, the new social regulation focused exclusively on regulating bad private sector behavior cutting across industries and sectors. Examples of the new social regulation include laws against discrimination on the basis of race, gender, or differential abilities; regulations on some greenhouse gas emissions (with carbon dioxide regulations in process under the Barack Obama administration); and endangered species protection.

Moreover, with states and localities typically viewed as lacking the will, resources, or both to address societies' problems, careers in federal agencies became especially attractive—as did educational preparation for those careers. Those who heard this call, in turn, helped to spark parallel job opportunities in states and localities so that the latter might apply, qualify for, and subsequently hand out grants that federal programs made available to them. These were heady days for persons such as you interested in public service, and they attracted the best and the brightest to the career service in Washington—and to public administration programs in university settings.

Were you enticed in these decades by the prospects of a public service career, you might have gone to Washington to help develop a host of incredibly successful federal programs such as Social Security, Medicare, or Food Stamps. You might have been involved in helping to expand greatly the number of grant-based programs for assisting states and localities with housing, transportation, or education problems or to issue and enforce regulations for protecting citizens from consumer fraud, environmental carcinogens, and public health threats. Indeed, by the time Richard Nixon left office in the early 1970s, you might have found yourself working in Washington or in federal regional offices among the nearly 2.8 million employees, running nearly 800 domestic and international programs, and administering over 400 grant-in-aid programs for assisting states and localities. Alternatively, you might have joined the public service in any of the 83,000-odd governments and administrative districts located in states and localities, many spawned to meet federal program requirements.

Nonetheless, as the 1960s dawned, were you an African American, a woman, physically challenged, or openly gay, positions were still largely open to you (if at all) only at the clerical or menial level of most federal, state, and local bureaucracies. But at this point came the civil rights movement that would produce the Civil Rights Act of 1964 and the Voting Rights Act of 1965, legislation that would propel slow but significant progress on these fronts. This was followed by nonwhites and women comprising significantly greater proportions of all workforces in the 1970s and 1980s; the increasing Latino presence in the United States and the globalization of markets during the 1980s and 1990s; and the rising influence in politics of the lesbian, gay, and bisexual community that we are witnessing today (along with transgender politics). Certainly, you will notice these trends in your classrooms today. Women, for example, comprise nearly 54 percent of Master of Public Administration (MPA) graduate students, while blacks and other minorities comprise approximately 17 percent of MPA students. Still, even after years of progress in moving into mid and high-level positions in government, representation of these groups is conspicuously lower at the highest levels of federal, state, and local governments.

The Assault on Public Service Begins. In the wake of all this activity and social turmoil, critics also began simultaneously questioning traditional definitions of what constituted public service, the values it should emphasize, and its legitimacy. Some critics coming from the democratic administration tradition were "friends" of public service but felt it was continuing to lose its way. Nor were they against efficiency as a value—only efficiency as the *sole* value of public administration. They argued that too much attention was still being given to economy and efficiency. It was, they claimed, distorting constitutional values in America. Members of this so-called "New Public Administration" movement again questioned agencies' responsiveness to the broader range of values cherished in a democracy.[57] Especially marginalized by instrumental concerns, they felt, were considerations of social equity, fairness of treatment, and representativeness of the bureaucracy.

To other critics less sympathetic of activist government, however, a *lack* of attention to efficiency, effectiveness, and economy in either domestic or international settings by public servants was the real problem. The root of what they called the "bureaucracy problem" in the United States was the large swaths of discretion granted administrators. Known as "public choice" theorists, scholars such as James Buchanan, Anthony Downs, Gordon Tullock, and Vincent Ostrom believed that professionals in government agencies had become insular, were responsive to their own rather than the public's needs, exaggerated budgets to enhance their own power and influence, and clung to the status quo.

Premised on theory rather than research and actual practice (but subsequently refined by research), this negative framing of public service had profound consequences. Coupled with Lowi's concerns, public choice theory gave intellectual heft to President Ronald Reagan's mantra in the 1980s that public servants were the source of, rather than the solution to, society's problems. Nor was the image of public service helped when a first generation of researchers studying the implementation of public policies partly attributed gaps between the promise of federal programs and their results to self-interested "games" that public managers played at the state and local levels of government.[58]

This critique flipped mainstream progressive principles of administration on their head by portraying overlap, duplication, and markets as the solution to government problems. Hamiltonian visions of good government took a backseat to what we covered earlier as Jeffersonian and Jacksonian visions of government. Moreover, many of these critics argued that the public interest was best served by *lowering* expectations about what government agencies could do, by cutting back on the number of agencies that had to cooperate to get something done, and by eliminating as much direct delivery of services by public agencies as possible. Also necessary, they argued, were decentralizing authority outside Washington and within agencies, defunding and cutting the number of professionals in domestic agencies and programs that remained while increasing military spending, delegating responsibilities to private contractors and nonprofits, and placing greater numbers of political appointees in the agencies that remained to "control" the career bureaucracy. Thus, the early progressives' embrace of neutral competence was replaced by a quest for "responsive competence" to elected officials. Produced also in some very vocal quarters by archconservatives, however, was a dysfunctional antigovernment rhetoric, as well as successful efforts to increase the legal liability of civil servants for their actions and to increase judicial scrutiny of agency rulemaking.

All this, of course, produced a strong negative reaction within the public administration community. For example, in the 1980s, scholars offering what became known as the "Blacksburg Manifesto" attacked the aggressive push toward responsive competence mounted by the Reagan administration. They also argued that sensitivity to citizens' perceptions, needs, and deliberative capacities had been marginalized by the instrumental focus of our field and needed to be restored in practice and in our educational programs. Echoing Waldo, they contended that public service education and practice had to be grounded in larger democratic values. Their concerns, however, could not compete with the Reagan juggernaut.

Consequently, your attraction to particular public administration programs and public service jobs in that era might have been to learn how to rein in what are called "bureaucratic pathologies" (or "bureaupathologies") so that a public interest might yet be advanced. As such, you might have been attracted to a variety of policy programs that took Waldo's values, policy choices, and politics as "givens." These policy schools offered students the microeconomic, statistical, and operations research tools to find the most efficient and cost-effective ways to attain the policy goals given to them by elected officials. Some of the programs you might have considered at the time (and even today) made a nod toward viewing public servants as leaders and implementers of programs by adding "public management" and policy implementation courses. Yet, the interests, emphases, and strengths of many programs lay clearly in decision analytical techniques and on welfare economics.

But even if you were not so disposed, you would have noticed other significant changes in where and what you studied during this era. Most pronounced was a still-ongoing trend away from locating public administration programs in political science departments. This break began in the 1960s as public administration scholars chaffed at their historical status as an "inferior" subdiscipline of political science. They also saw political science as too divorced from the applied and normative concerns of public administration, while political scientists saw public administration as too applied and lacking methodological rigor.

As such, some public administration programs began migrating to business schools (a trend since reversed because of public/private differences), established their own independent schools, or were joined to schools of public affairs. At the same time, and reflecting the multidisciplinary nature of the field, programs began returning to public administration's historical roots by incorporating courses and faculty from other fields in their curricula. These were courses and faculty hires that traditional political science departments would never allow or could not afford without disrupting existing salaries in departments (e.g., economists or operations research faculty).

Toward the Networked State

Not surprisingly, in the wake of the Reagan Revolution, and reminiscent of the early progressive reformers, concerns began mounting in the 1990s among those with an activist approach to government that a shifting political and policy environment merited a fundamental rethinking of government. Only this time, it was the administrative state launched by those early progressives that required fixing by what your professors may call a "post-bureaucratic" model of administration. Joined sometimes by more conservative political elements, they argued that ascendant in an era of fiscal stress and economic globalization were a host of "wicked" policy problems. These are problems such as climate change where no accepted definitions of either the problem or solution to it exist and where one problem is interrelated with others, thus requiring cross-disciplinary, cross-jurisdictional, interorganizational, and cross-sectoral policy and management approaches.[59]

Solving wicked problems required a high degree of flexibility, learning, cross-sectoral participation, and informed and meaningful stakeholder involvement in the deliberations of public agencies trying to cope with them.[60] Or, as Hugh Heclo puts it, such problems require public servants to engage with affected populations in "collective puzzlement on behalf of society."[61] But these were not traits, critics argued, for which public agencies were known.

Also required was a rethinking of the civil service system itself at all levels of government. For most, this did not mean doing away with merit principles but, rather, gaining more agency discretion and flexibility to recruit and retain top-notch professionals with the new skills required to deal with them. Many agencies opted out of, or were removed from, the traditional civil service to create policies and procedures more attuned to their particular personnel needs while still offering merit protections. Indeed, by 1996, only 56 percent of the federal civil service were covered under the full panoply of civil service regulations.[62] As such, you might today find yourself in one of many "exempt service" positions in the federal government.

Meanwhile, at the state and local government levels, a similar rethinking was going on but with some jurisdictions doing away with many civil service protections. Thus, you might have found yourself—and will continue to do so today—working as a public servant who could be dismissed "at-will" in states such as Georgia, Texas, or Florida. Similar efforts were unsuccessfully pursued by the George W. Bush administration in the post-9/11 era for the Defense and Homeland Security departments.

Many of these pragmatists also saw economic globalization further straining conventional government-centered models of public service.[63] Globalization brought a need for administrative strategies that crossed national boundaries (geographic challenges), for rapid decision making in a world of 24-hour markets and media (temporal challenges), for different types of knowledge (multidisciplinary challenges), and for institutional credibility (legitimacy challenges).[64] Critics claimed that these, again, were not characteristics on which public agencies were highly rated.

Proponents of this position—especially the Democratic Clinton administration in its "reinventing government" initiative—joined the chorus arguing that the bureaucratic, hierarchical, government-centered approach to governing was now anachronistic. You should understand, however, that many of these ideas were born in the states, because the balanced budget requirements under which most labor, and that the federal government does not, brought a focus on economy and efficiency to the states first. These so-called "New Governance" administrative reformers saw public servants as agents for setting agency priorities, transforming agencies into information-driven "learning" organizations, and becoming more responsive to clients and citizens (or, as they were called, "customers"). In turn, and in exchange for being given more flexibility, agencies and their public managers were to be held accountable and rewarded more for outcomes and results than they had been in the past.

These critics were preceded by others less positively oriented toward activist government in what is called the "New Public Management" (NPM) movement. The NPM was a bit of a Rorschach test that has taken different forms in developed nations (e.g., Australia, New Zealand, the United Kingdom, and the United States), and it borrows eclectically from various public choice, scientific management, and economic theories that we will cover in greater depth in chapter 4. Also incorporating elements of the separation of policy making from administration, NPM offered an economics-based view that accords no special role for citizens, the public service, or the public interest, aside from what market forces allow or dictate. Although you might not hear practitioners refer to it by name when you join an agency, you can recognize the NPM by its aims to: (1) have governments deal solely with core functions and devolve the rest to the private or nonprofit sector; (2) wean public agencies as much as possible from the treasury and have them raise their own sources of revenue; and (3) ensure as much competition for resources as possible among those remaining agencies.

Together, the New Governance and NPM movements helped to foster further an administrative apparatus in which an ever-growing proportion of the federal bureaucracy no longer directly makes or implements policy. Rather, civil servants in these agencies often arrange, coordinate, and monitor networks of public, private, and nonprofit organizations that pursue public actions with or on behalf of them. Moreover, in the process of pushing federal responsibilities ever "downward" to state and local governments, "upward" to international bodies and nongovernmental actors, and "outward" to the private and nonprofit sectors, a full-blown networked state (some say a "hollow" state) now overlaps the conventional administrative state.[65] Thus, an interest in advanced degrees or academic concentrations related to nonprofit management has also occurred, a phenomenon reflected in spiraling percentages of graduate students in public administration programs pursuing public service careers in that sector. In the process, flourishing within the public service that you are thinking about (re)joining requires that you cultivate abilities linked to learning how to "network in the shadow of administrative hierarchy."[66]

What may surprise you is that public servants at all levels of government and across the public, private, and nonprofit sectors are still learning how best to operate in today's networked state. Indeed, one exciting part of a career in public service today is that you will be helping to determine how best "to run a constitution" amid the challenges, choices, and opportunities afforded by the networked state. Further complicating this task, as a public manager you will have to figure this out while incorporating the often competing values treasured in a democratic republic. And you will have to do so while restoring a sense of political efficacy to them, lest the legitimacy of government itself be lost. Helping to run a constitution demands no less of you in the twenty-first century.

Stovepiped Worlds, (Mostly) Stovepiped Curricula, and Your Public Service Education Today

Regardless of the path taken by your career in public service, your coursework in public administration is likely to be the last chance you will have to think holistically about public management, the forces driving it, and their policy implications for the nation and its values. The problem historically in coursework, in many otherwise excellent introductions to the field, and within public agencies is that the subfields are studied or worked in separately (e.g., human resource management and public budgeting and finance). To help get your arms around our field, we are going to use what might be called a "6R" framework as we think broadly about the different tasks facing public managers today. The 6Rs we will emphasize are: reconceptualizing purpose, reconnecting with citizens, redefining administrative rationality, recapitalizing personnel assets, reengaging financial resources, and revitalizing a sense of common purpose infused with democratic constitutional values. More precisely:

- *Reconceptualizing purpose* refers to calls for agency and program missions to be rethought in light of the changing circumstances we have just reviewed.
- *Reconnecting with citizens* refers to calls for agencies to engage in what is called a "coproduction" ethic. This concept impels public servants to become more inclusive, participative, and collaborative in their decision-making styles.
- *Redefining administrative rationality* refers to calls, in the wake of the alleged "bureaupathologies" noted earlier, to create priority-based, customer-focused, information-driven, results-based, learning organizations to cope with today's and tomorrow's wicked public problems. It also means identifying opportunities to work collaboratively in networks with other agencies, as well as with private and nonprofit vendors of goods and services.
- *Recapitalizing personnel assets* refers to reconsidering how well existing agency personnel resources are aligned with present and future mission needs. You will be called upon to redress shortfalls in these assets that jeopardize efficient, effective, and equitable approaches to addressing today's and tomorrow's public problems.
- *Reengaging financial resources* refers to calls for changing resource allocation amid the aforementioned downward pressures on tax revenues, the shifting purposes of organizations, the evolving nature of public problems, and our understanding of what works and does not work in addressing them.
- *Revitalizing a sense of common purpose infused with democratic constitutional values* refers to pressures you will feel to think more in terms of democratic administration than bureaucratic administration. This does not mean you can forget about economy and efficiency as a public manager. Indeed, doing the "good" you want to do as a public servant in an era of budget challenges depends partly on you and your agency being as efficient as possible. Moreover, public revenue is not yours to squander but rather to steward responsibly. But, as noted earlier, bureaucratic administration has tended to dominate the thinking of administrative reformers in the United States, with only occasional nods toward democratic administration. As Maarten Hajer and Hendrik Wagenaar write, however, your role in a twenty-first-century world where policy and administrative choices are contested in the face of often incompatible or contradictory values will instead be "to assist [citizens] in the discovery of new policy [and administrative] options and the formulation of compelling arguments" for learning what to prefer as a society.[67]

What Follows

With this as background, the next two chapters are designed to orient you to why calls for the 6Rs have arisen in the first place and why realizing the nation's policy aims depends so much on getting public management right. Chapter 2 illustrates how a convergence of changes in what John Gaus called the "ecology" of public administration over the past 50 years has helped pave the way for calls for reform and why they are likely to continue in the future.[68] Chapter 3 then shows how these changes manifest themselves in calls for the 6Rs in three wicked policy problem areas that have both domestic and international implications (i.e., they are "intermestic" policy): global aging, global security (namely, food security, terrorism, and economic security), and global ecological threats. With this as context, the next six chapters illustrate how and why the first 5Rs are manifesting themselves in major tasks facing public managers in the twenty-first century. Offered in the process are the sources of resistance to change that these tasks involve (positive and negative), as well as strategies for coping with them. Chapter 10 then refocuses our attention on the big picture of what revitalizing a sense of common purpose infused with democratic constitutional values will entail, while offering strategies and caveats for doing so.

CHAPTER 2

Thinking Ecologically

Writing in 1947, John Gaus argued that changes in the "ecology" of society helped to explain the ebb, flow, and substance of the growth of the administrative state in America during the first half of the nineteenth century.[1] More precisely, Gaus tells us to pay attention to changes in people, place, technology (hard and soft), public philosophy, and crises if we want to understand these dynamics in the United States. They are no less powerful today in helping you understand the long-term (or "secular") forces that have helped to shape the contemporary context of public management that we discussed in chapter 1.

As you will see in this chapter, many of these trends are both domestic and international—that is, "intermestic"—in scope. How you are affected by them will depend on the positions you hold during your public service career (e.g., budget analyst, personnel specialist, or policy analyst), the type of program you work in, and the various levels of authority you hold. Regardless, understanding these forces using Gaus' framework will afford you a larger context for appreciating why your agency is doing what it is doing.

It will also help you think strategically about how best to position your agency to advance a sense of common purpose infused with democratic constitutional values as your career unfolds. As noted, a commitment to democratic constitutionalism means nurturing those aspects of American government and politics that have democratized the original constitutional design of a democratic republic.[2] These include, but are not limited to, the Bill of Rights, freedom of information, open meetings, the Administrative Procedure Act of 1946 (Public Law 79–404), citizen participation, and the expansion of individual rights through constitutional law.

Changes in People

Three profound sets of changes in people have prompted—and will continue for the foreseeable future to prompt—pressures on governments and their public managers for redress: exponential growth in the world's population, significant class divides in the United States, and the rise of professionalism in labor markets.

The Global Population Explosion

You may already know that it took all of humankind's history for the Earth's population to reach a billion persons in 1800. It then took another century for the world's population to top 1.7 billion persons. Yet, as the twenty-first century dawned, sweeping mortality declines caused by penicillin and other antibiotics, plus improved medical knowledge and services, catapulted the world's population past the six billion mark.[3] Current projections are that the world's population will hit 8.5 to 9 billion by 2050, although small adjustments to these projections are regularly made.

These exponential growth rates have triggered fears that economic development strategies failing to incorporate the true social and natural resource costs of development will produce disaster. These concerns found their initial impetus in popular culture in 1972 with publication of the controversial Club of Rome's report, *The Limits of Growth*.[4] Growth limits had to be imposed, for example, because population would exceed food supply. In ensuing decades, similar Malthusian claims followed by Paul Ehrlich and others, as did counterclaims by critics such as Julian Simon, who stressed that technological fixes would attenuate these problems. Today's emphasis on sustainable development—the idea that humankind can expand economic growth while simultaneously limiting ecological and human harms—is equally contested. Yet uncontested is mounting evidence that economic growth is raising public health and safety concerns around the world; straining public services; and exacerbating ethnic, regional, and national conflicts—problems public managers at all levels of government must tackle.

On the population side of the equation, the United Nations' Millennium Development Goals (MDGs) set in 2000 aimed to cut the 1990 rates of maternal and child mortality by 75 percent and 65 percent, respectively, by 2015. So far, we have fallen far short of these goals.[5] Still, over the past 20 years, the global extreme poverty rate (defined in 2014 as living on less than $1.25 a day) has been cut in half, meeting the UN's goals five years ahead of schedule. Moreover, some experts estimate that a realistic chance exists to move one billion people out of extreme poverty by 2030. This could occur because of what your coursework may call a "virtuous" (rather than "vicious") cycle; as more people increase their income, they have rising consumption demands, which lead to more jobs, which lead to further consumption.

Nevertheless, serious and potentially destabilizing global poverty will be with you during the remainder of your career, as will population trends that could reduce projected progress and put strains on US blood and treasure for military or peacekeeping operations. The US Census Bureau reports that the world is adding the equivalent of a new Egypt, Israel, Jordan, and the West Bank plus Gaza each year.[6] In the process, world population is still expected to soar to 8 billion persons by 2025 and to 9.3 billion persons by 2050. In addition, 90 percent of global natural increase in population (the difference between births and deaths) is projected in the world's poorest countries. Where most of the globe has seen falling family sizes and fertility rates, sub-Saharan Africa and the Middle East are laggard, with only one-tenth of all women in these regions having access to family planning.

In turn, the poor health and sanitation conditions rampant in less-developed countries with "youth bulges"—explosions of persons under age 25—mean potentially higher rates of infant mortality and, hence, more appeals for international aid that public managers must find ways to deliver. In these countries, a normally quite positive development—rising educational levels—has already interacted with a lack of employment opportunities to create an alienated younger generation ripe for terrorist recruitment in teeming urban areas. And in nations without legitimate governing institutions or a monopoly of military force, public managers and contractors associated with US foreign *and* domestic policy agencies have assumed administrative support positions in so-called military "operations other than war."[7]

When these population trends interact with a predicted 2 percent annual increase in global per capita income through 2020, the stress on natural resources and ecosystems will increase further, especially if—as we have seen in countries such as Brazil, Russia, India, and China, the so-called "BRIC nations"—additional incomes go into buying a Western lifestyle.[8] Despite somewhat slower levels of growth than expected, estimates are that today's "emerging" nations (including the BRIC countries, plus the so-called "MINT nations" of Mexico, Indonesia, Nigeria, and Turkey) will comprise 19 of the top 30 economies in the world by 2050.[9] Thus, also prompting calls for government redress will be natural resource scarcities that pit regions, nations, and users against each other for water, oil, gas, and precious metals.

Even one of the potentially positive aspects of global climate change—the possibility of enhanced access to untapped Arctic resources such as oil and natural gas—will cause international competition requiring the expertise of public sector professionals to sort out, negotiate, and oversee. Such calls have already arisen to ensure and secure oil and natural gas supplies from the strategically important South China Sea, sub-Saharan African nations, and in the Urals in South and Central Asia. They have also been made for the securing of supplies and the transporting of metals vital for economic growth and national security, such as copper and zinc for fiber-optic cables on ocean floors connecting the world's internet systems and computer chips. Indeed, these even now have lifted the visibility of—and sometimes raised animosity toward—public managers and contractors affiliated with such public agencies as the Agriculture Department, the Interior Department, the US State Department, the US military, and USAID, as well as employees and contractors with the World Bank and International Monetary Fund. And in mineral-rich nations such as the Democratic Republic of Congo, legacies of colonialism, government corruption, and ethnic rivalries are likely to continue to stifle the potential for peacefully realizing their economic growth potential.

At the same time, a set of changes in population aging, fertility, and mortality trends also promises to continue putting additional, albeit sometimes indirect, stress on domestic, foreign policy, and defense agencies and their managers for redress. These include, but are not limited to, a global aging wave known as "the gray dawn," "below replacement" fertility rates in over half of the world's nations, and "mortality spikes." In terms of the gray dawn, if present trends persist, demographers project that countries in the *developed* world with advanced economies will experience an unprecedented growth in their elderly populations and a precipitous decline in the number of their youth. In 2003, for example, 20 percent of Italy's population had exceeded the age of 65, a figure that Japan hit in 2005 and Germany in 2006. France and Britain will hit that mark in 2016, and the United States and Canada in 2021 and 2023, respectively. In Asia, fertility rates have already plummeted, too, from 5.8 percent in the 1960s to 2.1 percent in 2014. Meanwhile, Latin America as a whole has experienced the same magnitude of decline. In the Middle East, fertility rates in Iran have declined from 6.5 percent in 1980 to 1.9 percent in 2005.[10]

Declining fertility rates in and of themselves are quite positive. For instance, what is called a "demographic dividend" arises. Fewer younger and older citizens mean a broad working-age population that increases economic growth. In fact, some estimate that almost a third of Asia's economic boom is attributable to this phenomenon over the past 50 years.[11] However, if fertility rates fall below replacement rates, too few workers are available to maintain social support systems. In China, for instance, officials predict a decline of 30-million wage earners to support their system. As such, China's leadership has eased its one-child policy in the hopes of increasing fertility rates and its wage-earning population.[12] Nor are these trends confined to these nations. Demographers project "sub-replacement" fertility patterns in 83 nations with 44 percent of the world's population, including countries as disparate as the United States, Guadeloupe, Japan, Thailand, Tunisia, and most of Europe.[13] Interestingly, a decade-long improvement in European fertility rates that began in 2002 has recently halted, a casualty some experts say is due to the worldwide financial collapse of 2007–09.[14]

An aging population also means increasing health care and pension challenges and costs. Experts estimate, for example, that developed nations will have to pay anywhere from 9 to 16 percent of their respective gross domestic products (GDPs) over the next quarter century just to meet existing national pension commitments.[15] Meanwhile, low and declining fertility rates prompted by trends toward smaller families are occurring in many countries, further rendering tax bases short of funding for health care costs and pensions.

In the United States, declining fertility rates have been staunched by the influx of Latin American immigrants, to an extent reducing prior downward trends. However, they raise new issues regarding immigration, the rising social and political tensions over immigration laws and enforcement, the stress immigration (both legal and illegal) poses on local service delivery systems and taxes, and the low-income and low-skilled nature of immigrants in need of educational and training programs. A 2010 count by the National Council of State Legislatures of immigration-related state statutes—both protecting and restricting illegal immigrants—exceeded 1,400 laws and resolutions, including initiatives related to education, employment, health, law enforcement, legal services, identification/driver's/other licenses, public benefits, and voting rights. Each of these must be interpreted and enforced by public managers at the state and local levels, then coordinated and conflicts resolved with federal agencies.

Yet another challenging demographic trend that will impact your work directly or indirectly in the public sector is a downward spike in lifespans in over 50 nations and territories worldwide. Affected by this "mortality spike" is approximately one-sixth of the world's population, many of whom live in sub-Saharan Africa and Asia and suffer from the HIV-AIDS pandemic.[16] But the mortality spike is not only a product of the HIV-AIDS pandemic. As Gro Harlem Brundtland, former director general of the World Health Organization, states, poverty, homelessness, ethnic conflicts, poor nutrition, and overcrowded living conditions are culprits as well.[17] In addition, an epidemic of obesity is not only posing health challenges in the United States. In China, for example, nearly 30 percent of adults are now overweight.[18]

Were these looming challenges not daunting enough, the demographic trends noted above regarding rising health and pension liabilities are expected to contribute significantly to federal budget woes in the United States that we will review in greater detail in chapters 5 and 9. It suffices presently to note that from 1946 through 2007, the unified federal budget has been in surplus only 11 times; looking only at on-budget operations (generally excluding the social insurance trust-fund operations), there has been a surplus in only eight years. This continued a trend in which the federal government has not been able or willing to raise enough money to pay for what it spends. Overall, the US national debt stood at $17.9 trillion in 2014, although economic recovery from the 2007–09 crisis and across-the-board cuts in the federal budget (excluding, for example, entitlement programs) were slowing annual deficits down somewhat.

Regardless, politicians have shifted huge amounts of potentially debilitating debt to later generations and have left debt financing to foreign creditor nations such as China. Nor do things look better in the longer term. The Simpson-Bowles Committee appointed by President Barack Obama to examine America's fiscal plight and make recommendations for addressing it laid out in 2010 the following politically, economically, and socially challenging scenario that you will have to deal with during your career in public management: "The Congressional Budget Office (CBO) projects if we continue on our current course, deficits will remain high throughout the rest of this decade and beyond, and debt will spiral ever higher, reaching 90 percent of GDP in 2020."[19] Spending on health care alone is estimated to reach $4.8 trillion in 2020. This will amount to 19.6 percent of the nation's GDP, leaving tax revenues in 2025 able to finance only interest payments, Medicare, Medicaid, and Social Security.[20]

The preceding scenario is, of course, economically and politically unsustainable and will require wrenching shifts in taxing and spending the longer Congress waits to address them. The specifics of how this distressing curve will be altered are unclear. But what *is* clear is that public managers such as yourself will be involved in helping elected officials discern the most effective and equitable means for doing so, and living with the consequences of these decisions.

Emerging Class Divides

The past three decades have seen an appreciable redistribution of political power, economic resources, and religiosity in America that will profoundly shape the contexts and tasks of public managers going forward. Beginning in the 1980s, massive income inequities have occurred that have led some to refer pejoratively to a "New Gilded Age."[21] Especially noteworthy is that income gains soared for the top 1 percent of earners in the nation.[22] The Congressional Budget Office reports that half of the post-1979 rise in wealth inequality in America is attributable to the "pulling away of the richest 1%."[23] This, after a durable, decades-long coalition of economic elites—which we will discuss in greater detail in later chapters—reconfigured tax codes, financial regulation, corporate governance, and industrial relations to create a "massive, long-term transformation of the structure of economic rewards" in the nation.[24]

Nor can you ignore emerging trends in the United States showing the direct and indirect consequences of generational and intergenerational social equity issues. As Table 2.1 illustrates, the past quarter century has witnessed a serious and growing intragenerational gap in income distribution. Put most simply, the top 1 percent of wage earners has witnessed steep gains in net worth, while most citizens have experienced a decrease.

Partially responsible for this gap, as well, is the reality that traditional marriage rates in the United States and other foreign nations are declining, a trend placing new demands on government for services and changing consumption patterns.[25] For example,

Table 2.1 Impact on Average Incomes of Change in Income Distribution between 1979 and 2009

Income Group	Income in 1979	Income in 2009	Income in 2009 If Incomes Had Grown at Equal Rates Since 1979	Gain or Loss from Income Shift Since 1979
Bottom Fifth	$16,100	$23,300	$24,600	−$1,300
Second Fifth	$30,300	$40,500	$46,200	−$5,700
Middle Fifth	$43,100	$57,100	$65,800	−$8,700
Fourth Fifth	$56,400	$79,600	$86,100	−$6,500
82–99th Percentile	$85,900	$136,200	$131,100	$5,100
Top 1%	$339,800	$866,700	$518,800	$347,900

Note: Uses the Congressional Budget Office's after-tax income measure, which is a comprehensive measure of income that includes the value of government benefits. All figures in 2009 dollars.

Source: Center on Budget and Planning Priorities (cbpp.org) calculations based on Congressional Budget Office data.

single-person households drive up housing costs, consume more energy per capita than dual households, and require more social services. These households now comprise 15 percent of all US households, up from 4 percent in 1950. In the United States, for example, the rate of unmarried adults has risen from 20 percent in 1950 to nearly 50 percent in 2012; nearly 40 percent of all white births in the United States are to single women, as are nearly 75 percent of all births to minority women; and approximately 40 percent of all births are funded by Medicaid.[26] The reasons for some of these developments include later marriage by professional women who are pursuing career advancement; widows and widowers living longer; and traditional marriage payoffs such as financial security, sexual relations, and stable relationships no longer confined to betrothal.

Whether you view these trends as positive or negative, you cannot dismiss the significant challenges they pose for government and the management expertise they will require of public managers. For example, 25 states that responded to the Patient Protection and Affordable Care Act of 2010 (aka "ObamaCare" and, henceforth, the ACA) by expanding Medicaid eligibility saw their service demands jumping by 3.9 million persons in the initial enrollment period alone in late 2013. This happened because the ACA expanded Medicaid coverage in states that adopted this reform from children, low-income parents, and impoverished elderly and disabled persons to some in the middle class.[27]

What is more, if current trends continue, the implications for future generations are profound. A recent study examining intergenerational economic mobility between 1979 and 2000 found that a child born into the top socioeconomic quintile had a 55 percent chance of remaining in the top 20 percent and only a 1 percent chance of falling into the bottom 40 percent of income earners.[28] The comparable mobility figures for children born into the middle quintile were 13 percent and 31 percent. More recently, Anthony Carnevale and Stephen Rose analyzed family background data for students who attended the top 146 colleges in the United States. Seventy-four percent of students came from the top quartile of family socioeconomic status.[29] Only 10 percent came from the bottom half of the distribution. A mounting body of research thus indicates that the top 1 percent enjoy many advantages in gaining entry to the most selective institutions of higher education.

The Rise of Professionalism, Specialization, and the Achievement Gap

As we reviewed in chapter 1, the aim of progressives in the early twentieth century was to bring "professional administration" to governments in the United States in light of political corruption, the inability of states alone to address the nation's social changes, and economic and military competition abroad.[30] And American public administration still "live[s] off the intellectual capital generated by the Progressive founders" and, most especially, its focus on professionalism.[31] However, two problems immediately arise in this "professional state" that will affect you as a public manager. In the public sector, citizens increasingly feel that they have little input into government policy making. In the private sector, gaping income and social distances have emerged between a professional, highly educated workforce and working-class citizens.

How has this occurred? As we also alluded to in chapter 1, the origins of the professional state are traceable to the Gilded Age of the late nineteenth century and the rise of corporate industrialism in America. A veritable "corporate reconstruction of American capitalism" occurred that provoked a major need for professionally educated and trained staff in the developing industries. In 1883, only 20 corporations were listed on the New York Stock Exchange; by 1904, estimates are that nearly 300 industrial consolidations were in existence, with a capitalization value of about $7 billion.[32] Wrought in the process was a growing demand for professional managers to run these enterprises, including trained accountants, statisticians, engineers, and legal professionals.

As we also noted, the highest "value" pursued by many of these professions—and, most especially, by the engineering professionals who led this revolution—was "efficiency." And efficiency was advanced by taking advantage of emerging mass-production technologies that kept wages down and by keeping prices consistent through protectionist policies involving tariffs on imported goods. Consequently, social tensions arose between owners and workers, a situation exacerbated by the inflow of low-paid, uneducated workers coming largely from southern European countries and laboring in unsafe shop floors. Sparking a working-class "national strike day" in 1886 to demand an eight-hour workday, wage cuts also contributed to a growing number of strikes involving hundreds of thousands of workers in the peak years of 1877, 1886, 1892, and 1893.[33]

Into this social maelstrom strode another set of highly educated professionals: the members of the newly established social sciences, with their professional associations and embrace of scientific methods, measurement, and hypothesis testing to address social problems. As Guy Alchon writes: "The pre-World War I development of the technocratic social sciences was…punctuated by economic and social surveys, by the organization of research institutes, and by other exercises in data production that were designed to meet the need for greater enlightenment and better *social management* [emphasis added]…To [social scientists], poverty, disease, unemployment, and social discontent were…the effects of an unstable, ill-managed, but improvable corporate capitalism."[34]

This measurement-driven "technocratic progressivism" soon morphed into the idea that sorting all these data out and interpreting their meaning meant one could decipher an objective "truth" that no one could dispute, thus putting stale political debates aside.[35] The quest was for a fact-driven, neutrally competent public administration that would impose "order" amid what Robert Wiebe called a "chaotic" world.[36] As we will review in greater detail in chapter 4, trained professional engineers were to do these analyses, sitting in offices removed from the shop floor and, thus, taking control of job design away from the workers. Resentment quickly followed, which translated into congressional hearings, as workers saw "measurement engineers" as just another way to lower wages in the interest of corporate profits.

But so powerful and broadly accepted was the logic of scientism for the remainder of the twentieth century that its application was extended from the shop floor to society at large. We have already reviewed in chapter 1 how scientism and instrumentalist thinking were central to the progressive and associationalist movements of the 1920s and 1930s, and continued apace for the remainder of the twentieth century. For example, as Great Society programs expanded government's concerns with health, safety, and the environment during the 1960s, President Lyndon Johnson turned to universities and private foundation funding (e.g., the Rockefeller Foundation) for social science expertise to inform their construction and development.

In subsequent years, much of that expertise was brought inside government agencies, where they issued rules implementing statutory requirements.[37] So, too, as we will review in chapter 6, did the number of organized interest groups doing policy analyses spiral in Washington and in state capitals to challenge the experts in public agencies. Although positive in so many ways for the nation, among the downsides of this binge of professional specialization has been that only those with expertise could follow and influence legislative and agency deliberations.[38] Moreover, research evidence is mounting that business participation dwarfs that of other groups at every stage of the agency rulemaking process that you will be participating in, informing, or implementing during your careers.[39]

Nor was this the only downside of this secular trend. Just as rising education, professionalization, and related wage gaps played a role in creating social tensions at the turn of the twentieth century, by the end of the first decade of the twenty-first century, they were major contributors to the significant income inequities in America. In addition to what we just reviewed regarding income inequities, the performance gap on test scores needed for advanced educational and professional opportunities between low-income and affluent children is now double the testing gap between blacks and whites.

Also, a stunning imbalance between rich and poor children in college completion rates has increased by 50 percent since the 1980s. Importantly, college completion rates are the single best predictor of employment success and income during a person's working life. High-school graduates can expect, on average, to earn $1.2 million during their working life; those with a bachelor's degree, $2.1 million; and people with a master's degree, $2.5 million. Persons with doctoral degrees earn an average of $3.4 million during their working life, while those with professional degrees do best at $4.4 million.[40] Even then, evidence exists that women have to attain a PhD to earn more in their lifetimes than men who have only attained a bachelor's degree, and women with bachelor's degrees earn nearly the same over the course of their careers as men with some college experience but no degree.

Nor will you be surprised to read that, in the postindustrial era of specialization, the biggest education-related income gaps fall disproportionally on minority and single-female-headed families. The Bureau of Labor Statistics in the Department of Commerce reported in 2011 that African American and Hispanic families were significantly more likely to have an unemployed member (18.9 and 16.3 percent, respectively) than white and Asian families (10.4 and 10.9 percent, respectively). In addition, more than 70 percent of all mothers and more than 60 percent of mothers with children under three years of age are in the workforce, with two-thirds of them earning less than $30,000 a year and 90 percent making less than $50,000. As such, public managers such as yourself will be seeking ways to manage this exacerbation of trends toward a permanent underclass in America.

Changes in Place and Technology

When John Gaus wrote about changes in place affecting demands for government responses, he focused largely on population movements. They will be equally salient for you as a public manager for the foreseeable future. So, too, however, will be changes in place related to business location and tax mobility that, in turn, are related to changes in technology. Changes in technology have always brought both significant progress and policy challenges that generate calls for government redress. In the future, the following trends in technology and migration will be felt mostly by public managers such as yourself, because they will mean downward pressures on public taxing, dislocations demanding social service delivery, and a ginning up of spending.

Population Migration

As your coursework will repeatedly demonstrate, population migrations have been a driver of needs and demands for social services and either volunteer or government redress throughout US history. For starters, population growth and movements during the colonial era helped spawn what one leading historian calls the "fragmentation of households, churches, and communities."[41] When settlers began migrating within and away from the Atlantic seaboard into the Appalachians and the Mississippi Valley between 1760 and the early 1800s, losing lifelines to their original homes, their needs prompted the creation of voluntary associations across the Eastern seaboard.

Likewise, the westward migration of evangelicals in the 1830s meant the forming of thousands of voluntary associations to handle social problems, including slavery and temperance issues.[42] Indeed, by 1837, the so-called "evangelical united front"—national associations led by the American Bible Society—encouraged local associations to "work to better their communities."[43] Moreover, the federal government fostered these networks by means of grants and subsidies until unity was fragmented by the Civil War's sectional conflicts.[44] And by establishing confederated associations linking Americans across the continent during the nineteenth century, "they effectively brought ordinary people, including women and African Americans, into the imagined and actual life of the nation."[45] Meanwhile, confrontations with aggrieved Native American tribes having their lands and cultures stripped from them as Western migration accelerated during the remainder of the century prompted calls from settlers to Washington for federal troops.

You should also be aware that, in some ways, the field of public administration owes its origins to population migration, including religious migration. First, as migration from Ireland and Germany occurred from the 1830s to 1850s, the corruption and incompetence of the patronage state prompted the reform coalition that produced the Civil Service Act of 1883. Subsequently, during the first two decades of the twentieth century, you will recall that progressive reformers—many with evangelical Protestant roots—saw existing administrative structures as unable to cope with health, safety, and crime problems in urban areas, as well as the corruption of political machines dependent on immigrants for electoral support.

Migration also sparked concerns for social justice and calls for equal opportunity in the twentieth century. For instance, African American migration, first to the North for jobs and then back to the South for the same, animated racial tensions that wrought the civil rights movement in the 1960s. Likewise, military service overseas in World War II for many rural and noncollege-educated whites brought the GI Bill that helped to create the US middle class in the postwar era.

In turn, population migration over the last half of the twentieth century and continuing today has produced a series of major demands on government for action and administrative reform. We see it within the United States (e.g., northerners from the Frostbelt states moving into the Sunbelt states), into the United States (e.g., from Mexico and Southeast Asia, and in terms of Islamic immigrants), and among or within other nations (e.g., into England, France, and Germany). In 2014, for instance, the total number of international refugees and domestically displaced persons due to conflicts and sectarian violence in places such as Syria, Libya, Eretria, Afghanistan, and Somalia was estimated at nearly 50-million persons worldwide. Various European Union nations became favorite short-term and long-term destinations and were challenged to deal with humanitarian crises within their borders.[46] Meanwhile, the United States faced similar problems on its southwestern border with Mexico as nearly 50,000 children unaccompanied by adults from Central America were placed in illegal immigrant camps after evolving US immigration policy was incorrectly interpreted to mean they could automatically become US citizens.

Certainly, in the long run, the ethnic diversity that results from employment-driven immigration affords the kinds of new skills, talents, work ethic, and cultures that have always advanced US economic and national security interests. In the short run, however, problems arise that the private sector and nonprofits cannot handle alone. For example, migration places significant tax, service delivery, and cultural strains on society that you will have to cope with either directly or indirectly as a public servant in the twenty-first century.

During your career, you will also continue to face the challenges, choices, and opportunities spawned by a "migratory" success story that government helped to foster: the "suburbanization" and "ex-urbanization" of America. It did so with the best of intentions through such programs as government-backed home loans (VHA and FHA loans) and the construction of highways connecting those homes to jobs. But, in the process, the out-migration of residents helped to erode the tax bases of inner cities, thus making it harder to provide needed services for low-income and minority residents excluded from home loans and left behind. This, in turn, created a vicious cycle of raising central city taxes for individuals and businesses, resulting in further out-migration, leading to further tax increases, and so on.

Given the political activism of suburbanites—especially suburban women—relative to inner-city voters, migration has also made it difficult for elected officials in inner cities to compete for resources in Congress and state legislatures. At the same time, as migration from Frostbelt to Sunbelt cities increased over the past half-century, a decrease occurred in the numbers of congressional representatives in Washington representing the concerns of older Northern and Midwestern cities. So, too, did the electoral votes of states in these regions decrease in presidential elections, giving the more conservative

Sunbelt states a decided advantage in shaping the nation's political agenda during the last quarter of the twentieth century.

International Job Migration

Another secular trend relates to technological advances enabling the outsourcing of jobs to other nations to take advantage of lower wage rates than in the United States. Nor is this trend limited to manufacturing; even high-technology jobs are fair game in the global economy. A reversal in the collective bargaining power of unions worldwide might help attenuate this trend somewhat, as might rising wages in developing nations as capitalism takes root and educated workforces become critical to business. But the former is unlikely and the latter will take considerable time to have an impact.

After three decades of neoliberal labor policies pushed by conservatives in Congress, the United States has labor laws that make it the "most difficult place to organize workers in the advanced world."[47] The share of union membership has fallen to approximately 7 percent of all workers from a peak of one-third of all workers at the beginning of the Cold War and one-fourth in the early 1970s.[48] And although public sector unionization is the most vibrant part of the labor movement today with a 30 percent share of the workforce, we shall see in greater detail in chapter 7 how they are under assault today. Moreover, the combination of adverse labor union legislation, offshoring of production lines, and those assaults on public sector unions have placed downward pressures on union power, wages, and political clout.

Consequently, transnational corporations will continue for some time—implicitly or explicitly—to either threaten or actually move operations or parts of business lines to other nations or to jurisdictions within the United States with lower labor costs (e.g., to so-called "right-to-work" states in the Sunbelt). In the process, they will continue to pit regions, states, localities, and nations against each other to gain tax subsidies, tax preferences, and infrastructure commitments. These will boost their profits while reducing the revenue available to governments—and, hence, to you as a public manager—to address public needs. Interestingly, a new movement called "economic gardening" has arisen in some cities to move away from trying to lure corporations to their jurisdiction. Favored instead is helping smaller, local businesses to prosper and survive through grants and contracts.[49] You might even be a part of helping to shape or implement such initiatives, or create new ones, depending on where you work during your career.

Further exacerbating these trends is the urgency that worldwide competition places on raising business productivity while cutting labor costs. Threatened industries have turned to employing part-time, temporary workers in the "24-hour workday" that a global economy has created.[50] Nor do these jobs typically provide health or pension benefits, which means that some public managers such as yourself will face continuous pressures to address the needs of persons who fall through the social safety net in America.

Although the labor supply issue alone is important, so, too, are the challenges related to entrepreneurship and the immigration of skilled professionals into America. You may not know that 18 percent of all Fortune 500 companies in 2010 were founded by immigrants to the United States. Indeed, when the children of immigrants are included, 40 percent of those companies were founded by new citizens. And when one considers only high-tech engineering companies founded in the United States between 1995 and 2005, 20 percent were founded by immigrants.[51] Since 9/11, however, the United States has sorely restricted—and made more onerous—the awarding of visas to international students studying in the country. Consequently, many have returned home or moved to countries such as Canada, China, or India that are actively encouraging immigration to bolster their economies.

Tax Migration

A third change in place related to technology involves the location of where transnational corporations pay their taxes. This is a function of the globalization of business product lines that is made possible by computer network advancements. These allow "real-time" monitoring of product lines, wherever in the world they are located. Indeed, the consensus among economists is that approximately one-third of the United States' world trade deficit that you hear so much about now comprises *intra*-firm sales made to subsidiaries in foreign countries.[52] In the process, the globalization of product lines has afforded opportunities for corporations to engage in what economists refer to as "income shifting." Corporations claim deductions for costly production expenditures that they incur against the taxes they owe to countries with higher corporate tax rates. Conversely, they assess high profits to production facilities in nations that have lower corporate tax rates.[53] On an individual scale, you may have heard in 2014 about the outcry in Ireland when it was learned that the rock star and humanitarian, Bono, and his band U2, had shifted millions of dollars in income to the Netherlands to take advantage of its significantly lower tax rates.[54] But actual income shifting by companies and individuals need not take place to affect public sector revenues; merely the potential for corporations and individuals to do so will continue to put downward pressures on corporate tax rates worldwide.

The "Continuous Election" in Financial Markets

Because of technological innovations, nations worldwide now have an unprecedented chance to capitalize on the economic, social, and cultural opportunities produced by international financial markets. However, to do so, they must first convince investors that they are prepared to privatize state-owned enterprises, cut subsidies to those that remain, lower trade barriers, remove restrictions on foreign direct investment, balance their budgets, and cut the size of the public sector. As such, influence over macro-level economic decisions now migrates to an unprecedented extent from the US Federal Reserve to foreign investment and exchange capitals.

So, too, does control over US money supply move partially, albeit indirectly, from the Federal Reserve to the fiscal and monetary policies of foreign capitals and international financial traders. And, in a global economy, what happens in other nations—inflation or recession, high growth or low growth—has to be considered by policy makers in the United States. Thus, what governments such as China, Germany, or Japan do may mean as much, if not more, than what the national government in the United States does. As a result, although voters cast their vote on election days, financial markets in effect "vote" every day and can reinforce or repudiate what governments are doing by deciding where in the world to keep their money to get the greatest monetary return.

Depending on your area of specialization, you may be involved in helping to analyze these trends and making policy recommendations to adjust to them. However, regardless of specialization or level of government in which you work, the general economic climate affected by these factors will affect your agency's work. And because the global economy puts consistent pressure on companies to cut costs and downsize their workforces in order to remain competitive, governments and public managers such as yourself will find that the social costs of resizing corporate structures to meet these needs will largely fall upon them. This, in turn, means that cash-strapped governments increasingly will turn to the partnering systems of the networked state to leverage their resources for meeting these social costs.[55] For you as a public sector employee, this means honing your skills during your program and career for understanding how best to work in these partnering relationships.

The Rush to Product Standardization and Financial Market Deregulation

Technological innovation leading to a global economy has also affected the location of regulatory responsibilities. Over the past three decades, government and business elites have agreed on the need to standardize technological, product-line, and environmental regulations for global markets to function effectively, rather than having different standards in different nations. Consequently, nations have frequently turned over responsibility for standards and trade regulations to international associations such as the International Organization for Standardization, which is comprised of representatives from business, government, and (less prominently) nongovernmental organizations and the World Trade Organization.

This internationalization of responsibilities has both advantages and disadvantages. It can be useful in breaking down protectionist barriers to trade in a global economy. It can also have a leavening effect on lax product and environmental standards in both developed and developing countries by increasing stringency and making regulatory compliance a business advantage. But the downside risks include the possibility of compromising standards to the lowest common denominator of quality or safety, setting standards stringent enough to drive smaller competitors out of business who cannot afford to meet them, and using standards for protectionist purposes through what are called "nontariff barriers to trade."[56] The negative side effects of any of these will fall on governments and public managers, as will the task of working in international regulatory networks or adjusting regulations to those developed in other nations.

In terms of regulatory networks, consider the results of efforts to deregulate financial markets that occurred during the 1980s and 1990s and that fostered the Great Recession of 2007–09 in the United States and Europe. Regulators had created "market-friendly" accountability structures that "trusted private actors to self-regulate."[57] In 2000, for example, Congress ratified a veritable laissez-faire regulatory environment for over-the-counter derivatives trading. In the process, elected officials and regulators privatized the tasks of valuing market risks and assets to credit-rating firms whose compensation schemes depended on undervaluing risk. Also consonant with the early progressives' focus on taking politics out of administration, the 1990s saw elected officials worldwide shifting financial regulatory power to their treasury departments.[58]

Globalization of Local Economic Development

As alluded to earlier, were you to pursue a career in state or local government, you will also be affected by the globalization of economic development. You will either deal directly in developing or be affected by targeted, place-specific policies for attracting investments to your states and communities. Some argue that economic globalization has diminished the importance of location as a competitive edge in fostering economic growth.[59] American communities no longer have a great innovation advantage, they argue, because technologies such as the internet and wireless communication increasingly allow anyone, anywhere on the globe, to be a player in the global economy, particularly in places where wages for highly educated and skilled persons are still lower. In these locales, a business-centered strategy for economic development must come first to lure information-age types—one wherein localities reduce the costs of doing business through subsidies and incentives for regulatory relief.

Still others contend that cities trying to lure economic development to their areas "need a [friendly] *people climate* even more than [and before] they need a [friendly] business climate."[60] Policy makers first need to attract creative information-age people; economic development will then follow. This means offering amenities such as the arts and creating an acceptance of ethnic, minority, and gay lifestyles that appeal to this creative class of young, upwardly, and geographically mobile professionals who tend to stay single longer and look for community instead.[61]

Then there are those who counsel you to focus on regional economic development, as the most economically successful cities are regionally embedded and not locality-based. In the process, however, what policy analysts call "collective-action problems" arise among decentralized governmental authorities still seeking to create competitive economic advantage over others. At best, "coopertition" occurs.[62] Regardless of your field of specialization, and whether or not you work in local or state governments, you will be affected by these developments due to their impact on tax revenues and demands for particular types of services.

The IT, Social Media, AI, and GIS Revolution in Government

Wherever your public service career takes you, you will also have to deal effectively with the positive and negative effects of the information technology (IT), social media, artificial intelligence (AI), and geographic information systems (GIS) revolution underway worldwide. Not only does their development have the potential to make cross-agency collaboration and data sharing possible to an unprecedented extent, it makes what you do and the consequences of your actions as a public manager decidedly more visible and potentially more transparent to citizens. As such, the possibilities they offer have the potential for revolutionizing public sector work, especially in terms of enhancing opportunities for citizen participation in agency decision making.

But technological and social media breakthroughs such as these can also limit citizen input to those with network access. If your agency does not anticipate and compensate for this limitation, it will result in giving less input to disadvantaged citizens and more to better-off and organized interests. We already have a democratic deficit in America that you do not want to exacerbate and, hopefully, are committed to redress. A recent analysis of 25 years of survey research by Kay Schlozman, Sidney Verba, and Henry Brady concludes that at all levels of government "the individuals and organizations that are active in American politics are anything but representative. In particular, those who are not affluent and well educated are less likely to take part politically and are even less likely to be represented by the activity of organized interests."[63] These breakthroughs also raise critical legal and ethical issues that you will have to address with IT and legal professionals during your career, not the least of which are related to invasions of privacy, data access and sharing, commercial cybersecurity, and national security risks.

Prior research on e-government, IT, and social media initiatives in public agencies suggests that reaping the potentially immense benefits of these technologies has been quite challenging up to this point.[64] For instance, the most common use of e-government has involved information sharing and service transactions rather than collaboration or civic deliberation.[65] Moreover, most IT applications have focused on monitoring the status quo to make it run better. Also, because the quantitative measures used in IT systems simplify real-world complexity, they can narrow policy makers' focus to policy problems that are quantifiable and for which data are available. This diverts attention from issues and solutions that may deserve equal or more attention. As a public manager, overcoming this resistance and compensating for these tendencies will be primary areas of attention for you if we are to realize the benefits to deliberative democracy that these technologies can afford and that remedying citizen estrangement from government makes critical.

What is more, if computer scientist and best-selling author Jaron Lanier and colleagues of his persuasion are correct, as a public manager you might be involved in regulating, helping to reform, or dealing with the social and economic consequences of the current business model of social media moguls.[66] He writes that Americans (and persons worldwide) are freely giving their personal data to social media enterprises such as Facebook and private commercial businesses such as insurance companies, Google, and Amazon, who then engage in so-called "Big Data" analyses for huge profits. With incredible speed, Big Data analyses identify patterns (e.g., consumption patterns or networks of individuals) in the voluminous amounts of information provided by citizens that otherwise would not be detected.

In effect, consumers are exchanging their privacy without monetary compensation for entertainment, other forms of consumerism, and the promise of future benefits (e.g., better coordinated and personalized health care or protection from terrorists). In 2013, kickback from citizens regarding "data mining" by the National Security Agency and other government agencies occurred in the wake of the Edward Snowden affair, requiring experts within and across government agencies to develop policies that try to protect against such abuses. But so far, the basis for Big Data analyses—the personal information collected without compensation from citizens—has not struck a similar chord with the American public. Neither has widespread concern been aroused by the "winner-take-all" reality—and thus potentially anti-competitive nature—of the business model underpinning it. Writes Lanier, to be powerful in today's information economy means "information superiority," so power flows to those with the "biggest and most connected computer... [W]e shouldn't fall into the illusion of thinking of computers as great equalizers."[67] Given Moore's Law that the information-processing capacity of computers doubles every two years, dealing with the privacy, income redistribution, anti-competitive, and possible political power distortion of technology is likely to be a persistent agenda item for you as a public manager.

Similar dual-edged issues arise in the use of GIS technology in government. On the positive side, GIS is being used for planning and community development, environmental protection, integrated public safety, infrastructure management, transportation planning/modeling, assessments, facility siting, vehicle routing, permitting/licensing, election management, and parcel/real estate management.[68] On the negative side, issues related to democratic governance arise, including the same privacy, governance, information-hoarding issues that you will have to struggle with in the IT and social media areas.

But it is in the area of potential AI and robotic applications that technology's most profound opportunities and challenges for society arise and, thus, for you as a public manager. On the very positive side for society, AI promises to revolutionize every aspect of our lives. For example, among many other things, it already has changed how hazardous waste sites are cleaned up, routine surgeries are performed from remote locations, fires are fought, airplanes are flown, space is explored, warfare is performed (by drones), and automobiles are driven. But what some experts and futurists say might be right around the corner is quite astounding, from robotically driven cars, personal flying cars, microbot surgery, and crowdsourcing our medical diagnoses and prescriptions to isolated areas around the world. Take robotic cars. Just think how they might reduce auto accidents, allow longer periods of self-sufficiency for senior citizens, and deliver meals-on-wheels to the needy.

The potential downsides of AI and robotics, of course, also can be mind-numbing. As Lanier again warns, the replacement of many low-skill—and even some higher-skill—jobs can combine with the continuing concentration of wealth in America to further increase social inequities in the nation.[69] None of these futuristic scenarios, opportunities, and challenges are necessarily going to happen. But if they do, their development and consequences will be affected by decisions made or actions taken by career civil servants such as yourself for decades to come in America and abroad.

Changes in Attitudes but Consistency in Public Philosophy

Both the persistence of a public philosophy in the United States and major changes in attitudes and beliefs over the past three decades promise to continue challenging public management in the twenty-first century.

A Preference for a "Compensatory State"

As Aaron Friedberg argues, the American "Founders succeeded, in effect, in encoding a strong strain of antistatism into the new nation's political DNA. It is a strain that would reproduce itself and continue to fulfill its protective function in future generations [as well as a fear of] the dangers of excessive concentrations of governmental power."[70] Adds Gordon Wood, the "emergence of the liberal, individualistic, commercial, and interest-ridden world of early nineteenth-century America" remains today "part of the nation's understanding of itself."[71]

But you may be thinking that we *do* have a substantial administrative state in America. Certainly, your reading of chapter 1 confirms the accuracy of that impression. So how does a country infused with these values—what we alluded to in chapter 1 as American exceptionalist values—politically garner the administrative capacity to meet national challenges such as the ones with which we have been routinely confronted and with which we have dealt?[72] Since the nation's birth, the visible size of the national state has been hidden by creating a "compensatory state." This is a state that—as vividly illustrated in chapter 1—hides itself by acting indirectly through state and local governments, as well as networks of public, private, and nonprofit sector actors.[73]

Certainly, building a "government out of sight" at the federal government level was the default option of American leaders in the eighteenth and nineteenth centuries.[74] To this end, they relied on tariffs collected at US ports rather than internal taxes or income taxes, and they depended on the decentralized nature of state and local governments to advance national aims. They subsidized and gave tax-free deals for settling and developing Western lands and infrastructure. And they did not distinguish "between state and civil society or, for that matter, public and private roles for citizens."[75]

Attesting to the resiliency of this public philosophy, for instance, the United States did not pursue a classic European welfare state. Instead, the nineteenth century saw Americans build a "social service" state of political parties and voluntary associations, established primarily by politically disenfranchised women working in volunteer associations enabled by the federal government.[76] Likewise, as also alluded to in chapter 1, during the two world wars of the twentieth century, the nation relied on the private and nonprofit sectors for war mobilization and fighting.[77] Then, during the Cold War, "state capacity was expanded by appending the capacities of private-sector associations on to the state."[78] Be clear, however. Deregulation, privatization, and devolution of responsibilities to laissez-faire markets, states, localities, and counties do not indicate that the American state is a weak one. When the interaction of these actors is taken collectively, the "power of the U.S. [state] to regulate, study, order, discipline, punish [and support] its citizens—as well as other nations' citizens—has never been greater" than today.[79]

That said, in addition to helping to manage your agency's day-to-day operations during your public service career, you will either directly or indirectly be working on solving three puzzles related to networked governance in the compensatory state. The first is figuring out how best to accomplish your agency's purposes through leveraging the various tools at your disposal to get network actors to do what is necessary to fulfill its mission. The second is trying to ensure accountability in this complex, sometimes opaque, and loosely connected network of actors who do not perceive themselves as anything but private or nonprofit employees. Finally, you will be informing, making choices, or living with choices made by others concerning when your agency should directly carry out the implementation of programs as opposed to "buying" the services of others to do them for you. Helping to run a constitution will require no less of you as a public manager.

A Dispirited Citizenry

As we touched on earlier, public confidence in government at all levels has fallen significantly since the 1970s, with only a brief respite after 9/11. Federal agencies have usually been ranked more favorably than other government institutions such as Congress. However, the rankings of seven of 13 agencies covered in surveys between 1997 and 2007 fell significantly, including the Food and Drug Administration, the Department of Education, the National Aeronautics and Space Administration, the Centers for Disease Control and Prevention, and the Social Security Administration. Nor were these downward trends limited to the federal government, as the percentages of respondents who held positive views of the impact of state government on their lives dropped from 62 percent in 1997 to 42 percent in 2007.

As we will review in greater detail in later chapters, mounting empirical research exists in political science, policy analysis, and sociology that links the design of administrative structures, policies, and procedures with citizens' perceptions of self-worth and political efficacy (i.e., their sense for being able to influence government). These perceptions, in turn, have been shown to affect the propensity of citizens to pay attention to government, to value what it does, to participate in the political process, and to be mobilizable for political action. A disaffected, if not estranged, citizenry is not only normatively troubling for the reasons already mentioned in this chapter regarding the inequities it can breed through a distorted representation of interests. It is also an obstacle for you as a public manager trying to discern the needs of citizens, to marshal coalitions for supporting those needs, and to avoid disgruntled citizens in courtrooms. As such, and as this book will repeatedly emphasize, you should always be cognizant in your career of the impact of your actions on citizen perceptions of government more generally. You should reflect not only on program and career success but also on your role in helping to run a democratic republic.

Dueling Political Preferences

You will also see your work as a public manager affected by a changing materialist-post-materialist divide, culture wars, and dysfunctional levels of party partisanship. Ronald Inglehart has identified what he calls a surge of "postmaterialist values" worldwide.[80] As a rule, the higher the income and education levels of a nation, the greater the level of concern that its citizens have about issues requiring government intervention. These include support for ensuring strong social safety nets; improving the general quality of life—namely, investments in social amenities; ensuring gender, race, and ethnic equality; and protecting the environment. In the United States, for example, Jeffrey Berry sees postmaterialism driving the rising number and power of citizen groups pursuing a "new liberalism" agenda.[81] Also reflecting postmaterialist values are the participation of green parties in Europe and the impact of nongovernmental organizations on government policy throughout Europe, Africa, Latin America, and Southeast Asia.

But interacting with these activist government trends is a third political trend with which you will have to contend: the rise of a conservative populist strain in America. Until recently, conventional political wisdom in the United States was that the higher the education and income levels of Americans, the more likely they were to vote Republican. Yet, the 2000 elections began a trend that continues in which well-educated, higher-income, and non-church-attending white professionals (e.g., academics, doctors, lawyers, and scientists) are now among the Democratic Party's most reliable voters. In contrast, lower-income whites without college degrees who attend church regularly are among the most reliable Republican voters.

This reversal of partisan fortunes is also the product of shifts in religious attitudes, affiliations, and policy orientations in the United States. Analyzing survey data since the 1950s, Robert Putnam and David Campbell identify various "shocks" that have occurred among the religious that have had political implications which will affect your work directly or indirectly.[82] In the aftermath of evangelical Protestantism expanding beyond its fundamentalist roots in the rural South to the world via television broadcasts such as the Billy Graham crusades, the initial shock was the way denominational splits among Catholics, Jews, and Protestants morphed into liberal–conservative splits. Most responsible for this was the "countercultural" social revolution of the 1960s and early 1970s as summarized in that generation's "sex, drugs, and rock and roll" mantra and extended later to abortion and gay rights battles.

Putnam and Campbell's analysis of survey data documents how conservatives in all religions joined with evangelicals to condemn this perceived assault on traditional values and authority structures. The influence on politics of the so-called "Religious Right" and the "Christian Right" as part of the Republican Party base became a constant drumbeat in the press. But you should also not forget that many churches and church members were at the forefront of the civil rights movement and were—and remain—active in providing needed social services and counseling to the poor. Indeed, many churches were—and are—active in the climate change and sustainable development movements. Interestingly, though, membership in the Tea Party movement in the United States over the past decade indicates somewhat of a more libertarian streak in these voters, at least on social issues.

But a second aftershock occurred in the 1990s, this time in reaction to the perceived excesses of the Religious Right. A spike was witnessed from 7 percent to nearly 35 percent in nonaffiliation with traditional religions, especially among the millennial generation (ages 18 to 29). Indeed, although millennials continued to shift toward a more conservative position on abortion, they were more antiestablishment and accepting of gay lifestyles and gay marriage. In this, they reflect a significantly growing portion of survey respondents of all ages who show—as noted above—a more libertarian political stance, one incorporating a less activist government agenda domestically and internationally. And, politically, the shocks and aftershocks of religion and the polarization of politics accompanying them have contributed to the "stop-and-go" policy and budget brinksmanship that makes managing agencies and implementing programs challenging.

Both of these trends also have contributed to—but are not the sole reasons for—astounding and dysfunctional levels of ideological party divides in Congress and in many states. In 1950, a celebrated report done by a committee of the American Political Science Association argued that political parties as constituted were not up to the challenges facing America. They called for a "responsible two-party" system in the United States.[83] Just as some early progressives had coveted parliamentary government for their executive leadership and presumed speed of operation, these political scientists embraced the unified, program-based political parties in parliamentary systems. "An effective party system," they wrote, "requires, first, that the parties are able to bring forth programs to which they commit themselves and, second, that the parties possess sufficient internal cohesion to carry these programs out."[84] Party members ran on unified policy platforms, and the majority party (or the dominant party in a coalition with concessions to its minority partner or partners) governed on that basis until the voters threw them out of office.

Well, in effect, we have that system today in Washington—and we now lament the results: partisan polarization, an unwillingness to bargain, a tendency to demonize opponents and impugn their motives, and legislative gridlock. Indeed, as two leading critics of what has happened diagnose the reasons for gridlock in Congress, we have parliamentary parties trying to operate in a Madisonian system—a recipe for disaster.[85] Certainly, balanced budget requirements—no matter how subject to gamesmanship (see chapter 8)—in most states tend to breed more compromise. Moreover, in 2013, 36 states had single-party control of both the governorship and the state legislature. Republicans dominated 23 of these states, while the Democrats dominated 13 states.[86] Polarization still arises, however, when state governments as a whole are considered. Indeed, you need look no further than the nearly 50/50 ideological divide in state governors on the ACA.

Most Republican governors opted out of Medicaid expansion as an option, as well as out of creating exchanges in their states. Most Democratic governors did precisely the opposite. And similar philosophical divides can be seen at all levels of government when it comes to climate change issues, expansion of other social programs, and social security reform.

As you probably have heard from political analysts, there are a variety of reasons for how and why we got to this point. These include, but are not limited to, the shift of conservative Democrats to the Republican Party and the defeat of moderate Democrats; the capture of election primaries by extreme wings of both parties; the "sorting out" of Americans geographically into socioeconomic and political enclaves of likeminded persons; generational replacement; the Voting Rights Act; and the fragmentation of the media, which allows citizens to avoid views that contradict their own. Its causes aside, as a public manager, you will be affected by these secular trends. Regardless of what level of government you serve, you will be affected by gridlock in Washington in the form of programmatic and planning uncertainties, budget uncertainties, and efforts by chief executives to politicize the bureaucracy in order to advance their policy aims administratively when legislation is blocked. And depending on the state in which you live, these constraints will vary in severity. But as later chapters will show, these challenges will necessitate choices and create opportunities for the best of your generation of public managers to help shape a democratic republic.

Conclusion

Using Gaus' "ecology" of public administration as a framework, you now have a good sense for the long-term secular trends that are animating the challenges, choices, and opportunities currently facing public managers. You also now have a framework for assessing these trends as they evolve throughout your career, trends that you can use strategically and tactically to inform your program and agency goals. What you still lack, however, is a sense for how and why these challenges require public agencies to reconceptualize purpose, reconnect with citizens, redefine administrative rationality, reengage financial resources, recapitalize personnel assets, and revitalize a sense of common purpose infused with democratic constitutional values. It is to this task that we turn next in chapter 3 by reviewing three sets of major global policy challenges with intermestic policy implications.

CHAPTER 3

Linking Problems, Policy, and Public Management

As noted in chapter 1, had you begun or resumed your coursework in public administration as the Cold War dawned in the late 1940s, you would have learned that a number of scholars were worried about what the growth of the administrative state in Washington was doing to democratic values such as responsiveness, equity, equality, due process, and constitutional rights. These so-called "traditionalists"—leading lights of our field such as Paul Appleby, Charles Hyneman, and Norton Long whose research you may read in your coursework—joined Dwight Waldo in fearing that these values might get shortchanged, if not displaced entirely, in the late twentieth century by a premature, narrow, and myopic focus on economy and efficiency by technocratic specialists.[1] Posing a fundamental question for a democratic republic, Appleby asked: "How can we be a complex society and yet be a democratic society?"[2]

Today, these queries take on even more urgency. As illustrated in chapter 2, many of the most important policy challenges of our day are what your professors may call "multiattribute" (having many dimensions), "multidisciplinary" (requiring expertise from different academic disciplines), and "interdependent" problems. What is more, they are rife with what some scholars call "value pluralism." These are situations where a range of competing values predominates, conflict is prolonged in crowded policy and administrative spaces, and "solutions" are not objectively "right or wrong." Rather, solutions depend "upon the setting in which they arise" and the values that have to be traded off.[3] Moreover, a greater tendency exists for domestic and international policy to affect each other in a global economy requiring Heclo's "collective puzzlement on behalf of society" informed by public managers at all levels of government.[4]

But when you hear that the government is gridlocked, do not be fooled. For example, at the federal government level where concerns about congressional gridlock are daily fodder in the media, a robust agenda awaits you. Researchers studying decades of legislative activity in the United States find that although the number of *major* pieces of legislation decreases during periods of divided government, *overall* legislative productivity does not.[5] Moreover, the media is mostly looking in the wrong place for the policy "action." According to a May 2013 Congressional Research Service Report, "While 78 pieces of legislation were passed by the most recent Congress, the average number of rules [by federal agencies] issued annually is between 2,500 and 4,500."[6] Each of these rules is followed by guidance documents to federal agencies about how to implement them. In turn, state agencies may then be involved in additional rulemaking and guidance efforts in which public managers will have varying levels of involvement. Thus, while the media camps out in front of the White House, Congress, or the Supreme Court, most of the action is really happening in federal, state, and local agencies where anything but grid-lock is occurring!

As a career public servant, you will be contributing to this process—hopefully posi-tively! The citizens you are sworn to serve and protect, and the constitution you pledge to support, will expect you to embed your actions within the broad framework of Waldo's "consciously held values" in a democracy.[7] What is more, within the networked compen-satory state, complex problems expand exponentially, the keys to unlocking gridlock do not always fit the locks, and you may not even know where or how to find them. Pretty exciting stuff, right?!

Before applying the 6R framework of challenges, choices, and opportunities to specific tasks you will be asked to perform as a public manager in the twenty-first century, this chapter affords a glimpse of why they are important and how they interact in three wicked problem areas with domestic and international implications. These intermestic problem areas are global aging and public health policy, global food security, and global environ-mental security. From this, you should leave the chapter appreciating how and why public managers must play critical roles in helping to resolve their concerns. You will also see why thinking systemically during your career about how various administrative processes interact with each other is essential for building a sense of common purpose infused by democratic constitutional values in dealing with today's and tomorrow's problems.

The Gray Dawn and Public Health Policy

You have already read in chapter 2 about how demographers project countries in the developed world to experience an unprecedented growth in their elderly populations and an unprecedented decline in the number of their youth.[8] As is typical of wicked prob-lems, this "generational crossover" is attributable to a confluence of otherwise positive developments reviewed earlier, including declining fertility rates and longer lifespans.[9] Still, the least-developed nations increasingly are left behind their peers in the devel-oped world, because the economic challenges of health problems vary appreciably. For example, 90 percent of all malarial cases worldwide now occur in sub-Saharan Africa, nations such as the Philippines and Thailand are especially vulnerable to communicable diseases, and the average income ratio of the richest to the poorest nations has grown to 60-to-1 (from 9-to-1 at the end of the nineteenth century).[10]

Moreover, although optimal fertility rates are two births per woman of childbearing age in the developed world, and are even lower in China, one-seventh of the world's pop-ulation lives in countries with fertility rates of four births or more per woman. According to the United Nations, if family planning is not made more readily available to these nations, their populations will soar from 850 million in 2010 to 1.7 billion in 2050.[11] Analysis also indicates that should a woman conceive within 18 months after having a baby, child and maternal health suffer. The probability of miscarriages, stillbirths, low birth weights, and stunted child development increases appreciably.[12] This, in turn, means greater financial challenges and, likely, more calls for United States and international assistance.

As Douglas Wolf and Anna Amirkhanyan report, the impact of generational crossover also varies across the 50 states in the United States. Thus, were you to serve at the state or local government level, you might be more or less affected by these trends.[13] For example, in 13 states, unusually large increases in the dependency index are expected to occur. But where the greatest amount of variation exists is within states. For example, if you work in Arizona, you are likely to witness the second largest increase in senior population in the nation. And depending on where you work in the state's 15 counties, you may witness anywhere "from a low of -0.24 percent to a high of 67.2 percent" in negative or positive growth.[14]

Thus, as is typical with wicked policy problems, addressing the aging problem requires a concentrated effort across public, private, and nonprofit organizations. We will focus on only one aspect of this issue to illustrate this point—the public health dimension. The bottom line for you is that public agencies will face the difficult challenge of dealing with health issues that they have not faced before and for which they are presently not equipped to handle. Moreover, whether or not you work in a public health agency, the strains on finances and service delivery systems that these health issues pose will directly or indirectly affect your agency's operations as well.

For affected societies and agencies such as the US National Institutes of Health, state and local public health agencies, and many nongovernmental organizations (NGOs), this means shifting a portion of their focus and resources from population control, childhood diseases, and immunizations for younger populations to identifying, monitoring, treating, and managing chronic diseases (e.g., obesity, diabetes, cardiovascular diseases, hypertension, and cancer) associated with older populations. Indeed, the World Health Organization (WHO) has calculated that death rates from noncommunicable diseases have already overtaken those from communicable diseases (e.g., infectious and parasitic diseases) in all parts of the world except Africa. They also are seven times higher among middle-age workers (or those in so-called "prime labor-force ages") in developing nations than in the developed world. Lost in the process are the most productive economic years of citizens, which further promotes poverty and diminishes the tax revenues needed for capital investments in health systems transitioning to chronic diseases.

As such, public managers in these agencies will have to help *reconceptualize the purposes* of their existing programs. The longstanding focus on eliminating communicable diseases in children increasingly must be reconceptualized to incorporate a focus, as well, on identifying, monitoring, treating, and managing chronic diseases in middle-age adults and senior citizens. Reconceptualizing agency purposes in this way, in turn, will often mean *redefining administrative rationality* as personified in existing agency and interagency structures, processes, and procedures. Domestically, for example, in 2011 and 2012, the Government Accountability Office (GAO) found significant opportunities to eliminate duplication in health care by better case coordination and management in the departments of Defense and Veterans Affairs. Cost savings would also accrue with better information sharing among these two departments and the National Institutes of Health.[15]

Internationally, consider for a moment the path of the transmission of the virulent SARS (Severe Acute Respiratory Syndrome) epidemic in 2003 from Guangdong Province in China to the United States. No better example exists of why it is necessary to abandon single-agency thinking. Initially, secrecy prevailed in China, even after doctors in the province noted the contagiousness and high death rates of SARS. It was only through emails that the WHO found out about these deaths. Subsequently, one of the doctors treating patients in Guangdong traveled to a family wedding in Hong Kong and became ill during his stay at a hotel in one the busiest shopping areas in the city. He checked into a hospital where he died ten days later. Within a week, 386 persons living on three continents were infected. Aside from the human tragedies unfolding, China and Hong Kong lost approximately $15 billion, as tourist visits slowed dramatically. In Canada, over 2,000 reported cases requiring investigation soon outstripped the supply of doctors and new facilities to isolate patients, while public health officials tried heroically to go outside normal organizational boundaries, standard operating procedures, and bureaucratic routines to address these issues. Indeed, the more they fell back on their normal bureaucratic routines, the worse the situation became.

By its end, SARS had infected over 8,000 persons in two dozen countries on four continents. The reason was quite simple and was summarized in an advisory committee report provided to the Canadian government. Partnerships had to be voluntary and put together on the fly, because no steps had been taken in advance by relevant agencies to ask what they would do when "non-normal" crises occurred.

To be sure, these kinds of problems do not have to exist, and part of your job as a public servant working in or affected by these issues is to reduce their prevalence. Indeed, examples do exist of successfully bridging these gaps. Geographic information systems (GIS), for one, have allowed multiple jurisdictions to work together on a common front in the public health area. For example, the Birmingham, Alabama, county health department—in collaboration with the Environmental Protection Agency (EPA) and the University of Alabama at Birmingham—has undertaken the task of putting ozone information on GIS maps at the university's website.[16] Likewise, research on the creation of what are called "public sector knowledge networks" (PSKNs) for sharing information across agencies has shown great promise.[17] For instance, PSKN-related initiatives for sharing public health data exist, such as the BioSense system supported by the Centers for Disease Control and Prevention (CDC) and the Department of Health and Human Services. But PSKNs can be challenging, facing as they sometimes do subtle boundaries related to ideology, professional norms, and institutional divisions.[18]

Added to the need to reconceptualize purpose and redefine administrative rationality are the imperatives of *reconnecting with citizens and stakeholders in order to help reengage resources and recapitalize personnel assets.* As the gray dawn proceeds, managerial, political, and technical savvy is needed by policy makers and managers to find ways to leverage corporate pharmaceutical development adroitly for both communicable and chronic health diseases in the developing world. Currently, a market-driven disconnect exists between pharmaceutical supply and health needs in the United States and abroad.[19] Moreover, this disconnect is rife with social equity issues.

How so? Less than 1 percent (only 8 out of 1,233) of all drugs licensed worldwide between 1975 and 1997 were developed for tropical diseases in humans; for every 1,000 references in scientific papers to diseases in 1998, only 15 referenced diseases prevalent in the developing world; in the 17 poorest nations in the world, less than $10 per person was spent in 1998 on all health care, including pharmaceuticals; and less than 2 percent of spending for drugs dealing with cardiovascular diseases occurred in six nations (namely,

China, Egypt, India, Indonesia, Pakistan, and the Philippines). Although some progress on this front has occurred over the past decade, significant gaps still exist.

On top of this, two-thirds of US foreign assistance for health programs in the developing world is targeted for children's diseases and population control. As you might expect, the constellation of political actors surrounding these programs is formidable, resilient, and ill-disposed toward change. As Susan Raymond notes, "Concentrating huge resources on narrow problems over long periods of time has created both tunnel vision and significant vested interests in those problems among those who disburse the funds and those who win the contracts to implement the programs."[20]

Still, as global aging progresses, administrators considering responsiveness, cost-effectiveness, and equity in addressing the health care needs of "citizens as individuals" will be hard-pressed to overlook the need for a reconceptualization of purpose with its attendant need to finance and recapitalize personnel assets for new skills. One point of leverage for change is that although many of these nations are poor, they are biologically rich and potentially bountiful in ingredients for new medicines. But this means that public managers must also be at the forefront of developing strategies for reconnecting with foreign citizens who feel that corporations are unfairly "bioprospecting" their ecological bounties for pharmaceuticals without due compensation to them.

Meanwhile, in the United States, public managers will have to play a role in grappling with the Medicare and Medicaid frauds that have reached epic proportions and that must be curtailed substantially in an era of fiscal stress. GAO has consistently found weaknesses in Medicare's enrollment standards and procedures, which increases the risk of enrolling entities intent on defrauding the program.[21] The Centers for Medicare and Medicaid Services has made progress in addressing this by developing screening procedures for different categories of providers at each level. Nonetheless, GAO concluded in 2012 that much more needed to be done.

Similarly, the Patient Protection and Affordable Care Act (ACA) requires public management at all levels of government to work as envisioned by the law's proponents. Among other things, they will have to (1) help devise systems for determining which providers will be required to post surety bonds to ensure that fraudulent billing payments can be recovered, (2) contract for fingerprint-based criminal background checks, and (3) develop regulations specifying provider compliance with the law. You only need to think about the horrid rollout of the ACA in 2013 to appreciate how critical it will be for information technology specialists and their managers at all levels of government to make this law work effectively, as well as to regain and maintain citizen confidence in the system, whether it survives in whole or in part.

At the same time, recapitalization of personnel assets will be required to address health issues in the United States and overseas. Illustrative are the managerial challenges facing the CDC, challenges reflective of the plight of all public health agencies. GAO recently identified six key challenges the CDC faces in its efforts to sustain a skilled workforce to fulfill its mission and goals.[22] They include adjusting to changing workforce demographics, involving retirements of skilled personnel; dealing with a limited supply of skilled public health professionals nationwide to meet expanding workloads and responsibilities; overseeing the increasing diversity in its workforce; and managing a spiraling number of contractors, because expertise and staffing levels cannot handle the work in-house.

Nor can success be obtained without *building a sense of common purpose informed by democratic constitutional values* among agencies in this policy arena. As you are probably sensing, not only must the privacy of medical and other personal information be protected while knowledge networks are being created, but legal protections for medical staff against suits must be ensured. So, too, must procedural due process be built into the system, as well as processes of transparency and measures of accountability, to ensure that finances affecting one-sixth of the economy are spent as stipulated and without waste, fraud, and abuse of authority. With these issues so complex, with value pluralism so rife, and with policy spaces so crowded, public managers with the talent for facilitating decision making focused on building a sense of common purpose will be essential.

Global Food Security and Biotechnology Regulation

A second set of wicked problems that is likely to face you either directly or indirectly as a public manager involves the Janus-faced consequences of the technoscientific advances that you read about in chapter 2. To illustrate the critical role that public management must play in leveraging public resources to address these technoscientific challenges and opportunities, we focus here on one major wicked problem area—food security—and its impact on the developing world. However, the link to the United States, its policies, and its public managers is nonetheless profound.

The problem worldwide is that some scientists estimate that "by 2020, increasingly wealthy and urbanized consumers and the 2 billion new [and overwhelmingly poorer] mouths [to feed] will demand 40% more food."[23] Jonathan Foley puts the dilemma in readily understandable terms:

> The world's food system faces three incredible, interwoven challenges, then. It must guarantee that all seven billion people alive today are adequately fed; it must double food production in the next 40 years; and it must achieve both goals while becoming truly environmentally sustainable... Demand will also rise because many more people will have higher incomes, which means they will eat more, especially meat. Increasing use of cropland for biofuels will make meeting the doubling goal more difficult still. So even if we solve today's problems of poverty and access... we will also have to produce twice as much to guarantee adequate supply worldwide... By clearing tropical forests, farming marginal lands and intensifying industrial farming in sensitive landscapes and watersheds, humankind has made agriculture the planet's dominant environmental threat.[24]

Moreover, we know what the consequences of price increases in food commodities are for political stability. In both 2007 and 2010, massive social unrest almost immediately followed food price surges. These increases, in turn, tracked market behavior with uncanny synchronization. According to researchers from the New England Complex Systems Institute, commodity speculation—investors betting on food prices—amplifies any regular supply-and-demand market signals, creating new food price bubbles with ensuing crises.

Is this a population control problem, thus requiring an enhanced focus on birth control while protecting reproductive rights? Is it a problem requiring regulation of food commodity markets? Does it require an alteration in diets on a widespread scale to reduce our intake of meat? Is it a distribution problem rather than a supply problem, thus requiring improvements in transportation, safety, and refrigeration technologies? Is it a nutrition problem, thus requiring a pharmaceutical response? Could it be a supply problem that could be attenuated by a move to organic food farming or biotechnology advances? Does addressing the problem require a combination of all these things? As you can see, these initiatives have many dimensions that are controversial and pit citizens and interest groups against each other. And even were they not, resources are limited and must be prioritized. How can this be done best while not undermining the values citizens cherish in a democracy?

To illustrate the conundrum facing policy makers and public managers in the decades ahead, let us focus on one of the most controversial approaches to dealing with food security problems: the use of biotechnology. The optimism of genetically modified (GM) food proponents has been fueled by trait technology under development at agribusiness corporations (historically, Aventis, Monsanto, and Syngenta) that promises to increase crop yields, at lower net costs to farmers, with greater health benefits to consumers, and in more environmentally benign ways.[25] Challenging these claims, anti-GM food campaigners worldwide stress the cataclysmic risks to public health, safety, and the environment that they say are inherent in GM research, production, and commercialization. They argue that most prominent among these risks for humans are the disruption or silencing of existing genes, the activation of silent genes, and the formation of new or altered patterns of metabolites. Critiqued, as well, is the potential for GM foods to create new allergies or harmful toxins with which the body is ill-prepared to deal, causing sickness and death among vulnerable populations.

For a variety of ideological, cultural, and economic reasons related to these concerns, the so-called "precautionary principle" has been applied in Europe to GM research, testing, and development.[26] US regulators put the onus on critics of a technology to prove that a significant harm exists. But the precautionary principle turns this logic on its head by shifting the burden of proof away from opponents of biotechnology to prove that the harms they allege will occur. Proponents must prove that those speculative harms will not occur.

In the wake of food regulatory scandals in Europe in the 1980s and 1990s (e.g., "mad cow disease"), and led globally by international NGOs (INGOs) such as Greenpeace, opposition to GM foods resulted in the European Union (EU) enacting, first, a five-year moratorium on new GM food approvals. Then, in 2003, the EU adopted a rigorous GM-regulatory regime predicated on the precautionary principle requiring costly investments that US corporate food and grain producers found scientifically indefensible. With developing nations dependent for large segments of their exports on trade with EU nations and with their biosafety screening capacity much lower than Europe's, the safest thing for their regulators to do was to meet EU standards.[27]

As such, many agencies, organizations, and actors in the United States and abroad involved in food production, consumption, and regulation are in the process of *reconceptualizing their purpose and redefining administrative rationality* when it comes to agricultural production to feed the world. Especially affected in the United States will be public managers and regulators in the Animal and Plant Health Inspection Service of the US Department of Agriculture (USDA), the EPA, and the Food and Drug Administration (FDA), which all have regulatory authority over various aspects of GM food production. They—as well as agricultural producers—can no longer afford to ignore regulatory strictures on the production and use of GM organisms. The costs to farm producers from the loss of soy crop markets alone have been in the hundreds of millions of dollars.

As you can see, then, a huge challenge exists in the United States and other nations that demands the political acumen of what Paul Appleby called "philosophers of administration" and Dwight Waldo called "complete administrators." They—and perhaps you someday—must help "reconceptualize" GM food regulation to protect public health, safety, and the environment. They must do so, however, without putting at risk humanity's ability to explore the promises and pitfalls of major technoscientific advances that might help address pressing food security (and other) challenges.

By the same token, and as alluded to above, the regulation of GM foods in the United States is badly in need of a redefinition of administrative rationality, as are several international organizations. Depending on your employer and responsibilities in the public sector, you might be involved in helping the USDA, EPA, or FDA figure out how best to coordinate their oversight and regulation of genetically engineered (GE) crops. Over the past decade, all three have improved these processes, but several areas of improvement are needed to ensure safety.[28] For instance, the USDA and FDA do not have a formal method for sharing information that could enhance the FDA's voluntary early food safety reviews for certain GE crops in the field trial stage and support the USDA's oversight. Also, the three agencies do not have a coordinated program for monitoring the use of marketed GE crops to determine whether the spread of genetic traits is causing undesirable effects on the environment, non-GE segments of agriculture, or food safety, as recommended by the National Research Council.

In doing so, administrators must also *reconnect with citizens and stakeholders* if their efforts are to pay off. As we noted above, other approaches to food security exist that minimize environmental harm (e.g., organic farming) and must be integrated for maximum effect. For example, 60 percent of tropical forest loss in the world is related directly to the ecologically harmful activities of impoverished, small-scale, subsistence farmers.[29] They are forced to cultivate "erosion-prone hillsides, semiarid areas where soil degradation is rapid, and cleared tropical forests where crop yields can drop sharply after just a few years."[30] Working with policy makers, INGOs, and agencies in related fields, public managers must find ways to "tip" these citizens' decisions to more ecologically sensitive ways of farming. Success will depend on the extent to which these subsistence farmers psychologically buy into the program and, thus, on the creativity public managers utilize to facilitate such discussions less for an objectively "correct" decision and more for contingent solutions that navigate the value pluralism involved in this issue.

At the same time, any contribution to GM food technologies will require reframing existing communication strategies with citizens. The underlying assumption of multinational corporations and US government campaigns in informing citizens worldwide of the advantages of GM foods has been straightforward: if citizens better understand GM science and its benefits, they will become less wary of it. Recent research calls this strategy into question and suggests yet another major role for public managers and the policy analysts with whom they work.

Risk analysts have offered two models that they say override simple cost-benefit models of risk assessment in citizens' minds. The first, a "risk assessment discourse" hypothesis, posits that people filter their risk perceptions through broader moral, philosophical, and cultural feelings.[31] The second, or "institutional" hypothesis, posits that citizens who oppose a controversial technological innovation are not so much risk-intolerant as they are fearful that regulators do not have the capacity and inclination to protect public safety as research advances. Moreover, several studies find that support for GM foods is more likely if citizens trust in the regulatory capacities of their government.[32] Thus, more effective information campaigns may be those stressing the building of regulatory capacity and a willingness to protect public health, safety, and the environment rather than merely leavening citizens' understanding of the genetic science and biotechnology informing GM foods.

All of which, in turn, illustrates the importance of *recapitalizing personnel assets and reengaging resources* within and across agencies and sectors. As Eric Montpetit puts it in a larger comparative policy domain sense, agro-environmental policy making in the United States in general does not measure up well with other industrialized nations, such as France and Canada, in terms of resource allocation and regulatory focus.[33] This is the case because of coordination problems stemming from our Madisonian system of checks and balances, separation of powers, and federalism. Montpetit writes, "Negotiations have not been held in the United States to link the intrusiveness and comprehensiveness of environmental regulations with financial assistance for farmers. Initiatives primarily aimed at protecting the environment have come from state governments, while the federal government's efforts have remained preoccupied with the economic performance of agriculture."[34]

Finally, and relatedly, management issues in the food security policy arena related to GM foods are rife with the need to *revitalize a sense of common purpose infused with democratic constitutional values.* Multinational corporations in this policy arena do not have a stellar record in many countries when it comes to the values we cherish in a democracy.[35] For example, in the late 1990s, Monsanto's then-new president said that the company had been "arrogant and secretive" in dealing with the public in the past and announced a "New Monsanto Pledge" to engage in public dialogue, transparency, and technology sharing.[36] Yet, in the early 2000s, even friends in developing nations said the company had reneged on its promises. Illegalities have also occurred in the United States and abroad. For instance, Star Link GM corn—approved only for animal feed—was found in Kraft and Safeway taco shells, leading to a multimillion-dollar recall. Similar recalls and significant fines were also incurred when ProdiGene-dumped soybeans harvested in two states contained traces of GM corn. This situation led to the USDA increasing the stringency of regulations to keep pharmaceuticals grown in plants out of the US food supply.

Meanwhile, at the state and local government levels, and despite a two-year lobbying effort by the biotechnology industry to prevent local governments from regulating GM foods, nearly 20 legislatures considered or enacted bills in 2008 reflecting both farmer (especially organic farmers) and consumer fears about GM contamination of the food supply. In each of these areas, the quality of public management implementation will remain vital for the foreseeable future in identifying threats, regulating them, and preventing new threats to food safety. With trust a missing ingredient in this policy area, public agencies at all levels of government will also have to play major roles in (re)building trust through cultural sensitivity, transparency, and capacity building. Heclo's "collective puzzlement on behalf of society" facilitated by the only actors in the system who can act with the sovereign authority of the state—public managers—will again prove essential for progress in the food security policy arena.

Environmental Protection, Climate Change, and Energy Security

Equally challenging for your generation of public managers in a world of wicked problems with intertwined domestic and international implications are those derived from what

Lynton Caldwell refers to as the "changing relationship of mankind's world to nature's Earth."[37] Zoologist Jane Lubchenco, then-president of the International Council for Science and, later, director of the US National Oceanic and Atmospheric Agency in the Obama administration, summarizes six accelerating anthropogenic impacts facing societies worldwide that are a cause for great concern.[38] First, ecological systems upon which societies depend (e.g., clean air and water) are being damaged as a result of large-scale transformations of the earth's landscapes. Second, carbon emissions from human activities (e.g., power plants and automobiles) are contributing to global warming. Third, because of agricultural runoff from factory farms, the amount of fixed nitrogen has doubled since 1992, leaving (among other things) approximately 50 "dead zones" of algae blooms that have stifled other life forms. Fourth, humanity's consumption of water is now approaching 50 percent of available supplies, with agriculture accounting for nearly 70 percent of consumption. Fifth, anthropogenic habitat degradation (e.g., logging, farming, and dam building) and overpopulation are resulting in a loss of biodiversity, with some claiming that we are entering the "sixth mass extinction" event.[39] Finally, two-thirds of the world's fisheries are depleted, overexploited, or fully exploited.

Redressing any of these threats is difficult, but interacting together as they do comprises the "mother" of all wicked problems facing or affecting you indirectly as a public manager in the twenty-first century. Successive reports at five-year intervals beginning in 1990 from the Intergovernmental Panel on Climate Change (IPCC) warn of global average temperature rises that threaten life on Earth as we know it. A 2001 IPCC report tracking concentrations of greenhouse gases (GHGs) in the atmosphere concluded that the planet is undergoing warming at faster and higher rates than previously thought.[40] Specifically, it predicted temperature rises by the late twenty-first century of anywhere from 2.5 to 10.4 degrees Fahrenheit. Among other things, rises at even the lower end of this scale would still be enough to alter weather patterns, water resources, ecosystems, and the cycling of seasons, while upper-level changes would redefine life on the planet. All this is of particular importance for US citizens. Even though China recently surpassed the United States in total GHG emissions, we nonetheless outstrip China by four to one on a per capita basis and the EU nations by two to one.

In March 2014, another IPCC report offered no less worrisome a picture.[41] It stated that earlier findings of climate change impacts are likely to increase as human emissions of GHGs continue to rise. The draft also reports the stunning impacts of continued emissions creating turmoil as plants and animals colonize new areas to escape rising temperatures, with massive specie extinctions likely. In addition, scientists say that although it is not too late for emission reductions to reduce risk, the costs will be immediate while the benefits will not emerge until late in the twenty-first century.

This is not to say that the United States has not made progress on this front. Indeed, though the EU has been rhetorically more committed than the United States over the past ten years and though it has exceeded its GHG-reduction commitments under the Kyoto Protocol, the United States has gone beyond the EU in reductions. What is more, declining natural gas prices over the past decade have caused many US utilities to switch significant amounts of coal and oil usage to gas. This alone means lower GHG emissions. And when coupled with the Great Recession of 2007–09, the United States is now ahead of international target levels.

Still, the US Congress has been unable to deal legislatively in any comprehensive way with climate change.[42] This is why, in 2013, the Obama administration decided to circumvent congressional gridlock by more aggressively advancing the President's climate change agenda administratively. The US Supreme Court ruled in *Massachusetts v. Environmental Protection Agency* (549 U.S. 497 [2007]) that GHG emissions from new motor vehicles are pollutants under the Clean Air Act and that EPA can develop rules to curb GHG emissions. Two years later, EPA found that GHG emissions endangered future generations and issued rules limiting emissions for new motor vehicles. It also issued rules to limit GHG emissions from new power plants.

States and industry groups challenged the EPA regulations on several grounds. They said the agency's conclusions on the dangers posed by GHGs were incorrect, but a three-person panel of the US Circuit of Appeals for the District of Columbia rejected these arguments. The Supreme Court has now accepted six petitions to review that decision. In the meantime, President Obama went even further by instructing EPA to begin what will be a lengthy rulemaking process to regulate GHG emissions from existing coal-fired and gas-fired power plants. These were proposed by the EPA in 2014, with a final rule and then approval of state implementation plans projected to take another two years, at least, with court suits likely.

Consequently, you may be involved during your career in finding ways to reduce GHG emissions by designing and managing emissions trading programs. Alternatively, you may be involved in helping your agency or political jurisdiction adapt to climate change with new infrastructure development, creating financing mechanisms for investment in renewables, or overseeing the contracts of private companies developing technologies to reduce the intensity and volume of GHG emissions. Also, because most of the legislative climate change action is going on in states and regions such as the Northeast and West, if you are employed in government agencies in those more active states and their neighbors, you may be especially involved in helping to meet these challenges, choices, and opportunities.[43] Simultaneously, you may find yourself coping with the consequences of a warming planet. This might mean planning or implementing mitigation and resilience efforts at the local government level, such as that launched in 2013 by then-New York City mayor Michael Bloomberg (PlaNYC). Collectively, 40 major cities around the world have taken nearly 4,700 actions to reduce these types of emissions or to adapt to the effects of climate change.[44]

Rising to the occasion in this policy area begins with *reconceptualizing the purposes* of environmental and natural resource (ENR) and energy regimes. Overall, this will require public managers such as yourself to find ways to create a *mission and results-based sense of common purpose* that involves citizens in agency deliberative processes. Most challenging is whether a "triple bottom line" of economic, social, and environmental values—what was alluded to as sustainable development in chapter 2 and with which you are probably familiar—will become the central animating purpose of development in the years and decades ahead. This, as opposed to a narrower focus on economic development alone.[45]

But sustainable development is a slippery concept, open to various interpretations, and readily framed by opponents in policy debates as a conflict-ridden redistributive policy that takes from some at the expense of others.[46] The UN Educational, Scientific, and Cultural Organization, for example, defines sustainable development as the imperative for every generation to leave air, water, and soil resources "as pure and as unpolluted as when [they] came on earth."[47] Others, such as Noble Prize-winning economist Robert Solow, find leaving the world as each generation finds it unwise. Today's generation, he argues, has a responsibility "to leave open the option or the capacity to be as well-off" to future generations, and this may require resource depletion. Whatever view, if any, of sustainability ultimately prevails, however, Appleby's philosophers of administration will have a challenging role to play in assessing its promises and pitfalls and implementing its aspects in the United States and abroad.[48]

This, in turn, will mean a focus on *redefining administrative rationality*. Since the environmental decade of the 1970s, the United States and other nations have embarked on their own 30-year quest to afford the most effective, efficient, equitable, and accountable ENR management possible. A so-called "first generation" of regulation was heavily bureaucratic, prescriptive, and adversarial in nature. Moreover, it focused on one pollutant at a time (e.g., sulfur dioxide), in one medium at a time (e.g., in the air), and through one source at a time (e.g., automobiles or power plants).

Beginning in the late 1970s and early 1980s, however, critics of first-generation regulation emerged.[49] Their argument was not that first-generation regulation had failed but that the kinds of environmental problems remaining were beyond its abilities to address efficiently, effectively, equitably, and accountably. Traditional command-and-control approaches were ill-suited for ENR problems caused by small, diverse, and numerous nonpoint sources of pollution, such as GHG emissions, toxic pollution runoff from urban and rural nonpoint sources, and emissions of ozone-depleting chemicals. Moreover, they failed to recognize that many ENR risks are inherently cross-border, multimedia (i.e., they arise in or impact air, water, and/or land), interactive, multiple pathway (i.e., they can enter the body from different sources), and cumulative in nature.[50]

Reformers argued that market and quasi-market alternatives to command-and-control regulation were needed, including emissions trading, halon banks, and forestry and habitat conservation incentive programs. Also favored were information-based regulatory strategies, such as the Toxics Release Inventory in the United States, and the integration of "environmental accounts" into a System of National Economic Accounts. Still others stressed free-market environmentalism or ecological modernization strategies. The former included creating property rights for individuals and groups, while the latter focused on nations investing in more efficient and pollution-reducing technological advances. These changes are still underway and will continue as your career unfolds as a public manager.

Similarly, global ecological threats beg a *reconnection with citizens* by agencies and their public servants in the twenty-first century that has proven difficult in the past. Effective ENR management depends on valuing, promoting, and extending deliberative democracy to the greatest extent possible in the ENR policy formulation, implementation, and evaluation processes. For example, this idea permeates the UN Local Agenda 21 initiatives underway in 2,000 municipalities in 50 countries around the world to implement sustainable development. So, too, is it the predicate for such initiatives as regulatory negotiations (so-called "reg-negs"), environmental dispute resolution, effective risk communication, and cooperative rangeland conservation agreements for critical habitat preservation.

Regardless of the specific deliberative model used, however, participation has to include those previously marginalized by race, class, ethnicity, or gender for environmental justice to prevail. Regulators must address, if not redress, any inequalities in benefits and burdens imposed by past and present ENR decisions. Yet, although proponents of environmental justice in the United States have mounted an aggressive effort over the past 30 years to make public agencies minimize the negative results that their decisions can have on disadvantaged communities, significant bureaucratic obstacles have emerged and must be dealt with by your generation of public managers. For example, emissions of six common air pollutants dropped by two-thirds between 1980 and 2012, despite a 38 percent increase in population and a 27 percent increase in energy use. Yet exposure levels for lower-income and nonwhite populations are significantly higher than for whites and higher-income citizens. In addition, race seems even more potent than income in exposing citizens to accompanying health risks. Nitrogen oxide exposures, for one, are 38 percent higher for minorities than for whites living in major cities.[51]

Complementing and further advancing these approaches, Appleby's philosophers of administration are needed in ENR management who see themselves as catalysts building, nurturing, informing, and brokering multi-sided bargaining processes among diverse citizens and stakeholders. Equally valued will be collaborative partnerships with public, private, and NGOs, as well as with ordinary citizens. Reconnecting with citizens and stakeholders, thus, will have to continue to incorporate what some call "civic environmentalism," as well as the often-competing values of a burgeoning property rights movement, while protecting the general welfare.[52] Proponents of civic environmentalism expect agencies to nurture and listen to alternative grassroots approaches, such as economic incentives, technical assistance to volunteer groups and citizens, and public education. To property rights advocates, however, civic environmentalism also means respecting the rights of individuals to profit from and enjoy the resources they own.

Reengaging resources will also have to be a major element of any effort to deal in serious ways with the environmental, energy, and climate change conundrum we have outlined. Public managers and policy analysts will have to play major roles in this effort. Let us start with historical patterns of transportation funding and focus worldwide. As we covered in chapter 2, automobiles and superhighway development in nations such as the United States have allowed persons to live far from their jobs in suburban, exurban, and country settings. Yet the internal combustion engines that run automobiles produce carbon monoxide, hydrocarbons, and nitrogen oxides. These compounds then pollute the air, threaten public health, diminish the aquatic vitality of waterways, destroy critical habitats, and fragment fragile ecosystems.

Further complicating matters, even innovative mass-transit systems developed decades ago to shuttle workers into downtown areas more efficiently are finding their systems inadequate for today's more common suburb-to-suburb commutes (e.g., the Metro system in Washington, DC). As a result, new suburb-to-suburb transit lines and carriers are needed. On the positive side, the American Public Transportation Association says that more and more US cities are turning to rail systems, with approximately 262 systems now in operation or in various planning stages.[53] Yet choosing transit routes often pits preservationists, neighborhood groups, developers, property rights proponents, and environmental justice groups against each other as they joust to protect their respective interests.

High population density in metropolitan areas also means solid and hazardous waste disposal problems, as well as ever increasing demands for new energy power plants. Nuclear power plants to meet these energy needs offer the promise of clean power production, a promise seized upon by several nations. In the United States, of course, nuclear power has long been anathema to most environmentalists for a variety of reasons, including the technically and politically formidable dilemma of nuclear waste storage. More recently, these concerns were amplified in 2011 by the Fukushima nuclear plant disaster in Japan in the wake of a massive 8.9-magnitude earthquake. But even when nonnuclear sources of energy are involved, controversies over site locations can produce the same passions and NIMBY ("not in my backyard") reactions that controversies over solid, toxic, and hazardous waste disposal have occasioned.[54]

Energy conservation, of course, is an obvious approach to resolving supply dilemmas, especially if what policy analysts call the "true social costs" of producing electricity can be incorporated into prices (e.g., carbon taxes) or if the logic of the ecological modernization movement becomes widespread in business. As you will learn, market prices tend not to incorporate costs, such as those to future generations, of the depletion of natural resources used in producing a good or the health costs of pollution. But carbon taxes, such as those proposed by the Clinton administration in the early 1990s and by others since, have thus far proven politically unpalatable. Moreover, with exceptions in some corporations, conservation efforts in the United States typically ebb and flow with crises. For example, when rolling power blackouts occurred in California during the summer of 2001, high-tech companies in the Silicon Valley found ways to become more energy efficient. Still, this commitment dissipated once energy pressures were off.[55]

Government financing for energy efficiency and renewable energy also has varied sharply over the past two decades. Highest at the end of the Carter administration when the nation faced a severe energy crisis, funding for these purposes reached its nadir during the Reagan administration. It then increased during both the George H. W. Bush and Clinton administrations but was cut by President George W. Bush (albeit with an emphasis on hydrogen power that has yet to be followed by significant funding commitments for research). Most recently under the Obama administration, however, investments in renewables have spiked significantly, but not without controversy.[56] The Department of Energy distributed nearly $9 billion for solar and wind projects between 2009 and 2011, selling the idea partially on the logic that new jobs would be created for a post-carbon era and that US competitors were gaining market shares that would be lost if we did not pursue a similar strategy. Launched amid the 2007–09 financial crisis and as part of controversial stimulus funding, the Department of Energy's National Renewable Energy Laboratory could identify only 910 jobs directly created, in effect costing $9.8 million per job created. Moreover, 19 companies receiving funds filed for bankruptcy. Thus, opponents had more fodder for their argument that subsidies distort markets, tend to be distributed on political grounds, and invite political corruption.

Finally, shifting investments from a carbon-based (largely coal and oil) energy future to a renewable energy future will involve considerable political maneuvering. Energy costs are, after all, key components of agency budgets. But should you be working in or with agencies dealing with these issues at the federal, state, local, regional, or international levels of governance, the questions that you will be helping to inform from, say, a human resource, budgetary, policy analysis, or organizational perspective are multiple, complex, and interrelated. And the challenges, choices, and opportunities presented are profound.

Consider what some experts see potentially as a coming "golden era" of natural gas from technological advances related to hydraulic fracturing, known popularly as hydraulic "fracking." This process makes possible an abundance of gas from shale oil deposits in Argentina, Brazil, Canada, China, Europe, Mexico, and the United States. World production rose by 40 percent between 1990 and 2009, and estimates today are that a 200-year supply is on hand for development.

Not only will such a shift require reconnecting with citizens (as we noted above, as well as in terms of the potential environmental threats some claim it poses), but it will require investing in the infrastructure to get it to markets around the world. Expensive investments will also have to be made in huge plants to turn the gas into liquid at the beginning of the process and store it in a fleet of special tankers. It will then have to be turned back into gas at its final destination. Moreover, extensive pipelines within and across national borders will have to be built, just as the same must be built for wind-powered generators. Thus, during your career as a civil servant, you may be involved, among other things, with contract letting, oversight, and management of such projects; with the data analyses and interpretation informing decisions as to the worthiness of such projects; or with local communities upset about or seeking the jobs that might come from completing these projects.

Under these circumstances, *recapitalizing personnel assets* in society at large and in public agencies is also a critical component of any effort to deal with energy, climate change, and environmental challenges. Independent observers have concluded that the number, kinds, and skill-based intensity of program responsibilities and administrative reforms that they are charged with implementing are already straining the skill bases of most agencies. As we alluded to in chapter 2 and will discuss in great detail in chapter 7, the aging of America will further complicate this issue in the short run in the form of waves of retiring federal, state, and local employees.[57]

As we will also review in greater detail in chapter 7, a graying government work-force, of course, offers both threats and opportunities. If addressed strategically by aligning agency recruitment, training, succession planning, and outsourcing initiatives with evolving ENR missions, retirements conceivably could be a boon to efficient, effective, and equitable ENR management as purposes are reconceptualized. Yet, if handled reactively, opportunistically, or ham-handedly, the graying of the workforce will combine with fiscal constraints, new governance responsibilities, and faulty administrative systems to put both traditional *and* evolving ENR responsibilities decidedly at risk.

Consider the mission–human capital gaps facing the EPA as a result of these trends over the past decade. Although EPA experienced an increase in personnel of approximately 16 percent between fiscal year 1990 and fiscal year 2002, the GAO reported in 2003 that "EPA hired thousands of employees [during the 1990s] without systematically considering the workforce impact of the changes in environmental laws and regulations, the technological advances, or the expansion in state environmental staff that occurred during [that decade]."[58] EPA's Chief Financial Officer and the GAO have highlighted how shortcomings in the agency's personnel succession and training programs are putting its diverse missions at risk. Cited, among other critical needs, are developing leadership, management, technical, and scientific skills at EPA that are commensurate with the expanded responsibilities it has assumed over the past decade in major amendments to the Clean Air Act, the Safe Drinking Water Act, and the Food Quality Protection Act.

Likewise, the GAO reports that the Department of Energy headquarter and field staffs already cannot adequately oversee cleanup of hazardous and radioactive waste sites, because they lack contract management skills; that the Nuclear Regulatory Commission's "risk-informed" regulatory approach is being jeopardized by a lack of skilled personnel in this area; that the National Park Service lacks the skills necessary to hold park superintendents accountable for the progress they make toward meeting natural resource goals; and that building "sustainable biological communities" will require the Bureau of

Land Management, the Fish and Wildlife Service, the National Park Service, and the Bureau of Indian Affairs to select, train, and evaluate a coterie of employees possessing collaborative negotiation, alternative dispute resolution, and team-building skills. Also, because many of these positions are likely to be outsourced, skills in grants management, financial management, contract management, and budget and performance integration will need considerable buttressing and improvement in the years ahead.

Our environmental and energy fate will also depend on how successful we are at recapitalizing personnel assets at the state and local levels of government, as well as our success in finding willing public and private sector actors as partners in this enterprise. State and local planning, zoning decisions, purchasing decisions, building codes, and other functions must be aligned with sustainability goals. These will require the hiring, training, and promotion of individuals across these functions who understand, appreciate, and implement a sustainability ethic.

Conclusion

Hopefully, you will take away from this chapter and its examples of intermestic policy a sense for how public management incorporating both bureaucratic and democratic administration generally is linked to public policy success in the twenty-first century. You should also have a better understanding of how and why the 6Rs comprising the challenges, choices, and opportunities for public managers are grounded in the changing nature of the public problems we face today, and how these 6Rs must be integrated in the networked compensatory state for policy success. Moreover, after reading the first three chapters, you should have a sense for the historical legacy of the public service that you are preparing to join, continue in, or rejoin; of the linkage between long-term secular trends and their link to the 6R agenda that we have been reviewing and applying; and of the interconnectedness of the wicked policy problems awaiting you. With this as background, we are ready to begin examining in chapters 4 through 9 how the first 5Rs manifest themselves in five critical and exciting sets of tasks facing your generation of public managers in the United States. As noted, the 6th R—revitalizing a sense of common purpose infused with democratic constitutional values—merits a separate discussion in chapter 10.

CHAPTER 4

Aligning Structure and Strategy

I s there anything more pervasive in society today and yet more reviled than bureaucracy? Moreover, most of this animosity is hurled at government bureaucracy. Despite periodic bouts to reform, "reinvent," or replace it, however, it survives. No better means for coordinating large-scale organizations exists than the conventional "monocratic" or hierarchical organization.[1] Yet, as noted repeatedly in chapter 3, many question whether we have reached the limits of our competency in addressing today's and tomorrow's public problems using the bureaucratic model. And going beyond these instrumental concerns of bureaucratic administration, at the heart of today's governance challenges, choices, and opportunities for you in the public sector is figuring out how best to reconcile bureaucracy with democracy to meet today's and tomorrow's complex policy problems.

This chapter introduces you to some of the ways administrative reformers in the United States have attempted over the years to address the perceived shortcomings of bureaucracy. At the center of these efforts most recently have been pressures to *reconceptualize the purpose* of bureaucracy from control to achievement. This, in turn, evokes calls to *redefine administrative rationality* by aligning the structures of our public agencies with their own missions and for the purposes of a networked compensatory state. Referred to academically as aligning strategy with structure, the aim is to lessen bureaucracy's tendency to create perverse incentives stemming from that misalignment that undermine a sense of common purpose. Also necessary is *reconnecting with citizens* by attenuating bureaucratic tendencies to marginalize them. This means shifting from reformers' traditional focus on what we have called bureaucratic administration in chapter 1 to an ethic embracing democratic administration. And were these not enough, public agencies must learn to *reengage financial resources* and *recapitalize personnel assets* through strategic planning, while implementing these plans by pursuing an "aggressive patience" approach that considers the realpolitik of such efforts.

You should leave this chapter appreciating the obstacles that bureaucracy poses to *revitalizing a sense of common purpose infused with democratic constitutional values* within and across organizations in a networked society. However, you will also be familiar with more recent thinking by adroit entrepreneurial actors who view rules, regulations, and structures not as constraints but rather as resources to renegotiate and recombine in order to get needed change.[2] In addition, you will have an understanding of how administrative reformers have historically tried to remedy bureaucratic shortcomings with a rationality-based approach that paradoxically offers greater amounts of bureaucracy! But you will also leave it with a sense for how you might help meet these challenges by making choices and seizing opportunities informed by a realistic, clear-eyed, and "dirty-minded" perspective on change itself that incorporates both bureaucratic and democratic administration.

Reconceptualizing Purpose

The mantra of those who argue that we need to rethink agency design in order to address recent, new, and emerging policy challenges such as those we discussed in chapter 3 is straightforward. Many have wanted to reconceptualize the purpose of public organizations from one focused on hierarchical control, procedural compliance, and inputs (e.g., getting additional resources, staffing, and equipment) to one of decentralized control, flexibility, and outcomes or results assessment.[3] They have also wanted to separate "steering"—the development of policy—from "rowing"—the implementation of policy.[4] Put most simply, they are asking agencies and their partners in the public, private, and nonprofit sectors to reconceptualize their purpose from one of control to one of achievement. The rub comes, of course, in doing so while still ensuring that the values we cherish in a democratic republic—many of which are safeguarded by bureaucracy's procedural rules—are protected. This task is even more difficult in networks, because (among other things) administrative law is geared toward single organizations rather than multiple organizations across sectors.

Bureaucracy as Control

Although challenges to the bureaucratic model have always been leveled, its principles were quite revolutionary as the industrial revolution unfolded in the late nineteenth century. As you will learn in your coursework, the great sociologist Max Weber argued that bureaucracy was a necessary replacement to two other historically powerful bases of authority to lead or govern: traditional authority and charismatic authority.[5] The former was premised on heredity, with leaders claiming authority by virtue of family, ancestral, or tribal ties. The latter was premised on the deference of followers to the personal magnetism of leaders.

Weber claimed that both of these bases of authority were inadequate for an industrializing age animated by the increasing "globalization" of economies. Whether a shop floor, an organization, or a state, leaders needed to justify their giving of orders to others in order to gain legitimacy for their actions, legitimacy that neither charismatic nor traditional leaders could ensure. Charismatic and traditional leaders often were unable to implement their vision; their regimes turned into either traditional hereditary regimes in searches for successors or they were succeeded by another charismatic leader. Lost in the process were the expertise, efficiency, and institutional memory necessary for businesses to run efficiently or for nations to compete successfully in Weber's globalizing world.

Required instead, he argued, was a "legal–rational" basis of authority, the predicate for which was what he called an "ideal model" of bureaucracy focused on control. Be clear, though, that by "ideal" he did not mean "perfect." As we shall see shortly, he thought his model posed significant dangers. Instead, he meant that a pure bureaucracy would have certain characteristics if it appeared in the real world. In practice, bureaucracy is characterized, first, by a specialization of labor. Organizations take a problem, break it into smaller and more manageable parts, and assign responsibility for those parts to various internal units with specialized expertise in the tasks required. Organizational leaders exercise their authority over those further down in the hierarchy (their subordinates) by virtue of the position they hold in the hierarchy rather than by personal connections or personal traits. You will hear this referenced in your coursework as "authority in the position" rather than "authority in the person." Moreover, experts and other employees have "tenure in office," meaning that they cannot be dismissed arbitrarily (e.g., after an election or at the whim of a supervisor). The ideal bureaucracy then uses hierarchy, rules, and regulations to—in effect—"put Humpty Dumpty back together again" by controlling and coordinating everyone's work.[6]

Later, the early progressive founders of public administration built on the bureaucratic model during the first three decades of the twentieth century by offering what they called "principles of administration." Were you employed in a public agency at that time (and continuing today), you would have heard that efficiency would be attained if you placed related functions together in one unit. For instance, you would put all environmental and natural resource agencies in one department or all employment training programs in one department. You would also gain greater efficiency if authority was commensurate with responsibility; that is, if persons in your agency did not have the authority to make decisions regarding specific tasks but were held accountable for them anyway, efficiency would suffer. Inefficiency would also occur if managers had too many persons reporting to them; what are called "narrow spans of authority" were critical to performance. Conversely, you would prompt inefficiencies if you failed to instill clear lines of authority, meaning that subordinates could not be taking orders from more than one person. Nor could efficiency—or prevention of fraud and abuse—be attained if your organization did not have accurate recordkeeping. And if hiring or promotions were based on favoritism, efficiency would be sacrificed as well.

Moreover, by the 1930s, you would have been hearing of the virtues of what our field's founders called "POSDCORB."[7] The functions of leaders in organizations—public, private, and nonprofit—were to apply the principles of administration to *p*lanning, *o*rganizing, *s*taffing, *d*irecting, *c*oordinating, *r*eporting, and *b*udgeting agency activities. These were viewed as being performed in that order. Were these principles ignored or applied badly, control would be lost and organizational efficiency and, thus, performance would again suffer.

As we reviewed in chapter 1, the early progressives during this era also believed strongly in the idea of progress through applying the bureaucratic form, the principles of administration, and the scientific study of the workplace. Indeed, the heirs of progressives have held this belief ever since. Nor was the scientific study of work and work processes effective only in the workplace; progressives thought it could also be applied to attenuate the social problems of their day. By buttressing administrative controls, greater efficiencies would be realized and the sometimes violent labor–management conflicts in the industrial workplace would diminish, if not go away. The emotionalism they saw animating these tensions would diminish also—by using administrative controls informed by what your professors may call "scientism" or, more likely, "scientific management."

As you will learn, the father of scientific management at the shop-floor level was Frederick Winslow Taylor.[8] Taylor disparaged the "rule-of-thumb" thinking that characterized industrial relations in the early 1900s and that effectively gave workers in industry the power to control work productivity. In his view, workers took advantage of this by "soldiering"—that is, taking it easy. Instead, he envisioned a "science of work" that experts trained in work analysis could apply in the private or public sector to routine tasks, such as shoveling coal, loading pig iron on a rail car, and clerical work. Analyses included time-and-motion studies, which meant studying how workers did a job and analyzing how it could be done more efficiently by reducing it to the minimal number of actions needed for completion. Discerned from their analyses would be the "one best way" to organize work processes and, thus, maximize efficiency through administrative controls. A rising tide of profits from these actions could then be shared with workers, thus reducing tensions.

The initial attractiveness of Taylor's work was the control it would give to these specially trained work planners. Both managers and their subordinates would have to follow specific procedures to improve productivity, regardless of a person's partisan connections, personality, or subjective evaluation of a situation. As the now-legendary Mary Parker Follett emphasized, an impartial "law of the situation" would arise out of these analyses that all would have to agree on, because they would be based on objective, data-driven analyses by experts.[9] Presented with objective facts, "creative conflict" would result: reasonable people with different interests would come to a solution that was different from their initial position and that would refocus the debate in a more constructive way.

Although still a prominent and powerful theme of consultants around the world today, the irony of scientific management was that it sparked more, not less, labor–management conflict! Workers worried—accurately—that they would not share in the additional profits made and that they would actually lose jobs. So controversial did scientific management become that Taylor was forced to testify before Congress and later saw his techniques banned in the federal bureaucracy.

That said, you should not forget another major focus of the progressives and their vision of how scientism would lead to a better life in America. As Frederick Cleveland wrote in 1913, "Mak[ing] agency administrators more efficient was synonymous with asking how to make them more responsive."[10] As alluded to in chapter 2, progressives saw business competition as inherently inefficient, sought cooperation and coordination among firms as a means to eliminate inefficiency, and placed their faith in the ability of scientifically derived data applied by experts to bring about socially beneficial ends.[11] The nation, progressives argued, would be rescued from "moral anarchy" by placing human affairs where they "never yet have been placed, under the control of trained human reason."[12]

The "Wicked Problem" Challenge to Bureaucracy as Control

As we indicated in earlier chapters, the idea of top-down bureaucratic control over the development and implementation of policies has been linked to the nature of problems facing societies. For the early progressives, you will recall from chapter 1, urbanization, legislative corruption, and industrialization required a shift of power to the executive; Roosevelt's New Dealers and public administration scholars later argued that the "president needed help" to coordinate the myriad of programs addressing the social problems of the Depression; and, much later, the Cold War and 9/11 required the building of a national security state that further necessitated shifts of power to the executive branch and the White House.

However, beginning in the 1980s and 1990s, both liberals and conservatives argued that the complexity of contemporary "wicked" policy problems had severely undermined the ability of the classic bureaucratic model to address them.[13] Recall from chapter 3 how these types of problems require public agencies to do some things that they were not noted for doing historically. These included being flexible, information-driven, results-oriented, and learning-based organizations. As we will review more thoroughly later in this chapter, for example, crabbed and distorted information flows develop among units and different levels of the hierarchy. These stymie timely, accurate reconnaissance of turbulent organizational environments such as those characterizing wicked problems. Otherwise beneficial budget controls focused on subunits of organizations further reinforce fragmentation, balkanization of effort, and a lack of information sharing so necessary to learning. In turn, management information systems—so critical to informed priority setting and evaluation in learning organizations—tend to be equally balkanized because of turf battles over control of information. Lost in the process is the control element envisioned by Taylor and the progressives' focus on the principles of administration.

The Realpolitik Argument

One of the first lessons you learn upon beginning your career in the public sector is that public agencies are not designed for efficiency, economy, or even effectiveness. Rather, they are designed overwhelmingly for responsiveness to a variety of actors in their external environment, and their current structures—both the organization chart and their coordination processes—also reflect the results of infighting among programs and personalities over time. As such, although hierarchy matters, it does not ensure control because of the political dynamics involved. In Harold Seidman's now classic phraseology, organizational structure is about "politics, position, and power."[14] Thus, political rationality trumps Weber's and progressives' rational–technical (or means–ends) rationale when it comes to bureaucratic control from the top down in public agencies.

As you will likely learn in your courses, organization is literally the mobilization of bias, as political actors try to ensure that structures created guarantee their access to present and future policy deliberations and implementation. As you will read more in chapter 5, legislators sitting on committees that oversee agencies care deeply about programs that affect their reelection chances, as do related interest groups. Indeed, legislators seek out membership on these committees because they oversee policies that affect their constituents. Thus, anyone advocating a reorganization or change in organization structure is, in effect, trying to reorganize legislative oversight systems as well. These committees and interest groups will fight back. And even if successful in reorganizing agency structures, little behavioral change can be expected as long as the existing oversight committees remain intact to block new initiatives. Attesting to this reality are the difficulties experienced by the Department of Homeland Security in revamping the missions of various agencies incorporated into their department since 9/11.

Moreover, you need to understand that the organizational location of your agency or program is not an accident.[15] You may even be working in an agency or program that is deliberately designed by opponents to underachieve or that has been placed there because of legislative bargaining or a legislator's effort to place a program within her committee's jurisdiction. One of the oldest tactics used by opponents of agencies or programs is to place them in departments (or agencies, if programs) hostile to their missions or without the budget or personnel resources to implement them effectively. For example, assigning responsibility for implementing the Endangered Species Act to the Fish and Wildlife Service in the Department of the Interior, a predevelopment department that is chronically underfunded and understaffed, has meant huge backlogs in listing species. Other tactics are to place them in agencies that have experienced frequent reorganizations—an indicator that they lack a strong constituency to protect programs—or to place them deep within organizations without direct line reporting to assistant secretaries and the resources they allocate.[16]

In addition, agency structures have been designed by prior winning legislative coalitions to increase the political and administrative difficulties (what economists call "transaction costs") for those who wish to change policy or organizational behavior significantly in the future. Winning coalitions do so because they fear that electoral shifts in Congress or changes in legislative oversight committees will divert policy implementation to their own ends (what is called "coalitional drift") or that agencies implementing statutes will do the same (what is called "bureaucratic drift").[17] Conversely, opponents of a policy seek to hinder implementation by adding multiple reporting requirements to slow things down, by requiring annual budget reauthorizations in the hope of limiting agency resources in the future, by imposing significant analytical requirements that also slow down rulemaking and implementation, and by giving states major responsibilities so that policy making and implementation will be uneven.[18]

Your professors are also likely to emphasize the difficulties of controlling the behavior of what they will call "street-level bureaucrats" in organizations.[19] These are employees such as police officers on the beat, welfare caseworkers, or public health inspectors working in the public, private, or nonprofit sectors who deal directly with clients. As many scholars argue, all governance regimes have to "create or allow for substantial discretion and influence at the front-line levels of public organizations, where the primary work of service delivery and regulation is performed."[20]

Relatedly, in US executive branch politics, presidents, governors, and mayors must rely on bargaining strategies to ameliorate what economists call "information asymmetries" that they encounter in relation to their staff and agency-level subordinates.[21] Career civil servants are said to have more knowledge than political appointees, chief executives, and legislative oversight committee members. Because the severity of this information asymmetry problem increases as one moves from the chief executive to street-level bureaucrats, the slippage that occurs in the chain of command can be a significant barrier to control—as well as to achievement.

Redefining Administrative Rationality

The arguments summarized in the preceding section call for reconceptualizing the purpose of organizations from one of control—which is intensely unlikely—to one of accomplishment based on a sense of common purpose. But, as alluded to, doing so successfully requires us also to rethink conventional notions of administrative rationality. This is not to say that it is unimportant or impossible to apply various "rational comprehensive" (i.e., means–ends) techniques, such as strategic planning, to create a vision for an agency, to align organizational structure with that vision, and to reengineer processes and procedures to facilitate it. Indeed, we will review strategies and tactics for doing so later in this chapter, as well as critiques of it in chapter 6 on decision making in public agencies. It suffices presently for you to understand, however, that you will spend your career either trying to link strategy to structure or living with the frustrations and under-achievement of policy goals rendered by their misalignment. What your organization theory and organization behavior courses will do is give you a sense for the obstacles inherent in aligning strategy with structure, what their sources are, and how you might deal with them.

One of the most telling indictments of the "rationality" of the bureaucratic model offered by Weber was done by Jack Knott and Gary Miller.[22] They urged us to see bureaucracy as offering perverse incentives militating against efficiency and effective-ness. Produced instead was individual rationality for the actors involved but collective irrationality for the agency as a whole. To see how and why, let us return to research since the 1930s in the United States that supports their argument. As alluded to earlier, this is a body of research, according to Robert Golembiewski, which indicates that we have reached the limits of our competence within the conventional bureaucratic model.[23] Others agreed, and off we went as a nation to "reinvent" government and create a "post-bureaucratic" model of organizations.

The Technocratic Case for Redefining Administrative Rationality

The need for a post-bureaucratic model was premised on the idea that the same charac-teristics of bureaucracy that make it attractive also produce considerable downsides such as those noted above. To illustrate this point for you, consider five major characteristics of the Weberian bureaucratic model in the left-hand column of Table 4.1, as well as the bureaupathologies they provoke—alone or in combination—in the right-hand column. In the center of the table, you will see arrows connecting pairs of bureaucratic charac-teristics to clusters of bureaupathologies. Many of the arrows could go to other clusters of pathologies, and the pairs listed are not the only combinations of "virtues and vices" for organizational effectiveness. They do, however, give you a sense for how the perverse incentives created by bureaucracy create the individual rationality and collective irratio-nality identified by Knott and Miller.

Depicted, for example, is how both division of labor and professionalization of agen-cies by experts can produce—alone or in combination—coordination problems (stove-piping), information-hoarding, and turf protection. Although addressing a homeless person's problems, for example, officials working in separate units of an agency may not share the required information to cover all the needs of the situation. Nor might they work together on the whole problem instead of focusing on their own "piece" of the puzzle. They might even see coordination of their efforts as a threat to their individual programs as they compete for resources (bureaucratic pluralism). Lost in the process is a sense of common purpose for addressing homeless problems, which produces suboptimal results.

Unfortunately, these perceptions are often reinforced by an incentive structure within agencies that rewards information hoarding and coordination. The social and emotional attachments of employees to their programs or subunits—reinforced by budget pro-cesses, personnel systems, decision rules, and performance measures directed toward subunits—divert their attention from overarching agency goals and cooperating with others outside their unit. For example, a clean air program may be rewarded with larger

Table 4.1 Bureaucratic Characteristics and Pathologies

Ideal Bureaucratic Characteristics	*Machine Model Creates Bureaupathologies*
Division of Labor	Fragmentation
	Bounded Rationality (tunnel vision)
	Information Hoarding
	Program Capture by Interest Groups
	Trained Incapacity
	Subcultural Conflict among Units
	Turf Protection
Expertise/Professional	
	Dual Systems of Authority
	Professional Fiefdoms
	Expertise-Based Models of Service Delivery
Coordination by Hierarchy	
	Tendency for Top-Down Control
	Rigidity Cycle
	Distortion of Information Flow
	Rule Compliance Displaces Goals
	Organization as Routines and SOPs
Rules and Regulations	
	Functional "Silos" or Stovepipes
	No "Big Picture" Focus
	Subunits Compete for Resources
	Goal Suboptimization
Organization by Function	

budgets and personnel promotions for filing greater numbers of enforcement actions. At the same time, it is not rewarded for willingly giving up a portion of its budget to the water program, even if political appointees or air program officials believe that the money might be spent more cost-effectively in the water program. Again, individual rationality—the pursuit of greater amounts of resources by one unit—leads to collective irrationality—a less cost-effective distribution of resources across all units.

Likewise, an organization's focus on expertise can interact with coordination by hierarchy to produce what your professors may call "trained incapacity" by followers and leaders, hierarchical distortion of information, and dual systems of authority and accountability (too many bosses). Experts are trained narrowly during their education to understand their specialty. This results in their bringing to jobs a definition of how the world works, what the critical problems are, and what tools they can use to address them.

Here is an example. Economists in an organization faced with a workplace hazard tend to define solutions to problems in terms of the marginal utility of the last dollar spent to address that workplace hazard. In contrast, lawyers in the same organization will view proposals to address a workplace hazard through the lens of whether or not they will pass judicial scrutiny. Meanwhile, an environmental engineer will see the proposals of the economist and the lawyer as insufficient and will want to redesign the entire workplace to protect employees according to best engineering standards. These differences will have to be reconciled through bargaining, negotiation, and compromise before an agency can issue rules and regulations on any proposals.

Moreover, trained incapacity can prevent experts from seeing or supporting novel solutions to problems that lie outside their professional worldviews. This problem is compounded when they are isolated in separate units and pitted against each other for resources, power, and access to top decision makers. Little wonder, then, that some see the administrative orthodoxy as paradoxical: the more successfully one applies its tenets to public organizations for purposes of behavioral control, accomplishment, and accountability, the less one achieves these results. What occurs instead is responsiveness to parochial interests organized around or within organizational programs or subunits.

Toward a Post-bureaucratic Era?

With these critiques of the conventional bureaucratic model widespread by the mid-1980s, you can imagine why it was not long before critics began calling for a "post-bureaucratic" model of bureaucracy. And part and parcel of this movement were the New Public Management (NPM) and New Governance models of administrative reform mentioned in chapter 1. You will recall that the latter was pushed by those favoring an activist state, while the former was driven by those with a decidedly less activist approach to government. Both schools of thought, however, had similar diagnoses of organizational problems.

B. Guy Peters summarizes these diagnostic commonalities in a succinct way.[24] They are that government bureaucracies were too centralized; were monopoly providers of services; were unnecessarily rigid and unresponsive; and were too focused on inputs rather than outputs, outcomes, and the relationships between inputs, outputs, and outcomes. Both schools also shared many prescriptions for agencies solving these problems, including becoming a more entrepreneurial, mission/priority-driven, market-oriented, customer-focused, flatter (by reducing levels of hierarchy), results-oriented, and learning-based agency.

They differed, however, in terms of the emphasis given to any of these reforms.[25] For the Clinton administration, activist government had to be saved from bureaucracy, because good public managers were trapped in bad bureaucratic systems with high transaction costs and a lack of focus on outcomes. Clinton offered more discretion to public managers in exchange for greater levels of accountability for the "outcomes" they produced (i.e., were the homeless now better housed, was the air healthier to breathe, were crime rates lower).

Reflecting their very different electoral bases and decidedly less-activist vision of government domestically, the NPM under the Reagan administration focused on market-based solutions emphasizing privatization and contracting out (or outsourcing). For Reagan, markets were the solution to government failures—especially bureaucratic failures—and, thus, required a less interventionist approach by government into markets. Indeed, as we covered partially in chapter 1, the NPM that his administration advocated was grounded in a combination of public choice, deregulatory, transaction cost analysis (TCA), separation of politics and policy from administration, and free-market principles.

Public choice theory portrayed public managers as rational-utility maximizing individuals bent on promoting their own self-interest by maximizing budgets, program sizes, and promotion opportunities for themselves and their friends. Although subsequent research that you are likely to read in your program has called these assumptions into question, they remained powerful in popular minds. TCA, as noted above, focused on the amount of effort required to complete tasks and concluded that too many "hand-offs" in the conventional bureaucratic model caused inefficiency, ineffectiveness, and unresponsiveness by public agencies.

At the same time, the NPM and New Governance reform prescriptions called for, in effect, a return to the policy–administration dichotomy that we mentioned in chapter 1 and will review extensively in the next chapter. Elected officials—and their political appointees—would make policy and public managers would only figure out how to implement those policies. Both schools of reform also touted the need to cut rules and regulations, reduce levels of hierarchy requiring clearances, and decentralize implementation authority to frontline workers.

Finally, and most importantly, NPM proponents argued that free-market principles needed to be infused into the public sector in order to improve the efficiency, effectiveness, and responsiveness of agencies. Consonant with public choice principles, they argued that the competition provided by markets—especially contracting out—was critical. Public agencies were monopoly providers of services, and competition would overcome their tendency not to share information (internally among units or with external customers), to get away with wastefulness, and to not be mission-driven or priority-based.

As noted, the Reagan administration emphasized significantly more outsourcing of government functions than did the Clintonites. The next Republican president—George H. W. Bush—continued this trend, as did Democrat Bill Clinton, but with decidedly less intensity. Republican George W. Bush then greatly expanded the contracting out of government from 2001 to 2008. The Government Accountability Office, for example, reported in the mid-2000s that "acquisition of products and services from contractors consume[d] about a quarter of discretionary spending government-wide."[26] The next Democrat president—Barack Obama—then took a more Clintonesque approach. Obama, for example, reduced noncompetitive contract bidding, reassigned some previously contracted work to federal agencies, and tried to rebuild administrative capacity within government agencies.

Although we will come back to contracting in several subsequent chapters, it suffices to say presently that it has contributed significantly to what Larry Terry has called the "thinning" of public agency capacity to perform its tasks.[27] It has also created significant accountability challenges for us as a nation because of the difficulty of monitoring contracts that are typically "bundled" (one contractor with multiple subcontractors). It has also made the building of a common sense of purpose infused with democratic constitutional values more difficult than ever given the profit motive of private contractors.

The Challenges of the "Post-bureaucratic" Era

Although straightforward in the abstract, aspects of the NPM and New Governance administrative reform movements faced strong headwinds. As such, and putting aside the experiences of contracting until later chapters, the results at all levels of government have been rather halting, halfway, and patchworked. Still, because of the obstacles that conventional bureaucratic structures pose for dealing with many of today's and tomorrow's policy challenges, your agency will continue to feel pressure to move to post-bureaucratic forms while protecting the democratic constitutional values that citizens expect. To see how and why this is the case, let us review three key components of the post-bureaucratic agenda.

Reengineering. As we covered, realigning agency structures with their mission is premised on the notion that inefficiencies, ineffectiveness, and diseconomies are largely the product of the transaction costs imposed on balkanized conventional bureaucracies as they try to meld the tasks they need to produce a product. Reducing these costs is the goal of any reengineering effort by eliminating unneeded, duplicative, or non-value-added "hand-offs" among actors (e.g., reducing excessive middle-management reviews of employee work product).[28] Prior research on reengineering public agencies, however, identifies several factors that have compromised their success and that you should be aware of as a public manager, because they offer lessons for future efforts. Among those that you will be exposed to in your coursework are the following:

- what seems to matter most for effecting behavioral change and enhancing policy and program effectiveness is consolidating programs, not departments and agencies;[29]
- a focus on "flow-of-work" processes, not discrete functions, is most advantageous[30]—in other words, you are more likely to be successful if you think of the "assembly line" of actors who need to contribute to producing a good, service, or opportunity to citizens and reengineer those processes, rather than proceed one function at a time;
- the amount of "delayering" (i.e., the number of hierarchical levels reduced) that takes place in bureaucracies is critical for reinventing them—less important are the number of employees cut or functions devolved to states, localities, or private and nonprofit sectors;[31]
- delayering or reducing the number of hierarchical levels in an agency is not sufficient to make them more effective—reformers must also cut the layers of political appointees produced by executive and legislative efforts to politicize the bureaucracy.[32]

Results-oriented and Customer-focused Management. Researchers have identified sets of facilitating and inhibiting preconditions for success with which you should become familiar.[33] Among the foremost "necessary but insufficient" conditions for success that you should be aware of are the following:

- external pressures from central management offices such as offices of management and budget;
- heightened expectations among key legislators (e.g., oversight committee chairpersons) that managing for results is critical;
- external pressures to jettison current input and output-based performance measurement systems that are not linked to outcomes, including budget crises, inordinate or unexpected demands on service delivery systems, and an unfavorable policy outcome that arouses cries for reform;
- statutory requirements for change, such as the Government Performance and Results Act of 1993, although these have to be backed up with budgetary consequences for results;

- strong leadership from the top of the organization—and cascading through teams at different organizational levels—by a coalition of actors who support a results-oriented approach to performance evaluation;
- use of a limited number of performance or outcomes measures that are well-linked to agency mission and program goals;
- use of numerical performance targets to chart progress toward goals or procedural "milestones" for accomplishing key tasks.

To these, you should know that prior research adds the following list of factors that will make a successful transition to results-oriented management problematic:

- inadequate training opportunities, especially when technical know-how for developing performance measures is missing;
- different expectations among elected officials, managers, and employees about what performance measures are designed to do and for what they will be used;
- developing outcomes measures for results that are not easily measured, shaped by factors outside their control (e.g., long-term socioeconomic trends), or not amenable to assigning responsibility to particular actors;
- agencies with competing goals (e.g., the Forest Service has to promote timber sales and protect wildlife);
- agencies without adequate databases and compatible software programs to afford performance and outcomes measures in a timely, useable format to inform budget and management decisions.

Partnering. In recent decades, partnering with other agencies has been a major focus of public managers and scholars. Although always a part of the compensatory state since the nation's founding, the reasons for partnering have mounted. For one thing, with the ascendency of wicked policy problems that cut across agencies, political jurisdictions, and areas of expertise, partnering becomes attractive to agencies. At the same time, budget cutbacks, personnel retrenchment, and inadequate types of expertise within agencies render attractive the leveraging of resources across them. Both partnering and collaborating meet these needs. Recent decades have seen a variety of types of partnerships that you are likely to find yourself engaged in during your public service career. These include collaborative partnerships or networks for information exchange, building agendas for action, research, information systems development, and mutual program development.

What is more, some partnerships you will be involved in are mandatory (forced by law on your agency). Others are initiated by actors within and outside agencies who see opportunities or unmet needs that only partnering can address. And some collaborative arrangements "emerge" quite naturally from a sense of common purpose recognized by all involved. Importantly, however, the chances of partnership successes are uneven. As Table 4.2 summarizes, researchers have begun identifying when they are more or less likely to be successful.[34]

Regardless of their origins, however, prior research also suggests that building and maintaining successful collaborative partnerships in the networked state depend on the abilities of public managers such as yourself to engage in "catalytic leadership."[35] In a social service context, for example, catalytic leadership means identifying problems in

Table 4.2 Collaborative Partnering

Collaboration and Partnering Are More Difficult When:

- No history of trust exists among potential partners
- No focus exists on long term by partners
- The opaqueness of the partnership makes monitoring difficult
- A divergence of interests among partners is likely
- Harm to citizens would result if the partnership breaks down
- Prospects for future interaction among partners are minimal
- Partners do not view dependence as critical or complementary
- Rewards to partners are not linked to cooperation
- Large program goals cannot be broken into smaller ones to avoid defection of partners
- Government fears loss of control over final product quality

getting jobs for welfare clients, mobilizing support for action by actors in all sectors, placing clients in jobs, and keeping them employed. Thus, partnering is an integrative and coalition-building enterprise comprised of such typically balkanized tasks as: interviewing clients, assessing their skills, working with them to determine the obstacles they must overcome to become employable (e.g., personal habits, lack of transportation, inadequate training, and daycare problems), marshaling resources and cooperation among disparate actors to address these shortcomings, mentoring clients once they are on the job, monitoring their work habits, and taking corrective action with them if necessary.

Even if started under optimal conditions and done well, however, partnerships in a democratic republic face the challenge of ensuring accountability for partners' actions. When Woodrow Wilson spoke in 1887 about the virtues of large powers and unhampered discretion for public administrators, he placed his faith for accountability in hierarchical structures.[36] But when public–private–nonprofit partnerships are involved, any use of "large powers and unhampered discretion" takes place in networks that are often dense, complex, and opaque.

It is possible, of course, that these risks might be worthwhile to your agency in light of the pathologies we have covered, the acquisition of skill sets that it does not already have, the seasonal nature of some aspects of its tasks, or its budget shortfalls. But although "results" measures are touted for their ability to monitor both agency programs and partnerships, the loss of managerial accountability that these networks can afford is a serious concern. Moreover, a focus on results rather than on compliance with procedures designed to ensure due process, fairness, and equality of opportunity can mean that values central to democratic constitutionalism are lost in the process. Your responsibility as a public manager is to minimize these problems.

Toward "Structured Agency" and "Creative Syncretism" in Public Agencies

Although the preceding may sound daunting to you, mounting evidence exists that structures, rules, and regulations are not as confining—at least for entrepreneurial actors—in and across agencies as once thought. Indeed, this will be the continuing theme of this book! Thus, the research we have just covered is accurate and affords you a compass for diagnosing potential obstacles to change. But it also needs to be understood and grounded in longstanding debates in organizational studies about how much "agency" actors have in organizations. "Agency," in this case, means how much ability actors have to make things happen and control their fates.

Historically, and as the preceding illustrates, scholars have focused on the constraints and limitations that structures, rules, and regulations impose on agency, which minimize the prospects for change. Yet, we all know of cases where changes are made, so this theory alone is unsatisfying. However, we also know that changes are often foiled in organizations by these factors, which again limits the power of this theory.

Into this theoretical breach have come two related perspectives on change. The first is a "structured agency" model that portrays actors as having agency but having to develop strategies to cope with, navigate, and change organizational constraints on action. This is done in a variety of ways which we will discuss in later chapters, including mobilizing outside actors, reframing issues, and taking alternative routes to change.

The second perspective—going by the fancy name of "creative syncretism"—argues that structural obstacles are nowhere near as powerful a constraint as portrayed when you look at everyday behaviors by creative managers in organizations. For them, organizational diversity "makes change a constant feature of organizational action" and life.[37] What do proponents mean by "diversity"? In this case, it means that structures, rules, regulations, and the "habits" they produce in organizations are oftentimes multiple, partial, incomplete, ambiguous, incongruous, and do not cover all experience. Put most simply, situations and change proposals do not fit neatly into existing structures, rules, and regulations. As such, adroit public managers—hopefully such as yourself!—routinely pursue change through creative (re)interpretation and recombination of these to advance their causes.

Reconnecting with Citizens

As we reviewed earlier in this chapter, just because Weber offered an "ideal model" of bureaucracy did not mean it was literally "ideal." Indeed, he had profound concerns about the impact of bureaucratization on the world, on organizations, and on people. John Patrick Diggins summarizes Weber's pessimistic theories of bureaucracy and history in this way: "Eventually equitable administration becomes corrupted as the bureaucracy responds to specific interest groups demanding special programs and other advantages."[38] Moreover, in the end, Weber saw bureaucracy triumphing over democracy because of a combination of its own inner tendencies and the technical imperatives of organizations. For Weber, these led inexorably to a power asymmetry favoring bureaucracy and the "castration of charisma"—which today would be translated into a lack of entrepreneurialism. In the process, the effectiveness of democracy would be compromised as elected officials became dilettantes—bystanders—in the face of an expert bureaucracy.

These and other concerns were voiced in later decades—first in the 1930s and 1940s—by calls from political science and public administration scholars to reform public agencies in ways that would revive democratic constitutional values in agency policy making. For example, scholars in the so-called "traditionalist school" (noted in chapter 3) argued for a focus on democratic rather than just bureaucratic administration. And as you will see in the next chapter, by the 1960s, you would have been reading about calls from other eminent scholars to control public agencies that had continued to marginalize democratic values by responding only to organized interest groups.

Theodore Lowi, for instance, argued for what he called "juridical democracy": the limitation of congressional delegation to agencies absent clear standards set by Congress to prevent this problem.[39] Emmette Redford called for greater sensitivity for understanding the moral dimensions of agency decision making (democratic morality).[40] Similarly concerned, and as we reviewed in chapter 1, others from the so-called "New Public Administration" community urged the abandoning of technocratic rationales favoring efficiency and economy through bureaucratic controls in favor of the primacy of social equity as a value animating agency administration and policy making.[41] Meanwhile, coming from a very different perspective, Vincent Ostrom called for abandoning public administration's embrace of centralized government, bureaucratic control, and the principles of bureaucratic administration as ill-suited to the US Constitution's focus on decentralized policy making.[42]

More recently, researchers in the 1980s and 1990s—such as Gary Wamsley, Kenneth Meier, Laurence O'Toole, and George Krause—argued that the focus of executive and legislative control of the bureaucracy is shortsighted and compromises effectiveness and accomplishment. In offering what was alluded to in chapter 1 as the "Blacksburg Manifesto," Wamsley and his colleagues returned to the arguments of settlement women in the early 1900s, progressive reformers, and "traditionalists."[43] They emphasized the necessity for public managers to understand that they are in reflexive relationships with citizens and that they must be "sense makers" for citizens, translating the complexity, turbulence, and discontinuities of the postmodern era to them. Likewise, Meier and O'Toole argued that politicians do not merit absolute bureaucratic control over public managers; bureaucrats within agencies respond to interest groups, so they, too, represent citizens.[44]

A final normative assault related to the bureaucracy–democracy nexus recently has come from what scholars call "postmodernists." As you now know, bureaucratic control is premised on the idea of technoscientific rationality as the most effective means of policy making. In fact, Donald Schon and others have argued that technical rationality has been the most powerful influence in our society when thinking about both the professions and the institutional relations of research, government, and business.[45]

Rather than this kind of means–ends rationality—what we have called "instrumentalism"—that seeks the solution to problems, postmodernism uses what its proponents call a logic of "problematizing." That is, instead of getting a "correct" solution to a problem—an aim at the heart of bureaucratic instrumentalism—postmodernists reject "the haste of wanting to know."[46] Instead, they embrace the idea that public agencies are not instruments or "tools" for solving problems, but, rather, their role is one of governance: figuring out how best to create conditions conducive to resolving conflicts over values and deliberative democracy. As we will review in greater detail in chapter 10, in a world of wicked problems and value pluralism (multiple and competing normative values) where conflict is endemic, public agencies should create safe, deliberative "spaces" where contingent agreements can be worked out. Agencies—and you as a public manager—are to be facilitators, not instruments, who allow space for citizens to give voice informed by their own expertise regarding personal and local circumstances.

Augmenting this perspective is the postmodernist critique that political and policy questions are too often turned into neutrally sounding administrative issues. As leaders in this movement, Ralph Hummel and Camilla Stivers write: "Modernist critics point to the replacement of societal values by the values of bureaucracy. What the American founders called 'the genius of the people'—their belief in political and religious freedom, in progress, in community, in human dignity—has been submerged under bureaucratic norms of stability, calculability, discipline, impersonality, and procedural equality."[47]

We will flesh out this thinking and its implications in each of the following chapters. But, for now, you should understand that many of the leading scholars in our field—as well as an increasingly disenchanted and estranged citizenry—are pressing for greater and more meaningful roles in public agencies than they have been willing to give in the past. And before you leave this book, you will know why you have a role to play in this transition, as well as how and to what ends your efforts must be focused.

Reengaging Resources and Recapitalizing Personnel Assets

Challenging enough in their own right, the preceding pressures for organizational change inherently involve calls for maximizing the funding and personnel assets that you may have for cost-effectiveness. Subsequent chapters will address additional ways for you and your agency to make such choices and seize the opportunities they provide for the other key tasks public managers need to perform in the twenty-first century. In this chapter, we will review the political and power realities associated with one of the most common prescriptions offered today for reengaging resources and recapitalizing personnel assets: strategic planning and management.

As you will find in your coursework and during your public service career, not everyone defines strategic planning the same or sees its virtues. One leading critic of its application in business and government organizations, Henry Mintzberg, argues that strategic planning rarely produces true innovation.[48] Nonetheless, other scholars find merit in the approach, and elected officials at all levels of government see it bringing the wisdom of the business sector to public agencies and requires it of them. The most recent iterations at the federal government level have come in the aforementioned 1993 Government Performance and Results Act (GPRA), the President's Management Agenda of the George W. Bush administration, and the GPRA Modernization Act of 2010 under the Obama administration, all of which we will return to in chapter 8. This logic then both cascades downward and bubbles upward from states and localities, and subsequently moves outward to requirements for nonprofit agencies to do the same kind of strategic planning for their efforts.

As the chapters in this book make clear, not thinking strategically is hardly a recipe for organizational or program effectiveness—or perhaps even survival. Moreover, to be successful, strategic planning must be followed by strategic management of any plans developed. Where problems arise for critics, however, is in strategic planning seldom paying enough attention to the realpolitik of implementation. When this happens, plans sit on the shelf because of opposition, which then saps employee morale, enhances the cynicism already there in most organizations about the planning process eating up time with no follow-through, and brings additional opprobrium from elected officials for failing to carry out the plan.

Consequently, after reviewing the strengths and weaknesses of a generic approach to strategic planning, we will examine what some call an "aggressive patience" model of strategic management.[49] From it, you should appreciate that strategic planning and strategic management should really be done at the same time and adjusted to each other using a "dirty-minded" perspective that anticipates and tries to attenuate obstacles to change. Thinking about one without the other courts failure.

Linking Strategic Planning and Strategic Management

As outlined by John Bryson, the conventional approach to strategic planning has the following logical, time-bound, and sequential ten steps:

- Initiate and agree on a strategic planning process
- Identify organizational mandates
- Clarify organizational mission and values
- Assess the external and internal environments to the organization to identify strengths, weaknesses, opportunities, and threats
- Identify the strategic issues facing the organization
- Formulate strategies to manage the issues
- Review and adopt the strategic plan
- Establish an effective organizational vision
- Develop an effective implementation process
- Reassess strategies and the strategic planning process[50]

Although not Bryson's intent, the media, elected officials, and citizens often expect or demand a "straight-ahead," heroic, transformative leader who brooks no hesitation, takes no prisoners, and does not suffer fools gladly.[51] More technically, "transformational" rather than "transactional" leadership is what they expect and what they celebrate. As you will learn in your studies, the former means rethinking an organization's goals and processes from the ground up, quickly linking new structures and processes with the new goals, and, thus, transforming the organization into something very different from what it was before in a short period of time. The latter views leaders bargaining, cutting deals, trimming their sales, and pursuing a much slower and less ambitious set of changes over time—one where political rationality trumps instrumental rationality but which is still goal oriented.

That said, you will immediately notice from the ten steps the centrality of clarifying goals, the popular assumption being that the goals of public agencies are less clear than those of private organizations. This, despite the fact that surveys of public and private sector managers—conducted in the 1990s by Hal Rainey, Barry Bozeman, and their colleagues—find no difference in their perceptions of organizational goal ambiguity.[52] Sectoral differences in goal ambiguity aside, you are correct in probably thinking that goal ambiguity is likely to vary across agencies, policies, and programs. Content-analyzing the strategic plans required by GPRA, Rainey and various colleagues find less goal clarity in larger agencies, in older organizations, when problem complexity is high, when regulatory policies are involved, when programs have high public salience, and when agencies are faced with competing demands.[53]

Regardless, elected officials and then offices of management and budget typically impose top-down strategic planning across all agencies and programs.[54] Leaders are to conduct strategic planning exercises premised on comprehensive, means–ends, and largely hierarchical approaches to change.[55] These are intended to be "disciplined effort[s] to produce fundamental decisions and actions that shape and guide what an organization . . . is, what it does, and why it does it."[56]

For leaders in public agencies today, this often entails identifying core competencies (what do we do best?) and then trying to reengage funding and personnel to buttress these ends. This is accomplished by recommending contracting and devolving responsibilities to lower levels of government, measuring agency behavior against best-in-class performers, better aligning functions to advance agency goals, and collaborating or partnering with other organizations for resources and talents that agencies do not have. The problem, you will learn in your coursework, is that nearly 80 percent of all large-scale organizational changes fail.[57] Failures occur often because change "shifts roles and capacities of different actors, which in turn shifts the existing bases of power."[58] Thus, what are central to any chance of success is anticipating these dynamics and having an implementation strategy with persons skilled in combining both transformational and transactional leadership.[59]

Interestingly, evidence from the private sector indicates that top-down, one-time, and comprehensive strategic planning is neither useful nor necessary for public agencies to bring about fundamental reallocations of resources and personnel linked to their vision. Instead, truly innovative companies rely on what is called "time-paced evolution" (i.e., gradually rolled out change) that incorporates a "wide variety of low-cost limited [and repetitive] probes into the future."[60] In other words, they incorporate what might be called an "aggressive patience" approach in their strategic thinking.

The ABCs of Aggressive Patience

Unlike traditional strategic planning efforts, aggressive patience starts from the assumption that organizations behave more like *diffuse* bureaucratic systems or "polities" than hierarchical ones. As noted, the implied assumptions of strategic planning are that clear lines of authority exist, that orderly top-down and nested decision making and implementation can result during a plan's execution, and that adaptation and alignment of goals throughout the organization will follow. These are totally unrealistic assumptions, as experience during your career in public service will confirm. Yes, hierarchy in organizations is real and will affect how your agency runs. But public agencies are not "machines"; as we covered earlier, they are polities with very delicate political economies—that is, internal and external political and economic bases of power and support. Thus, they are reluctant to change, because it means significant funding and personnel reallocation that might disturb that basis of support.[61] Those at the top of the hierarchy—or leading strategic planning efforts—ignore this reality at their peril.

In contrast, the aggressive patience model assumes that nodes or clusters of power and authority reside both inside and outside of the organization to complicate strategic planning and management processes. Organizational actors with differing mindsets and agendas have different bases of power and authority and work in a system where issues, rules, and priorities are constantly questioned, negotiated, and changed. In diffuse systems, comprehensive rational decisions and straight-line implementation actions might work some of the time for routine changes but not for those requiring significant reallocations of finances and personnel.

To reduce this risk of failure, aggressive patience involves actively watching, listening, and learning with the aim of creating or seizing opportunistic moments for acting to advance the plan's goals. It also involves accepting progress on parts of one's goals or strategy while still keeping the whole in mind; knowing how to create and watch for windows of opportunity to make progress; and collecting and celebrating accomplishments as they occur rather than awaiting total success. All this entails being alert to possibilities for change while maintaining a multiyear timeframe for action, communicating this to employees, and reminding them constantly of how short-term actions relate to long-term goals. It also means taking short-term tactical retreats calculated to placate opposition in order to meet longer-term strategic goals. Thus, near-term actions are always pursued within the context of a more enduring guiding vision, a view often called "guided" or "logical" incrementalism.[62]

By the same token, however, aggressive patience diverts from strategic planning by not assuming that the agency's political environment—internal or external—is a "given." Aggressive patience is no fatalistic approach to strategic action. Rather, it sees environments as multiple, divisible, and potentially "enacted" by leaders—that is, created or modified to suit their goals. Thus, it borrows extensively from public policy research on what is called "issue framing"—and that we will address in greater depth in chapter 6. In doing so, aggressive patience models see leaders advancing their strategic initiatives by (1) issue (re)framing that mobilizes supporters for their cause and subtracts from their opponents' coalition; (2) using "fixers" strategically placed to cut through bureaucratic barriers that arise to realize their strategic goals;[63] (3) linking their strategic initiatives to other more popular or accepted ones; and (4) reducing complex problems to more manageable sizes, thus making it easier to deal with obstacles to their initiatives.[64]

In doing so, aggressive patience incorporates aspects of what Karl Weick calls a "small wins" strategy for change.[65] These help to build momentum for change, reduce opposition to it, lead to the learning of effective strategies for later wins, and can result in qualitative change over time, despite their smallness in scope.[66] Thus, small wins not only can build momentum but, more importantly, can help reset power balances. As Weick notes, "Small wins stir up settings, which means that each subsequent attempt at another win occurs in a different context" of politics and power that is more favorable to a positive outcome.[67]

Small wins also "bring new solutions with them and old opponents change their habits. Additional resources also flow toward winners, which means that slightly larger wins can be attempted [later]."[68] As such, small wins not only signal intent and competence when key choices are publicized, but the "confidence that flows from a pursuit of small wins frequently enacts environments in which the original [strategic] problem becomes less severe and the next improvement more clear."[69] Moreover, dividing a big task into "manageable chunks" can lessen the tendency for people to become "paralyzed by the magnitude of needed changes...so that interim success is possible."[70]

Still, such strategies mean that subordinates often need someone to show them how intermediate actions relate to ultimate goals. To employees who are not paying attention every day, initiatives may look random and strategic retreats can be interpreted as things gone wrong—as cynics claimed would happen. Thus, as alluded to earlier, aggressive patience requires leaders to make connections for their employees. Metaphorically, were you leading or involved in such an effort, you might offer employees a glimpse of the completed change "puzzle" by showing them the corner and side pieces. This makes it easier for them to see how their efforts and other components of your strategic initiatives fall into place with broader goals.

In this way, aggressive patience also shares some common premises with what Michael Barzelay and Colin Campbell call "strategic visioning."[71] Proponents embrace the importance of context and the centrality of what they call "backcasting": mapping back to the present from a desired future and not merely forecasting the present into the future, as traditional strategic planning entails. In chapter 9, we will call this backward mapping and get more into its details for doing so.

The bottom line for you as a strategic thinker using strategic planning and management to pursue goals requiring the significant reallocation of agency funding and personnel is the need to reconfigure existing political forces. This is done in ways leading to what political scientists call "slow-moving, less visible, but longer-term secular shifts" in context and power relationships to implement strategic goals.[72] And part of this strategy involves creating internal coalitions or "idea champions" and external actors who support the changes you envision and deftly combining bureaucratic with democratic administration.[73]

Conclusion

After reading this chapter, you should now have an appreciation for the strengths and weaknesses of the conventional bureaucratic model; for why it is important to link organizational structure and strategy; and for why doing so will present you with challenges, choices, and opportunities throughout your career as a public manager. You should also be familiar with why many have argued for the need to move toward post-bureaucratic governance models linking strategy to structure, as well as some of the obstacles to doing so in today's networked compensatory state. Finally, you should leave this chapter with the basics of an aggressive patience model for linking strategic planning and strategic management as you try to make these connections in a clear-eyed way, noting both the constraints and tactics for dealing with them. With this largely internal and interorganizational perspective on aligning strategy and structure, we will turn next in chapter 5 to the challenges, choices, and opportunities awaiting you in public agencies' external political environments as you try to participate in or build a sense of common purpose informed by democratic constitutional values during your career in public service.

CHAPTER 5

Shooting the Political Rapids

As you will learn during your coursework, nowhere have old ideas in public administration so consistently lost their hold than in our thinking about the politics/policy–administration dichotomy (henceforth, the PPA dichotomy) discussed briefly in chapter 1. And perhaps no body of knowledge will prove as useful to you when trying to understand what your agency is doing, why, and at what chance of success or peril as you move into positions of agency leadership during your public service career. As Norton Long famously wrote in 1949, "The lifeblood of administration is power. Its attainment, maintenance, increase, dissipation, and loss are subjects the practitioner and student can ill afford to neglect. Loss of realism and failure are almost certain consequences" of not doing so.[1]

Nothing has changed since to make Long's analysis any less fitting today for appreciating the challenges, choices, and opportunities you will face as a public manager involved in building a sense of common purpose infused with democratic constitutional values. Pursuing these ends in today's networked compensatory state is no less a task than it was in Long's day. It is not a task for the meek, the impatient, or the politically unastute.

What *has* changed from Long's day, however, are the dynamics driving what your coursework will call "bureaucratic politics." At the center of *reconceptualizing purpose* for you today is appreciating, first, how our field's understanding of the relationship between politics, policy, and administration has evolved since the early Progressive Era. In the wake of this development, you will also have to understand and cope with the persistent efforts elected officials undertake at all levels of government to *redefine administrative rationality* to gain "responsive competence" rather than "neutral competence" from civil servants. Pressures to *reconnect with citizens* will also be on your plate as a public manager as these developments have, in turn, helped spawn an era of citizen estrangement from government. What is more, this has to be done in ways that do not render democracy "the multiplication of ignorant opinions."[2] Likewise strong for the foreseeable future will be the need for public managers such as yourself to develop tactics and strategies for dealing with pressures to *reengage financial resources* in light of the unsustainable spending and taxing ways propelled by interest group politics. Finally, you will have to cope with the significant challenges, choices, and opportunities posed by the negative "bureaucrat bashing" of contemporary politics for *recapitalizing personnel assets* at all levels of government with the best talent available in today's competitive job market.

You should leave the chapter with an appreciation for how bureaucratic politics affect policy and how policy affects bureaucratic politics and the larger political environment over time. In the process, you will see why, during your career, you should strive to acquire a firm understanding of the history of any organization in which you work, its policies, and the interest groups surrounding it and your program. Gained as well by you should be a basic understanding of how the political environment of the nation—as well as the immediate political environment of your agency—in today's compensatory state affects everything you do. You should also appreciate how and why, because of this, your agency can be a battleground for control between chief executives and legislators with the courts often called on to resolve disputes.

Reconceptualizing the Purposes of the PPA Relationship

As noted in chapters 1 and 4, it was Woodrow Wilson in 1887 who urged the United States to adapt administrative principles derived from historically autocratic European nations to public agencies in America.[3] Recall, too, how he claimed this would not pose a threat to democracy in the United States, because you could separate politics from administration. This "separation" quickly morphed into a "policy–administration" dichotomy in the early Progressive Era of the twentieth century for reasons that we will discuss later. By the mid-1940s, however, the fallacy of separating politics or policy from administration was clear descriptively, instrumentally, and normatively. And yet, by the 1990s, administrative reformers tried unsuccessfully to revive a PPA dichotomy. Let us see how and why this occurred.

The Realpolitik behind the PPA Dichotomy

Recall that Wilson's rationale, which was adopted by the early progressives, was simple: Americans should not worry about autocratic influences, because politics would take place among elected officials in legislatures who pass legislation. Agencies would merely carry out those laws in an effective, efficient, and economical manner by applying their subject matter expertise and objective principles of administration. In essence, career civil servants would be what scholars call "neutrally competent": they would follow the policy directions of elected officials regardless of their party affiliation and apply their expertise to making those policy directions work. Moreover, a theme of Wilson's era was that a politically neutral and competent civil service would also be a "bridge-builder" between citizens and their government, thus advancing democracy in the process. Therefore, were you entering the public service in the early Progressive Era, you would see yourself as an expert making decisions that citizens would make themselves if they only had the time, knowledge, and ability to do so.

But there were also a variety of political reasons—other than those linked to immigration in chapter 1—driving the progressives' politics–administration dichotomy and its normative claim of neutral competence. For starters, progressives' focus on the centralization of power in, and professionalization of, the executive branch also sought to shift power from corrupt federal, state, and local legislators to the executive branch led by presidents, governors, and mayors. As such, in the early 1900s, it was aimed toward bringing about "new patterns of interest [group] intermediation" through the chief exec-utive.[4] Progressives saw interest group efforts to influence policy as inevitable and even democratic. But limiting the "access and influence of interest groups" to legislators would overcome the electoral timidity, inefficiencies, and corruption that precluded energetic, effective, and coordinated policy making from the legislative branch.[5] What is more, doing so would produce more public interest-oriented policies, because presidents, gov-ernors, and mayors must please a broader electoral constituency than legislators elected by districts or states.[6]

Progressives also justified on practical grounds both the separation of politics and administration and the concentration of power in the chief executive. They argued that all governments throughout history had relied on administrative structures to be effec-tive. The legislative branch was itself too highly fragmented into committees and sub-committees to be able to coordinate anything. Grounded in the Hamiltonian view we covered earlier that "energy in the executive" was necessary—and admiring a parliamen-tary system of cabinet government in Great Britain and Europe wherein ministers of departments could be elected members of parliament (something precluded by the US Constitution)—progressives sought to buffer administration from politics.

You should also be aware, however, that some progressives went further and indicted as anachronistic and dangerous the principles underlying the US Constitution itself. In that era, one of the founders of public administration as an area of study, Frank Goodnow, wrote that the Madisonian system was based on an inordinate "fear of politi-cal tyranny" that had "led to the adoption of the theories of checks and balances and of the separation of powers" that were "unnatural" in living organic systems.[7] Likewise, Charles Merriam argued that the Madisonian system of checks and balances resulted in "Hide and Seek Politics."[8] They were joined by William Willoughby who contended that executive-centered public administration would remedy the "greatest failure" of the framers: not "locat[ing] authority and responsibility in a single organ . . . [Thus] . . . our entire constitutional history has been marked by a struggle between the legislative and executive branches as to the relative parts that they should play in the exercise of this [administrative] power."[9]

In addition, you should be aware that although the politics–administration dichotomy was "sold" as a means for increasing efficiency, it is the not the efficiency that you will talk about in your policy analysis classes. As Leonard D. White put it in 1933, "When we say efficiency we think of homes saved from disease, of boys and girls in school pre-pared for life, of ships and mines protected against disaster . . . We do not think in terms of gadgets and paper clips alone."[10] Armed with research, facts, and measurements as guides, and with their criteria of efficiency linked to the relationship of expenditures to social outcomes, progressives were confident they could produce a true public interest untarnished by corruption, crass political power, and mass emotionalism.

It was not long, however, before the *politics*–administration dichotomy was conflated into a *policy*–administration dichotomy, partly because of the resource dependency of the field on wealthy patrons such as the Rockefeller Trusts. The nascent New York Bureau of Municipal Research and its counterparts in other cities deemed it too politically and financially dicey to take on an explicit link between public administration and social issues. Potential funders for their operations, such as the Rockefeller Trusts, feared that what was called the "efficient citizen" movement—the idea of municipal bureaus con-ducting research identifying social problems and teaching immigrants how to participate in the political process—might further inflame an already politically incendiary era of private sector labor–management unrest.[11] Consequently, they were not willing to fund social research that might either play into the hands of rabble-rousing anarchists and socialists or spark further calls for government intervention in markets.

For the same reasons, between 1927 and 1936, securing the Rockefellers' continuing largesse and public administration's quest for legitimacy cemented the ascendency of the PPA dichotomy. It also meant a focus on bureaucratic administration over democratic administration for that era.[12] As we will cover later in this chapter, the marginalization of democratic administration would later be expanded to the present because of what might be called a de facto "enduring coalition" of progressive, business, and social science interests.

The High Noon of the PPA Dichotomy

Although the early Progressive Era ended abruptly in the 1920s, the attractiveness of the politics–administration dichotomy did not wane in the public administration community. As was alluded to in chapter 1, it was not until the late 1940s that scholars who had served in administrative/policy positions during the New Deal and World War II distilled from their experiences that the PPA dichotomy was an unrealistic description of how public agencies actually worked. In the interim, however, some of the foundational figures in public administration went so far as to urge experts in the bureaucracy to consider themselves as, variously, a new "governing class,"[13] practitioners of the "master trade of all" specializations,[14] and "research technicians who possess the just, wise, and omniscient qualities of Plato's guardians."[15] None, however, were so bold as H. G. Durham who wrote of the necessity of public agency experts accepting "their destiny as a Democratic Ruling Class"![16]

Less pompously and more pragmatically during the 1930s, E. Pendleton Herring saw the PPA dichotomy as unsuited to the policy realities of his day.[17] Agencies given broad discretion by Congress, he said, were bombarded with pleas from private interest groups to respond to their narrow parochial needs. As such, they had to make policy decisions with political implications, decisions that hopefully redounded to a broader public interest. However, Herring also kept alive the early progressives' faith in shifting power to the executive. He argued that the only responsible way to ensure the public interest was to enhance the power of the president, a perspective that would become famous in 1937 with the publication of a report of the President's Committee on Administrative Management (PCAM).

Convened by President Roosevelt ostensibly to find a way to coordinate the huge number of federal agencies and commissions created during the New Deal, PCAM's most famous line in the report was "the President needs help." This recommendation eventually lead to the creation of the Executive Office of the President (EOP) in 1939. Initially comprised of four offices, the EOP today consists of 15 offices where you might one day work, interact, or follow their guidance. Most notable among these are the Office of Management and Budget (OMB), the Council of Economic Advisers, the Domestic Policy Council, and the National Security Council.

The PCAM report—put together by public administration luminaries Louis Brownlow, Luther Gulick, and Charles Merriam—was also a political document, however. It was steeped in what your professors may call the "public administration orthodoxy" of separating politics, policy, and administration; of the aforementioned centralization of power in the chief executive through creation of the EOP; and of the principles of administration we covered in chapter 4. The report also laid the foundation for a doctrine dramatically different from that of neutral competence: a doctrine of *responsive competence* of the bureaucracy to the president rather than Congress. Not surprisingly, a Senate select committee report—the Byrd Committee Report informed by the so-called "Brookings group"—argued that the framers of the US Constitution gave administrative power (as opposed to executive power) chiefly to Congress, not the president.[18] Still, the PCAM perspective prevailed. Before discussing that shift to responsive competence and its implications for the PPA dichotomy, however, it is important for you to understand why and how a revolt against the dichotomy took place in the late 1940s, a revolt that totally reconfigured our understanding of the relationship between politics, policy, and administration.

The Dichotomy Loses Its Legitimacy

As reiterated above, leading scholars who were "graduates" of the New Deal and World War II argued that politics and policy were not severable from administration.[19] Elected officials, they observed, passed legislation that was vague, ambiguous, or even contradictory. This happens in order to attain winning coalitions, because problems are so complex that only experts can make judgments, or because elected officials wish to shift politically risky questions to the bureaucracy. Because this happened, passing legislation was not the end of the political battle but just the beginning—as we will cover extensively in chapter 9 with its focus on policy implementation.

Also clear to scholars studying bureaucratic discretion in the 1950s and 1960s was that so-called "iron triangles" were driving policy making in agencies. These are cozy relationships that develop between agencies, interest groups, and the legislative committees charged with overseeing agencies.[20] As you will learn in your coursework, this type of "subsystem politics" revolves around the idea of mutual self-interest among actors. Agencies need interest group support in budget hearings and as sources for information they need to make decisions. In turn, members of legislative committees need interest group contributions and information to counter agency claims, as well as to allocate whatever resources they are giving to their states or legislative districts. Likewise, interest groups need agencies to make decisions in their favor. The stakes involved are material (e.g., funding) and, hence, divisible among interest groups, with all actors sharing an interest in keeping policy conflict low and dividing the benefits. The last thing any of them want is the attention of other actors with different policy values and ideas.

As you will likely discuss in your bureaucratic politics class, this recognition quickly morphed, first, into the idea that agencies could quite easily be "captured" by dominant interest groups. For example, regulatory agencies did the bidding of the actors they regulated. Then, beginning in the late 1970s and continuing over the next two decades, research support began waning for the iron triangle as a driver of the dynamics of politics, policy, and administration. Hugh Heclo described the iron triangle not so much as wrong as "disastrously incomplete" in explaining bureaucratic dynamics.[21] More accurate, he claimed, was the idea of "issue networks" of actors on various sides of policy issues motivated less by material stakes and more by normative or value issues. This made compromise among actors more difficult and sometimes impossible.

Heclo also argued that neither the career bureaucracy nor the president was advantaged in the policy process by these dynamics. For the career bureaucracy, the prior

influence of mid-level public managers in closed subsystem politics was reduced significantly. Policy knowledge rather than pure administrative skill was now the coin of the
realm in the legislative process. Moreover, policy knowledge extended beyond agencies
to nongovernmental actors, such as the growing number of policy think tanks at all
levels of government that we will discuss further in chapter 6. In practice, many of
these actors would be "in-and-outers," alternating between positions in think tanks,
businesses, or universities and government agencies as political appointees and advisors.
In effect, though, agencies no longer held as much of a monopoly on policy and program
knowledge, a major source of leverage in traditional subsystems.

Likewise, these developments further exacerbated existing concerns of presidents, governors, and mayors about being held accountable electorally for a policy apparatus they
really did not control. Heclo noted that dominating the PPA nexus were what he called
"technopols"—"policy politicians" and "entrepreneurs"—working in those universities
and think tanks—plus the media, interest groups, congressional staffs, associations, and
other nongovernmental organizations.[22] Based on their shared knowledge, continuing
policy agendas developed that were very difficult for elected officials to penetrate. Because
of their narrow expertise, moreover, technopols contributed to a stovepiping of perspectives on policies (albeit one broader in scope than traditional iron triangles), making it
challenging to coordinate across policy arenas when wicked problems were involved.

Were these problems not enough, Heclo also saw technopols having negative implications for democratic administration. He wrote that the "trouble is that only a small
minority of citizens, even of those who are seriously attentive to public affairs, are likely
to be mobilized in the various networks . . . [while the] sophisticated claims and counterclaims [of experts got] to the point that the non-specialist [became] inclined to concede everything and believe nothing that he hears."[23] And his analysis remains prescient
today, even in local government where policy decisions are made "closest to the people."
A recent national study of citizen participation in local government by the National
Research Center, for example, found that only 19 percent of respondents had contacted
elected officials in the previous year, while only 25 percent had attended a public meeting. Among racial groups, Asians had the lowest participation rates, while low-income
residents also were not as active as those earning six-figure incomes.[24]

In the 1980s and 1990s, Heclo was joined by policy analysts stressing the power
of ideas, ideologies, belief systems, and knowledge in policy making. These scholars
identified enduring networks of interacting interest groups, agency bureaucrats, journal-
ists, academics, and public managers who, over time, develop core beliefs and ways to
approach problems. In these "advocacy coalitions," those with competing views on issues
(e.g., pro-life versus pro-choice coalitions) again show little willingness to compromise
their core beliefs, but they may be open to compromise on the means to address problems.[25] As you can imagine, these dynamics only further frustrate elected officials bent
on making substantial change, as well as citizens who see policy making as gridlocked
by experts who marginalize them.

Nor were these conceptualizations of the PPA relationship limited to any one level of government. Your coursework will note that intergovernmental relations scholars had their own
version of subsystems. These resulted from the explosion to over 400 federal grants to states
and localities launched during the Great Society of the 1960s. As depicted in Figure 5.1,
and as we will cover in greater detail in chapter 9, these are identified metaphorically as a
"picket fence" having vertical slates of subsystems of actors organized around programs

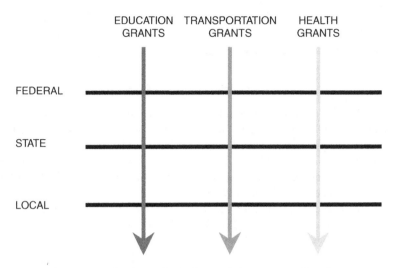

Figure 5.1   Picket-Fence Federalism: The Professional–Bureaucratic Complex

stretching from federal, state, and local levels of government.[26] Driving policy making in these subsystems is a professional–bureaucratic complex specific to each policy area.[27] The horizontal slats in the fence are elected officials at different levels of government trying to coordinate across different policy areas—and typically feeling quite frustrated by their exclusion from the vertical professional–bureaucratic complex.

Vertical PPA relationships are best understood as like-minded experts in various policy areas—such as health, education, or welfare—developing rules and regulations at the federal or state government level and pushing grant money through the system to address professionally determined needs. These PPA relationships and regulations grew even more complex in the aftermath of the Great Society programs, throughout their expansion in the 1970s under the Richard Nixon and Gerald Ford administrations, and during the substantial increase in cross-sectoral networked governance from the 1980s to the present. As later chapters will illustrate, with over 700 categorical grants in place today, figuring out how to bring these actors together, keep them together, and hold them accountable for their actions are things your agency will have to deal with throughout your career.

Observers of administrators operating in picket-fence federalism soon noticed the same erosion of the PPA dichotomy that we reviewed at the federal government level. Prior research vividly shows that state "administrators deal with different orders of policy making that ... [range] ... from routine administration to pure politics."[28] More than five decades of survey research by the American State Administrative Project also consistently reveals that state administrators see themselves spending roughly equal times between routine administration, policy development, and building public support for policies.[29] Likewise, at the local government level, research over the years has repeatedly shown that even city managers—the epitome of the early Progressive Era aim of separating politics from administration—see themselves as heavily involved in policy development.[30]

In combination, these realities caused many to question the top-down, neutral-competence connotations of the PPA dichotomy. Indeed, in elected officials' minds, many felt that they had little choice but to sharpen their focus on gaining responsive competence.

To see how this happened and the forms it has taken to advance their policy preferences administratively, you have to appreciate the efforts over the past three decades to redefine administrative rationality at all levels of government.

Redefining Administrative Rationality

Since the 1980s, a succession of presidents, governors, and mayors turned aggressively to management tools to gain traction for their policy agendas. Although we will review the philosophical pros and cons of doing so in chapter 7, for now, let us focus on a key instrumental component of this effort: the "politicization" of the career bureaucracy at all levels of government. Since a great degree of variation exists in the number of elected (as opposed to appointed) department and agency heads across the 50 states, we will focus on the politicization of federal agencies. These relationships have also been the most studied by researchers. But the same dynamics driving politicization at the federal level exist in many states and localities where you might work.

Prelude to Politicization

Recall from chapter 1 that inherent in the merit principles of administrative reform at all levels of government since the Civil Service Act of 1883 was the idea of neutral competence. Members of the civil service would respond to the preferences of elected officials, whether or not they were politically or substantively sympathetic to them. Career civil servants were, as British prime minister Winston Churchill said of scientists, to be "on tap, not on top."[31] But after 20 years of Democratic presidents "blanketing in" personnel—that is, extending merit protection coverage to federal employees originally hired on a partisan basis by presidents Franklin Roosevelt and Harry Truman—Republican President Dwight Eisenhower believed that careerists would not share his policy agenda. Consequently, he wanted his own people in agencies to gain compliance.

To these ends were created what are called "Schedule C employees." They were—and remain today—involved in confidential duties and/or policy advisory roles and include management positions just below the political-appointee level in agencies. Although nominally appointed by agency heads, presidents ever since have regarded Schedule C employees as White House appointees to gain more leverage over the career civil service. Someday, you may even be a recipient of such an appointment. By 2004, there were 1,596 Schedule C appointees to go with 550 slots appointed by presidents and confirmed by the US Senate (or PAS appointees) to the highest levels of departments and agencies.[32] Of these, 1,137 PAS positions were in the executive branch, with nearly 1,000 of these in policy-making positions.

But it was under President Nixon that efforts were launched to expand significantly the depth and breadth of politicization of the federal bureaucracy. Dubbed the "administrative presidency" by political scientist Richard Nathan, Nixon's strategy involved selecting political appointees who shared his policy aims and placing them as deep as he could into the career bureaucracy to help protect and advance his policy agenda.[33] These appointees would then try to align agency structures, personnel decisions, budget allocations, and decision rules within their discretion (i.e., that Congress would not have to approve) with Nixon's policy agenda. Nathan argued that this was a low-visibility strategy offering what economists call significant "first-mover" advantages to presidents.[34]

Consider the Nixon administration's efforts to politicize the OMB, previously known as the Bureau of the Budget. The bureau was originally created in 1921 via the Budget and Accounting Act and located in the Treasury Department. It was then moved into the EOP (as PCAM had wanted) in 1939. In 1970, the Bureau of the Budget was renamed the Office of Management and Budget by President Nixon. The administration then politicized the OMB by creating program associate directors (PADs). Today, each PAD is responsible for several departments and agencies with related missions—for example, human resource or community development programs. PADs negotiate with congressional members and staff on appropriations and authorization bills affecting the budget, sometimes with and sometimes without agency appointees!

To these duties have been added two major responsibilities in the years since. First, the Paperwork Reduction Act of 1980 created the Office of Information and Regulatory Affairs (OIRA) within the OMB. Designed originally to establish information policies and reduce agencies' collection of information from the public, OIRA's role was expanded under the Reagan administration to the screening of agency regulations. OIRA examines them for consistency with the president's policy preferences—and remands them (i.e., sends them back) to the agencies for further development if they are not consistent. Second, and as we will see shortly, OMB has played a significant role in efforts by presidents to implement their strategic planning initiatives.

As you probably know, the Nixon administration left office in disgrace in 1973 over the Watergate scandal, so it did not have enough time to complete its agenda. That would be left to the Reagan administration. And most responsible for allowing the Reagan administration to use the administrative presidency to an unprecedented degree and scope was the enactment of the most comprehensive piece of personnel legislation since the Pendleton Act of 1883: the Civil Service Reform Act (CSRA) of 1978. We will discuss this important act in other ways in chapter 7 and chapter 10, but for now it suffices for you to know that it gave presidents more appointees for placement deeper into the bureaucracy than ever before. It also gave them greater flexibility to apply standard techniques from the private sector, such as pay for performance (albeit to little effect, as we will cover in chapter 10). Finally, the CSRA created a Senior Executive Service (SES) with up to 7,000 positions. Of these, up to 10 percent of appointments could be political appointees.

Presidents ever since have intensified efforts to politicize the career bureaucracy. In the most comprehensive analysis undertaken to date of the politicization of the federal bureaucracy, David Lewis examines the numbers of SES, Schedule C, and presidential appointees requiring Senate confirmation (PAS) across federal departments and agencies between 1960 and 2004.[35] Looking at number of appointees and their ratio to civil service appointees, he finds that the greatest number of appointees were in the Department of Defense, the Department of State, the OMB, and the Office of Personnel Management. Among those most highly politicized were programs in the Department of Housing and Urban Development and the Department of Education. Among the least politicized were the National Aeronautics and Space Administration and the Social Security Administration.

Lewis' analysis also reveals that variations in number of appointees are attributable to several factors. As a public manager, you are likely to encounter significantly greater numbers of appointees if you work in agencies implementing social regulatory policies, while policies that require high levels of expertise, such as the National Institutes of

Health, have fewer appointees. And policies where partisans differ most greatly, such as in the environmental policy arena, will have more appointees. Also, within these areas, you are more likely to see greater numbers of appointees during the first term of a president, when the same party does not control the presidency and Congress, and when intraparty policy differences exist.

You will also learn that politicization through White House coordination of policy making (i.e., agency rulemaking) has done nothing but increase over the years. For instance, the Nixon administration began review of agency rules on a limited scale for environmental regulation, the Carter administration required agencies and OMB to weigh the costs and benefits of major regulations, and the Reagan administration then required that benefits exceed costs before rules could be issued. Next, the George H. W. Bush administration (reviving the Reagan administration's defunct Vice President's Council on Regulatory Relief) created a Council on Competitiveness led by Vice President Dan Quayle. The council became a backdoor way for regulated interests to petition the White House directly for regulatory relief from agency regulations. The Clinton administration then disbanded the council and returned its authority to OIRA. It did so, however, by issuing an executive order mandating the primacy of federal agencies in the regulatory process.

The George W. Bush administration then jacked up OIRA review. For example, it issued 23 "return" letters opposing proposed agency regulations during his first six years in office (compared to nine during the Clinton years). The administration also initiated "prompt letters" prodding agencies to reconsider *existing* regulations, created regulatory policy offices headed by political appointees in agencies, and tried to make guidance documents from agencies to regional offices reviewable by OMB.

The Obama administration has continued some of these trends, while also expanding the practice of prior administrations to appoint White House "czars" in various policy areas to coordinate initiatives across agencies (with mixed success). Moreover, its use of OIRA regulatory review has followed in the footsteps of prior administrations in terms of accelerating or decelerating rules and regulations with reelection concerns in mind. For instance, announcement of rules that might have been politically damaging to President Obama's reelection chances in 2012—related to health care, the environment, and workplace safety—were delayed until after his reelection. These included rules deciding which health plans would be accepted under the Patient Protection and Affordable Care Act and who qualified for federal subsidies if they opted to enroll in a state or a federal marketplace plan.

All in all—for good or ill—the last century has witnessed through these initiatives a centralization of policy making within the White House and the EOP. Agencies are seen too often as merely implementers of presidential preferences—much to their chagrin and the Congress' pushback. In terms of your career, you can count on the politicization of the career bureaucracy continuing apace. Chief executives at all levels of government understand that administration is policy, that no dichotomy exists between politics and administration, and that responsive competence has to be one of their aims.

Still, some important recent research finds claims of centralization, integration of initiatives, and strategic coherence wildly exaggerated. For example, Andrew Rudalevige's analysis of trends in the sources of policy proposals from 1949 to 1996 found that only 17 and 11 percent, respectively, of policy proposals considered by Congress originated exclusively in the White House or the EOP.[36] Instead, he offered a contingency theory:

the greater the number of issues involved, the more novel the policy, and the more necessary the reorganization of agencies to implement them, the more likely presidents will
want to avoid those transaction costs and opt for centralization of policy making in the
White House.[37]

Recent work by public administration scholar William West on OIRA regulatory
review also challenges the conventional wisdom that centralization is designed by presidents to obtain cohesiveness, coordination, and rationality across bureaucratic policy
initiatives.[38] West argues that OIRA has neither the goal nor the capacity to ensure overall planning and coordination. He found that "little if any effort is made in the review
process to think about the implementation of different programs in a comprehensive and
comparative way."[39] Thus, just because clearance of regulations is centralized in OIRA,
strategic cohesiveness and coordination across all programs may be an illusion. As such,
the degree of discretion your agency may have is much more substantial than you might
think, given all these centralizations of policy efforts.

Nor should you think that Congress (or state legislatures and city or county councils) is bereft of tools for dealing with efforts by chief executives to politicize the bureaucracy. Indeed, they engage in their own version of gaining responsive competence from
the career civil service. As we have reviewed in chapter 4, for example, appointees'
reorganization efforts often run pell-mell into preceding legislative efforts to "insulate"
agency programs from executive control. They do so by requiring annual rather than
multiyear budget authorizations; by placing responsibilities in commissions (e.g., the
Nuclear Regulatory Commission) and independent agencies (e.g., the Environmental
Protection Agency) rather than within executive departments (e.g., the Department
of the Interior); and by limiting the number of political appointees in a department or
agency.

Reconnecting with Citizens

As the descriptive validity of the PPA dichotomy has waned, calls for public managers to involve citizens more directly in agency policy making have periodically arisen.
However, with few exceptions, the results of these calls for democratic administration
have been disappointing. During the 1960s and 1970s alone, for example, nearly 155
federal mandates for citizen participation were imposed on local administrators as they
implemented federal programs.[40] You will learn in your coursework, though, that all of
these participatory efforts "suffered from a lack of resources for their implementation,
and administrators' logical response was to comply at the minimally required level so
as not to drain resources otherwise allocated for the operation of their programs... to
do just enough to comply with the legal mandates but not enough to make them work
well."[41] And although scattered successes occurred,[42] little comfort arises when considerable evidence suggests "that these efforts [were] not effective... some because of poor
planning or execution... [and others because] administrative systems that are based
upon expertise and professionalism leave little room for participatory processes."[43]

Moreover, the persistence of the early progressives' "bridge-building" mentality
model for linking bureaucracy with democracy has ever since made success in efforts
such as these strikingly uneven and wanting. As noted earlier, the dominance of organized interest groups—and especially business interests—in administrative policy deliberations has prevailed. To be sure, you might be thinking that these groups reflect the

preferences of citizens who otherwise lack the time, resources, and understanding to navigate the administrative process. But prior research, which we will examine next, suggests otherwise.

The Political Economy of the Rise of the Progressive–Business–Social Science Nexus

To understand fully the marginalization of average citizens in the policy process, you need to start with the early Progressive Era's focus on scientism, expertise, and bureaucratic over democratic administration which we covered earlier. You will recall how the resource dependency on business and private foundation funding of our then-newly emerging field of public administration put us on a path that was further amplified by a de facto coalition of progressive, business, and social science associations. This coalition sought to establish the legitimacy of their nascent movements and professional fields.

Nor is it possible to overstate the importance in fostering this outcome of the conjunction of these efforts with the two world wars of the twentieth century. Ellis Hawley writes that the aim of the first world war effort was "not only a managed economy but also the management for war purposes of the home, the workplace, the playground, the school, the church, the community, and the social service agency."[44] Thus, consistent with the idea of a compensatory state noted in chapter 2, boards consisting of economic interest groups were created to compensate for inadequate federal agency capacity and were attached ostensibly to federal agencies. During World War I, these included the War Industries Board, the War Finance Corporation, the National War Labor Board, the Food Administration, and the War Labor Policies Board. They, in turn, created commodity groups and war service committees that were "organized and certified by the U.S. Chamber of Commerce as being representative of the industry in question."[45]

Moreover, as we covered in chapter 1, the associationalist model of government further entrenched representatives of the business class in government deliberations. This idea was then amplified as the 1930s witnessed the advocacy in leading business schools, such as Harvard's, of a "management elite" of experts from both the public and private sectors to address the social problems of the Depression and beyond.[46] Once again, democracy would be saved and social harms reduced by experts wielding objective scientific knowledge and representing the true interests of citizens if they only had the expertise, time, and inclination to do so.

Of course, still needed to realize the progressive dream of policies led by bureaucratic expertise were empirically grounded data and analyses. Into this information chasm came the newly established social sciences. As alluded to in chapter 1, the two world wars offered the social sciences the rationale, resources, and legitimacy gains they sought by contributing to the mobilization effort. In the process, they also created politically supportive networks of cross-sectoral professionals in new associations. Developed "in the wake of [the second world] war" were "new models of state-economy relations and newly developed administrative capacities [that] existed side by side with a new universe of industrial organizations and elites experienced in working with the federal government to control and direct economic activity."[47] No talk of citizenship, let alone democratic administration, passed from policy-makers' lips.

Indeed, World War II spawned in America the greatest and longest-lasting amplification of bureaucratic over democratic administration that our field has witnessed. As

Marc Allen Eisner argues, "State capacity was expanded by appending the capacities of private-sector associations on to the state."[48] This approach had significant effects on policy making and implementation by providing sustained access and influence for organized interests pursuing their agendas and, most especially, for corporate interests. As we reviewed earlier in this chapter in our discussion of subsystems and issue networks, this effect was not limited to defense research and development policy at the end of the Cold War. And collectively, these efforts "favor[ed] the best organized competitors, specializ[ed] politics around agencies, [and] ultimately limit[ed] participation in agency deliberations to...pre-existing groups."[49]

Further influencing business to get better organized in order to affect subsystem politics—and marginalizing the participation of nonexpert citizens—was the new social regulation of the 1960s and 1970s that we reviewed in chapter 1. You will recall that the new social regulation—laws pursuing equal employment opportunity, environmental protection, and consumer protection—threatened business with aggressive and costly enforcement. As Richard Stewart argues, "Faced with the necessity of regulating very large numbers of firms, agencies shifted from case-by-case adjudication to adoption of highly specific regulations of general application."[50] In turn, the "large numbers of firms and industries affected, and the conflicts of interests among them, made negotiated solutions more difficult" and often displaced "political decision-making mechanisms by bureaucratic and technocratic ones."[51] These only further marginalized unorganized interests. Business interests also turned repeatedly to the courts to challenge the regulations issued by these regulatory agencies, efforts that further increased the opacity of government to ordinary citizens and advantaged well-organized and legally and technically savvy interest groups.[52]

More recently, and reminiscent of Progressive Era reformers, H. George Frederickson and Kevin Smith write that underlying network relationships today

> are *professional concepts of the public interest* and an obligation among public servants to represent an *inchoate public* outside of a particular jurisdiction. The end result is not just coordination among the various units of the disarticulated state, but the reappearance of the meaningful representation that has leaked steadily from elected offices as jurisdictional borders become less relevant to policy problems...Thus, citizens may get their interest represented in decisions that impact their lives only on the bridges of administrative conjunctions.[53] [emphases added]

Represented, perhaps, but these are interests as seen through the eyes of agency experts, thus further marginalizing citizens from the highly technical, legal, and interest group dominated administrative processes, subsystems, and issue networks that drive policy making.[54] Be clear, though. Corporate interests do not always get their way.[55] Moreover, the attention that they pay to public policy tends to vary over time, sometimes showing intense interest and other times none at all.[56] What typically happens is that once lack of attention turns out to hurt their interests, they mobilize and become intensely involved, as Stewart describes.

But you may be asking at this point, "So what? Don't these organized interests represent citizens who don't have the time, expertise, or resources to participate?" To be sure, tremendous growth in the number of interest groups dealing with more liberal causes has spiraled to reduce the advantage of business interests.[57] Still, these liberal groups tend to emphasize quality of life rather than economic issues of concern to broad swaths of working and lower-middle-class voters who in the past supported public agency capacity building.[58] Theda Skocpol also finds that many of these associations speak more for social service "institutions" and "professional elites" (see more below) than on behalf of average citizens.[59] Indeed, as alluded to in chapter 2, Kay Schlozman, Sidney Verba, and Henry Brady's analysis of survey research covering 35,000 interest groups operating at all levels of government finds that "the political voices of organized interests are even less representative than those of individuals" voting.[60]

Democratic Administration and the Paradox of Procedural Accountability

In the aftermath of World War II, Congress took steps to enhance the participation of citizens in agency decision making. Realizing that delegation of their legislative authority to agencies could not be avoided for the reasons we have reviewed, Congress stated that agency rulemaking had to be as open to political persuasion as the legislative process. To these ends, it enacted the Administrative Procedure Act (APA) of 1946. The act serves as a basis for administrative due process in agencies, and various statutes have added additional requirements to it over the years. At the same time, "little APAs" have been adopted and extended in most states.

The otherwise necessary and beneficial APA was not without its ironies for citizens, however. Created during its implementation was what Michael Sandel calls the "procedural republic."[61] Fostered was what some scholars call the "judicialization" of rulemaking and adjudicatory processes that marginalized most citizens even further. As you will learn directly in your public service career, the APA requires agencies to publish a notice of proposed rulemaking in the *Federal Register* to inform interested actors (1) that a new rule or rule revision is being considered, (2) of the statutory authority under which the agency is proposing a new rule, (3) of the substance of the rule they are considering, and (4) who to contact at the agency for further information.

Next, agencies have to offer "appropriate time"—usually a 30–60-day period—for public comment. Known as the "dialogue requirement," the public comment period is designed for the agency to have an interchange with the public about the specifics of the regulation and to respond to critics' reaction to it. The number of positive and (mostly) negative comments received for any proposed rule or rule change depends on how controversial the rule is, and they have ranged from none to thousands. Then, by classification of complaint, the agency must respond to these issues in the *Federal Register*. They may accept some criticisms and address them, or they may disagree (more likely) and give their reasons why. These exchanges then become part of the official record that a federal judge may review if the rule is challenged in court. The final rule is then published in the *Code of Federal Regulations*.

To challenge a rule in federal court, one must have suffered (or be reasonably expected to suffer) real harm on a variety of grounds. These include, but are not limited to, charges that the agency (1) did not adequately follow the rulemaking procedures of the APA (or any additional procedural actions required by a specific statute); (2) did not have the authority to issue such a rule (known legally as an ultra vires action); (3) accepted communications from interests after the period for public comment expired without being included in the record (known legally as ex parte communications); or (4) issued a rule that was unconstitutional.

If the courts agree with the charges, they do not amend the rule or substitute their judgment for it; rather, they "remand" the rule back to the agency with their decision for further consideration. All this can, of course, make for a prolonged period of uncertainty for the affected public, private, or nonprofit actors. This is especially true if decisions are appealed, different federal or state appeals courts render conflicting decisions, or appeals of their implementation are made directly to the state or federal supreme courts.

Thus, you might be wondering how anyone can say that the public is marginalized from agency deliberations given the extensiveness of the APA procedures and their focus on a dialogue requirement enforceable in court. But, again, the APA and its progeny in the states require "resources, organization, and sophistication" that most citizens lack and corporate interests find less daunting.[62] Indeed, recent research suggests that businesses, and the trade associations that represent businesses and professions, were (and are) involved in rulemaking more often than other groups.[63] This is especially true in the pre-notice period, where tremendous influence on the agency can occur without transparency to the public or their elected officials. Although some find that this influence varies across stages of the regulatory process, it nonetheless shows the marginalization of unorganized citizen interests, with bureaucratic as opposed to democratic administration continuing to prevail.[64] To be sure, citizens may be represented in class-action suits. However, this in no way is tantamount to the tenets of democratic administration where citizens actually engage in agency deliberations or public managers take the time to ensure that citizens understand the issues involved.

Part of the Problem or the Solution?

Scholars have identified many reasons for the decline of trust in government in the United States since the early 1970s. Some cite elevated citizen expectations following the government's success in World War II, anger in the wake of the Watergate scandal and the travails of the Vietnam War, and the unleashing of pent-up frustrations with the end of the Cold War masked by our previous focus on containing the former Soviet Union. Others identify more immediate culprits, such as long-stagnant wages for the working and lower-middle classes, anger over repeated threats to shut down the federal government, the polarizing partisan effects of the so-called "permanent political campaign" in Washington, and the destabilizing effects of economic globalization on local communities.[65]

How much public managers and public administrative theorists have played a role in either citizen satisfaction with or estrangement from government is currently unknown, given a paucity of public administration scholarship on this topic and despite the role agencies play in bringing "stability and change in political life."[66] Yet, as alluded to in chapter 2, researchers have recently linked the design of administrative structures, policies, and procedures with citizens' negative perceptions of themselves, public agencies, and their own sense of political efficacy.[67] Andrea Campbell, for instance, demonstrates how the erosion of direct service provision fostered by the compensatory state creates "interpretive effects" that undermine citizen perceptions of self-efficacy and political involvement.[68]

These negative perceptions, in turn, have been shown to reduce the propensity of citizens to pay attention to government, value what it does for them, participate in the political process, and be mobilizable for political action in support of agency initiatives. The

less citizens perceive policies affecting them directly, and the less they participate in decision processes, the less likely they are to see support for these programs as important to
their lives. Moreover, when private and nonprofit organizations are contracted to deliver
public services, research indicates that citizens do not associate the benefits they receive
with government but, rather, with the private or nonprofit provider of the service.

The same is true when what your public budgeting and finance professors will call
"tax expenditures" are used to implement policy agendas, rather than direct service provision. As we will review more thoroughly in chapter 8, these include such things as
subsidies for health insurance, loan guarantees, and tax deductions for interest on home
mortgages.[69] In identifying what she calls America's "submerged state" of tax expenditures, Suzanne Mettler argues that corporate interests—especially the real estate, financial, health, communications, and energy and natural resource sectors—have spent the
past three decades using indirect policy tools to shift economic resources from lower and
middle-class citizens to themselves.[70] Examples here include some programs from which
you, your friends, or your family may presently benefit, such as the Home Mortgage
Interest Deduction, the Retirement Savings Contributions Credit, the Lifetime Learning
Credit, the Coverdell Tax Deferred Savings Credit, and federal student loan programs.
These, as opposed to more "direct" tools such as food stamps and the GI Bill.[71]

Together, the networked and submerged states reduce the average citizen's sense of
awareness of government support and political self-efficacy, and improve the influence of
elements of the business community. As alluded to in chapter 2, one major example is the
role these efforts played in fomenting the Great Recession of 2007–09. Recently, Jacob
Hacker and Paul Pierson have shown us how conservatives and probusiness elements
comprised a decades-long "durable policy coalition" of actors beginning in the 1980s
that quietly shaped regulatory and tax policy regimes to stack the deck in their favor—
and against the lower and middle classes.[72] Their success meant that even when their
opponents won elections or even passed new legislation (think the Dodd-Frank Wall
Street Reform and Consumer Protection Act of 2010, Pub. L. 111–203, as a response
to this Great Recession), they had to work within the new rules of the game that placed
aggressive regulation and tax increases at a political disadvantage.

That policy, politics, and administration interact with each other, and that citizens
tend to be marginalized in the deliberative processes of government agencies at all levels
of government, might be consonant with our field's "bridge-building" role for administrators. But it also flies in the face of public administration norms to advance democracy
and is instrumentally a poor strategy for advancing your agency's policy or program
agenda. More normatively, if you are dealing directly with citizens or developing policies or programs that affect them, you have a responsibility in a democratic republic to
minimize the alienation of citizens from their government, if not to help build their sense
of political efficacy.

To these ends, you should know that the persistent decline of public faith in and distrust of government since the early 1960s has wrought a significant call for bringing the
public back into agency deliberations. The Alfred P. Sloan Foundation, for example, has
funded a number of initiatives to encourage municipal governments to involve citizens
in developing and implementing performance management systems. Examples of these
initiatives include Iowa's Citizen-Initiated Performance Assessment project, the Fund for
the City of New York's citizen-based assessments of the effectiveness of city government
services, and Rutgers University's National Center for Public Productivity. These projects

focus on municipal governments as a key starting point because of their opportunities for direct connections to citizens in management processes. As one Utah mayor at the forefront of such approaches, Jack Thomas, puts it, "If you want to have a government that's rooted in the community, you better start that way [with direct citizen contact]. It's all about trust."[73] As such, they revive the call of some early progressive reformers, such as Jane Addams and William Allen, to develop "efficient citizens," as well as Woodrow Wilson's call for cities to be laboratories for citizenship in America.

Meanwhile, at the federal government level, both the second Bush and the Obama administrations have seized upon technical innovations in the information technology and social media world to emphasize increasing transparency. In advancing the "open data movement," for instance, the Obama administration has sought to enhance the responsiveness and timeliness of agencies to Freedom of Information Act requests, as well as to release hundreds of thousands of new agency data. However, as we have already covered, the overall record of success in generating meaningful citizen involvement at all levels of government is disappointing to date.[74] Moreover, cybersecurity to prevent hacking into these information bases and the theft of personal, business, and national security data is imperative, even as transparency efforts expand.

As Jane Fountain writes, the "outcomes of technology enactment are...multiple, unpredictable, and indeterminate...[because they]...result from technological, rational, social, and political logics."[75] Given the ubiquitous nature of social media, the quick breakthroughs in technology, and the potential these hold for democratic administration, however, your agency will have an opportunity to build an "e-sense" of common purpose infused with democratic constitutional values that was not possible for your predecessors in the public service.

Anecdotal evidence suggests, however, that public agencies are going to have to become much more adept at dealing with social media, because if handled clumsily, it can get them in trouble. As illustrated by its use during such recent catastrophes as Hurricane Sandy and the Boston Marathon bombings, social media offers public managers such as yourself a way to connect quickly and directly with citizens. As such, "the future of public-sector communication lies in clouds and ether—Twitter, Facebook, Instagram, Pinterest and their ilk. Public officials had...better get used to it."[76]

But as social media experts Missy Graham and Elizabeth Johnson Avery note, "Participation in social media makes organizations vulnerable to both internal and external crises. On an internal level, organizations have to be concerned about online behavior that could potentially damage [an agency or government's] brand."[77] Consequently, it takes a "sophisticated and nuanced approach to shape and manage government's message,"[78] as well as intra-agency communication that cuts across the government silos and stovepiping we discussed in chapter 4 for a consistent "one-government" message to emerge.

Reengaging Financial Resources

Nowhere does the PPA dichotomy break down more visibly than when reengaging financial resources. As such, you should understand both the political constraints and the opportunities you will witness and need to navigate as a public manager in the decades ahead. Chapter 8 will delve deeply into the challenges, choices, and opportunities you will confront in US public budgeting and finance. For now, let us focus on how politics has wrought—and is likely to continue to do so—the intergenerational equity battle looming ahead of you that we noted in chapter 2. This battle will set the general context for the politics of public budgeting and finance at all levels of government for the foreseeable future.

As you may recall, the 1990s produced not only a balanced budget from 1998–2001, but also, for a brief moment, the potential for a sizeable budget surplus going forward. As we will discuss more fully in chapter 8, most responsible for this was the so-called "dot.com" technology bubble of the 1990s that brought in hundreds of millions of tax dollars because of capital gains on rising stocks and higher salaries producing more tax revenue, as well as congressional budget deals in 1990 and 1993 that cut spending. But a number of sizeable tax cuts, the deregulatory agenda reviewed earlier in this chapter, the war on terror, and the invasion of Iraq and Afghanistan launched under the George W. Bush administration wiped out those surpluses during the first decade of the twenty-first century. These deficits—and the national debt—then soared to $17.3 trillion during the Obama administration, partially as a result of the Bush and Obama administrations' efforts to cope with the 2007–09 financial crisis. The national debt is comprised of both the accumulation of annual budget deficits (excess spending over tax revenue) and intra-governmental debt that the government owes itself after borrowing from various federal trust funds (e.g., the Social Security Trust Fund).

Thus, between 1980 and 2013, the national debt increased by nearly sixfold. Although the national debt as a percentage of gross domestic product reached an all-time high of nearly 109 percent in 1946 (i.e., after the massive incurred debt of fighting World War II), the Congressional Budget Office (CBO) and the Government Accountability Office (GAO) estimate that the United States will exceed that within a decade. The national debt ratio will then spiral to over 200 percent by 2034 if Congress fails to take corrective action on the tax and spending sides earlier, a totally unsustainable rate economically and politically.

At the same time, interest rates on the national debt take dollars away from other spending needs. They must be paid when they come due, so that means that—like entitlements—they are in that sense "uncontrollable." The CBO estimates that until what the media calls a "grand bargain" is reached on raising taxes and cutting entitlement spending, interest costs will spiral.[79] In 2013, they were projected to comprise 6.6 percent of the federal budget. Combined with Social Security, Medicare, and veterans' pensions—along with the defense budget—that means over 70 percent of the fiscal year 2013–14 budget was uncontrollable.

Regardless, as noted in chapter 1, Republicans and Democrats have been unwilling or unable to address these deficits and the national debt through compromise. The two main negotiators in 2013—President Obama and Speaker of the House John Boehner (R-Ohio)—were not far apart in their negotiations. But fiscally conservative "Tea Party" members of Boehner's caucus and socially liberal members of the Democratic Party were unable to reach a compromise. For Republicans, increases in tax rates have been unacceptable; with the end of the Cold War, the party's single uniting agenda item has been an opposition to cutting tax rates. Meanwhile, the Democratic Party has resisted efforts to cut programs such as Social Security, Medicare, or Medicaid. And, yet, Congress has had no difficulty in creating unfunded programs for senior citizens, such as the Medicare Part D Prescription Drug, Improvement, and Modernization Act of 2003!

Following continued failure to arrive at a grand bargain after a presidential commission produced what became known as the Simpson-Bowles plan for deficit reduction that we noted in chapter 2, Congress—with President Obama's endorsement—turned to a budgetary technique known as "sequestration." This, after recommending a series of controversial cuts and tax increases. The former included a reduction in home mortgage deductions, a recommendation of Simpson-Bowles.

Under the terms of the sequestration agreement, if a grand bargain could not be reached, automatic spending cuts of 50 percent for defense and 50 percent for domestic programs (other than entitlement programs such as Social Security) would go into effect. Viewed as so draconian that no one would risk it, sequestration nonetheless went into effect in 2013 after another effort at a grand bargain failed. In fact, the total federal workforce, including postal workers, fell by 20 percent to 2.7 million employees from its high of 3.4 million employees in 2010. Excluding postal workers, the federal workforce fell by over 9,000 employees, its lowest level since 2009.[80]

In combination with increased revenues derived as the economy gradually began to improve in 2013 and lower-than-expected increases in medical costs, sequestration narrowed the expected short-term funding gaps that CBO predicted only months earlier. Then, in late 2013, Congress moved to avert yet another impending government and debt-ceiling showdown in early 2014, as well as to avoid continuing across-the-board cuts hitting defense especially hard. It did so by approving a very modest budget package that failed to deal with larger economic issues facing the nation. The Ryan-Murray budget plan increased authorized spending by $45 billion in 2014 and $18 billion in 2015, split evenly between defense and domestic programs. To offset these increases, the plan made a variety of marginal adjustments, including lowering the rate of increase in federal and military pension benefits, raising fees on airline travelers for airport security, and reducing federal payments to states for mineral royalties.[81]

Still, as we have noted, long-term budget projections remain highly worrisome and will be with us for a long time. As such, recruiting the best and the brightest to government to meet the challenges, choices, and even opportunities these projections are creating will be critical for our nation's future. Although we will address this question in great detail in chapter 8, it suffices presently to address the challenges to doing so for hiring and retaining a talented government workforce at any level of government given today's partisan atmosphere.

Recapitalizing Personnel Assets

As the preceding sections suggest, realization is now widespread that politics, policy, and administration cannot be separated when it comes to the kinds of public problems faced by the United States in the twenty-first century. The rub is that it is becoming more and more difficult in an era of fiscal stress, politicization, bureaucrat bashing, and downsizing to ensure that we can recruit and retain men and women with the appropriate skills, knowledge, and public service values necessary to address these problems. Not that applications for employment are down or that agencies are not hiring, because they have been—in impressive numbers. The issue is recruiting and retaining the *most talented* workforce possible for critical skill areas capable of dealing with today's and tomorrow's wicked problem challenges amid a hostile political environment.

Most notably, morale problems among career civil servants occasioned by government contracting, cutback management, wage freezes, and changes in personnel policy threaten to make it more difficult for you to recruit to your agencies the best and the brightest personnel with the right technical skills. For example, federal government-wide job satisfaction has been in a slide for three years, "dropping to 57.8 percent, a decline of 7.2 points from its high of 65 percent in 2010."[82] Likewise, a 2012 survey of 347 members of the International Public Management Association for Human Resources and the National Association of State Personnel Executives indicates that state and local government agencies are having difficulty hiring engineers; credentialed environmental, chemical, and forensic professionals; finance personnel; police and firefighters; information technology professionals; librarians; nurses and physicians; middle and top management; skilled trades; and social workers.[83]

At the same time, consider alone the conundrum for hiring top-notch technical personnel at all levels of government because of contracting. Historically, one of the major attractions of public service was the tradeoff between receiving lower pay than in the private sector in exchange for greater job security and better pension benefits. Today, this covenant is strained in many jurisdictions, if not totally broken. As we will discuss in greater depth in chapter 7, unrealistic commitments made to pensioners by elected officials and union leaders—plus political raids on pension funds—over the past three decades are now coming due, and pensions in many state and local governments are significantly underfunded.

Because of this, making up for shortfalls out of general revenues will take either unpopular tax increases or big chunks out of funding for other needed programs. For example, a 2013 study of 173 cities done by the Center for Retirement Research at Boston College found pension costs averaging nearly 8 percent of city budgets, but with cities such as Springfield, Massachusetts (15 percent), Chicago (17 percent), and New York City (12.9 percent) in significantly more debt. Indeed, at the extremes, cities such as Chicago and Detroit are now cutting budgets for existing retirees, and states such as Illinois, New Jersey, and Rhode Island are either making cuts or considering them for future retirees.

Relatedly, for technical and scientific job recruits, a leading attraction for making a difference in society was doing cutting-edge work or research in one's professional area of expertise. Yet, often today one finds professionals becoming contract managers and monitors, overseeing the work of other professionals in their fields in the for-profit and nonprofit sectors who are doing the work they love—at higher salaries. Indeed, sometimes those contracted in this manner are sitting in the same office as civil servants in what personnel experts call a "mixed," "blended," or "just-in-time" workforce—and receiving higher pay!

The Obama administration's efforts to bolster the contract monitoring workforce, noted earlier, may help by contracting-back-in, but scaling up will inevitably lag contracting efforts at all levels of government.[84] In this new clerical state, too many—but not all—professionals become check writers, monitors, and dispersers of largesse. What is more, they become exposed at all levels of government to the perverse graft and corruption incentives of the "old" clerical state of the Jacksonian era.[85]

Yet another important question arises from all this. Elected officials continue to say that (and act as if) public service can be provided everywhere—in government, for-profit, and nonprofit organizations. So why would government employment that pays less, has increasingly less job security, and involves contract letting and monitoring of others doing the kinds of professional work one has been trained professionally to do be attractive to the best and the brightest in America? That such a question arises hikes to a new level of quandary perennial personnel management questions about how best to make public service entry and retention attractive to outstanding technical persons.

Quite astonishingly in light of these challenges, a stunning lack of strategic human resource management systems exists at all levels of government. Little political will has been expended for such purposes, despite the accelerating graying of the workforce noted earlier and the need for reconceptualizing purpose in many agencies. Again, we will discuss these issues in more depth in chapter 7. Presently, it suffices for you to be aware that GAO continues to report strategic human capital planning as a high-risk management area.[86] If anything, states and localities are even further behind.[87]

Yet another manifestation of today's political environment is what personnel specialists call "at-will" employment, a topic we will also cover more extensively in chapter 7. For now, note that unlike in traditional civil service systems, at-will employees can be dismissed without warning or reason. Also understand that some argue that lifetime tenure is not as important to rising generations of young people in America, many of whom already may be employed in either public, private, or nonprofit organizations. Indeed, some evidence from prior research indicates that younger workers in the United States no longer expect to form long-term psychological contracts with their employers.[88] You may or may not feel the same. Regardless, these employees may not represent the best employees in the workforce, may not be representative of the workforce as a whole, and may be self-selecting. And as a public manager, you will have to find creative ways to address these issues, something we will cover further below.

Finally, given the practical, budget, and political realities of our time, it is likely that contracts worth billions of dollars will continue to be let by public agencies and, thus, will require extensive monitoring capabilities at all levels of government that currently do not exist. Indeed, the scope and magnitude of federal contractor abuses is just now being revealed in a systematic way. Pressure on OMB by Congress and the Obama administration to root out waste, fraud, and abuse—as well as to assess contractor performance—has resulted in an increase of the number of suspensions and debarments of contractors from 1,900 in 2009 to 3,326 in fiscal year 2011.

Still, oversight shortages exist and will require agencies to continue to raise considerably the status and reward structures for contract managers in the public service. But it is not just pay and status that will solve these problems. Contract managers must have the right combination of skills that experts say are needed.[89] They must be relationship-oriented, with skills in team building and facilitation. They must also have project management skills. Contract managers are generally not the official program or project manager, but they are often the only ones with the business expertise required to do so. Moreover, they must be more than police officers who are consulted only on ethical or regulatory adherence or process enforcement.

Importantly, evidence culled from the annual Best Places to Work in the Federal Government survey conducted by the Partnership for Public Service offers lessons for you in dealing with morale issues that are applicable at all levels of government—at least once employees are hired. Aside from various theories of motivation, some of which we will review in chapter 10, management in agencies with the highest levels of employee satisfaction and, thus, with higher levels of morale tend to do various combinations of the following:

- promote a robust telework program;
- enhance training opportunities for employees and managers;

- better emphasize the importance for managers to communicate with employees and create avenues for feedback;
- launch web-based crowdsourcing where employees can contribute suggestions and have a dialogue around innovations at the agency;
- recognize and reward innovative performance;
- start reverse mentoring programs where junior employees mentor more senior staff on a particular topic area, especially related to social media and information technology;
- shift the weighting on all managerial performance plans to emphasize "leading people, building coalitions, and diversity and inclusion" rather than tasks;
- create committees with employee volunteers, each championed by a designated top executive, to address a range of topics;
- create a career paths webpage depicting career tracks for contract auditors, as well as a career development assignment program and improved mentoring and coaching programs.[90]

Basically, management in these agencies should pay close attention to what employees are saying and then respond by making changes to address some of the top concerns and problems.

Conclusion

From this chapter, you should now have an appreciation for how the political environment of public agencies in America's compensatory state has changed over the years, the forces driving it, and how elected officials at every level of government have adopted strategies and tactics to advance responsive competence in all aspects of public management. You should also be comfortable with the idea that politics affect policy, policy affects the nature of politics, and administration affects both policy and political opportunities. In the process, you should have acquired a basic sense for the political challenges, choices, and opportunities offered to you as a public manager trying to reconcile bureaucratic and democratic administration and some idea of how to deal with them. With this as background, we turn next in chapter 6 to examining the evolution of the knowledge, skills, and tools available for you to play a meaningful public management role in the policy process as you or your agency pursue the building of common purpose informed by democratic constitutional values.

CHAPTER 6

Informing Policy Decisions

One constant theme of the previous chapters is that public managers at all levels of government help to shape, interpret, and inform the policy process. But many policy analysts who will help inform your agency's policies have been trained traditionally to think and act as if the bureaucracy is a "black box" in which resources and demands are "inputs" to agencies, which then produce policy "outputs." What happens in between inputs and outputs within an agency are left to others to understand and consider.

Relatedly, many policy analysts also embrace what Deborah Stone calls the "rationality project."[1] Stone sardonically puts it this way in describing what she sees as an inherent paradox: although "passionately devoted to improving governance," the field of policy science has been "based on a deep disgust for the ambiguities and paradoxes of politics."[2] Although Beryl Radin is more charitable to the field, she nonetheless argues that it struggles to integrate two distinct cultures—politics and analysis.[3] This, despite the reality Stone notes that political necessity often trumps technically superior analysis. Moreover, "political reasoning is reasoning by metaphor and analogy."[4] As such, the results of advanced quantitative analytical techniques are important inputs into the policy-making process in the compensatory state. However, they are subjects of a contest over their interpretation by contending actors involved in that process.

Known as the "argumentative turn" in policy analysis, this perspective puts a premium on analysts' ability to engage in "evidence, argument, and persuasion."[5] To be sure, analysts need to know the assumptions, logic, strengths, and limitations of the well-honed quantitative skills and economic thinking offered by the policy sciences for diagnosing and addressing the problems confronting societies worldwide. And as a public manager supervising them or interacting with them on teams, you need to know the right questions to ask of policy analysts and their work products. But equally important for them—and for you as a public manager interpreting and applying their work—is mastering the skills of marshalling evidence, making cogent and compelling arguments, and persuading a crowded field of listeners with their own policy claims within and outside public agencies. These argumentative skills are just as analytical, expertise-based, and complicated to learn in their own way as the most sophisticated econometric techniques you will encounter in your studies. In fact, some analysts—and public managers—never master them, and their effectiveness suffers appreciably.

The argumentative turn thus requires agencies to *reconceptualize the purpose* of policy analysis from one of offering "correct" solutions to public problems to one of framing problems and solutions and marshalling evidence to support arguments. It also means *reconnecting with citizens* as deliberative partners in a true spirit of democratic administration and *redefining administrative rationality* by decentralizing rather than centralizing policy analysis units in public agencies and dealing with multiple outside voices. This also means recognizing that there exists no one "policy" dealing with a topic but rather clusters of policies that are typically uncoordinated and that may even work at cross-purposes to affect policy problems. Agencies will also need to figure out how best to *reengage financial resources* using existing analytical techniques but in ways that take more than efficiency into account. Finally, it means they will need to *recapitalize personnel assets* by learning to work collaboratively, integratively, and across functions in hybrid policy and administrative teams.

You should leave this chapter with a good sense for the history of the policy sciences field, its evolution, and its current debates. Garnered, too, should be an appreciation for the roles that public managers such as yourself play in the policy process, how those roles have changed as the compensatory state has evolved, and why they have changed. Moreover, you should leave the chapter armed with an understanding of how the argumentative turn requires you and policy analysts in your agency to acquire more skills and "mental mindsets" than those held by your predecessors. At a minimum, you will leave with an ability to ask the right questions as a consumer of policy studies. And, from all this, you should gain an appreciation for how instrumental thinking—that is, means–ends analyses of whether or not a policy or program works—is a necessary but insufficient condition for restoring a sense of common purpose infused with democratic constitutional values in America.

Reconceptualizing Purpose

We should begin our tour of the policy sciences and how they are being reconceptualized today by returning to their origins. The self-conscious study of public policy took root in the 1950s and was led by a leading political scientist of the day, Harold Lasswell. He argued that political science and public administration had failed miserably in their study of public policy and offered a solution to this problem.

The Rationality Project Begins

According to Lasswell, political science was focused inordinately on developing theories to explain and predict political behavior but without linking that behavior to the policy process, policy, or the policy outcomes produced. In addition, political science's embrace of what your professors may call the "behavioral revolution" stressed eliminating normative values from research (i.e., "ought questions" and judgments). Meanwhile, as you will recall, public administration in the 1950s focused on the inner workings of agencies and did not link them explicitly to policy outputs, let alone outcomes.

Lasswell's solution was to create a new field—policy science—that would integrate the value-laden aspects of political theory with the behavioralist study of what governments actually do to produce policy. This new field would be multidisciplinary, because policy problems do not fit neatly within any one discipline. But as you will learn in your course-work, policy science eventually split into two elements that continue to this day: policy analysis and policy studies.

Policy analysis is pursued through quantitative analyses informed by economic prin-ciples, especially welfare economics, and it is geared toward assessing the impact of poli-cies and their determinants. For example, an analyst might use data from the National Survey of Families and Households to evaluate the determinants of receiving a childcare subsidy, as well as the effects of receiving employment, school attendance, and welfare benefits. Policy studies engages in a more contextually grounded study of policy pro-cesses, their interrelationships, and their effects on outputs and (more rarely) outcomes. For instance, an analyst might start with how an airline safety issue is framed, how that affects the language in a law dealing with that issue, what difficulties and constraints the language poses for regulators writing regulations to implement the law, and the fate of the regulation as it is implemented.

It was not long, however, before the economics side of the field became dominant. Here, two assumptions serve as rebuttable presumptions. First, policy actors are rational utility-maximizing individuals and should be the primary unit of analysis. They seek to maximize their benefits and minimize their costs while pursuing their policy choices. Second, and driven by welfare economics, analysts start from the rebuttable assumption that markets are the most efficient way to allocate resources for the overall welfare of society. The only role for public policy is to establish the rules of the game for market operations so willing buyers and sellers will become involved and to prevent or minimize market failures such as "negative externalities." A negative externality occurs when a voluntary market exchange imposes social costs on society that are not incorporated into the price of an item, such as building a gambling casino that brings increased crime to an area. Market failures also occur when, for example, no competition exists to keep prices down while ensuring quality products or services (monopoly); whenever too few custom-ers distort market prices (monopsony); whenever customers cannot be excluded from something if they do not pay for it (a free-rider problem); and when self-interest leads actors to consume something before others do, which leads to overuse and depletion of resources (tragedy of the commons).

Moreover, the standard for evaluating policy in terms of efficient resource alloca-tion—and whether to pursue government intervention at all into markets—is something that economists call a "Pareto improvement." This occurs when a change in resource allocation prompted by a potential policy makes at least one person better off and no one worse off. In turn, what economists call "Pareto optimality" occurs at the point at which no further Pareto improvements can be made.

Pareto efficiency might strike you as a pretty high and unrealistic standard to meet for policy makers in a democratic republic characterized by topsy-turvy politics. It certainly will after you read chapter 8 in this book on public budgeting and finance in America! It definitely struck others as such, and many used what economists call the "Kaldor-Hicks criterion" to soften its stringency. Here, the same logic of Pareto optimality holds, but compensation to losers is allowed (though it does not actually have to take place!).

Reading these criteria for evaluating policy, you might also wonder what happened to the other democratic constitutional values cherished in America other than effi-ciency (e.g., equity and due process). Also disturbing for you might be both standards' assumption that the initial allocation of resources is fair or just. You are not alone. These reactions were—and remain today—just a part of the negative reaction to welfare economics that erupted in the wake of its dominance of policy analysis.

Questioning the Field's Direction

Critics immediately began nibbling away at the assumptions of the economic rationality project. Indeed, citing the exclusion of political variables from its models, welfare economics' most severe critics called it "a myth, a theoretical illusion"[6] that reflects "a false and naïve view of the policy process."[7] Contrary to the principle of utility-maximizing individuals, people do not have clear or fixed goals. Nor do they have an ordered set of preferences from least to most desired (i.e., a "transitivity" of preferences). At the same time, people often use what some call a "logic of appropriateness"; they not only consider monetary costs and benefits when making instrumental policy choices, but they also use existing norms, ethical and moral values, rules, and role descriptions. Others, including no less formidable a critic than Nobel Prize-winning economist Herbert Simon, noted that cognitive, resource, and time limits on individual decision makers cause them to "satisfice"—that is, pick the first acceptable alternative rather than choose the "one best way" to realize their goals.

Still others, whom you will probably read about during your studies, critiqued the economist's aim to attain what is called "parsimony" in prediction and explanation. Called "Occam's razor," the economist's logic is that the simplest of competing theories should be preferred to more complex ones. Critics attacked the simplicity of this argument for—ironically—its own simplicity. As the preeminent practitioner of parsimony, Albert Einstein, once said, a theory should be as simple as possible *but not simpler*! Otherwise, the theory loses legitimacy. These critics were joined by others who argued that econometric techniques might allow you to "predict" with some degree of probability that something will happen (e.g., a person would leave the welfare rolls), but you would not be able to explain *why* it happened. For that, you need to consider the history and context of preferences, choices, and behaviors—as is typically of interest to elected officials with competing policy preferences.

These "historical institutionalist" scholars urge you to pay attention to the sequencing of events—invoking what a group of scholars call the concepts of "path dependency"—as well as the "constitutive effects" of policies, programs, and administrative reforms. In terms of the former, they argue that choices or decisions coming earliest in a sequence of decisions shape, amplify, and constrain the path of available future policy options. In terms of the latter, early decisions are more difficult to dislodge later because of the constellation of political forces that coalesce around them—what we discussed in chapter 5 as subsystem, issue network, and advocacy coalition politics. And although we usually think of politics creating policy, *policy also creates politics*. Any new policy creates or expands existing constituencies and interest groups, or spawns new ones. The latter happens when the interpretation or implementation of a new policy creates conflicts even among original supporters, which leads to new interest groups representing the disaffected.

You should not take away from this the idea that policies get "locked in" or do not change. Policies frequently get amended, experience variations in funding and political support, and are reauthorized with specific changes. Moreover, external "shocks" to the system (such as 9/11) and slower-moving secular trends can bring cumulative change that become qualitatively different over time (e.g., demographic changes such as we discussed in chapter 2). In addition, the ambiguity of policy language, plus conflicts within policy coalitions and social movements, can prompt change.[8]

To these more scholarly complaints were added a drumbeat of political criticism against the sophisticated statistical models used by social scientists to inform social programs coming out of President Johnson's Great Society initiatives in the 1960s. Writes one critic sympathetic to these techniques, noted Brookings Institution economist Henry Aaron, "Social scientists, in emulation of physical scientists and mathematicians, seek simplicity and 'elegance,' though the question whether the problems of social science *can* be solved elegantly remains unanswered." He continues: "In order to [reach these goals], problems are separated into components that can be managed and understood."[9] But "such abstraction produces theory, apparently detached from reality, that often provokes the laymen's scorn" and undermines the legitimacy of the enterprise.[10]

The Argumentative Turn in Policy Studies

But the single, most profound challenge to business as usual that you need to appreciate is the aforementioned "argumentative turn" in policy science. As alluded to earlier, proponents agree that the policy process is fundamentally about evidence, argument, and persuasion. Why? Because, as Frank Fischer argues, all knowledge is "contestable."[11] Your role in the policy process as a public manager—and what you should expect from policy analysts who work with or for you—thus becomes ensuring that a range of problem definitions, alternative solutions, and values (including equity, due process, and equality) are debated and weighed. You will be more of a facilitator of democratic participation than the early Progressive Era's expert delivering correct answers or solutions to public problems.

Writes Fischer, political "arguments are only more or less convincing, more or less plausible to a particular audience. What is more, data and other evidence can be chosen in a wide variety of ways from the available information, and there are various methods of analysis and ways of ordering values" that make picking an objectively correct decision impossible.[12] Thus, objective data—for example, measurements of teen pregnancy, soil erosion, or China's military capability in ten years—are merely the fodder for battles over their implications and meanings by actors who "socially construct" reality. Put more simply, they "give meaning" to raw data and analyses, or, more negatively in today's terms, they "spin" the data to advance their interests and viewpoints. These actors in the policy debate serve as "claims makers," paying selective attention to certain aspects of the data "out there" while ignoring others and then going to battle with their adversaries.[13] <u>Lower unemployment rates</u>, for instance, can mean fewer persons looking for work rather than a growing economic recovery. Lower greenhouse gas emissions could merely reflect lower economic growth, not the success of cap-and-trade policies. Or lower numbers of illegals coming into the United States may reflect both an economic slowdown in the nation and a reduction in drug-dealer killings in Columbia.

You should anticipate that these "issue-framing" arguments will tend to fall into three "narratives" identified by Albert Hirschman: perversity, futility, and jeopardy.[14] These should become staples of *your* argumentative arsenal as well. For example, opponents of a policy will frame their arguments negatively to emphasize the perverse effects of policy (e.g., cutting welfare rolls will only hurt the innocent children of previous recipients), the futility of taking action (e.g., stemming drug traffic in one country will only shift the problem to another), and the risks of jeopardizing other values (e.g., legalizing marijuana may raise revenues and cut crime, but it will undermine the cultural fabric of America). Meanwhile, proponents of a policy will tell their own counter-narratives or "stories."

Do not interpret this as saying that policy making is only about "telling the best story." Rather, be cognizant that issue framing and contests over it are efforts to expand the strength of the coalition of forces supporting your position and to counteract that of your opponents. Sometimes this works and sometimes it does not. You should also understand that you and your opponents may engage in a series of issue-framing and reframing efforts during any single debate as you—and they—get a sense for the effectiveness of your story. Think here of George W. Bush's serial narratives justifying the invasion of Iraq and Barack Obama's series of threats and then pull-backs for sending troops to Syria.

Reconnecting with Citizens and Stakeholders

But thinking substantively, analytically, and strategically to advance policy goals in an era of argumentation is not all you will be doing. Your purpose in the policy process as a public manager can also be framed more nobly, especially if informed by a commitment to democratic administration. You will also have opportunities to foster civic deliberation and help build networks of social capital. Moreover, these are networks that could carry over into other policy debates in the future. Let us see how and why this is the case.

As you would certainly expect given the preceding discussion, your relationship as a public manager to the policy process—the steps involved in decision making on behalf of society—has evolved as well. It will continue to evolve during your career. For public managers, this goes well beyond the breakdown of the politics/policy–administration dichotomy we reviewed in chapter 5. It also means that, although civil servants are playing a less visible role in policy formulation today because of the factors we covered in chapter 5 and will add to in chapter 8, their impact can be felt throughout the policy process in today's compensatory state.

To fulfill these aspirations, however, public managers such as yourself will need to be sure that the technical analyses informing policy debates do not further marginalize citizens and that aspects of each "stage" of the policy process are informed to the greatest extent possible by the coproduction ethic we reviewed in chapter 1. You will recall that this means working with citizens to provide expertise-based solutions to mutually defined problems. Public managers must also return to "first-order" normative questions dealing with the appropriate relationship between citizens and the state, government and the private sector, and bureaucracy and democracy.[15] It requires your focus as a public manager on trust building, which, in turn, requires a focus on capacity building through administrative investments, transparency building, and cultural sensitivity at home and abroad. As such, you will have various opportunities to contribute to society's broader and longer-term capacity for problem solving while simultaneously protecting democratic constitutional values during your career as a public servant.

Doing all this effectively means that you need to avoid thinking about the policy process in traditional ways as a series of separate "stages," as depicted in Table 6.1. Formerly the dominate model of the policy process and still a useful analytical framework for you, by the 1990s, the stages model came under attack on several grounds.[16] Critics argued

Table 6.1 The Policy Process

• Agenda Setting
>   Data collection and studies identifying a possible public problem
>   Issue framing by different actors
>   Problem moves to legislative agenda for debate
>   • Identifying worthy agenda items
>   • Reality testing
>   • Highlighting "focusing events"
>   • Avoiding the negative stereotyping of target groups
• Policy Formulation
>   Specifying policy alternatives
• Policy Adoption
>   Who or what drives the statutory design and adoption of a policy
>   • Pluralist theory
>   • Power elite theory
>   • State theory
• Policy Implementation
>   Interpreting, operationalizing, and carrying out statutory goals, objectives, and design
• Policy Evaluation
>   Seeing if statutory goals and objectives were attained, why, or why not

---

that the stages are not really independent but actually overlap. And not only are they happening at the same time, they are not sequential—there is no particular order to them.

Still, the stages model affords insights about the policy process that an integrated model can mask. Of particular importance for you as a public manager is that policy making can actually begin during policy implementation—as vague, ambiguous, and contradictory statutory language is interpreted by state, local, and nonprofit agencies, or by private sector contractors. Because your role as a public manager in policy and program implementation is so profound, and because it is where your agency will have the greatest impact, we will cover it only briefly here and devote chapter 9 to a more thorough discussion of it. Also, our present focus is on policies pursued legislatively (rather than, say, executive orders or court decisions, which are important as well), because they afford the best view of the policy process as a whole, which is most beneficial to your thinking at this point.

Agenda Setting

The policy process begins with the identification of problems worthy of government to address, and public managers can play an important role in it. In particular, you and the policy analysts in your agency can improve the chances of moving an issue from what scholars call the "universal," to the "systemic," and then onto the "institutional" agenda. Respectively, these refer to all possible issues affecting a political jurisdiction, issues that are viewed as important to discuss but not currently under active consideration by elected officials, and issues that are currently being considered for adoption. In the process, you and your agency also have important roles to play in ensuring that citizens are connected and involved in that process. Four especially critical "coproduction" roles exist for you as a public manager to appreciate and use to the advantage of your agency, policy, or program. These include identifying worthy agenda items, reality testing, seizing on "focusing events" to call attention to problems, and avoiding the negative stereotyping of target groups.

Identifying Agenda Items through Analysis. As we reviewed earlier, since the early 1960s, the nation's major policy alternatives have been informed by social science research and expert opinion both within and outside public agencies. They have had notable successes and failures in getting important matters onto the institutional agenda for action. The former include helping to get HIV-AIDS, social inequality and discrimination, and national security-related privacy issues onto institutional agendas. The latter include econometric models consistently understating or overstating economic performance that raise or lower issue salience to elected officials. They also include expert opinions and social science-driven analyses failing to call legislative attention to the impending 2007–09 financial collapse; intelligence failures related to 9/11; the imminent fall of the Soviet Union in the early 1990s; and the Egyptian, Syrian, and Ukrainian crises in the twenty-first century. What seems critical in both success and failure is the ability or inability of public agencies to "connect the data dots" in compelling ways for elected officials and citizens to take seriously and want to take action.

More recently, the twenty-first century has seen the arrival of a major new tool for connecting those dots: the so-called "Big Data" analyses noted in chapter 2. These massive databases and the unparalleled analytical capabilities of supercomputers hold the potential for policy analysts within and outside agencies to identify problems, find correlations that predict issues, and develop policy alternatives that have been hidden previously from even the systemic agenda. But data mining also could reinforce and even amplify the citizen-marginalizing—and off-putting—problems that we noted earlier.

Thus, just as the "procedural republic" noted in chapter 5 produces marginalization, so, too, could the incorporation of Big Data analyses into the issue-framing process. This, as policy makers lose sight of the policy context that produced those correlations and rely more on policy making by statistical correlations rather than by citizen input. Therefore, not only will one of your major roles as a public manager be helping to develop, interpret, or be a consumer of Big Data analyses done by your agency or by others that will have the potential to put previously hidden, underappreciated, or deferred issues on the institutional agenda. Also central will be keeping the "people" behind and affected by those numbers in the foreground of policy makers and the democratic constitutional values they cherish.

Reality Testing. Another key role you and your agency can play in the agenda-setting stage of the policy process is dispelling "factoids" by claims makers that can either propel or stall movement of issues onto the institutional agenda. Factoids are incorrect statements of fact that enter into the debate but that are constantly repeated as facts and take on lives of their own. During the problem identification stage, the career bureaucracy in agencies can work with allies in the legislature and with citizens to help frame debates and inform controversies surrounding them in several ways by diminishing the power of factoids.

Consider, for example, recent debates over the adequacy of the Supplemental Nutrition Assistance Program (SNAP), the successor of the Department of Agriculture's Food Stamp program. Several dozen congressional opponents of proposed cuts to food subsidies for the poor or those temporarily unemployed due to the slow economic recovery mounted a publicity campaign that they called the "SNAP challenge." Together with public interest groups, these members of Congress demonstrated on camera what it was like to live on $4.50 per day for meals (the proposed allocation was $133.44 a month). Not to be outdone, proponents of the SNAP cuts did the same but showed how tradeoffs, smart purchasing, and focusing on nutritional products would be more than adequate under the cuts.

Each group was trying to frame the issue in such a way so as to expand the coalition of forces (i.e., interest groups and other stakeholders) supporting their side of the argument. They knew, as E. E. Schattschneider pointed out in the 1960s, that the "audience determines the outcome of the fight."[17] In the end for SNAP's fate, however, it took analysts in the federal bureaucracy to point out to broader audiences that SNAP is "supplemental" and, thus, not the only source of income that recipients have for buying food. Basically, they looked at the problem from the perspective of citizens affected by that program and stopped in its tracks what was rapidly becoming an agenda-setting factoid.

Highlighting Focusing Events. Another way for agencies to impact agenda setting is to look for what policy analysts call "focusing events" that identify new or previously marginalized items for the institutional agenda. These are events that afford opportunities to push policy solutions onto the legislative agenda for action, or to stop them. Focusing events include, but are not limited to, the tragic events of 9/11, a school bus or plane crash, a child molestation or kidnapping case, or a news story about the female sex trade. They tend to have a highly personalized quality understood and identified with by average citizens and elected officials and, thus, offer opportunities to you for building compelling "stories" about a need for policy action. Importantly, although they can catapult issues onto the institutional agenda, they may not produce ultimate results. To appreciate this point, you need only think about incidents such as the Columbine High School and Sandy Hook Elementary School tragedies, the IRS auditing of conservative political groups, and the leaking of secret documents on the National Security Agency's searching of social media for patterns of suspicious behavior.

The Social Construction of Target Groups. As we covered earlier in this chapter, part of the argumentative turn in policy science involves "giving meaning" to data, events, and other conditions. Another contribution of that perspective also involves giving meaning—formally called by policy analysts positive or negative "valencing"—to potential target groups for government redress.[18] For example, the poor are often classified into "deserving" or "undeserving" categories, with the former typically conceived as the white working poor and the latter as the nonworking and minority poor. Gender typifying is also rampant; for example, the idea that women are not as good as men in the science and technology fields.

Importantly, these categories are not objectively determined but are socially constructed, can expand for a particular group or contract, and can change over time. For instance, intravenous drug users, drug traffickers, and other felons have negative valencing. Likewise, the definition of "deserving" veterans for receiving benefits for their military service has expanded since the nation's founding. And persons of Japanese ancestry have progressed from being viewed as "problem minorities" early in the twentieth century to "model citizens" today.

What is significant for you as a public manager is that some of these categories are unfairly acquired, inadequately reflect the diversity of persons in each category, and, thus, perpetuate perceptions of differences among citizens that are nonexistent, hurtful, and deceitful. This, in turn, produces differences in the attention that the problems of negatively valenced populations get on institutional agendas. They also unfairly influence how policy benefits and burdens are ultimately allocated. Your role as a public servant should be one of eliminating unfair valencing for the constituents of your agency, strategizing for the most positively valenced image you can create for them when it is deserved, and, thus, ensuring a fair chance for their problems to move from the systemic to the institutional agenda.

Policy Formulation

Where career civil servants carry significant clout is in what John Kingdon calls the "alternative specification" aspect of policy formulation.[19] As you know, elected officials and their legislative staffs cannot be experts on every policy issue, and some issues are so complex (e.g., scientifically or financially) that only policy specialists can master them. Into this void step civil servants, and their views can be especially powerful as they specify alternative ways to approach a problem. Moreover, public managers do best at this when they include the perspectives of agency clients, constituencies, and citizens at large. In doing so, you will want to know the information upon which they are based, whether or not there are other ways to define a problem or disaggregate it to make it more "solvable" or politically palatable, and how citizens will react to various policies.[20]

Moreover, you should always be asking yourself or the policy analysts in your agency what the causal and technical theories are underlying policy proposals. Causal theories treat policies as hypotheses, much like those you will be testing statistically in your methodology courses. These are "if-then" statements regarding cause-and-effect expectations. Stated as a causal theory, for example, welfare reform in the 1990s might be understood by proponents as follows: "If we make welfare harder to obtain, then the culture of dependency that welfare has created among recipients will decline and welfare recipients will seek employment more aggressively." Alternatively, an underlying hypothesis of supporters of the Affordable Care Act (ACA) was that if we afford health insurance to the uninsured, they will make less use of emergency rooms for nonemergency maladies, and, thus, health care costs will be cut.

In turn, the technical theory underlying a policy addresses the validity—that is, the actual ability—of the tools used to affect the behavior that has to be either encouraged or discouraged to have policy success. For example, one tool of welfare reform was placing a lifetime limit on the number of years a person can receive welfare benefits: if we limit the lifetime benefit for receiving welfare benefits, current welfare recipients will look harder for work and the culture of dependency will decline appreciably. Or, returning to the ACA, if we allow more persons to join Medicaid, emergency room visits will decrease. As with causal theories, if "hypotheses" such as these are or appear invalid or incomplete, then the policy solutions offered are not feasible and should be rethought or abandoned altogether in favor of others. For example, early evidence from Oregon questioned the validity of the technical theory underlying parts of the ACA we just reviewed: *increased* use of emergency rooms actually occurred after insurance coverage and Medicaid expansion. But evidence can change over time as implementation adjustments occur; emergency room and hospital use eventually dropped while expanding coverage in the state after strict accountability measures kicked in.[21]

You should also be realistic, of course. Sometimes proposed policies are identified as worthy of attention because of their "symbolic" value, regardless of the validity of their assumptions. These types of policies are occasionally pursued for good reasons, such as for sending societal messages about behaviors it approves and those it does not (e.g., the drug interdiction war or marijuana laws). Similarly, in the aftermath of a crisis or shocking news story, governments have to calm their citizens and satisfy their demands for action, even if the causal and technical theories are unknown or invalid. Less positively, symbolic policies can merely be the result of elected officials pandering to their constituents for votes.

That said, getting the perceptions of affected citizens can lead to more realistic causal and technical theories. For example, surveys might be used to assess the impact at different levels of a tax on diabetes-related foods. The presumption of advocates is that such a tax would reduce consumption, but it may not be true and might shift consumption to other "bad" foods that are substitutable. Thus, it will be up to you as a public manager to put citizens front and center as much as you can during the alternative specification process. In a social media era, you may not have any choice but to do so. Even if not, however, remember this: you can meet citizens either up front in this stage of the policy process or in front of a judge later after policies are adopted.

Policy Adoption

Commenting on the state of civic deliberation in the United States in 1956, C. Wright Mills wrote that Americans know they are "liv[ing] in a time of big decisions; they [also] know that they are not making any."[22] The perdurability of this situation in the United States has more recently led some to conclude that we are in a "post-democracy" era.[23] Whether overstated or not, your studies will expose you to a variety of theories of policy adoption that offer reasons for optimism but also cynicism and a declining sense of political efficacy by citizens in today's compensatory state. All have implications for your role as a public manager. For now, we will just consider three theories that are directly applicable to help you in diagnosing, strategizing, and, hopefully, ameliorating citizen discontent: the pluralist, power elite, and state theories.

Pluralist Theory. The most benign of these theories for citizen participation is that held by proponents of pluralist theory. Early on, they saw government as having no independent role in the policy process except to serve as a referee responding to interest group pressure. Later, pluralists conceded the naiveté of a struggle among interests where each has a reasonable chance of winning the game. In compensating for this flaw, they offered what is called "polyarchy." This perspective saw the single most powerful force in policy making as clusters of various interests in a policy domain (e.g., in the economic development domain) but with dominant elites within each cluster (e.g., bankers, real estate developers, and construction firms).[24] This theory should give you pause for thought as a public manager. For example, do you or your agency merely respond to the most powerful, persistent, and politically potent pressure group(s), or do you speak for voices and values not represented in the interest group struggle surrounding your agency and its programs? Regardless, pluralist theory again suggests the need to use issue framing to expand or contract the audience of interests paying attention to the fight over policy to advance your cause or stop other things from happening that agency leaders do not think are wise.

Power Elite Theory. A more troubling theory of the policy process may also be useful to you in your diagnostic function and strategic thinking as a public manager. Rather than only focusing on the surface "noise" of interest group struggles, power elite theory calls your attention to identifying dominant social and economic *classes* as the most powerful factors affecting policy agendas and adoption. Power elite theory urges you to pay attention to how the elite controls the entry of policy items onto the institutional agenda, permitting only those policies that advantage them or do not undermine their privileges. Referred to as "nondecisions," those issues with no agenda access or adoption possibilities include such things as land redistribution from the rich to the poor in America. It also means that only certain types of citizens gain a hearing from policy makers and implementers such as yourself: the financially and socially well off.

But you might ask, "What about people who come from lower-class or more modest social or economic means who go on to hold political office, rise to the top of Fortune 500 corporations, or become public intellectuals who have an impact on public policy?" Conceding that this occurs, proponents of this theory claim that "elite circulation" is at work; in order to give the impression of social mobility open to all, elites identify persons who buy into the dominant values of the elite class and, thus, pose no threat to their interests. Relatedly, when critics of power elite theory point out the size of social programs geared toward the socioeconomically disadvantaged, proponents of this perspective argue that elites allow enough downward redistribution of wealth to prevent revolts. Others in this school say that elites give out these benefits to keep the lower classes dependent on those services and, thus, on a tight leash.

If you are interested in a career in state or local government, you should know that the idea of power elites has long dominated theories of politics, especially at the urban politics level.[25] Economic elites are said to be at the center of what scholars call urban policy "regimes": groups in a policy area that coordinate their actions through norms, rules, and other understandings. This perspective began with a pure theory incorporating networks of business, banking, and real estate elites controlling policy adoption. From there, a "growth machine thesis" evolved, with economic development actors driving the policy process as "boosters" in cities. However, regime theorists later took these claims—and prior elite theories—to task for focusing exclusively on localities and ignoring the impact of other levels of government on local politics.

In any event, elite theories of whatever kind afford yet another lens for you to use in diagnosing existing or potential pressures affecting your agency's policy or program adoption plans and as you think strategically about whether and how to advance their aims. You always want to know who might be offended or might be of use in pursuing your agenda, as well as how much interest they have in your proposal, how strong or influential they are, what their position on the issue might be, and how likely they are to work actively for or against it. You might also use issue framing to alter their original perception of your proposal and to make it more palatable to them. Regardless, power elite theory illustrates how your role in ensuring citizen voice in policy decisions—especially in the means for carrying out elite-driven policies—will be critical.

State Theory. In contrast to the power elite and pluralist theories, state theory offers a decidedly more positive and public service-oriented role for you as a public manager. The state—including public agencies at every level of government as key components of it—is said to have interests of its own that differ from elites and interest groups. What is more, it has the resources and power to pursue those goals on its own as a "semi-autonomous" entity because of two factors. The first is that conflicts exist among the owners of capital (primarily corporate enterprise) and interest groups, so there is no "unified" corporate or interest group sector to "capture" the government. Second, proponents argue that the bureaucracy is staffed by individuals who are not members of the dominant class and who engage in what we referred to in chapter 1 as "active representation" of the socio-economic and demographic interests from which they come. All this leaves the state—including agency personnel such as yourself—some freedom to pursue policies that favor the interests of subordinate classes, as well as its own conception of the public interest. Thus, state theory adds value to your diagnostic repertoire not offered by a focus solely on power elite or pluralist theories. It offers you more room for maneuver, more proactive and public interest-oriented strategic and tactical thinking, and more hope that involving citizens in agency deliberations will make a difference.

In sum, and as Claudia Scott and Karen Baehler argue, "No linear or cyclical model will capture the complex and volatile realities of the policy world, or their implications for [the policy process]. In practice, policy tasks are encountered as collections of imperatives, some deriving from the outside, some from the inside game [of politics], in various combinations and proportions, with varying degrees of urgency."[26] So you should both understand the dynamism of the various theories of the policy adoption and apply them as alternative frameworks as you diagnose the political realities of adoption of your agency's proposals. This activity is frequently referred to as doing a "stakeholder analysis."[27] In applying it, you identify the key actors who may have an interest in your policy proposal, what their interests are in it, their likely positions regarding it, the power each holds to affect it, any potential alliances they can marshal to either support or oppose it, and how important it is to get their buy-in. In the process of conducting a stakeholder analysis—which often involves interviews and surveys of stakeholders, if time allows—you can interact more effectively with key actors to help you modify (or even totally rethink) your policy or program proposal and enhance its chances of adoption.

Policy Implementation

Regardless of the political forces dominant or interacting in the policy adoption process, their participation and relative weighting will affect the statutory language that will determine by whom, how, with what resources, and when it will be carried out. This stage of the policy process—the one you will hear so much about in chapter 9 of this book—is known as policy implementation. Moreover, it is the stage of the process where you as a public manager will have the most influence.

Two elements of implementation—when a law gives discretion to implementers and the types of discretion given—bear noting at this point for their effects on reconnecting with citizens. Discretion, as we noted in earlier chapters, is a product of the legislative bargaining process when cobbling together majorities is imperative and elected officials often shift tough political choices to implementers. But when are legislators more or less likely to give discretion to implementers?

Prior research suggests that legislatures desire policy control, but they must and do temper this desire with the need for greater policy expertise and the institutional capacity of executive branch agencies.[28] Among other things, trying to lessen the risk of the bureaucratic and coalitional drift that we covered in chapter 5, they are likely to grant more discretion to executive branch implementers whenever (1) the same political party holds majorities in both the legislative and executive branches and their policy preferences are the same; (2) they are confident that supportive interest groups in policy subsystems are available to monitor the agency; (3) they need the expertise of career civil servants because the issue is too complex or to avoid blame, and they are sure that expertise can handle the issue effectively; and (4) agencies do not press legislators to give them discretion—for example, if they must invest in new types of expertise and, thus, strain existing resources. We also have some evidence that agencies choose policies closer to legislative preferences when they fear the legislature will sanction them with the tools we discussed in chapter 5.

This said, research by Helen Ingram and Anne Schneider advises you to think more about discretion varying across different components of the same statute.[29] Additionally, in each of these components, opportunities for reconnecting with citizens may be either required or something you may be free to pursue because of the discretion you are given in their implementation. More precisely, what your coursework will call the "policy design" incorporated in statutes may give you more or less discretion to set policy goals, policy objectives, who the targets of the policy might be, the tools you can use during implementation, and the applicable decision rules (i.e., the criteria for making decisions).

Thus, you might have more discretion to change decision rules than to alter the objectives of the policy you are implementing, or a statute might require you to hold public hearings to determine policy goals and decision rules. Ingram and Schneider also argue that you should expect the social, political, and economic pressures on an agency to affect policy whenever greater amounts of discretion are given to implementers. Consequently, greater discretion might enhance your abilities to "reconnect" with citizens directly through your conscious efforts at issue framing and the like to bring new audiences into the fight. Thus, and as we will review in chapter 9, as a public manager, you will be making policy as you implement it, placing a great deal of responsibility on you and your agency to do so in ways that advance rather than diminish the realization of democratic constitutional values in America.

Policy Evaluation

When most of us think about policy analysis, we often think first of policy and program evaluation. As noted, figuring out the impact of policy on desired outcomes is a major focus of policy analysis. Thus, part of your coursework will incorporate courses on statistics and research designs for evaluating programs. Before you graduate, for example, you will become familiar with the logic of experimental and quasi-experimental designs (and a variety of research designs within each), as well as some of the latest statistical techniques—for example, least squares regression, probit and tobit regression models, and interrupted time-series analyses.

At the same time, your coursework in policy implementation will alert you to how easy it is to misinterpret what look like statistically significant results as signs of either policy success or failure. As we will see in chapter 9, for example, successful policy implementation can be perceived as "learning," "evolution," and "mutual adaptation" over time. Thus, you should be wary about evaluating programs or policies only on the basis of prescribed or expected policy results, of thinking that non-implementation is necessarily bad, or of thinking that a result of either "no impact" or a "major impact" stems from the policy or program alone.

For example, policies that change over time may be the result of learning what really works, and, thus, the true impact of the policy will be delayed. Likewise, an evaluation that shows no impact can merely mean that the policy itself was never even tried or was traded off against higher values or policies. Conversely, positive results may not be the result of the policy or program itself. As such, it was not the policy itself that failed or succeeded. And although the prescribed goals of a policy may not be met, other benefits that stem from the program may be just as valuable to society. For example, aspects of individual Great Society programs that might appear to have failed instrumentally may mask their impact on other values. In this case, many previously disenfranchised and disadvantaged African Americans went on from these programs to hold elected and administrative positions at all levels of government.

This does *not* mean that you should not evaluate policies or programs, but only that you should be cautious in interpreting what their evaluations mean and be sure to incorporate process evaluations to get a complete picture of what happened. Moreover, you need to evaluate programs or policies on various dimensions and from a variety of perspectives before declaring them a failure or a success. But the single, most important lesson from prior evaluation research is that one of the audiences that matters most in evaluation are the citizens affected by policy. Avoid the tendency to focus solely on your own or your agency's definition of policy success; citizen perceptions are what matter most for government legitimacy. Thus, again, your role as a public manager should be one of not letting sophisticated output or outcome evaluations drive out efforts to assess citizen perceptions of program, policy, and agency performance.

Redefining Administrative Rationality

Another implication of the argumentative turn in the policy sciences that you need to appreciate is that the internal and external organization of the deliberative processes in public agencies has changed significantly over the past five decades. Policy analysis has evolved from a focus on formalization and hierarchy to one of adhocracy and competition among networks of actors. In the process, the field, the role of policy analysts in your agency, and your role as a public manager have been turned on their heads in the twenty-first century.

As Beryl Radin writes, were you involved in the policy process in the 1960s, what would have been striking to you was the near monopoly on the enterprise by government.[30] Government analysts in the 1960s typically saw their role as one of writing reports for an immediate supervisor who was, in essence, their only "client" and a primary decision maker. As Radin cleverly defines it, their role was primarily one of advising the "prince" and "speaking truth to power."[31] What is more, they were largely the sole advisors to the prince. Today, however, the policy world looks much different, both outside public agencies and within them.

Externally, one of the biggest changes you will face has come in the fracturing of the policy analysis world more generally. For starters, analysts now work directly for legislative bodies, for nonprofit organizations across policy areas, for various interest groups, and for think tanks focused on particular policy areas. Examples include state and local legislative budget offices, the Center on Budget and Policy Priorities, the American Association of Retired Persons, the Brookings Institution, the Heritage Foundation, the Century Foundation, the Congressional Budget Office, and the Government Accountability Office. As a consequence, and part and parcel of today's compensatory state, the "most visible analysts" participating in policy debates may not be working in your agency, thus reducing the monopoly that your agency's analysts once held over "advising" elected officials.

However, for you as a public manager, this need not be a bad thing; you will have alternative sources of information for making decisions. Still, you need to be very careful in sorting out this information. Some of these policy shops are inherently nonpartisan or nonideological and offer objective analyses, while others are not. For the latter, you do not have to read the research reports they produce to predict their "findings." Nor are the reports of these advocacy shops ever submitted for traditional blind peer review, the standard that upholds the integrity of any research process—and one you should demand. The last thing you want to do as a manager is quote statistics and findings produced by sources that are partisan or lack credibility—unless you can find other, more credible sources that support the findings or interpretations offered.

Internally, the most significant impact for you as a public manager comes from change in the organization of policy analysis shops within government agencies. As noted, the primary model of the 1960s involved policy analysts crafting reports for and serving in direct advisory capacities to those who had the authority to make policy decisions. This arrangement resulted in program offices getting quite jealous about the monopoly access that policy shops had with key decision makers who could affect their programs. Nor were program offices happy with the top-down nature of policy agenda-setting and funding that existed under this organizational arrangement. Centralization of policy shops created a situation where top agency executives and their senior staff were the only clients that mattered to analysts, and, thus, those clients "would define the perspective, values, and agenda for the analytic activity" produced.[32]

Bent on reducing their organizational disadvantage, individual units within agencies started their own policy analysis shops. By the 1980s, "any respectable program unit had its own policy staff—individuals who were not overwhelmed by the techniques and language of the staff of the original policy units and who could engage in debate with them or even convince them of other ways of approaching issues. Both budget and legislative development processes were the locations of competing policy advice, often packaged in the language and form of policy analysis."[33]

Not surprisingly, a free-for-all among these units was—and remains today—common. Analysts in centralized policy shops found themselves jousting with analysts in programs, to the point where the roles of analysts and program managers were hard to distinguish from each other. The former, in effect, became program advocates! As Carol Weiss puts it, congressional staff saw analysts "less as bearers of truth and clarity than as just another interest group beating on the door."[34] Much the same organizational points of contention also occurred in state and local governments that had any level of professionalism in this regard.

Thus, the argumentative turn was both a consequence and cause of the decentralized and duplicative structures established within departments and agencies. The role of the analyst became—and continues today to be—one of interacting with peers in a variety of offices rather than giving advice solely to managers, senior staff, and executives. Relatedly, rather than provide very technical analyses to hierarchical superiors, a range of types of analysts engage with a variety of "clients," including, but not limited to, decision makers. These are comprised of analysts who focus on issues relevant to institutional processes and organizational maintenance, as well as the conventional microeconomic and welfare economics analyses that have monopolized the field.

Reengaging Financial Resources

As noted, a key component in policy analysis is figuring out how best to raise new revenue or reengage existing resources to new or higher-priority purposes in public agencies. We will cover specific policy analytic tools for reengaging resources later in this chapter when we review the need to recapitalize personnel assets in public agencies, as well as in subsequent chapters addressing issues in public personnel management (chapter 7) and public budgeting and finance (chapter 8). Prior to that discussion, however, you need an overview of what the policy literature tells us about decision making in general in public agencies, with some attention to its implications for reengaging existing resources. Again, rather than select one model as best characterizing decision making, you should see them as diverse "lenses" for analyzing prior decisions or for creating strategies to reengage resources as agency or program purposes are reconceptualized in the twenty-first century.

The Rational–Comprehensive Model of Decision Making

As its name implies, and as alluded to in chapter 4, the rational–comprehensive decision-making model is most consonant with the rationality project of objective, evidence-based, instrumental (i.e., means–ends) decision making. Referred to metaphorically by Charles Lindblom as the "root" model of decision making, decision makers start with clear goals and objectives, identify alternative ways to reach these goals, weigh the costs and benefits, select the "one best way" to proceed, and then formally evaluate what happened to see if their goals were reached.[35] Proponents believe that organizations make better decisions about resource allocation using this model, because it affords the most thorough consideration of information possible.

The Incremental Model of Decision Making

But do people, let alone public agencies, really make decisions—including decisions to move resources from one project to another—in ways that proponents of the rational–comprehensive model purport? Lindblom, leading a legion of others over the years, said "no" and offered in its place the "branch" or "incremental" model of decision making alluded to in chapter 4. He called it the "branch method," because it took fundamental decisions made in the past as "givens" from which new decisions branch off. Moreover, he argued that the incrementalism model is more accurate, useful, and normatively preferable than the root or rational–comprehensive model.

Incrementalists offer evidence that organizations typically do not start with clear-cut goals and objectives and then select the most cost-effective ways to reallocate resources— or to make any other policy decision. Not only are their goals and objectives uncertain and a point of contention within organizations, but they are also often imposed after the fact as a dominant narrative becomes socially constructed by agency actors so that it looks as if rationality prevailed. Incrementalists also show that goals and objectives cannot be determined until decision makers know how they are to be obtained. For instance, national security might entail indiscriminate monitoring of all communications sent by citizens, but at what cost to personal privacy? Or efficiency in health care might partially involve the sharing of electronic medical records, but security issues must be considered first.

Nor would Lindblom want you to buy into the idea that policy and program decisions are the result of a widespread search for all the possible ways to accomplish whatever goals or objectives prevailed. In the case of reengaging resources for higher purposes, no comprehensive assessment of all programs takes place. Limits on the cognitive abilities of decision makers and the time parameters normally facing them preclude a "comprehensive" search for all the possibilities that exist. Rather, decision makers take an existing policy—or, in this case, existing budgets or personnel allocations—and make limited changes to it. As the jargon goes, they take "limited successive approximations" toward reaching their goals. And the goals themselves are discerned by a process Lindblom characterizes as "partisan mutual adjustment":[36] actors "mutually adjust" to each other's perspectives and strategize how best to pursue their interests in light of what other agency actors are likely to do in terms of position-taking and tactics. Put simply, they bargain over goals, objectives, and ways to pursue them, then "satisfice" rather than choose the one best way. Satisficing means that decision makers select the first option on which all or most can agree, or to which no one strenuously objects. Thus, actors from different offices and programs seek to protect what they have and get more for themselves.

Although you may be distressed by this approach to agency decision making, Lindblom counters that partisan mutual adjustment is actually the most comprehensive and efficient way for agencies to make decisions. Information is surfaced, he argues, that would otherwise not be known without the contest among actors. So, if you do not advocate for your unit's interests, you are actually curbing information flow that could provide important perspectives on the implications of policies that only your unit could know and understand. Thus, Lindblom argues that being an advocate for your program redounds to the benefit of your agency as a whole.

You may also wonder how evaluations of resource reengagement—as well as other policies—take place in the incremental model. For Lindblom, formal evaluations of policies or programs are themselves "bargained" among different evaluation units, typically sit on the shelf, or are not done in time to make a difference. Instead, incrementalists argue that the way agencies most efficiently "learn" about policy successes or problems is to wait for "noise in the system." That is, if you hear few complaints, assume everything is fine or, at least, good enough to not need reform. They then take any complaints that do arise and, if possible, do quick fixes or make policy adjustments in the next cycle of decision making in the agency—in this case, the budget cycle. However, they do not go back and revisit the assumptions of the policy itself.

As your coursework in public budgeting will no doubt review, this incremental model of decision making was the dominant theory of budgeting in the United States until the mid-1980s. Developed initially by Aaron Wildavsky, this model saw agencies, as well as programs within them, as developing their budget submissions in the following, almost unreflective, and economically irrational way. They started with the budget received last year, built in a factor for inflation, asked for a small increase above that level for new initiatives, and then added a small amount that those above (the central budget office or legislative committees) might cut to look as if they were doing their job.

As you will also learn, however, critics of the incremental model of decision making abound and may reflect some of your concerns after hearing Lindblom's arguments. For starters, they argue that slow, marginal changes to the status quo are often insufficient to resolve problems that require an integrated, coherent, and immediate approach (e.g., a national energy policy adduced in a rational–comprehensive analysis). To which proponents of incrementalism respond that small marginal changes to the status quo—in this case, existing budgets—are best for you to pursue as a public manager, because your organization avoids making "the big mistake."

Relatedly, incrementalists argue that a rational–comprehensive approach fails to take into account that the current organizational structure, task assignments, and goals of any agency reflect political "treaties" among actors that have been negotiated over time. Thus, they risk reopening many of those settled conflicts. But critics warn that not all the actors involved in this partisan process over the years are equal in power, so the "haves" repeatedly have won over those with less power. As they do so, they amass even more power that they then use to win future battles, and thus avoid needed policy change and resource reengagement.

However, prior research also suggests that all is not lost in terms of your efforts as a public manager to reengage financial and personnel resources to higher priority levels. Here, what your methodology professors may call the "unit of analysis" makes a difference. Budgeting scholars have found that focusing on the agency level masks significant resource reengagement over time *within* agencies and programs, and across them. Indeed, when total agency budgets are examined, only small changes are seen from year to year. Yet, if looking within and across budget accounts for agency activities and programs, you will often see fluctuations in resourcing, with programs gaining in some years and declining in others.[37] And sometimes these shifts are substantial. This occurs, as you would expect, given shifts of emphases over time stimulated by elections, political appointees, and objective need. Moreover, as we noted earlier, small marginal changes over time can result in qualitatively different programs and policies.

Related to unit of analysis arguments, proponents of rational–comprehensive decision making also point to today's information technology revolution as potentially rendering incrementalists' perception of cognitive limitations on policy makers anachronistic for budgeting and other administrative planning functions in public agencies. As a former chief financial officer and assistant secretary for administration at the US Treasury Department writes:

> With investments in new technology over the past decade such as Enterprise Resource Planning (ERP) solutions, agencies are now capturing the necessary data to understand agency performance. This data, combined with the emergence of advanced, predictive analytic technology and a focus on change management and execution, is enabling agencies to meet these efficiency challenges head on. They are starting to recognize how data-driven efficiencies can achieve targeted savings and better service delivery at a scale large enough to absorb cuts and sustain mission capabilities. While the data may at times point to tough choices, this analytically-supported, fact-based approach is superior to furloughs and other reactive measures to across-the-board spending cuts... By focusing efforts on creating value from existing data and the expertise of their employees, these agencies – and others like them – are charting a path to sustainable operational performance, savings and productivity improvements in a tough budget climate.[38]

The Mixed Scanning Model

At the same time, perhaps all this has left you wondering if both incremental and rational–comprehensive decision making might not actually coexist within public agencies.

If so, your instincts are correct. The analytical component of rational–comprehensive models performed in policy analysis shops has been—and will continue to be—thought of as an input into the larger political process within and across agencies, programs, and policy domains.

This might not produce the purely knowledge-based, analytically driven decision making that early policy analysts embraced in the rationality project and that would produce immediate results. But it certainly can have impacts in the longer run. One thinks of how rational analysis by economists was an input into the decision-making processes that produced airline and trucking deregulation in the 1970s or, more recently, how the analytical work of the Intergovernmental Panel on Climate Change has been an input into the debate over global warming and what to do about it.

Taking another angle on this, you are likely to read in your coursework about Amitai Etzioni's "mixed scanning" model.[39] He argues that both rational–comprehensive and incremental decision making occur whenever policy is being considered. He divides the process into two components. The first he calls the "pre-decisional" or "representative" stage of framing the problem. Here, incrementalism prevails—a limited search of alternatives occurs that looks to see if the problem fits into existing categories for action. Where rational–comprehensive thinking occurs for him, however, is in a second—or "analytical"—stage wherein the options generated in the first stage are dissected in-depth. The operational analytics discussed in the previous section are an apt illustration of this dynamic.

The Streams Model

Yet another model of decision making is designed to address a reality that you most assuredly have noticed: we see both incremental and non-incremental changes in policy decisions.[40] Developed by John Kingdon, the "streams" model alerts you to the importance of policy softening, policy entrepreneurs, windows of opportunity, independent policy streams, and the linking of these streams.[41] Policy softening is critical to change—including reengaging resources—because ideas need to be talked about and refined for long periods of time before they gain legitimacy as realistic options.

Therefore, even when there is little likelihood that a policy change can be enacted, it is important for you to have it discussed in various forums in policy circles, in agencies, and in legislatures. In that event, when "windows of opportunity" occur to adopt a policy—either because of a focusing event (such as 9/11), a change in political actors or political climate, or periodic events (such as budget decisions)—your proposal for reengaging financial and personnel resources is more likely to be viewed as legitimate rather than coming out of nowhere.

Policy entrepreneurs—and you might yourself be one at various times in your career given the argumentative turn in public policy—are also critical in the streams model. They either link—or fail to link—three independent "streams": the problem, policy, and political streams. So, first, you must understand what these streams are and how they operate. The first, or problem stream, requires you to picture a variety of problem definitions competing for attention by policy makers at any point in time. Concurrently, a second independent "solution" or policy stream also exists, with multiple solutions to policy problems. What is most critical for you to understand about these two streams is that a variety of problem definitions and solutions float around in each, advocated by various actors within the organization. For example, regardless of the policy problem to be addressed, advocates of vouchers will offer them as solutions. Have a housing problem? Vouchers are the solution. Have an education problem? Vouchers are the solution. Have a health problem? Vouchers are the solution.

Policy entrepreneurs such as yourself must then understand that a third stream—the political stream—exists where actors come and go. This turnover happens because of, among other things, elections, retirements, promotions, and scheduling difficulties in attending key meetings. Thus, as a policy entrepreneur, you must link all three streams together for a non-incremental change to occur. If the problem and solution streams are linked together, for example, the only possible outcome is either no change or incremental change. If the three streams are linked, however, major non-incremental change can happen.

Building on these insights in a series of sophisticated statistical analyses of various policy areas since the early 1900s, Frank Baumgartner and Bryan Jones consistently find that long periods of stasis—of relatively incremental changes to existing policies—are interrupted by periods of significant policy change. They call this phenomenon a "punctuated equilibrium" model of policy making.[42] What is critical here in terms of resource (re)allocation, however, is that this model has also been proven accurate by researchers studying the budgeting process. James True, Jones, and Baumgartner, for example, argue that when change proposals attract the attention of Congress, the presidency, and the courts, "policies and programs can make radical departures from the past, and budgets can lurch into large changes."[43]

They attribute these major shifts in budget and personnel staffing fortunes—what they call "earthquake budgets"—to such things as shifts in the image of a policy, its salience, and perceptions of its proximity to citizens. Illustratively, these refer, respectively, to nuclear power shifting from a positive to a negative image as an energy source after the Chernobyl accident, perceptions that anyone could lose their health care coverage, and perceptions of AIDS shifting from a disease of drug dealers and homosexuals to one affecting the heterosexual population. Thus, again, you can see that resource reengagement does happen, but it also requires you to be alert for—or to help bring about—changes in perceptions of problems by helping to link the three streams.

Recapitalizing Personnel Assets

Not unlike every other aspect of the policy field we have covered to this point, the kinds of skills necessary for policy analysts in your agency to thrive in an argumentative era—and for you as a public manager to seek in them—are quite different from those expected at the birth of policy science in the 1960s. At the beginning, "capitalizing" the field meant hiring persons for policy shops in government agencies with technical skills in areas such as cost-benefit analyses, systems analyses, and research methods rather than substantive expertise in a given policy area. You should know that these kinds of skills are just as relevant today, meaning that recapitalizing your agency with persons holding these skills will remain critical. Indeed, with so many claims makers wielding quantitative tools in an argumentative era, this grows more important daily.

By the end of the twentieth century, however, well-trained and successful analysts also had to possess organizational, evaluation, and specialized knowledge of a policy sector. Certainly, the multiplication of policy shops within organizations is one reason that agencies today need analysts who understand the bureaucratic and political dynamics covered in chapters 4 and 5, and who have an in-depth understanding of policy domains and the evaluative state of art within them. This situation also requires analysts who have the interpersonal and group decision-making skills central to the policy-making process today.

However, analysts in your agency also need to understand *interorganizational* dynamics because of what Carol Weiss terms a "decision accretion" model of decision making.[44] She writes: "Decisions on complex issues are almost never the province of one individual or one office. Many people in many offices have a say, and when the outcomes of a course of action are uncertain, many participants have opportunities to propose, plan, confer, deliberate, advise, argue, forward policy statements, reject, revise, veto, and re-write."[45] In the process, decisions can emerge in a piecemeal fashion, without conscious deliberation, and as the accreted total of a variety of discrete, uncoordinated actions taken in various levels or layers of an agency or across agencies. What is more, as our discussion in chapter 9 will make clear, the policy implementation process is rife with interorganizational dynamics that policy analysts and public managers must understand to work in and make informed policy recommendations.

As we have alluded to in this and earlier chapters, the argumentative turn also raises the importance of agency personnel with skills in fostering civic deliberation on an unprecedented scale. Again as we have reviewed in this and earlier chapters, public problems are normally multiattribute in nature (i.e., they have many dimensions and values)[46] and are embedded in *social contexts*. They are also highly "unstructured" in terms of problem definition—meaning that interlocking issues and constraints must somehow be reconciled. Consequently, problem definitions are less "objective truths" and more a reflection of bargaining among the diversity of active stakeholders involved. Analysis under these circumstances can only produce solutions that are "better," "worse," or "not good enough."[47]

Conceptualizing policy making and implementation as we have as "collective puzzlement on behalf of society"[48] or "communicative governance,"[49] recall how proponents of deliberative models argue that the only way to address multiattribute problems successfully is through building a sense among all stakeholders that the decisions made are legitimate. Legitimacy, in turn, is conferred not only when policy recommendations are steeped in quality data-based analyses, but also when those affected by the policies develop trust in the capacity and public interest-oriented predisposition of the public agencies, managers, and decision processes involved. This trust-building role, in turn, means your agency must have personnel with skills in identifying collective—that is, common—definitions of problems, building common identities as problem solvers through deliberative processes involving the public, and improving your agency's capacity to gain legitimacy with the public and key stakeholders. These will be predicates for acceptance of your program's or agency's most sophisticated analytical models and recommendations.

James Meadowcroft offers a useful summary of some of the major forms taken in deliberative models of governance around the world and, thus, the kinds of skills needed by policy analysts and others in public agencies in building trust.[50] He evaluates various participatory modes according to four criteria that you and policy analysts hired in your agency need skills in advancing. These include *modes of representation, scope of participants involved in deliberation, the character of outputs*, and *roles in policy execution*. Each dimension emerges with core elements of the deliberative democratic ideal that we have been reviewing.

The first criterion—representation of affected interests—should prompt you and policy analysts in your agency to ask the following questions: Have we ensured that all interests have an opportunity to express their views and influence proceedings? Who actually participates in the deliberative interaction? Is the process open to scrutiny by affected interests who cannot directly take part? The second criterion relates to the quality of deliberation and compels you to ask the following: Is the encounter structured to facilitate reasoned analysis, to give careful attention to expert opinions and those of citizens, and to encourage the emergence of shared understandings and new solutions? The third criterion refers to the decisional character of the exercise and begs the following questions: What is the character of the collective output? How is it linked to any broader decisional process? How significant are the substantive issues on which decisions are made? The fourth criterion deals with collective implementation, monitoring, and review. Questions you should ask include the following: To what extent are participants—experts and citizens—involved in implementing any decision? Are there opportunities to monitor progress or to revisit issues at a later point? Is the deliberative exercise a one-shot affair or an ongoing process?

Conclusion

Armed with the information in this chapter, you can now better appreciate how the role, responsibilities, skills required, and challenges of policy analysts have evolved over the past 40 years. Indeed, they mimic efforts to reconcile bureaucratic and democratic administration in public administration amid the evolving context of the compensatory state. From the rationality project, to the argumentative turn, and on to the potential of a "deliberative" turn for dealing with today's and tomorrow's complex and wicked problems, policy science has come a long way since its founding in the 1960s. So, also, have two components of management directly related to policy development and implementation—human resources and public budgeting and finance—that you must understand to flourish as a public manager. And given the critical role that people and resources play in policy implementation, we will turn to them first, respectively, in the next two chapters. As you will read, their evolution affords the same kinds of challenges, choices, and opportunities for you that are afforded by the argumentative turn in policy science and that make a career in the public service so exciting and important to America's future.

CHAPTER 7

Linking People to Public Purposes

On July 20, 2013, a *Washington Post* investigative team reported that Medicare reimbursement requests from doctors were being significantly overstated.[1] In addition to the possibility of fraud, two things were striking about this story. First, the government was not setting reimbursement rates. Instead, a committee of the American Medical Association was setting them. As Tom Scully, Medicare chief during the George W. Bush administration, said, the "idea that $100 billion in federal spending is based on fixed prices that go through an industry trade association in a process that is not open to the public is pretty wild."[2]

Wild, indeed, but it is just the tip of the iceberg in today's compensatory state. Although the Centers for Medicare and Medicaid Services technically oversees 20 percent of the US gross domestic product, it retains only .02 percent of all federal employees (4,400) who review programs that comprise 45 percent of the federal budget each year.[3] Nor is this case an outlier. As we reviewed in chapter 2, America's penchant for hiding the visible size of government pushes billions of dollars out the US Treasury door each year to third parties without adequate agency capacity to oversee expenditures.

During your professional career as a public manager striving to link people to agency and program purposes, you will have to deal with issues such as this one. Indeed, you will face a full panoply of challenges, choices, and opportunities regarding personnel management—or, as it is frequently referred to today, human resource management (HRM). As we covered in chapters 4 and 5, *reconceptualizing purpose* involves a continuing effort by elected officials to narrow your discretion by favoring "responsive competence" over "neutral competence." What you need now as we consider reconceptualizing purpose is an understanding of the debates over the wisdom of "outer checks" versus "inner checks" and the conditions under which elected officials are more or less likely to favor one set of these accountability mechanisms over the other. You will also be involved in or experience the *redefining of administrative rationality* from an emphasis on government-wide, centralized personnel offices to a more decentralized structure that delegates greater personnel authority to departments and agencies. Accompanying this shift are expectations that these decentralized offices will become full-fledged participants in agencies' strategic planning and facilitators of program operations, rather than purely "police officers" of agency personnel practices. Likewise, from a democratic administration perspective, you will encounter a variety of needs or pressures to *reconnect with citizens* by fostering what your professors will call a "representative" workforce. This is a workforce that reflects the increasing racial, ethnic, gender, and sexual preference diversity of the American workforce. And were these not challenging enough, you will have to *reengage resources* and *recapitalize personnel assets* amid the aforementioned coarsening of anti-public service rhetoric, the outsourcing of public sector jobs, and a diminution of job security.

Your coursework, once again, will not offer solutions to these problems. But it will give you the tools to influence and manage them effectively in a democratic republic. After reading this chapter, you will also have a sense for the significant roles that HRM must play in meeting the policy challenges—wicked or more mundane—you will face as a public manager in today's compensatory state. Linking the right people—talent-wise—to a sense of common purpose infused with a passion for democratic constitutional values is a must for government effectiveness and legitimacy in the twenty-first century.

Reconceptualizing Purpose

As we reviewed in chapter 4, the eminent sociologist Max Weber worried in the early 1900s that elected officials would become mere dilettantes in the face of an expert and unelected bureaucracy. With the demise of the politics/policy–administration dichotomy, scholars grappled with how best to ensure that Weber's fears did not become reality. The essence of these debates was distilled in one of the most important "exchanges" (a nice way of saying "arguments"!) in public administration history: the Friedrich–Finer debate of the early 1940s.[4]

Inner Checks versus Outer Checks

At odds in the 1940s were two visions of the purpose of the career civil service in America and how to ensure its members were held accountable for their actions. For Carl Friedrich, the unique technical and scientific expertise provided by careerists meant that the nation could only rely on "inner checks" to hold bureaucrats accountable for their actions. Basically, this meant relying on the norms and values they acquired during their education, their fidelity to professional codes of ethics, their consciences, their sense of duty to a public interest, and their ability to hold each other accountable through the competition of ideas. External or "outer" checks on careerists—such as strong legislative oversight—he felt were impossible because of the complexity of the tasks facing government and the expertise required to perform them. Notice that responsiveness to elected officials was not what Friedrich sought. Not only did elected officials lack expertise, but the electoral process often produced what he called warped or corrupt personalities. By inference, then, the role of the personnel office was to protect civil servants from political interference by enforcing the merit principles we discussed in chapter 5 so they could apply their expertise objectively.

In contrast, Herman Finer argued that only "outer checks" consisting of punitive controls by elected officials would be sufficient to hold civil servants accountable for their actions. Relying on inner checks was only as good as the consciences of the civil servants involved, and agency professionals might cover each other's backs. Wrote Finer, "Sooner or later there is an abuse of power when external punitive controls are lacking."[5] Although he thought some bureaucratic discretion was necessary and that opinions of citizens and interest groups—as Friedrich also claimed—were helpful to check abuses by careerists, these could never be as effective as elected officials in holding careerists to public interest-oriented values.

As we also reviewed in chapter 5, this predisposition for outer checks has, for the most part, prevailed in the United States since the 1980s, for the reasons we discussed. This preference for what we call "responsive competence" has limited the discretion of career civil servants, limited their flexibility to act, and spawned increased politicization of their operations. In the HRM area specifically, the most profound shift has come in refocusing personnel offices on facilitating the work of programs, which has largely meant advancing the agendas of political appointees representing those of presidents, governors, mayors, or other elected executives. This does not mean relieving them of their traditional merit protection responsibilities but, rather, adding on new duties and responsibilities to already understaffed and overworked personnel offices. The specifics of these responsibilities will be dealt with in the remainder of this chapter, but, presently, it should be noted that fear exists of a repoliticizing of HRM functions.

Redefining Administrative Rationality

Further stoking these fears, you should know, is a wider questioning of the merit system itself. Nor are critiques of the system limited to small government conservatives, some of whom call for an end to merit system protections altogether. Indeed, some of the best friends of the concept of a career civil service have long urged its reform. For example, in the early 1980s, one of the most accomplished and prominent of those friends, public administration giant Frederick Mosher, wrote that "the principles of merit and the practices whereby they were given substance are changing and must change a good deal more to remain viable in our society."[6] In the 1990s, the National Commission on the State and Local Public Service—known popularly as the Winter Commission—offered a comprehensive agenda for merit system reform.[7] Needed, the commission felt, was a rethinking of administrative rationality through legislative reform, administrative retooling, and strategic human capital planning (SHCP) in public agencies.[8] More recently, a 2014 report by the prestigious Partnership for Public Service argued that the federal civil service system was "obsolete and in crisis, and an obstacle rather than an aid in attracting, hiring, retaining and developing top talent."[9]

Rethinking Administrative Rationality through Legislation

As we reviewed in earlier chapters, reformers behind the Civil Service Act of 1883 felt that the corruption of their day was linked to political parties, that ending patronage would diminish their power, and that more efficient government awaited once "better people" were hired by agencies. To this end, the act created a three-person, nonpartisan Civil Service Commission (CSC), an entity largely untainted by scandal until the 1970s and the Watergate affair under President Nixon (see more below).[10] Until then, the CSC handled all merit protection issues, oversaw hiring, and advised agencies on HRM issues.

You will recall from chapter 1 that the merit system expanded slowly. Covering only about 10 percent of federal employees in 1883, coverage reached 46 percent in 1900 and 70 percent by 1920.[11] Civil service merit protections reached an apex of 86.5 percent in the 1960s. And although still giving merit protection to exempt employees, only 56 percent of all federal employees were protected by all personnel regulations associated with the traditional civil service system by the end of the twentieth century.[12]

As we reviewed in chapters 1 and 5, the 1930s and 1940s saw Democratic presidents expanding the number of government jobs substantially and "blanketing in" by executive orders former patronage appointees to extend them merit system protection so that they could not be fired by presidents of the other party when they took office. That era also brought new and expanding responsibilities, which meant hiring, among others, public health specialists to deal with disease; lawyers to write economic regulations; and planners, economists, and social scientists to deal with the economic hardships of the day.[13] With the Great Society programs of the 1960s further expanding this professional base, by the 1970s the federal civil service looked, at least formally, like a system resistant to political interference.

As we also noted in chapter 1, the spread of merit systems in states and localities was slow, uneven in coverage, and still awaits completion today in some jurisdictions. Most notably, coverage still varies across state and local jurisdictions on such things as administrative and legal due process rights involving compensation, dismissals, and protection from partisan pressures. For instance, although 99 percent of state government employees in North Carolina were covered by the merit system in 2007, only 60 percent were covered in Indiana. Overall, in the states, civil service coverage peaked in the 1980s, with three-quarters of the states and 60 percent of their employees part of civil service systems. Importantly, much of this was forced on them by the federal government beginning in the 1940s through tying the creation of state merit systems to the receipt of federal aid, with a big boost coming during the 1960s from the explosion of Great Society grant programs. In localities during that same era, 88 percent of all jurisdictions used merit systems. By the first decade of the twenty-first century, however, the most notable characteristic in states and localities was reform of the merit system. In fact, for the past two decades, civil service reform has dominated administrative reform initiatives in local government.

Amid all this, as you know from earlier chapters, came the single most important federal legislative initiative involving personnel management since the Pendleton Act of 1883: the Civil Service Reform Act (CSRA) of 1978. Partially in reaction to personnel abuses condoned and then covered up by the CSC during the Watergate affair, but also informed by dissatisfaction over the centralization of key personnel functions by the CSC, the CSRA split its responsibilities into two new agencies: the Merit Systems Protection Board to protect merit provisions of the original act and the Office of Personnel Management (OPM) to take over all other CSC responsibilities. The act also created the Federal Labor Relations Authority to deal with labor–management issues.

Recall also how the CSRA sought to emulate aspects of the British civil service by creating the Senior Executive Service (SES). Its aim was to produce a team of outstanding management executives who would move from agency to agency to bring their skills to bear wherever they were needed most and gain a broader perspective on government. Those joining the SES could, among other things, opt out of the civil service system, be evaluated on performance, and receive pay bonuses for outstanding performance. From an "outer check" perspective, of course, pay for performance also increased the leverage of political appointees over top-level managers in their agencies.

Revamping Administrative Rationality Managerially

To these legislative reforms of HRM have been added a variety of administrative initiatives to remedy perceived civil service or merit system shortcomings. In particular, you should be familiar with two major administrative reform efforts that have animated personnel administration at all levels of government. As alluded to in chapter 1, the first involves moving agencies out of the standard civil service system. The second involves decentralizing personnel authorities from centralized personnel offices to agencies. As a public manager, you will have to work effectively within this new administrative rationality and perhaps even refine or develop new approaches to the perennial HRM issues they address.

From Merit System to Multiple Merit Systems. As leading proponents of reform of the federal personnel system have observed, the "civil service system, which was devised to create a uniform process for recruiting high-quality workers to government, is no longer uniform or a system."[14] Yes, most civilian positions are part of the competitive service, where applicants must compete with other applicants for positions available in agencies. However, by the end of the twentieth century, that percentage had declined to a little more than half of all federal employees as agencies opted out of the civil service system or positions were removed from it.[15]

As alluded to in chapter 1, employees working in agencies or positions opting out of or removed from the traditional civil service are in what personnel experts call the "exempt service." These agencies have been granted exemptions based on their need for speed and flexibility in hiring and retention decisions that the civil service system cannot provide. Exempt status, for example, allows agencies to pay higher salaries necessary to hire and retain specialists who might otherwise go into the private sector (e.g., at the Nuclear Regulatory Commission). Exempt status is also used for positions where it is not as easy to judge a person's qualifications, such as special agents or policy advisors. Thus, were you to become a public manager in a national security agency—for example, the Central Intelligence Agency, the Department of State, the Defense Intelligence Agency, the National Security Agency, the Federal Bureau of Investigation, or the Department of Homeland Security—you would be serving in an exempt service status. You will not, however, lose merit system protection; each exempted agency has its own system.

From Centralization to Decentralization. Related to the growth of multiple merit systems is a focus over the past two decades on decentralizing personnel authority from central administrative units, such as the OPM, to agencies and programs. Decentralization is hardly a new idea; as Patricia Ingraham and David Rosenbloom point out, a cycle of centralization-decentralization that we will cover later in this chapter actually began at the federal level in the Classification Act of 1949.[16] This act decentralized some pay-classification responsibilities back to the agencies. Part of the logic of decentralization was—and remains—to give political appointees the authority to wield personnel policies in agencies that would advance the policy agendas of chief executives. But it was also a reaction to real management problems of delay, inflexibility, and unresponsiveness associated with centralized personnel operations. As Mosher put it, HRM systems "should be decentralized and delegated to bring them into more immediate relationship with the middle and lower managers they served."[17]

The CSRA of 1978 made some provisions for decentralizing personnel management authority to agencies, especially in evaluating and rewarding employee performance.

But it was during the 1990s under the Clinton administration that decentralization of personnel authorities was pushed most aggressively by the White House out into agencies and programs. Had you been working in a federal agency during that administration, you might have noticed three major and substantial changes affecting your organization's operations and mission in this regard.

To begin with, the Clintonites eliminated nearly half of OPM employees, dwarfing the downsizing of so-called "overhead personnel" in any other federal agency as part of their "reinventing government" initiative.[18] In 1996, the administration then radically decentralized hiring by creating almost 700 "delegated examining units" in federal agencies. Problems quickly arose, however. Agencies lacked expertise in the basics of handling personnel issues, thus causing substantial backlogs in hiring and other types of cases. Moreover, without a job application procedure to cover all federal government hires during those years, applicants were faced with nearly 200 hiring authorities, each with their own hiring procedure.[19] Furthermore, with most agencies foregoing written exams in favor of "unassembled exams"—hiring based solely on college GPAs and experience—the least predictive measures of job performance drove hiring.[20] Indeed, over 40 percent of all federal hires had no contact or interview with their immediate supervisor before being hired!

The second, and related, thing you would have noticed in this regard was the enactment in 2002 of the Chief Human Capital Officers Act. Among other things, it gave "direct-hire authority" to agencies. This meant that they could hire outstanding candidates *without* following civil service regulations. Almost immediately, the rate of direct-hiring in agencies tripled, and it continues to be very popular.

The third personnel dynamic likely to have captured your attention by the early 2000s was the increase in contracting out various HRM functions to the private sector. By mid-decade, surveys were finding that all federal agencies were contracting at least some of their personnel responsibilities to the private sector. This occurred partially for perceived cost savings and the prevailing conservative philosophy in Washington but also due to the agency personnel mismanagement issues noted above.

Lest you think all this was merely a federal phenomenon, you should understand that similar trends occurred at the state and local government levels. Indeed, many of these initiatives started at those levels and percolated up to the federal government. On the decentralization front, almost 80 percent of the states have devolved recruitment and hiring to agencies, while 16 states have contracted out at least part of their personnel functions to private industry. Meanwhile, at the local level, 8 percent of these jurisdictions contract out at least part of their personnel functions. However, they do so to a wider group of contractors, including nonprofits and other governments.

To be sure, efforts have been made during the Obama years at all levels of government to improve recruitment systems. For example, actions replicated by or borrowed from states and localities have included selecting from among a larger number of qualified applicants by using a "category-rating" approach rather than the "rule-of-three" approach. This allows agencies to avoid having to select from only the three highest-scoring applicants, as was the case historically. In addition, the administration's Hiring Reform Initiative has overhauled the federal hiring process. Among other things, OPM moved to a resumé-based system, eliminating the "KSA essays" (knowledge, skills, and abilities). Launched, too, has been the Pathways Programs, which were designed to recruit new agency talent by creating clear pathways to federal service for students and recent graduates. Targeted were "mission-critical jobs and professional careers where there are skill gaps."[21]

Still, significant glitches and embarrassments have occurred, some of which you may have heard about from friends or previous classmates trying to apply for federal jobs. The most infamous of these was the launch of OPM's USAJobs portal. In 2013, the OPM launched version 3.0 of USAJobs, allowing applicants to search and apply for federal government positions. The result of an 18-month collaboration between OPM and the Chief Human Capital Officers Council, enhancements were made to security, informational features, and search capabilities. Moreover, for the first time, applicants were allowed to submit their information only once to apply for multiple jobs. However, reminiscent of the recent website launch of the Patient Protection and Affordable Care Act, OPM reported problems with its search features due to high site volume, as well as problems with "its ability to allow people to build new saved searches."[22] Later, more problems arose with login and password-reset functions.[23]

Were all these but one-time glitches, the situation might be irritating but not cause for alarm. However, OPM—just as other federal agencies such as the US Internal Revenue Service—has had chronic issues with information technology (IT) development throughout its history. OPM inspector general Patrick McFarland testified before Congress in late 2011 that OPM lacks sufficient "institutional knowledge" to build information systems in a "very deliberate, structured, and methodical way."[24] Moreover, most states and localities are in worse condition, so your work in hiring talented personnel for your agency will be cut out for your cohort of public managers in the foreseeable future.

From Policemen to Strategic Human Capital Managers

Perhaps the most important cultural aspect of rethinking administrative rationality has come in the aforementioned shift at all levels of government away from the idea of HRM offices solely policing agency operations. Emphasized instead is collaborating with agencies and programs within departments to ensure a strategic approach to workforce development consistent with agency goals and needs. This typically manifests itself in the SHCP process. As Nicholas Henry writes, central personnel agencies at all levels of government had by the 1990s come to see themselves as "independent and powerful" entities, separate from the rest of government, and the unilateral authors of rules not subject to appeal by agencies.[25] Thus, after experimenting with a variety of different incentive structures in an attempt to encourage a collaborative rather than merely a compliance mentality in personnel offices, administrative reformers began calling for the formalizing of SHCP in public agencies.

Strategic human capital plans, in turn, are defined as a "coordinated set of actions aimed at integrating an organization's culture [symbols, norms, and underlying beliefs], organization [structure and job roles], people [skill and competency levels and potential], and systems [HRM or people-focused mechanisms]."[26] They are reminiscent of, but not as broad in scope as, the strategic planning model we covered in chapter 4. As Sally Selden describes, SHCP seeks to link in greater detail for the HRM function the larger goals enumerated in the agency's strategic plan.[27] This means that the traditional responsibilities of personnel specialists in public agencies—job and pay classification, hiring, discipline, performance evaluation, training, and retirement—are consciously integrated with agency goals, thus making personnel offices co-workforce planners, collaborators, and partners with agency leadership.

To help you envision how SHCP works in practice, Figure 7.1 depicts the SHCP process followed by the state of Georgia—evaluated by some HRM experts as among the

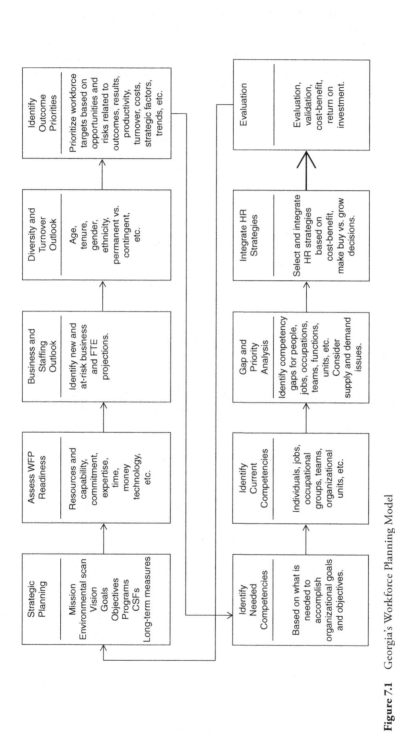

Figure 7.1 Georgia's Workforce Planning Model

Source: S. C. Selden (2009) *Human Capital: Tools and Strategies for the Public Sector* (Washington, DC: CQ Press), p. 27.

best in the nation. Emulating the Georgia approach means that your agency has to align those individual personnel tasks noted in the figure to advance agency goals. If any one component is not aligned with those goals—and the workforce plan designed to implement them—your organization risks underperforming in significant ways. Moreover, benchmarking what your organization is doing against "best personnel practices" in other agencies is a critical component for fulfilling its potential. Also notice how "action-oriented" Georgia's SHCP process is, as well as the time-specific nature of the tasks involved. As such, Georgia's planning follows the widely accepted SHCP rule of identifying the key activities that the personnel office will have to do well to attain its goals, measures of success, and clear action dates—or "milestones"—for holding employees accountable for performing needed tasks along the way.

Do not, however, think only of these milestones as accountability mechanisms; they are also "conversation points" for finding out why an activity could not be done on time before it is too late to get the process back on track. And because a variety of reasons can exist for why deadlines are or are not met, another noteworthy feature of Georgia's plan is its anticipation of what might happen to hinder success. This includes the bureaucratic politics of change we reviewed in chapters 4 and 5 (and that we will cover some more in chapter 9), as well as the symbolic, normative, and emotional obstacles to change that you might anticipate from employees.

Also worthy of special attention in Figure 7.1 are the critical roles played in SHCP of supply analysis, demand analysis, gap analysis, solutions analysis, and feedback analysis. These refer, respectively, to doing analyses of

- the skill or competency mix that presently exists in an agency;
- the competencies needed to carry out the plan;
- the difference between skills and competencies needed and those available;
- the short, medium, and long-term (ten-year) strategies for closing those gaps and aligning human capital systems with goals;
- the status of implementing the plan and adjusting it where necessary in light of obstacles that are arising and changes in the environment.[28]

The movement toward SHCP means that personnel specialists in your agency will need a variety of skills not part of the traditional HRM portfolio. And as a public manager, you will need to be an intelligent consumer of these analyses. Certainly, the courses that you will take in statistics will come in handy if you are working in an agency using what are called "human capital analytics." The best-managed agencies, for example, use regression analyses based on historical data and exit interviews to determine the most significant factors affecting employee turnover. And, most definitely if working in these agencies, you will be inundated by requests at all stages of the SHCP process for "human capital metrics," as well as continually pressed to manage by them.[29] Indeed, these may be critical in marshaling "evidence, argument, and persuasion" when promoting employees and justifying requests for personnel slots within your agency.

Reconnecting with Citizens

To this point, we have examined the instrumental dimensions of HRM that you will confront in the twenty-first century. However, as noted in other chapters, you will need to understand the existing instrumental, normative, and symbolic aspects of personnel management, especially as they relate to democratic administration. One of the most significant of these is what is called "passive representation": the extent to which the career bureaucracy reflects the social, demographic, and economic composition of the citizenry it serves.[30] You will also hear a great deal about the aforementioned "active representation." The focus here is on whether passive representation results in policy changes that better reflect the interests of the groups represented. Both are premised on remedying past discrimination against blacks, women, ethnic minorities, the disabled, and lesbians, gays, and bisexuals (LGB) in hiring and promotion patterns in private and public agencies, as well as the policy disadvantages they have suffered.[31]

Some Pros and Cons of Representative Bureaucracy

As you might imagine, complaints soon arose from some members of established groups that a focus on increasing diversity, first, through equal opportunity laws and, later, through affirmative action policies meant merit principles were being violated. Proponents countered by stating that "merit" was really a much broader concept than critics implied. Being competent to do a job involved more than having a specific set of skills.[32] For instance, a diverse police force was likely to hold more legitimacy—or, as proponents argued, "symbolic value"—in minority communities than a lily-white force of officers.

In addition, not only were favoritism and discrimination constants in personnel hiring and promotion decisions from the beginning of the nation, but competency alone had never been the sole aim of public service employment. For starters, jobs in the public sector have historically been an avenue of social mobility for immigrants (for instance, the Irish, Germans, Poles, and Italians) and for rewarding political supporters. Recall from chapter 1 our friend Roscoe's advice to political novices! Moreover, governments have historically put a thumb on the scale in favor of white males and against certain subpopulations. For example, and in addition to well-known instances of discrimination by race and gender, a series of studies by Gregory Lewis document a history of federal prohibition of the hiring of homosexuals during the Cold War.[33] Espoused fears of the blackmailing of closeted gay men prompted huge obstacles for them in obtaining security clearances during that era, credentials crucial for obtaining some federal and contracting jobs. Lewis' analyses compellingly show, however, that this policy owed more to negative stereotyping than to national security concerns.

The Long and Winding Path toward Representative Bureaucracy

As noted in chapter 1, the history of discrimination in federal government hiring is a long and embarrassing one. Consider the fate of African Americans. In 1810, Congress passed legislation stating that only free, white males could be hired by the US Postal Service, a major source of federal employment in that era. This law was not repealed until 1865. In fact, Rosenbloom notes that this policy infested all federal agencies, as he reports no evidence of blacks in the federal government until 1867.[34] Nevertheless, slow progress was made in ensuing decades, with a rough proportional representation of blacks in the general population working in federal agencies not occurring until 1928.

All this happened as the Republican Party initially appointed blacks to meaningful civil service positions during Reconstruction. And although Republicans gradually lost interest after the end of Reconstruction in 1876 as fears grew of losing Southern white votes, progress continued because the merit system made overt discrimination in hiring more difficult. Still, as we covered, the system offered no protection against either removals or segregation of agency workforces once hired, weapons wielded with ferocity by both the William Howard Taft and Wilson administrations during the first two decades of the twentieth century. The next three Republican presidents maintained this pattern, although President Hoover had, as secretary of commerce, desegregated the Census Bureau. Thus, by the time of the election of Roosevelt in 1932, the number of black clerks in the federal government dwindled from around 2,000–3,000 to hundreds.[35] This, despite some efforts to desegregate blacks in the departments of Commerce, Interior, and Treasury in the late 1920s.

As we also reviewed in chapter 1, during the remainder of the twentieth century, the Roosevelt administration then began a long series of initiatives to address racial discrimination. A series of federal policy initiatives were produced, commencing in 1939 with the Hatch Act and in 1940 with the Ramspeck Act. The former incorporated language prohibiting discrimination on the basis of race or color whenever funding for federal relief programs and projects was involved; the latter did the same more broadly for occasions such as appointments, salaries, and promotions.

Launched in this fashion, "equal employment opportunity" (EEO) became a federal government focus. The idea was to require actions that removed barriers to hiring the historically disadvantaged. When actual hiring fell short of aims, however, that policy then morphed into what we know today as "affirmative action." The latter requires organizations to demonstrate that they have actively recruited from these groups and that all affirmative steps have been taken to hire their members. Over the years, you will learn, these efforts have gradually expanded what is called "protected status" to include nondiscrimination on the basis of race, gender, ethnicity, religion, national origin, age, and disability.

Then, once affirmative action became vulnerable in the courts to "equal protection" violations of the US Constitution (as we shall see below), the rationale expanded from compensating for past discrimination to the nation having a "compelling state interest" in, and "narrow tailoring" of remedies for, fostering a diverse society. Importantly, you should be aware, however, that neither of these are relevant if a public sector affirmative action program is challenged on statutory (Title VII) grounds. Usually, though, challenges are based on constitutional grounds, and that standard is referred to as "strict scrutiny."

Although not without controversy, EEO efforts were generally seen by citizens as consistent with American sensibilities regarding fairness. However, affirmative action policies have proven highly controversial. As alluded to above, opponents categorize it as a shift from equality of *opportunity* to equality of *outcome*, a characterization not only inconsistent with American exceptionalist values but one repeatedly framed by opponents as "reverse discrimination" against white males.

Still, EEO had to be pursued initially by executive order, as congressional majorities simply did not exist to pass legislation. In 1941, for instance, the Roosevelt administration issued EO 8802 barring discrimination by race, religion, or national origin for federal contractors. Then, in 1948, the Truman administration integrated the armed forces by executive order. Legislatively, however, the pathbreaker for EEO was the Civil Rights Act of 1964, which made private or public sector discrimination illegal. Importantly, the act also expanded the protected-class designation to include gender discrimination against women. You should be clear, though, that the Civil Rights Act was not a direct mechanism for pursuing affirmative action. Its only reference to it was that a federal court could—not must—order affirmative action as a remedy.

In short order, presidents Johnson and Nixon launched a series of executive orders that began the shift from EEO to affirmative action as a primary recruitment goal of the federal government.[36] In what many describe as the single most significant administrative action taken, the Johnson administration issued EO 11246 in 1965 requiring all federal government contractors to use affirmative action—meaning "aggressive, proactive" efforts—to combat discrimination on the basis of race, religion, or national origin.[37] In 1967, the administration added women to this protected class of citizens in EO 11375.

Then, in 1969, the Nixon administration required all government contractors in the city of Philadelphia to hire minority workers. So-called "Order Number 4" issued by the Department of Labor (specifically, its Office of Federal Contract Compliance) was based on a plan developed during the Johnson administration and, for the first time, stipulated preferential hiring goals and timetables for the city. The policy was soon extended to other cities by "Revised Order Number 4," which survived a Supreme Court appeal.[38] Then, in 1971, the administration issued EO 11625, which committed all federal agencies to increasing the proportion of minority-owned businesses receiving federal contracts.

Congress also moved legislatively in 1967, 1974, and 1981 to offer a series of expanded protections against age discrimination, with the fundamental aim to ban compulsory retirement for those 40 years old and above. Alongside these efforts came affirmative action for Vietnam veterans in 1974 (building on previously adopted veteran preferences in federal hiring) and then protection for mentally and physically disabled citizens in 1990. Most recently, as we will review shortly, efforts to prevent discrimination on the basis of sexual orientation have taken place, including benefit protection for domestic partners (persons domiciled together but not married) and (now) married same-sex partners.

How Well Have These Policies Worked?

How successful have these efforts been in promoting a diverse workforce? You will learn in your coursework that initial studies on passive representation suggested that African American representation improved significantly as a proportion of the government workforce into the 1960s and 1970s.[39] However, subsequent research indicates that progress slowed at all government levels in the 1980s during the Reagan administration, with upticks coming later during Democratic administrations.[40] Today, women and some minorities are better represented in public organizations, but they are overrepresented in the lower echelons of bureaucracies and underrepresented in the managerial and executive ranks at all levels of government.[41]

Researchers also find that although gays totaled 6.23 percent of the workforce in 2012, they are underrepresented in local government jobs (4.03 percent) and overrepresented in both state (7.81 percent) and federal jobs (7.08 percent).[42] They are also overrepresented in nonprofit agencies, even when statistical controls are used for the absence of children and higher-paid partners.[43] Research by Gregory Lewis and David Pitts on government employment patterns by sexual orientation has also found some underrepresentation of partnered gay men, especially in the federal service.[44] Meanwhile, people of color are significantly underrepresented in nonprofit agencies, with minorities in 2010 comprising only 6.8 percent of executive board members and 10 percent of directors. They are, however, 18 percent of the nonprofit workforce.[45]

Although racism and homophobia explain discrimination against minorities and the LGB community, the forces driving gender-based disparities in passive representation are debated. Up to the 1960s, sexism was clearly the culprit and was officially sanctioned by governments. As Rosenbloom puts it, "Although the employment of women in government service in America actually predates the formation of the Union, historically, women have not generally been treated as equals."[46] Indeed, until 1920 and ratification of the Nineteenth Amendment to the US Constitution, women were excluded from 60 percent of all federal jobs, and until 1923, unequal compensation for women was provided by law. Nor did preferences for military veterans in hiring help the situation, as they went to men. Moreover, married women felt discrimination even more than women in general. For example, during the Great Depression of the 1930s, women were dismissed at three times the rate of men, a situation prompting a 1937 statute that precluded discrimination on the basis of marital status. And it was not until the 1960s, as noted, that a concerted effort to redress discrimination began.

Since then, overt sexism has been joined by other competing explanations. Institutional sexism (as with institutional racism) is certainly possible, as is pervasive societal stereotyping. Lending some evidence to the latter explanation is research suggesting that entry levels of women have more to do with their ultimate work grade than promotion rates at the federal level.[47] Indeed, women are just as likely as men at a comparable level to receive promotions, and they typically receive higher performance ratings than men. Nor are women more likely than their male counterparts to leave the federal service.

Still, organizational culture differences loom for women and minorities. For instance, SES women have more favorable attitudes than SES men toward policies that aid women in the workplace, indicating residual white male disaffection.[48] Similar disparities exist for LGB employees and the general federal workforce. Although one analysis of 2012 census data finds that gay–straight pay differences between comparable federal employees have basically disappeared, LGB employees in that study are significantly less satisfied than white males with the treatment they receive.[49]

Evidence also exists that minorities and women are significantly more vulnerable than their white male counterparts to economic downturns. For example, a recent study finds that the Great Recession of 2007–09 had disparate impacts on both women and African Americans in state and local government agencies. This is partially because of the "last hired, first fired or laid off" principle that occurs during downsizing in most organizations during tough times. Women experienced 69.1 percent of job cuts through March 2012.[50] Likewise, an analysis of data from the 2006, 2008, and 2010 Displaced Worker Survey indicates that the difference in the probability of displacement between African American and white public sector respondents increased from zero to a recession gap of 2.8 percentage points.[51]

But what about active representation? The evidence is a little more mixed, particularly for women. Scholars studying active representation consistently have found links between passive and active representation in a variety of policy areas where a particular demographic group benefits from implementation and/or when the issue is salient to the demographic group in question.[52] For example, studies have found that higher numbers of women in law enforcement agencies are associated with more reporting and convictions of sexual assault.[53] Others find that female representation in child support offices is associated with greater case enforcement.[54] The verdict is still out, however, as studies do exist that have found no linkage between passive and active representation for women, such as was found at the Equal Employment Opportunity Commission (EEOC).[55]

Research also has shown that representation of racial and ethnic minorities makes a real difference in how services are delivered and how program resources are allocated, but its ultimate impact on organizational performance is not as well documented.[56] Several studies find that increasing the passive representation of these minorities in teaching positions is associated with better educational outcomes for minority students.[57] Similarly, upper-level minority state bureaucrats are more likely than nonminorities to support policies that benefit minorities.[58] Researchers also find that higher levels of African American representation in the Department of Agriculture's Farmers Home Administration and in the EEOC are associated with better outcomes for African Americans.[59]

Currently, scant research exists on active representation of LGBs in public agencies— or elsewhere.[60] But what does exist suggests that passive representation can make a difference. Gregory Thielemann and Joseph Stewart, for example, find that people living with AIDS prefer service providers of their own sexual orientation.[61] Also, LGB-elected officials appear to shift policy in favor of LGB citizens, suggesting that LGB bureaucrats with policy discretion will do the same.[62] And in one of the first efforts to assess the link between LGBs in a bureaucratic setting and performance outcomes, David Pitts and Jon Weakley find that gay students having an openly gay faculty member in class or as a mentor attain higher GPAs.[63] Certainly, achieving a critical mass of 15 percent of LGBs in an agency to affect policy is difficult, given their much lower share of the public sector workforce. But the critical mass needed for LGB impact may be less important due to the generally more favorable societal attitude today toward gays.[64]

All in all, then, sufficient research evidence exists for you to suspect that representative bureaucracy is a way for public agencies to reconnect with historically disadvantaged citizens, as well as to impact the policy outputs and outcomes agencies produce. Moreover, many corporations are now aggressively moving ahead to improve their diversity as a marketing tool. Consequently, failing to address these issues could place your agency at a significant disadvantage for recruiting the "best and brightest" to public service. This will be true regardless of whether legal pressure to pursue affirmative action continues, wanes, or takes a different approach. But what are its prospects and under what conditions are courts likely to approve such strategies?

Whither Affirmative Action?

As alluded to earlier, affirmative action suits have increasingly found their way into the courts largely by asserting reverse discrimination. In its first full decision on affirmative action, *Regents of the University of California v. Bakke* (438 U.S. 265 [1978]), the US Supreme Court upheld the principle of affirmative action in university admissions but disallowed the use of "quotas."[65] Since then, court decisions affecting workplace issues involving disparate impact of remedial policies have been somewhat mercurial but are beginning to yield an identifiable doctrine for you and your agency to follow. For example, in the late 1980s, the US Supreme Court issued decisions on how to prove employment discrimination (see *Wards Cove Packing Co. v. Atonio*, 490 U.S. 642 [1989]), restrict the scope of civil rights laws (see *Patterson v. McLean Credit Union*, 491 U.S. 164 [1989]), and create a higher threshold for justifying affirmative action remedial programs (see *City of Richmond v. J. A. Croson Co.*, 488 U.S. 469 [1989]). In *Grutter v. Bollinger* (539 U.S. 306 [2003]), the Supreme Court ruled that the racial diversity of a student body can be a sufficiently compelling interest to use race-conscious admissions. But on the same day, in *Gratz v. Bollinger* (539 U.S. 244 [2003]), the Court struck down the use of affirmative action by the University of Michigan's undergraduate programs for not doing the same.[66]

From these and other decisions, if your agency pursues affirmative action programs, it must be prepared to show how that program can rectify past discrimination in the agency and that it is narrowly tailored to address the problem. The latter means you must choose the remedy that addresses past discrimination while doing the least harm to other populations. You must also ensure that agency contractors and nonprofit partners do the same.

You should also be aware, however, that movements are afoot to redefine affirmative action to emphasize economic disparities rather than—or just—racial disparities. Proponents argue that many beneficiaries of diversity policies come from the more economically well-off segments of protected classes, leaving the least advantaged no better off.[67] Thus, they see a focus on income as fairer for truly needy minorities, as well as for poorer whites. Opponents of this approach, however, argue that the unique experience of racism in the United States merits special consideration and that a residue of that discrimination still exists. Others argue that affirmative action on the basis of race will be less and less implementable in the future because (1) greater numbers of individuals are refusing to check off their race on census forms and (2) mixed-race children will blur racial differences.[68]

Regardless, the increasing racial and ethnic diversity of the country will require that you know how to manage a more diverse workforce. In 2012, for example, over one-third (36 percent) of the American workforce was Hispanic, African American, or Asian, a figure predicted to grow to 52 percent by 2042.[69] We are already seeing "majority–minority" localities in states such as California, Florida, and Texas and, thus, a more diverse recruiting pool.

As such, a portion of your time as a public manager is also likely to be focused on interpersonal challenges related to diversity. These may involve communication breakdowns, as well as misunderstandings and even hostilities, that can result in a work environment with persons from highly diverse backgrounds, age cohorts, and lifestyles. Indeed, your agency's success may depend on it, as well as on linking diversity planning and management into its SHCP. Also important to you as a public manager will be availing yourself of cross-cultural training exercises; learning what best-in-class organizations in all sectors do to manage diversity; and mentoring persons who are unique ethnically, racially, in gender, and in sexual preference. And once in official leadership positions, you will want to create processes that make people who are unique feel welcome and comfortable, obtain survey and interview data on organizational climate across demographic groups, and develop and deploy recruitment teams that have multicultural training.

Reengaging Financial Resources

As you may already know, personnel costs are often the single most expensive component of government operations at all levels of government in our Madisonian system.

Thus, figuring out how best to deliver the goods, services, and opportunities that citizens require, as well as reconceptualizing their missions in the twenty-first century, means finding ways to minimize personnel costs and reengage existing resources to those higher purposes. We have already covered one major tool available for doing so: strategic human capital planning. But three primary challenges exist today to doing so effectively while remaining focused on building a sense of common purpose infused with democratic constitutional values. These are efforts to move toward at-will employment, to recalibrate previously negotiated labor union pension plans, and, as previously noted, to outsource government responsibilities.

From Merit to At-Will Employment?

One way to deal with personnel costs and reengage existing resources is for agency leaders to gain greater flexibility on hiring, performance, promotion, and termination decisions. As we alluded to in chapters 1 and 5, one way elected officials have done this is to allow "at-will" employment in their jurisdictions. Recall that at-will employment means, unlike in merit systems, employees serve at the pleasure of a government employer. They can be dismissed without warning or reason. Proponents argued that since employees can quit at any time, at-will just evens the playing field for management. They also claimed it would produce more responsive competence to elected officials and their appointees and better employee performance. Moreover, flexibility in hiring and firing would save agencies money; they could shift the costs of employee benefits by outsourcing jobs to the private and nonprofit sectors. The response from public unions and many scholars will not surprise you: at-will employment would produce a return to the spoils system, as well as the loss of hard-won employee protections against unfair treatment of civil servants.[70] Nor did they believe the claims for greater efficiency; this they saw as a fig leaf covering proponents' real desire to shrink the size and capacity of government.

Unfazed, three states led the at-will effort during the 1990s: Florida, Georgia, and Texas. In Georgia, the state legislature abolished civil service protections for newly hired employees, as well as for those accepting promotions or transfers to other positions in state government. As of 2006 under the GeorgiaGain initiative, approximately 76 percent of Georgia's state employees were employed at-will.[71] Following suit, Florida placed upper-level managers in at-will status. Texas has long operated under a decentralized, at-will arrangement for delivery of human resource services and is the only state that does not have a central personnel agency, so the move to at-will was less of a break with tradition.[72]

You should be aware, however, that aspects of at-will employment have not been confined to these states. Indeed, a majority of state governments (28 states) have incorporated aspects or limited the scope of at-will employment.[73] In Kansas, for example, only higher-level employees have lost traditional merit system protection. In still other states, such as Delaware and Iowa, policy makers have exempted all workers in particular agencies (e.g., the economic development office in Iowa).[74] Additional research suggests that if you work in states with any of the following characteristics, you are likely to be exposed to some aspects of at-will employment: states with Republican-controlled governments, weak public unions, and high levels of administrative and legislative professionalism.[75] Even then, however, you should know that care still must be taken in carrying out terminations. They cannot be accomplished in such a way as to damage the employee's ability to find similar employment in another jurisdiction—so the systems implemented are not truly or fully "at-will" in this sense. Also, termination on the basis of illegal considerations (e.g., race or sex) are prohibited.

Under these conditions, have the claims of at-will proponents materialized? Given the ups and downs of the economy, it is hard to discern a clear picture. For instance, we know that anticipated cost savings have not always been realized. In Florida, for example, Convergys—the firm to which human resource processing functions were outsourced—experienced delays and "significant problems," including payroll and benefit errors.[76] In contrast, Steven Condrey and Paul Battaglio found that less than half of state human resource managers (47 percent) in Georgia thought that at-will employment had helped "ensure that employees are responsive to the goals and priorities of agency administrators."[77] At the same time, they found that only 3 percent believed that it made the "HR function more efficient," and only 34.9 percent reported that at-will employment provided the "needed motivation for employee performance."[78] Mixed findings for Georgia are also presented in other studies. Robert Sanders, for instance, disputes the efficiency claims of state officials.[79] In support, he finds that pay increases across all occupations have decreased, as have outstanding annual evaluations, and more "inadequate" employees have left Georgia government since at-will efforts were launched. At the same time, however, rates of exit for employees rated as average and above-average have also increased, calling efficiency gains into question because of the loss of good performers. Other surveys of state employees indicate that majorities contest the productivity gains touted by state-elected officials.[80]

But did the dire predictions of opponents pan out? James Bowman and Jonathan West found that at-will employment in Florida *was* spawning the "dissolution of the traditional social contract at work: job security with good pay and benefits in exchange for employee commitment and loyalty."[81] Still, evidence also exists that opponents' fears of at-will employment leading to violations of merit principles have yet to materialize. Jerrell Coggburn, for example, reports that fully 97.4 percent of state human resource directors in Texas agreed that "even though employment is at-will, most employee terminations in Texas agencies are for good cause."[82]

The Rise and Demise (?) of Public Sector Unions

As you might guess from recent media reports, one cannot talk about reengaging personnel resources without talking about public employee unions. Private sector labor–management tensions, as we reviewed in chapter 2, have been a constant in America since the industrial revolution in the late nineteenth century. Much the same has been true for public employee unions, thus posing a significant challenge for managers in public agencies.

As you will learn in your coursework, the labor movement faced early resistance to union representation for government employees. The general sentiment was that working for government was not a right but a privilege, meaning employees forfeited rights otherwise enjoyed by private sector employees.[83] For instance, collective bargaining for federal employees was not approved for federal agencies until President Kennedy issued EO 10988 in 1962, as employees gained the right to join public unions to represent their interests but without the ability to bargain over wages or benefits (restrictions that are still applicable today).

President Nixon subsequently expanded employee bargaining rights by issuing EO 11491 in 1969. It defined unfair labor practices and allowed binding arbitration to settle disputes. President Ford then expanded the scope of the issues that could be negotiated in collective bargaining to include agency regulations and approved secret ballots in elections. These were followed in subsequent years by the CSRA's creation of the Federal Labor Relations Authority; the Clinton administration's creation of Labor–Management Partnerships and their reversal by the second Bush administration; and the reinstatement by President Obama of Clinton's initiative through the creation of Labor–Management Forums.

By the same token, state and local government employees did not gain the right to bargain collectively until Wisconsin approved it in 1959. Once attained, however, unions joined their federal counterparts in negotiating with management over items previously under the exclusive prerogative of managers, such as pay, benefits, disciplinary practices, and working conditions. Currently, only eight states do not have collective bargaining legislation in all or some aspects of employee contracts: Arizona, Arkansas, Colorado, Louisiana, Mississippi, North Carolina, South Carolina, and Virginia.[84] North Carolina and Virginia alone proscribe collective bargaining altogether for public employees.

Still, public employees in 39 states and the federal government do not have the right to strike. States that permit public employees some modified right to strike include: Alaska, California, Hawaii, Idaho, Illinois, Minnesota, Montana, Ohio, Oregon, Pennsylvania, Rhode Island, Vermont, and Wisconsin. Even in these states, however, the balance of power is generally skewed in favor of management. Public sector unions maintain that, without this right, they can never be coequal partners in the labor–management relationship. Critics counter that strikes are improper, because essential public services are held hostage for employee gain. Some even contend that alternatives to the strike, such as binding arbitration, are inappropriate, because they unconstitutionally delegate policy-making power to private parties. Still, about half the states with collective bargaining statutes mandate binding arbitration, primarily for police and firefighters.[85]

The greatest assault on public unions today, however, has resulted from the unfunded public pension liabilities on state and local government finances. These have been produced over decades by collective bargaining agreements that committed future taxpayers to payouts without setting aside necessary revenues; the underfunding and diversion of pension funds by legislatures, governors, and mayors; and the aging workforce noted earlier. You may have read about the recent confrontations over these and related issues in states such as New Jersey, Ohio, and Wisconsin. Politics aside, the unfunded pension liabilities facing state and local governments are real and likely to accelerate as baby boomers retire in greater numbers over the next decade.

A 2013 report by Moody's Investors Service, however, shows that unfunded pension problems vary across states.[86] Moody's assigns ratings to states based on the ratio of adjusted net pension liabilities to each state's revenues. They range from a low of 6.8 percent for Nebraska to a high of 241 percent for Illinois. The median value for all 50 states was 45 percent. The top nine states in pension "distress" had ratios greater than 100 percent, while the nine least distressed had ratios less than 20 percent of state revenue. Following Illinois, the states with the worst adjusted pension liabilities were Connecticut (with a ratio of 189.7 percent), Kentucky (140.9 percent), New Jersey (137.2 percent), and Hawaii (132.5 percent). Following Nebraska, the states with the lowest ratios were Wisconsin (14.4 percent), Idaho (14.8 percent), Iowa (16.1 percent), and New York (16.6 percent).

Given all this, how much you are directly affected by these issues as a public manager will vary. If you are serving in a state or locality where it has been a problem in the past, you are likely to witness political pressures to cut the size and nature of future pension benefits, as is the case in Detroit and Illinois today. In the interim, the painful and con-flictual task of reengaging funds from other programs to offset unfunded pension com-mitments is likely to occur, a topic we will return to in chapter 8. Thus, the best, most creative, and most imaginative managers will be needed to help policy makers deal with these issues or cope with their consequences in the years ahead.

Toward a "Just-in-Time" Workforce?

The final aspect of reengaging resources for our purposes involves the aforementioned outsourcing of public sector jobs in today's compensatory state. As you know, the current civil service system was designed for a government in which, for the most part, agencies directly delivered most public services. However, as we have covered, privatization and devolution have in recent decades increased the number and importance of partnerships with private and nonprofit firms at all levels of government in the United States.

Thus, you might be surprised to learn that we often do not have accurate databases for estimating the total amount of contracting taking place nor how well contractors actually perform when hired. In 2002, for example, the Pentagon was unable to account accu-rately for the total number of contractors in even one of its units—the Army.[87] Moreover, as we also reviewed earlier, lack of transparency—and, hence, accountability—exists at all levels of government and is even worse at the state and local levels.

What we do know is that the projected cost savings of contracting are disappointing. This happens largely because the fundamental assumptions posited for contract savings are violated, most often due to an absence of competition. Moreover, even when savings are claimed, they are often calculated without taking the transaction costs of the process into account.[88] These include the costs of holding competitive bidding and monitoring contracts by individual agencies. In addition, savings claimed often stem from contractors' workforces being comprised of part-time employees, so companies do not have the expense of paying for their health care benefits. This brings to mind again the sad reality that contract monitoring is totally inadequate, and its inadequacy is a true national scandal. Agencies have few contract monitors relative to the number and size of contracts, a situ-ation not helped by the paucity of monitoring positions to oversee compliance. This will have to change during your career, as billions of dollars are going out agency doors without sufficient accountability, and you may be a part of remedying this situation at some point.

Granted, all this has prompted a rethinking of contracting out and a movement toward what is known as "insourcing" of previously privatized functions and services. As noted earlier, the Obama administration has focused on this with some success. Indeed, "insourcing has...gained traction in the federal government, as agencies includ-ing the Internal Revenue Service, U.S. Army, Department of Homeland Security, and Department of Defense are increasingly bringing contractor jobs back to the public sec-tor to successfully save money and reduce debt," after finding "problems with service quality and lack of cost savings when the service was privatized."[89] So have some states and localities. As Mildred Warner discovered, "From 2002 to 2007 the rates [of contract-ing and insourcing] were about equal (new contracts out were 11 percent, contracting back in was 12 percent)."[90]

Nevertheless, you should not conclude from this that you will be able to avoid participation in some way in the "contract state."[91] There are circumstances when contracting is imposed for political reasons on agencies, even when it is unwise or even nefarious. Less pejoratively, contracting may be the only option available, because agencies cannot or should not build in-house capacity due to a lack of competitive salaries with the private sector. Moreover, from a market perspective, contracting can work well if, among other things, competition among a sufficient number of bidders exists; seasonal variations in service are anticipated and a full-time workforce would sit idle during parts of the year; true "arms-length" relationships exist between government officials and contractors; outcomes can be clearly specified and progress measured; awarding contracts does not create future monopolies because of the size of capital investment costs; and service interruptions from strikes and other work stoppages will not harm public health or safety.

In addition, and contrary to the fears of many, preliminary research by Anna Amirkhanyan, Hyun Joon Kim, and Kristina Lambright finds that citizen participation in contracting decisions is quite good, at least in the five counties they studied in New York, Maryland, and Virginia.[92] They find, for example, that local governments and their nonprofit and for-profit contractors dealing with health and human services use a broad array of public participation mechanisms. Private contractors tend to take the lead in seeking client feedback, with the objective of improving customer satisfaction and overall program performance. Counties, on the other hand, are more active in convening advisory boards and public hearings and, in some cases, involving citizens in the contract renewal process. Amirkhanyan and her colleagues also find a lot of evidence that citizen feedback actually influences the implementation of contracts—in terms of staffing, rules, new services, and eligibility. However, they have found little evidence so far of the "general public" participating in or affecting the implementation of these services.

Still, much more research needs to be done on this and other aspects of outsourcing to understand the generalizability of these findings. And doing so is imperative. As Trevor Brown, Matthew Potoski, and David Van Slyke argue, to build a sense of common purpose informed by democratic constitutional values in the compensatory state, you also have to align these market considerations with legal values—such as equality of treatment, integrity of the bidding process, and transparency—and citizen and stakeholder preferences.[93]

Recapitalizing Personnel Assets

Coming out of the 2007–09 Great Recession is not the best time to examine hiring at any level of government. Still, you must go into the public service with a sense of both realism and optimism due to the longer-term trends. As you look around the country over the past two to three years, you see that budget difficulties and projections such as those discussed in chapter 2 and that we will cover with added detail in chapter 8 have had seriously negative effects on public employment, employee salaries, job security, and morale. You will recall that we addressed the political reasons for this unfavorable context in chapter 5, as well as some potential strategies for you to use to improve employee morale. Still, you will face three serious challenges that could actually be turned into *opportunities* to recruit and retain a quality agency workforce. These include (1) the graying of the workforce, (2) reducing pay classification obstacles to recruiting and retaining talented workers, and (3) reducing remaining pay and benefit inequities.

The Graying of the Workforce as Challenge and Opportunity

As we have reviewed, the challenges of the aging of the workforce are clear for public agencies. Let us fill in that statement with some additional numbers. In 2012, approximately 263,000 federal careerists were 60 years of age or older, and these numbers will continue to grow over the next ten years. Moreover, the over-60 crowd is only the tip of the retirement iceberg in the federal government. Roughly 650,000 federal workers are in their 50s. And historically, federal employees in their late 50s leave the civil service soon after they become retirement-eligible. Before the 2007–09 financial crisis, employees in their 50s accounted for roughly half of all federal retirements. By 2013, the number had dropped to 35 percent. So, during the past five years, tens of thousands of employees in their late 50s who might have otherwise left the federal workforce decided to stay. That leaves a huge backlog of employees ready to retire.[94] Indeed, the Government Accountability Office reported in 2014 that about 30 percent of federal employees on the job at the end of fiscal year 2011 would be eligible to retire by 2016—58 percent of whom were in senior-level positions.[95]

Moreover, in some specializations and agencies, the challenge will be acute. By 2016, nearly 45 percent of employees at the Department of Housing and Urban Development and the Small Business Administration will be eligible to retire, while two-thirds of all administrative law judges reviewing disability claim decisions at the Social Security Administration will be eligible to retire.[96] Likewise, at the state and local government levels, agency workforces are challenged by retirements, though not as much, as they generally have younger workforces. For example, the proportion of federal employees under the age of 29 has decreased since 1975 from 20 percent to 7 percent in 2013, with the average age of the federal workforce near 50 years old.[97] This, compared to 25 percent of the private sector workforce being under age 29 in 2013.[98] In contrast, 12 and 15 percent of local and state government employees, respectively, are under the age of 29. Still, about 36 percent of local and state government workers are over the age of 50, compared with only 24 percent of private sector workers and 26 percent of workers overall.[99] Some analysts argue that without increasing and retaining the number of younger employees in government service at all its levels, the facility, comfort level, and ability with new technology that agencies need will elude them and reduce their efficiency and effectiveness.[100] And well-trained graduates of public administration programs will be especially well-positioned to take on this challenge.

The graying of the public sector also offers an opportunity to align government workforces better with contemporary needs, especially if SHCP is aggressively pursued. This might, in turn, help reduce opposition to the reconceptualizing of purpose, reconnecting with citizens and stakeholders, and redefining of administrative rationality that we have been reviewing in this book. At the same time, the talents of retiring careerists might yet be re-harnessed for public purposes. Illustrative is the Office of Management and Budget's 2012 draft rule under which those employees eligible for retirement and meeting certain requirements could work part-time and receive half of their pension. While on the job, they would spend 20 percent of their time in "mentoring activities" with the employees who would step into their positions when they completely retire. The public comments for this proposed program showed employees eager to take advantage of this opportunity.[101]

Incredibly, in light of these circumstances, federal agency human resource professionals recently surveyed said "their agencies aren't planning to invest in [succession planning]. And even where they are taking action, too many agency managers are taking a piecemeal, 'siloed' approach to succession planning, according to experts who parsed the survey results."[102] To be sure, new directives from the Office of Management and Budget were launched in 2014 to link better what is called HRstat software to data collection efforts under the Government Performance and Results Modernization Act. Designed to cut down on multiple and largely static annual human resource trend reporting and to provide better real-time management of these data, HRstat involves quarterly review of such things as hiring, retention, and retirement trends. Even if fully funded by Congress, however, this effort first involves getting government agreement on what data to collect and in what format, a process that will take time and negotiation.

Still, HRstat is designed along the lines of two rather successful IT management software initiatives by the Obama administration—TechStat and PortfolioStat. TechStat reviews have been used to turn around failed IT projects, and PortfolioStat has helped managers get a better sense of coordinating IT purchases. Were you to join a federal agency, you might be involved in helping to design and implement any of these three initiatives, or to manage your program better through their use. Moreover, you are likely to be involved in or affected by similar efforts in states and localities.

Revamping Pay Classification Systems

Pay classification systems have long dominated public personnel management in the United States. First adopted by the city of Chicago in 1912 and then by the federal government in the Classification Act of 1923, the pay classification system was yet another effort by early progressive reformers to introduce scientific management to the federal government and to take power away from corrupt political machines and their minions in Congress. The 1923 act established in the federal government the principle of classifying like jobs together, standardizing pay for those positions, and providing common rating systems for performance. It also established the principle of rank-in-the-position (rather than in-the-person) in a further effort to bring a measure of equity to the system.

Problems in the administration of the act were uncovered in evaluations done in 1929 and 1935, however, sparking great levels of criticism of the system. But it was not until the Hoover Commission issued a biting report that Congress took action in the Classification Act of 1949. Although not considered to have taken great strides toward reform, this act did do some important things, including creating the General Schedule (GS) pay classification system (GS-1 to GS-18). Moreover, grades GS-16 to GS-18 were called "supergrades" reserved for top career civil servants. You will find similar pay classification systems based on the act's principles today in all 50 states.[103]

Additional reform would not happen again regarding the pay classification system until the 1970s. As covered already, the CSRA of 1978 eliminated the supergrades from the GS schedule and created the SES in their stead. Thus, today, the federal GS consists of 15 pay grades for white-collar workers, over 450 job categories (or "series"), and ten steps for within-grade pay increases premised on length of service. Graduated pay increases according to years in rank have also predominated in states and localities.

But as you will learn in your coursework, the GS system has long been criticized as an obsolete approach to job and pay classification. In a 2002 report, for example, the OPM identified the GS as a "system whose time has come, and gone."[104] The report noted that at the time the Classification Act of 1949 was enacted, "over 70 percent of Federal white-collar jobs consisted of clerical work" that was easy to classify.[105] But, as we covered earlier, for decades, "knowledge work" has since dominated public employment, and these jobs are less well defined and distinguishable from others.[106] And especially critical since the terrorist attacks on 9/11 and the IT revolution has been increasing the number and quality of federal government hires in so-called "STEMM"-related positions. These are professionals in the science, technology, engineering, mathematics, and medical professions. Indeed, in fiscal year 2013, nearly 40 percent of all new hires were in STEMM professions, nearly 80 percent of all hires were in national defense and security-related agencies, and 45 percent were veterans.[107]

A second area of concern is that the rigid nature of the GS system impedes organizational change in an era when agencies have to change in order to merely stay even in effectiveness. Thus, efforts at what is called "broadbanding"—that is, combining and reducing the number of pay grades—have been accompanied by efforts to reduce automatic step-in-grade increases based on length of service. In a 1995 publication, the National Academy of Public Administration noted that, "Broader bands allow managers to shift their workforce to new roles more easily."[108] Broadbanding also obviates the need to make fine distinctions in levels of job difficulty and responsibility. As a result, managers can play a larger role in classification decisions. It also provides recruitment advantages, as qualified recruits can be offered salaries anywhere within the specified range rather than only at step one of the position grade. As personnel scholar J. Edward Kellough argues, "The challenge is to get the number of pay grades 'just right'; that is, not too many and not too few. How many should there be? The number of grades should match the number of meaningfully different levels of work—a subjective determination, to say the least."[109]

Yet another criticism of the GS is that it is insufficiently sensitive to the market. This is in part due to its preeminent focus on "internal equity"—that is, on ensuring that pay levels are the same for jobs with equivalent levels of difficulty and responsibility. As OPM has observed, "Labor market shortages and excesses are described and analyzed in terms of occupations, skills, specialties, and locations, not grade level."[110] Needed, according to OPM, is a pay system that provides a better balance between internal equity, external equity (i.e., relative to the market price for an occupation), and "contribution" equity (i.e., individual performance rather than length of service). All this suggests that, regardless of what level of government you join during your career in public service, you will face these challenges and watch—and perhaps help design—at least the gradual transformation of today's GS system for the needs of a twenty-first-century workforce.

Redressing Pay and Benefit Inequities

One of the more contentious issues on the employee "rights" side of the personnel ledger over the past two decades has involved pay and benefit inequities. And as a public manager, you will be front and center in dealing with them as an employee or supervisor. These issues focus on disparities between the public and private sectors, genders, and sexual orientation. In terms of public–private sector differentials, and as we have noted, the traditional view—some say "covenant"—was that public employees received lower pay than in the private sector in exchange for more job security and better pensions. We have already covered how two aspects of this covenant—job security and pensions—are eroding. What remains is noting how pay differentials are not as clear-cut as they were years ago. Although "dueling" analyses drive the discourse about these issues today, the bottom line is that those at lower levels of the GS (clerical and other support skills) receive higher wages than their private sector counterparts, while those at the higher GS levels requiring greater skills are less well compensated.

Turning to gender-based pay discrepancies in both the public and private sectors, Congress sought to address pay disparities by enacting the Equal Pay Act of 1963. Yet, despite much progress in the interim, a half century later women in full-time, yearly jobs are paid approximately 77 percent of the pay received by their male counterparts. This amounts to a pay gap of nearly $11,500 annually. Much the same occurs in the states, although there are differences among them. A 2011 American Community Survey indicates that the largest gaps exist in Alaska, Louisiana, Utah, Washington, and Wyoming. What is more, women of color do even worse in pay comparisons, with African Americans and Hispanics earning 69 percent and 58 percent as much as all men, respectively, and 64 percent and 54 percent of all non-Hispanic men.[111] With the number of single female-headed homes spiraling, this disparity in pay has both intra and intergenerational implications that cannot be ignored.

Given these continuing disparities, the Obama administration pressed successfully for the Lilly Ledbetter Fair Pay Act of 2009, which amended the Civil Rights Act of 1964. More recently, the administration proposed the Paycheck Fairness Act to address several shortcomings in the Equal Pay Act. Among other things, the act gives the US Department of Labor greater authority to gather information from private organizations, including requiring employers to disclose differentials in pay grades for men and women employed in similar jobs. This is known as a "blaming-and-shaming" policy tool, one predicated on the assumption that the potential for embarrassment and even lost revenue if consumers react negatively to statistics showing discrimination will alter employer behavior.

Disagreements reign over the source or sources of pay disparity. Since we are not yet a "gender-blind" society, some pay disparity is attributable to discrimination. Moreover, some gender-based pay disparity certainly arises because of gender stereotyping. For instance, some employers implicitly assume that women with children are less commit-ted to their jobs than men, that women without children are likely to have them and leave the workforce, and, thus, that investments in training women are more likely to be wasted. But as you will learn in your coursework, a variety of competing explanations exist falling short of conscious discrimination by an employer that might explain gender-based wage and promotion disparities. These may be related, for example, to women not entering certain professions historically (e.g., math and science) or having been "pink-ghettoized" in others (e.g., nursing, clerical, and teaching), leaving a legacy of disparity today based on occupation.

Thus, although significant strides have been made over the past 40 years, and espe-cially within government agencies, much remains to be done. Research still shows that women are paid less than their male counterparts regardless of controlling for occupa-tion, industry, years of work experience, job tenure, number of work hours, time-off for childbearing, race, marital status, and education.[112] As such, being watchful for both overt discrimination and more subtle patterns of discriminatory behavior that are less conscious but real is important for you as a public manager concerned about democratic constitutional values of fundamental equity. Some of these factors may be beyond your control (e.g., the educational and occupational choices made by employees), but helping to ameliorate the results of these choices through, for example, aggressive personal or institutional mentoring is not.

Finally, regardless of the level of government in which you serve, your agency will no doubt find that gaining equal benefits for the partners and spouses of LGB employees is a major focus for public agencies trying to attract and retain first-rate employees. As of the end of 2013, 17 state governments and the District of Columbia recognized same-sex marriages, with an 18th—Utah—appealing a federal judge's ruling to overturn the state's same-sex marriage ban. At the same time, 37 states and the District of Columbia banned discrimination in employment based on sexual orientation, but only 16 states and the District of Columbia did so by law rather than by executive order. These jurisdictions account for 40 percent of the US population. Meanwhile, Colorado, Nevada, Oregon, and Wisconsin recognize civil unions, domestic partnerships, or other legal status for same-sex couples. Waiting in the wings are at least 31 cases about to hit judicial dockets petitioning to allow gays and lesbians to marry.[113]

Renewed salience at the federal level today stems largely from the US Supreme Court in *US v. Windsor* (133 S. Ct. 2675 [2013]) striking down the 1996 federal Defense of Marriage Act (DOMA) as unconstitutional. DOMA allowed states to deny recognition of same-sex marriages performed legally in other states, thus banning federal benefits for legally married gay couples.[114] In the aftermath of *Windsor*, several federal agencies announced that same-sex couples would be eligible for federal benefits, even if they live in states that do not recognize same-sex marriages.[115]

Likewise, the Internal Revenue Service announced that legally married same-sex couples "will be treated as married for all federal tax purposes," including for income tax filing, gift and estate taxes, individual retirement accounts, and other tax regulations where marriage is a factor.[116] Meanwhile, the Department of Health and Human Services issued guidelines stating that beneficiaries of Medicare can have equal access to coverage in a nursing home where their spouse lives, regardless of their sexual orientation.[117] More broadly, the OPM proposed extending the Federal Employees Health Benefits Program to domestic partners of *both* same-sex and opposite-sex couples to compete better with the private sector for talent.[118]

As of mid-2014, both same-sex and opposite-sex domestic partners who meet certain qualifications are able to receive some federal employee benefits—for example, using sick leave to care for an ill family member. However, gender aside, domestic partners cannot receive such major benefits as retirement survivor annuities and health insurance coverage. Further complicating the issue, some benefits that are available to domestic partners apply only to same-sex, not opposite-sex, partners—for example, eligibility for long-term care insurance. Thus, with battles still raging in the courts and at all levels of government, staying on top of issues and decisions related to same-sex marriage and domestic partners and adapting to the voluntary initiatives of private sector competitors for talent will be critical for you and your federal, state, or local agency in hiring the most talented workers possible.

Finally, and related to LGB health, privacy, and equity issues but affecting all employees, you also are likely to run pell-mell into the complexities of implementing the Genetic Information Nondiscrimination Act of 2008.[119] The act prohibits the use of genetic testing information in health insurance and employment decisions. This precludes your agency from denying health benefits to, or raising premiums for, employees on the basis of any predisposition to health problems that genetic testing might identify. The same prohibition exists against using genetic information in hiring, job placement, or promotion decisions that you make or that affect you as an employee. During your career, and especially as new breakthroughs in genonomic health research occur, you may help sort out these issues in ways that protect privacy and equity concerns, apply them as a public manager within these constraints, or have need yourself of protection from abuse.

Conclusion

You should leave this chapter with a general sense for the significant personnel challenges, choices, and opportunities facing public managers today. You will be called upon to align people with purposes in the midst of antigovernment rhetoric, shifting demographics, and pressures to diversify agency workforces and ensure constitutional rights for all. This reconciliation of bureaucratic and democratic administration will have to be done while competing with a private sector offering higher pay for badly needed specialists, amid calls for more outer checks than inner checks on agency discretion, and in circumstances where managerial updates to existing management systems are sorely needed. All these issues become critical as you engage in implementing policy in today's compensatory state, regardless of what level of government you serve. Indeed, in that process, the changing ecology, wicked policy, organizational, interorganizational, and personnel matters we have covered so far all come together. But before addressing your role in policy implementation, you still need a broad understanding of how the political, economic, and technical dynamics involved in stewarding the nation's financial resources interact with the others to affect policy implementation. It is to that topic that we turn next in chapter 8.

CHAPTER 8

Stewarding a Nation's Treasure

When you began this book, the thought of developing, implementing, and analyzing public budgets and finances as a public servant might have excited you. Hopefully, it still does! After all, could any single document express a nation, state, city, or agency's priorities, commitments, and concerns more than the budget it annually offers to its citizens? That budgets are the ultimate policy documents and set priorities is beyond dispute. But to the extent that those priorities are clear to citizens is problematic. Budgets can be opaque, laden with accounting gimmicks, difficult to navigate, and maddeningly unconnected from the policy outcomes sought.

To see how and why this is the case, we will review in this chapter the evolution of our thinking in the United States about what your public budgeting and finance professors may call "macro-budgeting" and "micro-budgeting." Macro-budgeting deals with the impact of fiscal (taxing and spending) and monetary (interest rates and money supply) policies on the nation's economic performance and sets the overall context within which micro-budgeting takes place. In contrast, micro-budgeting deals with the politics of budgeting within and across agencies, as politicians are cross-pressured to cut spending while simultaneously protecting favored constituencies.

As Sven Steinmo observes, the fragmented American political system makes the targeting of benefits (tax cuts and services) much easier than ensuring the general sharing of costs for broad benefits such as universal health care.[1] What is more, and as we reviewed in chapter 5, this is exacerbated by the tendency of the American political system to mask what it spends by using an arcane tax code rather than creating new programs on the books. Thus, some of the major financial challenges facing your generation of public managers will be finding ways to help frame, implement, and evaluate policies and programs at the micro-budgeting level within the macro-budgetary constraints imposed by unsustainable budget trends at the national level.

As public finance experts Daniel Mullins and John Mikesell argue, sorely complicating your task is that the federal government has been guilty of "intergenerational irresponsibility" for decades.[2] Between 1973 and 2014, for example, the federal budget has been in balance only four times. During that period, federal expenditures as a share of gross domestic product (GDP) have averaged 21 percent, while tax revenues have averaged only 18 percent.[3] And as we noted in chapters 2 and 5, these deficits have cumulatively bequeathed to your generation of public managers a $17.9 trillion national debt in 2014.[4] Moreover, because intergovernmental transfers of federal dollars comprise significant portions of subnational government revenues in the compensatory state, you will be affected by these trends—and the solutions offered to them—no matter where your public service career takes you.

As such, you will again be dealing with continuing pressures to *reconceptualize the purpose* of budgeting, with much more of a focus going forward on advancing economically sustainable policies. You will also have to *reconnect with citizens* by thinking about and involving them more systematically than budgeting offices have done in the past in budget development. This, in turn, will mean continually *redefining the administrative rationality* that has driven public budgeting and finance offices for decades. The nation has undergone alternating shifts from decentralization to centralization of budget processes and back again in efforts to impose rationality on an inherently political process. The focus today increasingly is on performance-based or outcomes-based budgeting. Likewise, the pressure to *reengage resources* and *recapitalize personnel assets* in today's compensatory state will mean—at the macro-budgeting level—fine-tuning revenue and spending forecasting techniques and—at the micro-budgeting level—incorporating more sophisticated ways to link budgets to the strategic planning efforts of your agency. But with them, as well, will come conflicts among the alternative purposes for which budgeting has been used historically: control, accountability for stewardship, and planning and evaluation.

You should leave this chapter with a good sense for how and why the politics of macro- and micro-budgeting interact not only to shape the overall context of public management in the United States, but for how they interact with the other challenges, choices, and opportunities we have reviewed in prior chapters. Garnered, too, should be an appreciation for the sources of our nation's current financial dilemma, as well as how and why tools of the rationality project of bureaucratic administration have typically come up short in our recent efforts to deal with it. Noting, too, how tools of democratic administration are being incorporated in public budgeting, you will then be prepared to deal with the politics of the implementation process that we will cover in depth in chapter 9.

Reconceptualizing Purpose

Since the nation's founding, the purposes of both macro-budgeting and micro-budgeting have been repeatedly reconceptualized. In terms of the former, these purposes at the national level have ranged from (1) controlling expenditures with little overall concern about the macroeconomic effects of budgeting, to (2) using budgets and monetary policy as countercyclical forces to the business cycle, to (3) emphasizing tax cuts and using interest rates to give economic stability to the nation, and now to (4) finding a path to a sustainable economic future for America.[5] Wrought in the process of these shifts, however, has been the national debt time bomb mentioned earlier that will be full of challenges, critical choices, and opportunities for your generation of public managers in the years ahead.

Budgeting for Balance and Control

You might be surprised to learn that balanced budgets were sacrosanct for Americans during much of US history. Between 1789 and 1835, for example, continuous surpluses paid off the nation's debt from the Revolutionary War. In turn, between 1835 and 1860, the federal government rapidly paid off incurred debt, with the only significant deficits occurring in the 1840s as the result of a devastating three-year depression. Otherwise, seven years of consistent budget surpluses incurred between 1850 and 1857 paid off all the nation's debt from the Mexican–American War. Debt rose, of course, during the Civil War, but war's end almost immediately brought retirement of about one-third of that debt.

But things began shifting at the micro-budgeting level in the mid-1880s after Congress decentralized appropriations authority from a single committee—the House Appropriations Committee— to eight major authorization committees. As foes of this reform warned, decentralization of spending powers to authorizing committees eliminated two important checks on spending in one fell swoop. The first was the spending check that the House Appropriations Committee historically had imposed on authorizing committees. The latter could start new programs (i.e., authorize them) but could not fund them (i.e., appropriate money for them). In the process, a second check disappeared: the single point of accountability that the Appropriations Committee provided. This made transparency of spending more difficult in a Gilded Age noted for members of Congress being "bought" by private interests such as the railroad industry. Major intervening events occurred over the next few decades to increase federal spending through this decentralized committee structure. These included military expeditions to facilitate westward expansion, the Spanish–American War, the enactment of the federal income tax in the Sixteenth Amendment to the US Constitution in 1913, and World War I. Spending as a proportion of GDP rose by 50 percent between 1885 and 1893 alone, turning a sizeable 1885 budget surplus into a deficit by 1894, following the Panic of 1893.

You will also recall that the early progressive reform movement arose in reaction to all this. Even profligate elected officials began noting that spending increases were unsustainable and that elected officials could not control themselves. Their efforts, begun in the bureaus of municipal research (BMR) that we discussed in chapter 1—and with spadework done by Teddy Roosevelt's Keep Commission between 1905 and 1909 and President Taft's Commission on Economy and Efficiency between 1910 and 1913—culminated in the Budget and Accounting Act (BAA) of 1921. Enacted immediately in the aftermath of the spending binge from World War I that piled additional debt on the nation, the BAA is most famous for creating a first-of-its-kind national executive budget, a model associated with the New York Bureau of Municipal Research and replicated in major cities across the country as part of the BMR movement. Also important, and as covered in chapter 5, was its creation of the Bureau of the Budget, placed at the time in the US Treasury Department. As we noted, it was later moved to the Executive Office of the President in 1939 and then renamed the Office of Management and Budget (OMB) in 1970 by President Richard Nixon (see more below).

Immediately prior to the enactment of the BAA, and related to the decentralization of appropriation decisions to authorizing committees that we just reviewed, individual agencies worked directly with their authorizing committees to pass their budgets, without any coordination with the White House. The BAA, however, required the president to put forth what is known as an "executive budget" to which Congress would respond. The act also created the aforementioned General Accounting Office (today, the Government Accountability Office). The scope of its responsibilities have evolved from inspecting vouchers to conducting financial, managerial, and performance audits and special studies.

In combination with Congress' recentralization of funding authority to each body's appropriations committee, balanced budgets made a comeback. Economic growth unprecedented since the Gilded Age in the 1920s did not hurt this effort. Produced was a series of 11 consecutive budget surpluses between 1920 and 1930. However, all this changed as the Great Depression of the 1930s brought a nation to its knees, and a new economic theory called Keynesian economics entered the policy and political fray.

Budgeting as a Countercyclical Device

It is hard for us today to conceive of federal government spending being as low as 3 percent of GDP. But that is what it was until roughly the 1930s in America. If you think about it, though, the absence of a federal income tax until 1913 meant that the federal government had relatively little to spend, reliant as it was on import tariffs. Nor was the idea of what your professors will call "fiscal policy"—using the taxing and spending policies of the United States as a tool for managing the overall economy—discussed until the 1930s. Moreover, until then, only 3 percent of Americans paid income tax.

Absent until 1913, as well, was the Federal Reserve System we know so well today that develops monetary policy for the nation.[6] As you may know, monetary policy is the process by which a country controls the supply and rate of growth of money in circulation, with the aim of maintaining stability of prices and full employment. Today, the Federal Reserve System (henceforth, the Fed) is comprised of a Board of Governors (the Federal Reserve Board), the Federal Open Market Committee (FOMC), 12 regional Federal Reserve Banks, privately owned member banks, and a number of advisory councils. The Fed chairman and vice-chair are appointed by the president and confirmed by the US Senate.

The FOMC, per se, is responsible for setting monetary policy and consists of the seven members of the Board of Governors and five of the twelve Federal Reserve Bank presidents. The latter include the president of the Federal Reserve Bank of New York and four others who rotate through one-year terms. Unlike in other nations, the Fed is not affiliated with the treasury ministry—in this case, the US Treasury—and is an independent body. The president does not approve its decisions, it receives no funding from Congress, and the terms of the Board of Governors are staggered so that they span multiple presidencies. This was done so—among other things—it would not become politicized to the point of increasing the money supply in the run-up to elections for incumbent reelection purposes. Indeed, one job of the Fed is to "take the punch bowl away" when the spending "party" becomes too raucous.

Still, with the share of federal revenues and expenditures so miniscule as a proportion of GDP in the late 1920s, there was neither the wherewithal nor the political will for the federal government to do anything more than seek budget balance and control over how its budget was expended. With the Great Depression of the 1930s resulting in unemployment for nearly one-third of the working age population in the United States, however, not acting to intervene in the economy became political suicide—as President Herbert Hoover learned in 1932. Enter President Franklin Roosevelt, who reluctantly accepted budget deficits, and later an economic theory offered by the legendary economist, John Maynard Keynes, which turned budget deficits into *good* things when incurred to stimulate a faltering economy.

Under Keynesian economics, the government acts as a "countercyclical" device to smooth out the business cycle. If the economy slows down, the federal government cuts taxes and increases spending to pump more money into consumers' hands in the hopes that they will spend it. Likewise, on the monetary side, the Fed buys bonds, thus further expanding the money supply for consumer spending. This spending, in turn, has what economists call a "multiplier effect," meaning that someone spends part or all of the additional dollars in circulation to buy something and that seller, in turn, buys something, and so on. Conversely, when an economy is "overheating" with too many dollars chasing too few goods to buy, thus pushing up prices, fiscal and monetary policy should raise taxes, cut spending, increase interest rates, and sell securities to take money out of the hands of consumers until the economy stabilizes (i.e., inflation comes down).

Thus, with Keynesian economic theory as its justification and with fears that unemployment due to a recession would soar after World War II much like it did after World War I, unbalanced budgets became legitimate. Indeed, Keynesian theory became, in effect, ensconced in law with the enactment of the Employment Act of 1946. A vague target of "maximum employment, production, and purchasing power" was set, and US fiscal and monetary policies were aimed at avoiding recession. You should also appreciate the political appeal of Keynesian deficits to elected officials: increasing spending would go into projects that members of Congress could target for their districts and claim credit for in the next election. Still, any spending that increased budget deficits when unemployment was under control was deemed unwise. Indeed, if what is called "structural unemployment" occurs, running up additional budget deficits as we have done for decades is especially unwise. Structural unemployment occurs when unemployment is caused by fundamental changes in demand patterns, obsolescence, or technology breakthroughs and cannot be offset by fiscal or monetary policy.

Budgeting to Stimulate Savings and Investments

By the late 1970s, two events occurred simultaneously that, according to Keynesian economic theory, could not happen together: the nation witnessed both double-digit inflation and double-digit unemployment. There are a variety of reasons that could help explain this anomaly, including an unprecedented influx of women into the job market and two Arab oil shocks that reverberated in higher prices throughout the economy. But for proponents of what was called "supply-side economics," the problem was that Keynesian economics was not incorporating the impact of "marginal" tax rates and business regulations on work and investment incentives. The higher you raise marginal tax rates and regulatory costs, they argued, the lower the amount of tax revenues you actually get and the more unemployment and underinvestment rises.

If you think about it in the pure utility-maximizing world we reviewed in chapter 6, this makes sense at a certain level. If you are taxed at, say, a 70 percent rate rather than 30 percent on every additional dollar you might earn—that is, the marginal tax rate— you may be less inclined to work or invest to reap these gains.[7] At another level, of course, we work and invest for a variety of other reasons—necessity, ego satisfaction, a sense of worth, family responsibilities—regardless of tax rates. So, too, do we invest in new businesses and plant equipment in this manner, oftentimes ignoring the odds against success. In addition, even if it existed, no one knew exactly where that "disincentive point" was to work or invest.

Its validity aside, supply-side economics was the perfect political platform for Republican Ronald Reagan. It brought into his camp so-called "blue-collar ethnic Democrats" with socially conservative leanings by arguing that tax cuts would trickle down to them. In a "rising economic tide lifts all boats" theme reminiscent of Frederick Taylor's in the early twentieth century and President Kennedy's in the 1960s, he argued that new business investments would mean more jobs for blue-collar workers, as well as decreases in inflation. Tax rate cuts, of course, would also keep the wealthier in his coalition satisfied. Moreover, by exempting Social Security and Medicare from spending cuts and pursuing the largest peacetime increase in defense spending in history, he kept senior citizens and defense hawks in tow.[8]

Regardless, with the economy on an upswing that he attributed to supply-side economics, Reagan swept 49 states in his 1984 reelection campaign. What you may not realize, however, is that after deficits mounted following his initial success in cutting taxes in 1981, Reagan acquiesced in four additional tax increases before he left office in 1988. For example, in 1982, Reagan accepted a tax increase that reversed approximately one-third of the individual rate cuts he gained in 1981, and in 1983, his administration increased payroll taxes for the Social Security and Medicare trust funds. Then, in 1986, the administration compromised with a coalition of Democrats in Congress to pass the Tax Reform Act. This act tried successfully, among other things, to eliminate many tax subsidies, loan guarantees, deductions, and exemptions. Since then, however, tax expenditure losses totaling approximately $1 trillion (as we will see later) have crept back into the tax code to advance further what we identified in chapter 5 as the "submerged state."[9]

Overall, and most significant for us today, even the "structural deficit constraint" mentioned above fell by the wayside. Supply-siders did not worry about deficits, arguing that the United States was nowhere near historical levels deficit-wise and that the debt incurred was merely an intragenerational transaction where one set of Americans owed money to another. Moreover, Reagan's two terms in office produced a change in the *composition* of tax revenue toward payroll (and, hence, working and middle-class earners) and away from higher earners, including cutting tax rates on capital gains and dividends.[10] In the process, federal revenue as a percent of GDP fell from 19.6 percent in fiscal year 1981 to 17.3 percent in fiscal year 1984, before rising to 18.4 percent by fiscal year 1989. Yet, expenditures remained at approximately 21 percent of GDP.

Some argued that the Reaganites were using a "starve the government beast" strategy. Deficits were not a concern of the administration, because less revenue and higher deficits would mean that higher spending would be more difficult to support politically. Moreover, deficits actually transferred future resources to bond holders (at higher interest rates), which benefitted most higher-income segments of the population. Rationale aside, the deficits occasioned by this strategy resulted in the national debt rising during Reagan's presidency from approximately $900 billion to $2.8 trillion.[11] Next, of course, came the dashing—some say squandering—of budget surplus projections (discussed in chapter 5) as a result of the United States fighting two wars (Iraq and Afghanistan), enacting two large tax cuts, and trying to reboot economically after the Great Recession of 2007–09. US debt held by other nations soared, too, affecting foreign policy. Thus, bequeathed to your generation of public managers are the public budgeting and finance stewardship challenges, choices, and opportunities that only a $17.9 trillion national debt can afford.

Redefining Administrative Rationality

Although these macro-budgeting developments are important in their own right, you also need to understand the micro-budgeting adjustments they occasioned. In addition, you need to know how these efforts to redefine administrative rationality, in turn, helped to create the macro-budgeting challenges, choices, and opportunities we just discussed. Once again, these budget reforms have typically been geared to the technical rather than the political side of the reform ledger. Yet, as Aaron Wildavsky put it nearly three decades ago, the "budget lies at the heart [of politics.] . . . The victories and defeats, the compromises and the bargains, the realms of agreement and the spheres of conflict in regard to the role of . . . government in our society all appear in the budget."[12] Thus, although rationality-based efforts gain traction in certain places at different points in time, they fail as a universal prescription for administrative reform at the micro-budgeting level. To see why, let us examine two major sets of efforts since the 1960s to rationalize technically the budget process and curb profligacy: (1) combining planning, programming, and budget systems and (2) linking budgets to performance as part of a strategic planning process.

Redefining by Linking Program Planning, Budgets, and Performance

As we have reviewed in earlier chapters, early progressive budget reformers such as Frederick Cleveland stressed that inefficiencies—broadly defined to include social inefficiency—had to be wrung out of existing systems through budget controls, the first being control through "line-item" budgeting.[13] During the early 1900s, this meant that legislatures at all levels of government focused on what the government spent on, for example, paper, desks, police weapons and uniforms, but not on what these items were used for or whether they accomplished program goals. The key questions were, "Was the money used as the legislature intended?" and "Could cost savings and efficiencies be realized through more effective allocation of funding received?" Nor was any element of planning ahead—or what we would today call "forecasting"—involved.

As you will learn in your coursework, line-item budgeting continues to remain popular—because it affords control over expenditures and understandability. In fact, it is inescapable as the fundamental element for assuring financial accountability, with subsequent reforms really attempts at overlays of line-item budgeting. Indeed, during your career in the public service, you will also encounter the legacy of efforts to remedy its shortcomings. After all, just knowing that the resources going into an organization (i.e., the dollar inputs) are done legally and spent as prescribed for items tells us nothing about whether they actually produce what we want done as a society.

Entering first in this reform legacy were "performance budgets" directed at managerial efficiency. These were followed by what are known as "program budgets," which are designed to promote program effectiveness and outcomes.[14] Today, as you will learn in your coursework and as alluded to earlier in this chapter, the dominant approach is a return to performance budgeting: a truncated reform program directed toward managerial efficiency and limited use of outcomes measures.

More precisely, reforms emerged prominently with the two Hoover Commissions' focus on government reorganization in the late 1940s and early 1950s and with their claims that performance budgeting was preferable to line-item budgeting. This was followed by the Budget and Accounting Procedures Act of 1950, which mandated performance budgeting for the entire federal government, and then the Planning, Programming, and Budgeting System (PPBS) initiative launched by the Kennedy and Johnson administrations in the 1960s. PPBS was subsequently replaced in focus by management by objectives (MBO) in the Nixon administration, only to be replaced by zero-based budgeting (ZBB) in the Carter administration. This, in turn, was followed by extensive OMB oversight by the Reagan and Clinton administrations, and finally by President George W. Bush's Program Assessment Rating Tool (PART) as part of the President's Management Agenda (PMA). And marbled among these were the 1993 Clinton-Gore National Performance Review and the aforementioned Government Performance and Results Act (GPRA), which were more management approaches than budget reforms.

Regardless, were you just finishing your career today in the federal government, you would have witnessed a host of "rationality-based" budgeting reforms. Nor would you have escaped them during a career in state or local government (where many of them originated). In 1998, for example, the National Advisory Council on State and Local Budgeting identified four principles that had been developed over the past three decades, with accompanying practices designed to "enhance the [technical] quality of decision making."[15] These budget principles revolved around (1) establishing goals, (2) identifying approaches for goal achievement, (3) allocating required resources, and (4) evaluating outcomes. What proponents of techniques such as PPBS, ZBB, and MBO that were premised on these principles did not talk about was something else you would have experienced during your career: the political control rationales behind them that stimulated kickback from those losing power.

As alluded to above, for example, the Kennedy administration introduced PPBS extensively into the Department of Defense with two aims. The first and more technical side of the equation was to establish a measurement tool for ranking alternative weapons systems in terms of cost-effectiveness. The second and more political side of PPBS was an effort by Defense Secretary Robert McNamara, briefly president of Ford Motor Company, to bring the Pentagon's weapons procurement system under his control. This system historically was controlled by the individual military services and their congressional allies.

Although McNamara enjoyed some success with PPBS in reining in the services at the Department of Defense, it proved totally inadequate as implemented when President Johnson tried to extend it to the social programs of the Great Society. Professionals in those agencies were not familiar with planning and evaluation techniques or with even thinking in terms of whether or not what they were doing was having the expected impact on the clients they served. Nor was adequate direction or training provided in most instances. In addition, these programs were more geared toward providing services to needy individuals, not making choices among them regarding the best means for doing so. And aside from the inherent difficulty of defining desired results and identifying methods adequate for the different functions to which PPBS was applied, the costs of full-blown implementation for social programs were huge.

As such, substantial resistance to PPBS emerged in these agencies, as well as on Capitol Hill, with resistance by the appropriations committees in Congress becoming a death knell for PPBS in all but limited circumstances. Nor is this an uncommon result with budget reforms because of the inherent tension between budget decision-making systems that inform presidential choices and those that inform congressional decision making. The committees saw PPBS as a threat to members' existing subsystem access and influence, and insisted that proposed budgets be sent to them in PPBS *and* traditional line-item and program formats. Nor did Congress feel that only the executive branch should set priorities and, thus, circumvent legislative–executive bargaining over them.

Next up, and similarly plagued by political games and implementation difficulties, was the Nixon administration's MBO system. Borrowed again from the business sector, the general idea behind MBO was that each level of an agency would show how its activities related to the goals of agency leadership. Resources would then be allocated in an "objective" way to those activities that best aligned with top-level agency goals. What will not surprise you by now is that managers and employees framed what they wanted done in ways that fit into the overall goals of the organization.

Similarly, ZBB was developed at Texas Instruments Corporation and brought first to Georgia state government and then to Washington by President Carter.[16] ZBB initially called for program managers to start their budget proposals from scratch rather than from existing program bases. They were then to decide what they could do with varying levels of funding. More precisely, agency leaders first had to identify decision units—that is, where the basic decisions on program budgets were made. From this, they identified a program manager to analyze each decision unit. Calculated were the cost-effectiveness and efficiency of each of these units. Next, decision packages were ranked by higher-level administrators in terms of priority across all units. Those that became high-priority items were then submitted for funding and the remaining decision packages discarded.

Thus, in theory—and not unlike PPBS and MBO—ZBB was a stunning contrast to the traditional politics of "incremental budgeting" that we discussed briefly in chapter 6.[17] In this process, you will recall, agencies start from last year's budget, increase it to incorporate inflation, add a small increase, and then include an additional sum for others above them to cut (e.g., the budget office and the appropriations committees in the legislature). Equally unsurprising was its undoing because of this and failure to grasp the enormous paperwork burden imposed on programs and agencies.

For starters, the scope of budgets and the time-intensive nature of the information gathering and analyses involved—in any of these techniques—brought resistance and gaming. Program managers, for instance, would rank programs as lower priorities that they knew agency superiors or elected officials would not defund—a strategy labeled the "Washington monument" or "firehouse" strategy. They would also be content to start programs small—what budget scholars call the "camel's nose under the tent" strategy—confident that once clienteles developed around them, they would be extended. At worst, all three techniques—PPBS, MBO, and ZBB—turned into "paper-generating" exercises full of gamesmanship and took time away from more important tasks. At best, the process of thinking through programs and their relationships to one another was—and remains—valuable, and those attracting less political attention likely got better sorted out in terms of priority. Moreover, remnants of each technique survive to an extent in various agencies where they have tended to be more workable. But, it is one-size-fits-all reforms such as these that may not be effective and with which you will have to live repeatedly during your career as a public manager.

Next came efforts to impose rationality on the congressional budgeting process itself by means of the Congressional Budget and Impoundment Control Act (BICA) of 1974. Signed by Richard Nixon in the waning days of Watergate, and as summarized in Table 8.1, BICA tried to centralize the budgeting process by creating a House Budget Committee and a Senate Budget Committee, created a timetable for steps in that process, and required it be informed by multiyear projections of tax revenues and expenditures. It also provided that the Congressional Budget Office (CBO) would serve as an analytic unit to allow Congress to even the playing field with what were

Table 8.1 The Congressional Budget Process Timetable

Date	Action to Be Completed
First Monday in February	President submits budget to Congress.
February 15	Congressional Budget Office submits economic and budget outlook report to Budget Committees.
Six weeks after President submits budget	Committees submit views and estimates to Budget Committees.
April 1	Senate Budget Committee reports budget resolution.
April 15	Congress completes action on budget resolution.
May 15	Annual appropriations bills may be considered in the House, even if action on budget resolution has not been completed.
June 10	House Appropriations Committee reports last annual appropriations bill.
June 15	House completes action on reconciliation legislation (if required by budget resolution).
June 30	House completes action on annual appropriations bills.
July 15	President submits mid-session review of his budget to Congress.
October 1	Fiscal year begins.

Source: Congressional Research Service, Library of Congress, www.senate.gov/reference/resources/pdf/98-472.pdf.

perceived by critics as politicized—and, hence, less trusted—OMB projections favoring the President's preferences.

We will get to the "rough-and-tumble" politics of budget projections later in this chapter. What is critical for you to understand at this point is that although BICA created the two budget committees to relate projected revenues to projected spending and then "reconcile" them (i.e., put them in balance), they could only send reconciliation figures back to the existing appropriations committees in each house of Congress. Nor were the so-called "cardinals"—that is, chairpersons—of the appropriating committees ready to see their power of the purse shift to the House and Senate budget committees. So they doggedly fought—and continue today to fight—centralization. And because the assumptions underlying budget projections are susceptible to challenge, the cardinals had ample grounds to challenge both committees. Moreover, timetables are routinely flouted. Indeed, the Congress passed its first budget since 2009 in 2014!

As budget deficits continued to grow in subsequent years, Congress took several steps within BICA processes to try to hold them down. For example, it enacted the 1985 Balanced Budget and Emergency Deficit Control Act—more popularly known as the Gramm-Rudman-Hollings (GRH) Act—during the Reagan administration. The act included what we are all familiar with today—a sequestration component—to achieve a balanced budget by fiscal year 1991. If $36 billion in deficit cuts were not made by

Congress annually, then across-the-board cuts would be made. The problem again, however, was that GRH excluded Social Security and Medicare—two major drivers of budget deficits. So GRH soon joined its predecessors in the dustbin of disappointing budget reform efforts—and budget deficits continue to mount.[18]

As we saw briefly in chapter 5, federal revenue sources soared in the mid- to late-1990s from a propitious, technology-driven economic and, hence, tax revenue upturn in America. What we did not cover specifically, though, were the legislative underpinnings at the micro-budgeting level that helped to reduce the rate of spending growth during that era: the Budget Enforcement Act of 1990 (BEA) and the Omnibus Budget Reconciliation Act of 1993 (OBRA). Under the first Bush administration, the BEA raised tax rates and introduced a pay-as-you-go decision rule—known as "PAYGO"—that remained in place until it was terminated by Congress in 2002 and then reenacted in 2010.

In addition to some increases in marginal tax rates that helped cost Bush his reelection, BEA's PAYGO provision stated that any increase in spending had to be offset by either increased taxes or cuts in spending elsewhere. But, again, entitlement programs such as Social Security and Medicare were excluded from PAYGO. OBRA, enacted under President Clinton without a single Republican vote (as the Democrats had done—to their political regret—to Reagan's first budget), then raised tax rates on the wealthy. But then came the revenue bonanza cited above from taxes paid by corporate executives with higher incomes and cashing in stock options from the high-tech boom. Left in the wake of these developments were projected surpluses that peaked at $237 billion in 2000 and then evanesced in the twenty-first century for reasons we covered earlier in this chapter.

Redefining through Strategic Financial Planning and Management?

It was also during the 1990s, however, that the business sector's embrace of strategic planning throughout the 1980s (discussed in chapter 4) found its way into the public sector at all levels of government. The most significant legislative installment in this version of the rationality project at the federal level was the GPRA of 1993. On paper, GPRA was straightforward. Agencies were first to develop five-year strategic plans containing a mission statement and long-term, results-based goals covering each of their major functions. Also required were annual performance plans incorporating performance goals for each fiscal year, with brief descriptions of how the goals were to be met and what measures were to be used to verify those results. Finally, agencies were to do annual performance reports reviewing their successes and failures in meeting those targets.

However, as you might guess, the political side of GPRA has made its implementation anything but straightforward. Beryl Radin offers the most comprehensive and trenchant litany of the challenges faced by GPRA, which she analogizes to trying to fit square pegs into round holes.[19] As she summarizes, the act's implementation has been plagued by a "tangled set of expectations and experiences that reflect quite different and often competing views about the process."[20] Nor did it help that GPRA focused on programs, while the Clinton administration's managing for results program launched as part of its reinventing government initiative focused on agencies. This forced agencies to do separate, time-consuming data collection when compiling these documents. Also, federal agencies chaffed at being held accountable for outcomes actually controlled by third-party actors in states, localities, and the private or nonprofit sectors in today's networked state.

Agencies also differed in the ways they organized to comply with GPRA requirements. Some gave authority to special units, others to management units, and still others to budget offices. This, in turn, produced different approaches and measures across agencies, making it difficult to render cross-agency comparisons or to crosswalk data from different agencies that had impacts on specific problems. And when agencies cracked the whip for consistency, the largely unintended result was a recentralization of agency decision making.

At the same time, the internal politics of Congress sorely compromised GPRA's implementation. For starters, GPRA was championed by members of committees overseeing government administration (e.g., the Committee on Government Operations), not by members of the crucial appropriations committees. The latter did not buy into the process and were not comfortable with agencies setting their own goals and measures. They also saw it as an incursion on their jurisdictions by the Committee on Government Operations and (again) were unwilling to concede policy priority setting to the executive branch. Radin also points out that the regular budget timetable for agencies did not fit into GPRA's five-year or annual performance plans, and the former always takes precedence for lawmakers and agency budgeters.

Undaunted, and with GPRA still in effect (as it is today, with amendments in the Government Performance and Results Modernization Act [GPRMA] of 2010), the next major iteration of strategic planning came in 2001 from the White House under George W. Bush. As we have noted, this was the PMA, included PART as a key component, and was implemented by OMB alongside GPRA requirements. This, not surprisingly, caused significant management problems and concerns. PART was different in several respects from its performance budget-based predecessors. First, it evaluated programs on five specific criteria: whether they had a strategic plan, had a performance-based budget, had a strategic human resource management plan (that aligned hiring with program goals), used their contracting authority aggressively, and effectively employed information technology (IT), social media, and mobile technology (smartphones and tablets). Overall, PART scores on these dimensions were weighted heavily toward results: program purpose and design (20 percent), strategic planning (10 percent), program management (20 percent), and program results (50 percent).

PART also differed from its rationality-based predecessors in two other respects. First, although the aim was to cover all federal programs, assessments were phased in gradually rather than all at once. Information on 67 programs was reported as a part of the fiscal year 2003 presidential budget, then 20 percent of the remaining programs were "PART-ed" each new fiscal year for review. Second, rather than a one-size-fits-all approach, separate sets of questions were created, for example, for regulatory programs, direct federal programs, competitive grants, block grant programs, and research and development programs.

How did programs do? As Radin notes, "Of the programs included in the FY-2004 budget document, 14 were rated as effective, 54 moderately effective, 34 adequate, 11 ineffective, and 118 results not demonstrated. In the FY-2005 budget document, 11 percent of the programs were rated effective, 26 percent rated moderately effective, 21 percent adequate, 5 percent ineffective, and 37 percent results not demonstrated."[21] Nice and tidy for budgeting purposes, right? Perhaps from a technical standpoint. But a closer look illustrates all the political—and sometimes technical—challenges faced by prior budgetary reforms.

Again, Radin offers the best summary of challenges facing rationality projects such as these when results enter the political process. Among a host of factors, she cites "institutional conflict between the legislative and executive branches; the fragmentation of responsibilities within the legislative branch; intergovernmental relationships; and tension between OMB and departments and agencies."[22] For instance, little indication exists that Congress used PART data to inform budget judgments, a not surprising outcome, as OMB failed to include members of authorization or appropriations committees in the process. Likewise, when it comes to the intergovernmental dimension of performance-based budgeting, states that already had performance measurement systems in place (which many did, because budget reforms tend to move up the system, not down) balked at moving to national measures. Moreover, institutional tensions between OMB and agencies also arose in the PART (as in the GPRA) process. Finally, some evidence exists that programs associated with Democratic Party constituencies (e.g., social programs) received lower PART scores than others from this Republican administration.

Most recently, the Obama administration set new performance goals for individual agencies and for cross-agency priorities as part of the 2015 budget preparations and the GPRMA.[23] The most significant aspect of this initiative—known originally as High Priority Performance Goals as PART's successor—is the recognition that, as we stressed in earlier chapters, public problems have to be addressed in a coordinated way across government agencies known for being stovepiped and resistant to cooperation. The cross-agency goals—115 in number—concern missions such as cybersecurity; insider threats; job creation; and science, technology, and engineering education. Agency goals involving each department are still emphasized, as are overarching administration goals such as open government, customer service, and strategic sourcing performance metrics. But many of the same obstacles are arising that have hindered success in prior efforts to link goal setting to budgeting. Consequently, OMB has launched a series of strategic reviews with federal agencies in an attempt to integrate better program performance with budget decisions. Queried is how well performance measures—within and across agencies—will inform long-term strategies, budget formulation, and legislative strategies.[24]

From all this, you again should not assume that rationality-based budgeting is without merit. As we covered in chapter 6, rational–comprehensive analyses can be an input into incremental processes and can affect policy change. Some evidence also exists that these efforts *do* frame and influence earlier decision making in the budget process within agencies.[25] Moreover, as we also reviewed in chapter 4, managerial value exists in these efforts. Agencies that do not have a sense for where they are going either go around in circles or merely drift. That said, redundancy, gaming, and nonuse of data—plus using the information gleaned to embarrass politically rather than improve agency operations—have been serious problems that your generation of managers will inherit, need to navigate, and, hopefully, be a part of resolving.

Nor should you think that rationality-based initiatives in the public budgeting process will wane in the future because of the issues we have reviewed in this chapter. No matter the gamesmanship that accompanies rationality-based initiatives such as these at all levels of government, elected officials gain in two ways. First, they get information about agency operations that they otherwise might not have gained, and, second, they can use this information for their own political ends—as political appointees have used PPBS, MBO, and ZBB for their own centralization purposes. So best you pay attention in your classes to the rationality-based budget tools—including the forecasting tools we will later discuss in this chapter. Just be alert to the inherent political component of their application and implementation, because you will not be able to escape them during your career.

Reconnecting with Citizens

Charles Lindblom and Aaron Wildavsky argue that just passing a budget is a testament to the quality of the outcome because of all the interests that have to be accommodated.[26] As such, their criteria for success are not premised on the outcomes but rather on the quality of the deliberative process itself. Did the process promote budgetary competition and debate and simultaneously confine conflict to a level sufficient for orderly budget development? Were the results seen as legitimate by participants and nonparticipants? Was participation broad enough to assure adequate representation of interests? In other words, was bureaucratic administration not allowed to trump democratic administration in the process?

A new wave of public budgeting and finance reformers argue that more positive responses to these questions can only be gleaned by reconnecting budgets with citizens, a movement that you will come to know in your coursework as "participatory budgeting." Although participatory budgeting has started to gain traction in cities and towns across the country, you should know that progress has been an uphill struggle. Consistent with the argumentative turn in policy analysis that we reviewed in chapter 6, proponents argue that participatory budgeting is needed today for a number of reasons. These include the unstructured nature of public problems, the need for budget offices to engage in "collective puzzlement on behalf of society," and the importance of gaining buy-in from citizens early to avoid meeting them in court later.

To these ends, the Alfred P. Sloan Foundation established a nationwide program in 2003 entitled "Making Municipal Government More Responsive to Their Citizens." Its results afford you a very nice overview of the logic and implementation of participatory budgeting in states and localities. When supplemented by the experience of the Los Angeles citizen charter law over the past ten years, you can get a peek into the challenges, choices, and opportunities involved in participatory budgeting.

Reports from both these projects clearly show that there are often a variety of disconnects between governments and citizens. You may already have experienced or observed this in local or state government agencies. Many budget offices, for example, believe that citizens are too busy, lack the expertise, or simply do not want to get involved. Yet, in the 70 jurisdictions participating in the Sloan Foundation's National Center for Civic Innovation (NCCI) projects, a sense emerges that if citizens do feel that way, they have "learned" to feel that way by being excluded by government agencies.[27] Researchers find that citizens who participated in budgeting focus groups wanted to be involved in the future, regardless of the decisions made. Participation also offers hope for change, because many budget offices altered or added to the performance budgeting measures they were using based on focus-group comments.

To elaborate further, data from the NCCI and Los Angeles projects also show that decision outcomes matter less than citizens' perceptions of how they are treated. They are fine with outcomes as long as they feel respected, public employees are courteous, and they are treated in an evenhanded manner. They also want to see evidence that their opinions matter, even if they do not carry the day. Documented more broadly, however, have been rude and discriminatory behaviors by "street-level bureaucrats" at all levels of government and across different kinds of agencies.[28] Indeed, the proportion of Americans who believe that all public officials do not care what people think rose from 36 percent in 1964 to 66 percent in 2014, with similar increases in persons who believe that public officials lie or are corrupt.

Findings from the NCCI projects also should disabuse you of the idea—held in most budget and finance offices (and in other offices)—that your responsibility to include citizens in deliberations stops with citizen satisfaction surveys. As you will learn in your data and methods courses, surveys are only one-time snapshots of opinions that can change over time. Moreover, citizen preferences can evolve as the choices they face evolve, questions asked can generate opinions that really do not exist, and surveys typically do not afford the kind of context needed in making choices among different budgeting priorities. In addition, surveys are subject to wording biases, selection biases, sampling errors, and statistical manipulation.

Even were these not issues, survey respondents who lack context and understanding of the budget processes, issues involved, and tradeoffs are not offering informed decisions. Participatory budgeting proponents, like the early progressives such as Woodrow Wilson, Jane Addams, and William Allen, did say that local governments can be laboratories today for citizens learning how to participate in a democratic society. This means that budgeting and accounting officials in agencies—as well as all public managers such as yourself—can and should when possible "tutor" them in the ways, whys, and wherefores of key practices such as public finance.

A related lesson for you derived from both the NCCI and Los Angeles projects is this: budget analysts think they know what information citizens want, how they want it presented, and what the unit of analysis is that they prefer. But they may be wrong. For example, even offices committed to citizen responsiveness have tended to collect performance information that serves more to justify their own actions or delves into issues that interest them rather than what citizens find useful. With participatory budgeting, the focus is broadened to outcomes that *citizens* deem important. Moreover, research into those attitudes reveals that your agency may have to drill deeper into budgets and operations when developing performance measures than is typically the case. Both, of course, can frighten budgeters and program managers, causing resistance. One indicator of the dilemma is reflected in the NCCI's Government Trailblazer Program. Although deciding to opt into the program, 58 of the 70 jurisdictions participating said that they did not involve the public in developing performance budgeting measures, and 64 of the 70 did not even allow public comment on performance reports.

Thus, what we earlier called a bureaucratic rather than democratic mentality of administration has dominated agency budget thinking and operations. What is more, even in those jurisdictions where experimentation with participatory budgeting has taken place, typical launch problems occurred. These included limited and declining fiscal resources for doing so; difficulties in deciding which of a variety of methodologies for citizen involvement works best for different communities; reluctance to report bad news, despite it making performance reports more credible to citizens; and concerns by elected officials and appointees about political repercussions occasioned by enhanced transparency of budget processes.

Despite these challenges, these participatory projects also offer broader lessons for you to consider as a public manager. For instance, budget offices learned that citizens were less interested in the duties of particular departments and more interested in identifying the major "themes" (e.g., poverty reduction and public health) addressed by various departments. They also wanted shorter reports, more graphs, and greater context in terms of tradeoffs that have to be made than agencies were used to providing.

Finally, the NCCI and Los Angeles projects suggest that you should also weigh the following as you think about your agency trying to build a sense of common purpose infused with democratic values:

- using mutually agreed on—or "coproduced"—measures less as penalties than as "beginning points" to launch into a discussion of possible budgeting priorities or reprogramming;
- framing budgeting deliberations in terms of those measures and making budgeting adjustments accordingly;
- explaining more of the "Why?" behind data presented in committees in which citizens are participating and in reports they are given;
- affording greater flexibility for traditional online and mobile iPhone and tablet users and offering the ability to drill down into data as little or as much as users wish;
- not only giving citizens access to background information on the basics of government and the budget process, but giving agencies data that can help them understand their citizen "audience" better;
- making clear to citizens the limits of their authority, so as not to raise their hopes unrealistically and cause greater problems of distrust;
- making sure that racial, ethnic, and socioeconomic diversity are reflected, so that the effort has credibility with all citizens.

Approaches aside, participatory performance budgeting is part of the continuing pressures you will face to reconnect with citizens during your career in a social media age.

Reengaging Resources and Recapitalizing Personnel Assets

As the preceding sections of this chapter have made clear, the world you will face in the immediate future as a public manager will be challenging but also wrought with new possibilities. You will be asked to help make or implement hard decisions about budget priorities, with both elected officials and citizens demanding high levels of performance within tight budgets. By the same token, however, fiscal stress and technology advances may help bring down many of the obstacles to building a sense of common purpose that we have covered so far.

At the macro-budgeting level, there are those in the business community and beyond who foresee an impending American economic rebound in the decade ahead. They see it propelled by such things as its leadership—and maybe even independence—in energy production through the fracking technology available for extracting oil and gas in North America that we reviewed in chapter 3. This depends, again, on being able to do it in environmentally sustainable ways. Others claim that a so-called "Smarter Planet" will be led by the United States. These optimists see "Big Data" analyses as a "natural resource which promises to be for the 21st century what steam power was for the 18th, electricity for the 19th, and hydrocarbons were for the 20th."[29] Moreover, they view the United States as holding a decided "innovation advantage" over its international competitors, positioning it to reap the economic and tax benefits of a global economy.

At the micro-budgeting level, these optimists also see the potential for a so-called "smarter enterprise" to break down silos in business and, perhaps, within government. As chief executive officer Virginia Rometty of IBM recently wrote, smarter enterprises "will do the things that organisations have always done...But they will do them in new ways" that will reduce the transaction costs of doing business.[30] For example, Big Data-driven, decision-support systems—some of which we have already reviewed in this book—will counter incremental decision making in business and government by allowing managers to "captur[e] data and apply predictive analytics, rather than just relying on past experience."[31]

Perhaps. And you may play a role in bringing these initiatives to fruition by helping to design and implement, say, tax subsidies for getting them off the ground. Or you may be instrumental in bringing these and other innovations to government and by being involved in their implementation. But it will not happen quickly. The history of short-term success in high-tech initiatives in government agencies is not encouraging, and optimists underestimate the social, organizational, and financial constraints of taking such efforts to scale in government. Thus, although the promise remains and IT advances are already underway in different agencies, they will not be as automatic as claimed by some companies selling these IT tools.

Nor does this IT revolution mean more jobs in government or elsewhere. The history of technological innovations in the short run has been a substitution of capital (machines) for labor—although they also wrought greater numbers of jobs elsewhere in the long run. Moreover, and as noted, applications of IT and social media in government agencies so far have involved little beyond mundane transactions rather than, for example, increases in civic deliberation. Thus, some of the other challenges to the stewardship of the nation's treasure that you will face and that we have reviewed in earlier chapters may actually be exacerbated, requiring further government expenditures. For instance, were the transaction costs of doing business really reduced to zero, the result is likely to be more networked governance rather than a rebuilding of government capacity.

So, while awaiting the IT revolution to blossom in government agencies at all levels (and it no doubt will in time), it is better for you at present to prepare for "doing more with less." Getting your bearings in doing so will be helped by understanding the sources of revenue that exist today, where our current tax dollars are going, and the technical–political nexus that has driven these allocations in the past. You must understand the current allocation of financial and personnel assets before you can understand the realpolitik involved in reengaging and recapitalizing them in the future. How and why they got to this point historically will be covered in chapter 9 as they relate to policy implementation, but a broad overview of the status quo today is important for you to grasp at this point.

The Ecology of Tax Revenues Today...and Tomorrow

Existing federal tax revenue sources and expenditures are a good place for us to start. As Figures 8.1 to 8.3 illustrate, the largest source of federal revenue is the income tax, while the largest sources of revenue for state and local governments are sales taxes and property taxes, respectively.[32] Property taxes are controversial, because other types of property— such as stocks, bonds, and bank accounts per se—generally are not taxed as such. Those who hold "real" property, then, pay a disproportionate share of the taxes. It is important to understand, however, that states and localities vary in terms of the specific rates they

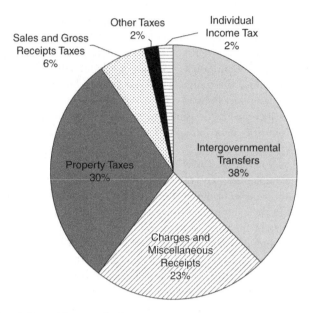

Figure 8.1 Local General Revenue by Source, 2010

Source: Tax Policy Center, State and Local Government Finance Data Query System, http://www.taxpolicycenter.org/taxfacts/displayafact.cfm?Docid=530.

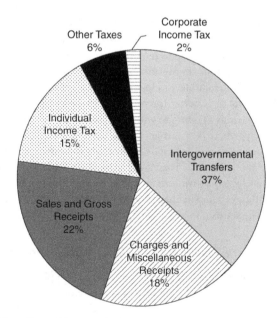

Figure 8.2 State General Revenue by Source, 2010

Source: Tax Policy Center, State and Local Government Finance Data Query System, http://www.taxpolicycenter.org/taxfacts/displayafact.cfm?Docid=528.

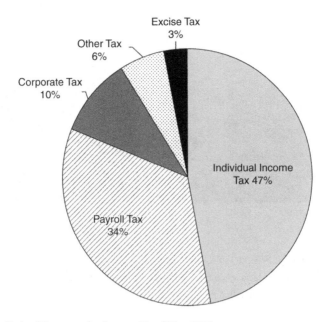

Figure 8.3   Federal Revenues by Source, Fiscal Year 2012

Source: Office of Management and Budget, Budget of the US Government FY 2012, Historical Tables, Table 2.2.

set, since both sets of taxes at least partially affect where businesses and families may locate. So, depending on where your career takes you, you may be more or less advantaged by these differences in terms of the revenue with which you have to work.

You should also note the relatively small proportion of revenue at all levels of government that comes from corporate income taxes relative to individual and property tax revenues. As noted in chapter 2, this also reflects the competition among nations, states, and localities for the economic growth and jobs that luring businesses can bring. At the federal level, and as we covered in chapter 5, it reflects the persistent effort since the 1980s of a coalition of financial, banking, real estate, and energy industries who contribute large sums to the campaign coffers of elected officials to create a friendly tax and regulatory environment for themselves. Indeed, as Figure 8.4 illustrates, were you reading this book in the 1950s, the relative tax burden on corporations and individuals would be almost reversed, as would the relative tax burden of high-income versus middle-class wage earners. Still, the US has a higher corporate rate than other nations.[33]

When debates begin over relative shares of tax effort at the federal level, you should also be aware that the combatants are often not defining taxes in the same way. Two types of taxes fall on individuals: payroll and income. When political figures argue that large percentages of Americans do not pay taxes, they are correct only in terms of income taxes. Everyone pays sales and payroll taxes, and lower and working-class individuals actually pay a higher percentage of their income on these than do more well-off Americans. When that occurs, taxes are said to be "regressive" rather than "progressive."

Finally, as Figure 8.5 illustrates in the health policy arena, and as we have noted earlier in chapter 5 for the compensatory state in general, you should understand that states and localities are highly reliant on federal revenues in certain areas. In that chapter, we noted

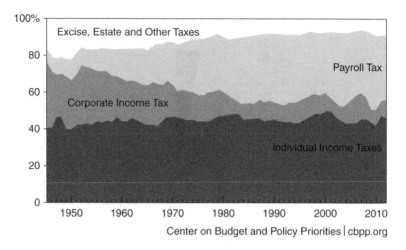

Figure 8.4 Sources of Federal Tax Revenue, 1945–2012

Note: "Other taxes" category includes profits on assets held by the Federal Reserve.

Source: Office of Management and Budget, http://www.cbpp.org/cms/?fa=view&id=3822.

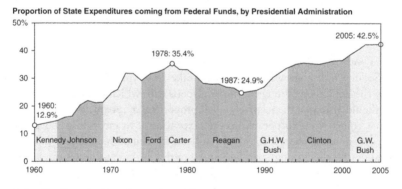

Figure 8.5 Tracking the State Dependency Rate

Note: The state dependency rate is a measure of how dependent states are on federal funds. Among recent presidential administrations, only the Reagan Administration saw a significant decrease in the rate.

Source: Calculations based on US Department of Health and Human Services, Centers for Medicare and Medicaid Services, "National Health Expenditures by Type of Service and Source of Funds, Calendar Years 1960–2006," at http://www.cms.hhs.gov/NationalHealthExpendData/downloads/nhe2006.zip (April 29, 2008), and U.S. Department of Commerce. Bureau of Economic Analysis, National Income and Product Accounts Tables, Table 3.3 at http://bea.gov/national/nipaweb/SelectTable.asp?Selected=N#S3 (April 29, 2008). *Author source*: http://www.heritage.org/~/media/Images/Reports/2010/b2136_chart1sm/b2136_chart1.ashx.

how these revenue transfers have spiked to over 700 categorical grant programs today, in the process creating their own version of intergovernmental subsystem politics and inflexibility. In contrast, the national government provides little state and local funding for general public services. Overall, approximately 20 percent of total state and local resources comes from the federal government, with about 50 percent of this funding for Medicaid.

Despite some significant funding cuts during the 1980s under the Reagan administration, the share of state and local budgets has increased ever since. As a percent of general revenue of the state and local sector (a smaller number than total revenue), the national government contributed 19.7 percent in 2001, 20.1 percent in 2007, 22.2 percent in 2009 (up due to the stimulus), and 24.7 percent in 2011 (again up due to stimulus construction spending).

But you should also know that although the federal government transfers large amounts of dollars to states and localities, those recipients frequently complain about the "unfunded mandates" imposed on them as well by the federal government. Going beyond normal grant rules and regulations, unfunded mandates stem from the perverse incentives offered to federal elected officials to vote for popular programs and then pass responsibility to the states to pay for them. Congress addressed these complaints to an extent in the Unfunded Mandates Reform Act (UMRA) of 1995. In brief, UMRA required the CBO to estimate the costs of federal legislation for state and local governments and the private sector as bills emerged from committees.[34] Nevertheless, in 2006, the CBO identified 37 unfunded intergovernmental mandates enacted in that year alone.[35] Moreover, in a review of three programs, the Center on Budget and Policy Priorities estimated $73 billion in unfunded mandates from 2002 to 2005 and $175 billion in increased state and local government costs due to federal policy changes.[36] Consequently, unfunded mandates will be with you as a public manager for as far as the eye can see.

The Ecology of Public Spending

In terms of public expenditures, Figure 8.6 illustrates that the four largest spending items at the federal level in fiscal years 2013–14 were health, social security, defense, and income

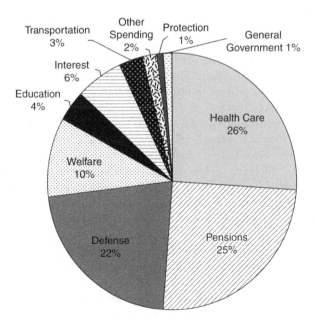

Figure 8.6   Federal Spending for the United States, FY 2014

Source: http://www.usgovernmentspending.com/US_fed_spending_pie_chart.

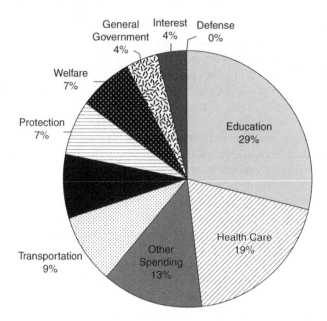

Figure 8.7   State and Local Spending for the United States, FY 2014
Source: http://www.usgovernmentspending.com/US_statelocal_spending_pie_chart.

security. They constitute more than 75 percent of annual expenditures. And as Figure 8.7 shows, the single biggest expenditure in all states is education, with the average state—and the localities within it—spending more than one-quarter of its budgets on public schools.

Funding for education comes primarily from state and local governments. Contrary to popular perceptions, state governments on average provide slightly more education funding than local governments due primarily to education finance reforms over the past two decades to protect against possible court suits. The latter involved legal challenges contending that local property taxes—the primary source of local funding for education—discriminated against low-income minority school districts. You should also appreciate that average state funding for education masks substantial variation across states. For example, Hawaii provides more that 92 percent of school funding, while Nevada provides 31 percent.

Other big budget items for state and local governments are expenditures for public welfare, health care, highways, police and fire protection, interest on debt, utilities, and liquor stores.[37] Each of these items is less than 10 percent of state and local expenditures in most states, but, together, they make up a good portion of their expenses. In addition to this highly visible spending, you can see from Figure 8.8 that the tax expenditures we have discussed are a significant source of revenue loss at all levels of government. Since the enactment of the BICA of 1974, the federal budget has had to include a statement of federal tax expenditures, and more than 30 states also prepare tax expenditure budgets. Nonetheless, as we covered earlier, the costs are substantial. Moreover, if the intent of expenditure budgets is to constrain their use by Congress, they have not fulfilled their purpose.

The first listing of federal tax expenditures in 1972 included around 60 items. By 2007, 170 tax expenditures were listed.[38] Moreover, based on OMB definitions, tax expenditures equaled an amount 129 percent larger than total nondefense discretionary

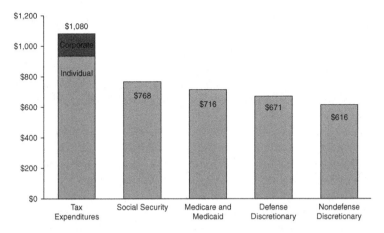

Figure 8.8 Tax Expenditures Are Very Costly: Tax Expenditures and Outlays for Other Major Spending Categories in 2012, in Billions

Note: Tax expenditure estimates do not account for interaction effects; estimate does not include associated outlays ($94 billion) or the effects on excise and payroll receipts ($112 billion).

Source: Office of Management and Budget, Historical Tables 8.5 and 8.7 and Analytical Perspectives Table 16–2, http://www.cbpp.org/cms/?fa=view&id=4055.

spending ($514 billion) for 2007. Thus, tax expenditures far surpassed spending for social programs and other purposes in the federal government. You need to understand, though, that these figures are based on what is called "static" rather than "dynamic" budget scoring. The former does not consider the economic stimulus that tax expenditures can have, only their costs.

Proponents of dynamic scoring argue that some of the costs of tax expenditures are offset. A subsidy to employers for hiring and training unemployed workers, they argue, might lose the government $500 million in revenues, but it also can stimulate additional economic activity, such as contracts for trainers and purchases made by trainees. More importantly, these amounts do not consider the behavioral change that will occur if the preference is removed. That is, people will purchase smaller homes or invest monies differently when the tax preference is removed. Thus, by removing it, behavior will change, allowing you to recapture some of the estimated revenue loss. Still, critics argue that these "dynamic" effects are too speculative, and, consequently, static scoring still prevails at all levels of government.

The Necessity and Perils of Budget Prognostication

As was alluded to earlier, budget forecasting has been required since the 1974 BICA, with its requirement for multi-year revenue and expenditure projections. It is also a necessity at the state government level, because most states have balanced budget requirements that apply to their operating budgets and that necessitate at least annual revenue and spending projections. What is more, advances in computer technology are exponentially and continuously improving our ability to run forecasting models that approximate the complexity of factors involved in macro-budgeting in the United States.

Still, you need to understand that these technical models are only as good as the assumptions and interaction terms built into them. If one predicts, for instance, that unemployment will be 7.6 percent and it rises to 8 percent, any projections you made about total revenues versus expenditures will be off by millions of dollars. You will be paying out considerably more money in unemployment, welfare, supplemental nutrition assistance, and other social service benefits, while taking in substantially less revenue because fewer citizens are working.

Projections are also based on constantly changing numbers that often are adjusted up or down depending on circumstances. Nor can one be certain that what happened in the past will happen in the future. For example, just because senior citizens historically racked up high health care costs does not mean that future seniors will be as unhealthy for as long. However, costs might actually increase if chronic diseases such as dementia interact with medications that extend the lives of these patients. In addition, of course, projections themselves can cause behavioral changes (e.g., lifestyle changes involving more exercise can reduce some chronic diseases) that, in turn, can reduce Medicare and Medicaid costs.

Also, consider the challenges and imperfect nature of the first step of the budget projection process itself as specified by BICA and required in state and local projections: computing baseline budgets. Doing so involves estimating the costs of a program if nothing is added to or subtracted from it legislatively or in regulatory terms in future years. But what, for instance, if new threats arise in the war on terror? To provide the same level of protection to US citizens that, say, the Department of Homeland Security is providing today requires new activity and likely more or reengaged dollars and personnel. How can an agency possibly anticipate these changes in advance without building in some guesswork? Likewise, if the Centers for Disease Control and Prevention fails to anticipate a new viral strain, their baseline budget will be inaccurate. And what if the target population of your program increases, also leaving your estimates understated to meet, say, the needs of the unemployed at the same level you provide existing recipients?

All this, of course, has produced a variety of budget "games" that actors in the compensatory state routinely play to advance their policy interests. You should understand that elected officials and agencies at all levels of government are able to use projections to claim budget cuts, even while spending increases. In making projections, they claim cuts produced by lowering the rate of spending in future years if current trends continue, not real cuts in today's programs.

Another common strategy is assuming that things will happen without any real expectation that they will. For example, the federal government has repeatedly "sold" various government properties to get them off the federal books for any given year and then "sold" them again during the next budget year when original sales never happened.[39] Likewise, states use many additional tactics that federal actors use, only this time to arrive at "balanced budgets." These include cutting maintenance or deferring the replacement of assets, raiding trust funds, and shifting fiscal obligations to out-years or to other governments. Moreover, because "balanced" does not include capital investment budgets (which are financed by bonds and typically improve needed infrastructure), sources of funding can be shifted off-budget to attain balance.

In addition to these political games, the technical rationality of forecasting is complicated by the seemingly "bipolar" patterns of spending and taxing in the states. Prior research, some of which you will encounter in your studies, shows how rapid and sustained revenue growth tends to encourage unsustainable spending increases or tax cuts. Then, when a recession strikes, states look for federal bailouts and rob from their future by raiding trust funds after first using contingency funds (better known as rainy-day accounts).[40]

Still, as we noted in chapter 6, models of public budgeting have now settled on several common assumptions that should be encouraging to you. Recall how the punctuated equilibrium model that we discussed in that chapter applies to the budget process. That model advises you to expect long periods of stability in macro-budgeting punctuated by significant shifts in resource allocation in terms of overall agency budgets. Moreover, when crises occur, agency operations become fodder for sustained attention by chief executives, legislatures, and the courts, often resulting in radical departures from the status quo. Arguably, the unsustainability of today's fiscal and monetary situation augers the preconditions for such "earthquake budgeting."[41] In addition, the literature on policy analysis that we reviewed in chapter 6 also suggests that you can help create these conditions as a public manager by reframing the image of a policy, its salience, and perceptions of its proximity to citizens.

Conclusion

The British statesman Edmund Burke once wrote, "If we command our wealth, we shall be rich and free; If our wealth commands us, we are poor indeed."[42] By that standard, the United States is in trouble and will require the best minds, political courage, and some good luck to fix the situation. In some ways, the public budgeting and finance challenges and choices we have reviewed at the macro-budgeting and micro-budgeting levels of our system are daunting. But as we have also covered, there are optimists who, in effect, are predicting a new American century that—like the dot.com or high-tech bubble—could produce revenue, efficiency, and economy without the pain of drastic spending cuts for entitlements. But even if the projections of optimists are wrong, opportunities are available to you as a public manager or budget analyst in the compensatory state to help address longstanding, pernicious, and needed changes in the budgeting focus of the United States. Moreover, you could do so in ways accommodating both bureaucratic and democratic administration that advance a sense of common purpose informed by democratic constitutional values and leave a lasting mark on our nation. However, that mark will, in many respects, depend on how well your generation of public managers link public problems to organizational purposes, budgets, and human resources during policy implementation in politically savvy ways. Such is our focus in chapter 9.

CHAPTER 9

Networking in the Shadow of Hierarchy

The last half of 2013 brought heartburn to the Obama White House. First, an employer insurance mandate that was a centerpiece of the President's Patient Protection and Affordable Care Act (ACA) of 2010 had to be delayed from 2014 to 2015. Rather than provide insurance, many employers laid off employees or reduced their hours to slip below the 50-full-time employee mandate. For instance, approximately 29 percent of employers surveyed in 2014 set a cap of 29 hours per week to maintain part-time status for employees and, thus, avoid having to provide insurance coverage for them.[1] Meanwhile, at the US Securities and Exchange Commission, officials explained that an analysis comparing corporate executive pay to average employee salaries as required by the Dodd-Frank Act was much more complex to do than expected.[2] This came after three years of not being able to produce these comparisons. Then, in October, the opening of the federal website for registering uninsured citizens under the ACA suffered repeated crashes, as hundreds of thousands of citizens whom the President repeatedly said would be able to keep their existing policies received notices that they were losing their coverage. And although the governors of the states of Maryland and Oregon trumpeted their commitment to being leaders in running state insurance exchanges under the ACA, the same computer problems and delays surfaced in both states, causing them to abandon their initial efforts at the costs of millions of dollars.

Perhaps you have heard economics referred to as the "dismal science." As the above examples suggest, to an extent, the public management equivalent is policy implementation. Indeed, two leading implementation scholars characterize much of the early research done on policy implementation as "misery research."[3] But as you will read in this chapter, "dismal" and "misery" are overstatements and depend on one's perspective of the purpose of policy implementation. Recent research looking at cases of success, comparing successes and disappointments, and exploring large numbers of cases statistically (what your methods class will call "large N" studies) offers more hope.

Discerned are the conditions under which implementation difficulties are likely to emerge. As such, the words of British statesman and philosopher Edmund Burke again should be etched into your brain as you begin your career in the public service and prepare to play a major role in policy implementation: "Never despair; but if you do, work on in despair."[4] You should also heed the words of Max Weber: "What is possible could never have been achieved unless people had tried again and again to achieve the impossible in this world."[5]

Let us start by getting on the same definitional page, because a wide variety of definitions of implementation exist. We will proceed in this chapter with an understanding that implementation comprises those sets of activities performed by public, private, or non-profit organizations that are needed to translate policy aspirations into concrete achievements.[6] But we will also keep in mind that implementation is always "evolutionary"; implementers will "inevitably reformulate as well as carry out policy."[7] Why? Because "policy is made as it is being administered and administered as it is being made."[8]

As such, implementation, too, is not a task for the meek, the impatient, or the politically unastute. Enacting a statute is not the end of politics but, rather, the starting gun for a different kind of politics involving strategy, bargaining, and compromise among implementers. Implementation will tax your acumen as a public servant, because it is a process of stops, starts, steps back, and steps forward in an iterative process. What is more, the challenges of implementation have become more pronounced in the networked state.[9] As public management scholar Fritz Scharpf puts it, implementation now involves learning how to "network in the shadow of hierarchy."[10]

Thus, consistent with the argumentative turn in the policy sciences discussed in chapter 6, many scholars have *reconceptualized the purpose* of implementation from one of control to one of learning. Likewise, *reconnecting with citizens* in the networked state does not mean thinking solely about interagency implementation structures but rather moving toward a more citizen-centric perspective focused on a coproduction ethic and facilitated by innovations in social media. At the same time as this foregrounding of democratic administration occurs, *redefining administrative rationality* in this implementation setting means agencies need to become more collaborative, cross-jurisdictional, and facilitative than they have been historically. However, in doing so, they must learn to navigate the existing maze of bureaucratic, procedural, and control-oriented cultures that can complicate collaboration, which we reviewed in chapter 4. This again requires thinking strategically and tactically about how best to create contexts allowing for collective puzzlement by all. Finally, *reengaging financial resources* and *recapitalizing personnel assets* for a networked state require a "dirty-minded" diagnostic perspective that this chapter will help you to begin developing.

You should leave this chapter with a realistic historical sense for the evolution of our thinking about policy implementation, both in theory and practice. You will be armed, as well, with a set of analytical frameworks for prospectively anticipating implementation difficulties and retrospectively explaining why difficulties occur. You may find yourself modifying—and even abandoning on occasion—past perceptions you have held of policy implementation or railing in frustration against the games played that can derail it. As in prior chapters, however, the focus on problems is not to discourage you but rather to convey how essential it is for you to think systemically, strategically, and tactically to excel in our profession. Building a sense of common purpose informed by democratic constitutional values that produces positive policy results requires no less of you.

Reconceptualizing Purpose

It is difficult to exaggerate how much scholarly perceptions of the purposes of implementation have shifted in America over the past half-century, yet remain in conflict. Equally difficult to overestimate, however, is how little the perceptions of elected officials, the media, and citizens have changed. Moreover, this "stickiness" of perceptions is something that you will have to cope with and, hopefully, help to change as a public manager through your actions and those of your agency.

Implementation as the Rationality Project on Steroids

Today it might sound odd to think of states and localities as administrative extensions of the federal government. Yet such was the implicit assumption of many of the Great Society programs enacted during the 1960s in the United States, of elected officials and citizens, and of the scholars studying implementation. These assumptions were based partially on a hierarchical and normative view of governance: states and localities *should* faithfully carry out national priorities passed by Congress to deal with issues and problems affecting all citizens.

Thus, by the late 1960s and early 1970s, a widespread perception existed that there was a gap between the promises of President Johnson's Great Society programs and their actual performance. Those supporting the aims of the programs were dismayed by a failure to implement them the way they had envisioned; those opposed saw these gaps as yet another instance of federal policies reaching too far. And rather than look at the policy design crafted by the legislation, both camps identified the "bad guys" frustrating national initiatives as public agencies at all levels of government.

These perceptions then garnered intellectual heft from the scholarly community. The complexity of the implementation process was first extensively documented in 1973 in a now-classic book provocatively titled, *Implementation: How Great Expectations in Washington Are Dashed in Oakland; Or, Why It's Amazing that Federal Programs Work at All, This Being a Saga of the Economic Development Administration as Told by Two Sympathetic Observers Who Seek to Build Morals on a Foundation of Ruined Hopes.* In this book, Jeffrey Pressman and Aaron Wildavsky focus on an urban economic development program begun in 1965 and led by the federal Economic Development Administration (EDA). The EDA decided to give $25 million to the city of Oakland, California, and to use Oakland as a national model for combating poverty, racism, and urban unrest. Yet, three years after its launch, only $3 million had been spent, with most of that going to architects' fees and an overpass to the Los Angeles Coliseum that likely would have been built anyway.

Thoroughly challenged in this study—as well as in a series of case studies by scholars across different social policy arenas[11]—was the validity of a "machine" model of top-down control of the implementation process by the federal government. Such efforts were foiled partially by what Pressman and Wildavsky called the "complexity of joint action" in our Madisonian system and the invalidity of the causal and technical theories underlying policies or programs. The former refers to the substantial number of actors involved in implementation efforts, how these actors have to bargain with each other during the process because of the ambiguity of many statutes, and, hence, how each is a potential "veto point" over all or part of the implementation process by not cooperating. The latter two were mentioned in chapter 6 and refer to the importance of thinking about policies as "hypotheses"—or "if-then" statements. These often proved invalid and, thus, produced a great deal of activity with little policy accomplishment.

We will discuss more about both of these later, but, for now, you might wonder why the federal government had to bargain with the states—and the states with localities and all three with private actors—to get federal laws implemented. Would not the federal government have the power to insist upon its will, since it held the purse strings funding these programs? In a pathbreaking study that you are likely to encounter in your studies, Helen Ingram notes several reasons why and how subnational actors had significant bargaining power with the federal government during implementation.[12]

Ingram begins with the practical reality, noted especially in chapter 2, that the United States has had to resort to a compensatory state involving third-party actors to mask the visible size and power of the federal government. In taking this approach, states were granted major implementation roles in order to obtain the votes necessary to pass a bill, given the nation's penchant for federalism and states' rights. Finally, the nature of the problems that government began to address required state involvement, because they were "closest" to problems, understood better how policies might affect local communities, and had resources that the federal government did not have. Thus, the federal government needed the states, localities, and private actors to implement policies—and continue to do so today—and this gives strong bargaining power to state actors.

As such, you, too, need to embrace the idea that implementation involves bargaining that takes place in nonhierarchical implementation structures and is animated by intendedly rational actors. Always remember, also, that implementation is not just a process of implementing a single policy but, rather, a process of "portfolio management." Implementers are simultaneously carrying out a number of policy initiatives and have to choose where to put their time, effort, and resources. Moreover, although implementation "monsters"—large variations from policy intent—seldom occur because of the legal standing of policies enacted, difficulties still arise.

Many of these stem from what Eugene Bardach calls "implementation games"—some of which you may play yourself or have others play on you one day![13] These are the equivalent of the budget games we covered in chapter 8. One game is known as "delay." Sometimes delay occurs merely because it takes time to put all the administrative "pieces" together to get a program up to speed. But, at other times, delay is caused when implementers extend negotiations over resource or personnel commitments or procrastinate on moving ahead on implementation until they get what they want or it looks like they will be left behind (known as the "odd-person-out" game). And, sometimes, it occurs as they pursue their own personal, program, or agency's perceived self-interests while carrying out other policies. Moreover, delay can occur when opponents of a policy try to change or modify policy as it is implemented.

Another game involves diverting resources to other purposes unrelated to the policy; for example, by spending dollars received for policy implementation in other areas. Likewise, games are rampant that deflect the goals of the policy by, for instance, compromising and watering down the impact of a policy to prevent maximum impact. Moreover, a timeworn approach by opponents of a policy—dissipation of energies—involves wearing proponents down by, for example, engaging in turf wars until a compromise emerges that is suitable to advance their interests.

Thus, early implementation research produced a host of initiatives focused on foiling these realities by limiting the discretion to act. We will review these contingency approaches later in this chapter. It suffices presently for you to note three things produced by this early scholarship. First, some urging "benign neglect" argued that raising expectations that could not be met because of the foibles of implementation only dashed the hopes of the poor and increased citizen cynicism about government. They cautioned restraint in enacting new legislation. Second, the "conditions" for success identified by researchers could rarely ever be met in our Madisonian system, so government activism should again be restrained. Finally, with public agencies the culprits, eliminating them as much as possible as "middlemen" by using market-based approaches such as the ones we have covered in earlier chapters became a mantra of conservatives.

If all this sounds familiar, it should, because it contributed mightily to the intellectual foundation and legitimacy, first, for the Reagan Revolution of the 1980s and, then, the New Public Management of the 1990s and beyond. This is not to suggest that what this early research offers you in the way of implementation advice is not worthy of your close attention. Rather, as we shall see shortly, the prescriptions offered in this research should lead you quite wisely to take a "dirty-minded" perspective when new policies are proposed. This means anticipating what can go wrong and how to cope with these obstacles by, among other things, rethinking the policy, who will be implementing it, and what tools and resources they need to be successful. The point for now, however, is that the normative implications of top-down control of policy implementation—and of third-party governance—had both policy and political implications that we still live with today.

Bottom-Up Implementation as Learning What to Prefer

Not surprisingly, the premises of top-down implementation were soon widely challenged by what you may learn to call a "bottom-up" normative perspective. This perspective finds virtue in the messiness of the policy implementation process that top-downers try to avoid. Thus, in contrast to the Hamiltonian underpinnings of top-down proponents, bottom-up proponents reflect both the Madisonian faith in checks and balances and the Jeffersonian antagonism toward concentrations of power in Washington.[14]

Pragmatically, they argue that control is not only infeasible, but that the tools—largely mandates—of top-down control often do not affect the "behaviors" that have to be influenced to attain policy goals. Moreover, and quite paradoxically, bottom-up proponents claim that the more top-down control is exerted—for example, by rules on how government grants are spent, for what and in what manner, and for whom—the less likely policies will be successful. Success, they argue, often requires that implementers such as yourself have *more* rather than less discretion to adapt policy to local circumstances and problems unanticipated by looking from the top down.[15]

Consequently, when research findings indicate that implementation is a bargaining process between or among federal, state, or local implementers, bottom-up scholars are decidedly less worried that a compliance problem will arise. Rather, they see *democracy* at work.[16] They argue that perspectives, interests, and values not represented or that could not be anticipated in Washington—or in state capitals when state-initiated policies are involved—find a voice in the implementation process. Bottom-up proponents also point out that policies are often not based on a valid causal or technical theory, so carrying them out faithfully is a mistake. Implementing a bad or ill-conceived policy well only means continued failure in dealing with the problem you are trying to solve.

Policy success, as noted above, often requires tweaking a policy or program to fit local or state circumstances better.[17] As such, what top-down advocates call a policy failure is actually "learning what to prefer"—implementation's ultimate purpose. Think, for instance, about implementing a youth unemployment program that is uniform across all US cities.

Certainly, giving a young person job experience is a worthy goal—especially inner city or rural youth where either discrimination has occurred or jobs do not exist and families depend on the extra income a job might provide. But now think about the same program in an area where the overall unemployment rate is high. In this situation, subsidizing or hiring a person 15 to 18 years old may mean taking a job from a family breadwinner who has been unemployed and whose family desperately needs the income.

All of which is not to say that bottom-up proponents are totally opposed to top-down controls or performance measurements. Their default option is, however, giving more discretion to implementers over more control by Washington. Their argument is that successful implementation often requires what they call "mutual adaptation" or "mutual accommodation."[18] For example, federal officials charged with implementing a policy have to modify their goals and procedures to adapt (i.e., tailor) policies to state and local contexts for success, while state and local actors have to modify their preferences to accommodate federal preferences. Both also have to engage in mutual adaptation with private contractors and nonprofit grantees in the networked state.

Still, you may be thinking that accountability mechanisms—controls—*are* necessary in a democratic society. Much like Herman Finer's arguments regarding "outer checks" on the federal bureaucracy that we discussed in chapter 7, couldn't mutual adaptation lead to ignoring the national will or goals while sustaining bad policy because of local preferences? As top-down critics of the bottom-up perspective point out, what would mutual adaptation have led to when it came to implementing antidiscrimination policies in the South in the 1960s or mitigating anti-gay or misogynist local preferences today? In response, proponents of bottom-up thinking argue that it is the aspirational level of a statute, executive order, or court decision that matters (e.g., making the waters fishable and swimmable or ensuring employment for Wounded Warriors), not the means specified to realize those aspirations. The latter may change and be adapted to local circumstances or experience, as long as the steps taken during adaptation are reasonably linked in outside evaluators' eyes to the aspirational level or goal expressed.

Moreover, some implementation scholars recommend what is called a "contingency" approach to resolving the top-down/bottom-up conundrum. One leading theorist, Richard Matland, says that the interaction patterns of two variables should determine which approach to use: the amount of policy ambiguity and the level of political conflict expected.[19] To the extent a policy exhibits low levels of each, top-down overhead controls are appropriate; if both are high, policy makers should expect a highly politicized process, use a bottom-up perspective to identify sources of opposition and support, and act accordingly to advance their policy. Otherwise, a top-down approach is likely to be feasible.

Others urge policy makers and implementers to evaluate how tight or loose controls should be by how certain or controversial a policy's cause-effect relationships (explicit or implicit) are. For example, one hypothesis of enterprise zones under the Reagan administration in the United States (and amended and "Opportunity Zones" during the Clinton administration) was this: if we offer tax subsidies to businesses to move into inner cities to create jobs, they will move and hire local residents. Or take President Obama's version of this policy tool, "Promise Zones." Announced in 2014, the program calls for the federal government to reduce administrative obstacles to gaining federal funding assistance for 20 economically hard-hit cities. The hypothesis: if we reduce administrative obstacles, cities will qualify for more funding and apply for it. In either case, if you are uncertain that the hypothesis is true, then you should allow implementers more discretion rather than strict guidelines.

In doing so, different approaches would be taken and we would learn what to prefer—that is, we would find out through experimentation the best way to reach our goals.

Wicked Problems and Networked Implementation

As you might expect, learning what to prefer and policy implementation as evolution took on added attraction as governments began tackling the wicked policy problems that we discussed in chapter 3, cutting the visible size of government, and moving more aggressively toward networked government in the compensatory state. As we have covered throughout this book, "solutions" offered to these problems are not simply "correct" or "incorrect" but, rather, "better," "worse," or "not good enough."[20] Thus, a key component for addressing these kinds of problems is seeing implementation as a learning experience, not merely a control device. On the one hand, this may not be as inspiring a notion of policy making as you had in mind when you first entertained a career in public management, but it is also a bracing reminder that you or your agency will not have all the answers when addressing today's public problems. On the other hand, your role as a public manager in helping to engage with stakeholders in collective puzzlement on behalf of society when implementing policies should be an exciting prospect. This, in turn, will also require you to help constantly rethink administrative rationality in your agency during your career in ways we are now ready to explore.

Redefining Administrative Rationality

Implementation scholars refer to an "implementation structure" as the assembly-line of actors who have to do something, stop doing something, or do both in order for policy goals to be met. Historically, as we noted, these structures were intergovernmental in nature. As described in a series of classic articles over the years, the nature of these relationships has changed over time and will continue to evolve during your public service career.[21] Produced by this evolution to date has been a series of administrative structures whose rationality you will often hear criticized but within which you will have to become strategically and tactically savvy as a public manager.

Baking the Federalism Cakes

As we covered in several chapters, selected federal grants-in-aid with attached requirements to states, localities, and volunteer groups have been used by the United States since its inception to prompt them to do what national governments do themselves in other nations. Still, leading scholars have metaphorically characterized the era prior to the Great Depression of the 1930s as, first, a "layer cake" and, then, a "marble cake." In terms of the former, each level of government was said to have its own unique responsibilities. For instance, public health, safety, police, and education were the responsibility of states and localities variously, while national defense was the federal government's responsibility. Recall from chapter 8, for example, how small a percentage of GDP federal expenditures were through the 1920s.

From roughly the 1870s to the New Deal, this layer-cake federalism metaphor began to shift in comparatively small ways to a sense of mixed responsibilities, captured in the metaphor of marble-cake federalism.[22] The number of grants remained small (less than

50 or so), and they were mostly "project" grants dedicated for specific purposes, such as transportation or water sewage treatment. Importantly, however, the priorities for determining what project grants existed were largely identified by the states rather than by the federal government.

The magnitude and scope of these efforts spiked significantly during the Great Depression of the 1930s. States and localities lacked either the will or the wherewithal to provide basic social services to a nation figuratively on its knees economically and spiritually. Extending the early progressives' notion of a positive state charged with helping citizens battered by large-scale social and economic forces beyond their control, federal grants multiplied. Importantly, project grants did not go away but, rather, were supplemented by "categorical" grants. These were grants for broader purposes, such as housing, job training, and other social services. Still, the general needs identified largely originated at the state and local levels.

Although these changes and continuities were important in recognizing the practical necessity of shared federal, state, and local responsibilities, variations existed across policy areas. For example, the strong historical legacy of local responsibility for education and public safety continued apace, with federal grants only a very small percentage of local government budgets. Greater percentages of federal assistance were seen, however, in state and local government budgets for housing, job training, and infrastructure projects. For instance, San Antonio, Texas, had large portions of its vaunted river walk paid for and staffed by workers employed by the federal Works Progress Administration during the New Deal.

When Fences Do Not Make Good Neighbors

All this changed dramatically in source, scope, and aims during the Great Society of the 1960s. President Johnson and an overwhelmingly Democratic Congress believed your quality of life and life chances should not be determined by where you live. Consequently, as we reviewed in chapter 5, the federal government had to help ensure that inequalities in tax bases and service provisions across states and localities were addressed. As the Venn diagram partially illustrates in Figure 9.1, our federal system thus began to consist of both discrete and shared responsibilities.

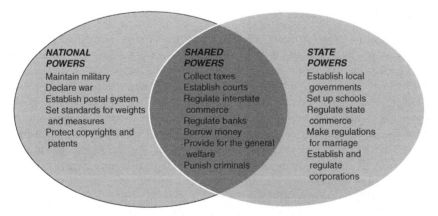

Figure 9.1 Americans Live under Both National and State Governments

As we covered in chapters 5 and 8 when discussing the increasing amount of federal assistance to states and localities, an explosion of top-down federal grants for programs ensued during the 1960s and 1970s. By the late 1960s, over 400 categorical grants existed, and they today total nearly 700 in number for implementing national priorities. These grants did several things that are quite important and that you will deal with during your public management career. Our discussion of the top-down and bottom-up implementation structures has also touched on this.

First, and as we noted in chapter 8, receipt of categorical grant funding brought with it a myriad of rules and regulations regarding how the money could be spent. And why would it not? If you are a taxpayer from Massachusetts, you might not mind having a portion of your taxes sent to Mississippi to help provide better education to its children, but you would want to be sure that this money is targeted at poor school districts and not more financially well-off districts or for subsidizing gambling casinos. Nevertheless, so great a number of restrictions and requirements were stipulated in these grants that they soon became part of the inflexible, difficult to coordinate, and marginalizing (to state and local elected officials) nature of picket-fence federalism that we covered briefly in chapter 5 and that bottom-up proponents so vocally lament today.

Consider the poverty problem in America. A mayor trying to deal with this issue would obviously need to address a wealth of problems to be successful. As jobs move from the inner city to the suburbs, transportation becomes necessary. And as jobs require higher levels of skills, education funding is needed. Moreover, workers cannot take advantage of job opportunities if they are unhealthy. But the rigidity of categorical grants too often precludes a mayor from coordinating these services, allocating funding to higher priority needs in their jurisdiction, or tailoring services to the needs of various citizens.

In light of these trends, so-called "public interest groups" (labeled with the unfortunate acronym of "PIGs") representing elected officials—such as the National Governors Association, the National Conference of State Legislatures, and the United States Conference of Mayors—pressed Congress to consolidate categorical grants into "block grants." The latter have to be spent in the general categories noted, but they afford state and local agencies and elected officials more discretion to act—and, thus, more credit claiming for politicians for resulting state and local projects.

Theoretically, greater amounts of coordination can also occur within these general policy areas. For example, the Community Development Block Grant Program took a variety of categorical grants (such as police patrol, housing rehabilitation, and recreation grants) and put them into one package with fewer constraints on how the money could be spent. The same was done for programs addressing drug addiction, homeland security and infrastructure protection, mental health and substance abuse, and children's health. At least a dozen proposals for additional block grants exist today. However, in a dynamic that will not surprise you, the vertical intergovernmental subsystems surrounding the existing 700-plus categorical grant programs have posed great barriers to consolidation. Placed on top of these vertical subsystems come the horizontal networks that we have consistently covered in prior chapters—and for the philosophical, political, and budgetary reasons we have discussed.

One additional dimension of which you should be aware that has driven networking comes neither from the federal government nor the states. Partially to fill gaps in problem coverage because of picket-fence federalism and jurisdictional boundaries ill-matched to public problems, local officials and grassroots groups have engaged in what Robert

Agranoff and Michael McGuire call "jurisdiction-based" and "networked" models of intergovernmental regulation.[23] The former involve local government officials creating partnerships to address problems that cannot be addressed as a whole by government programs and that would otherwise fall through the cracks. The latter are often initiated by civic groups and bring together community leaders, local business people, frontline staff of state and federal agencies, and ordinary citizens to address a problem area.

Mapping It Out

Amid all this, several scholars and practitioners have offered strategies to increase the likelihood of policy implementation success. Most innovative for you as a public manager engaged in policy or program implementation is what bottom-up proponents call a "backward-mapping" perspective to implementation analysis. They contrast this approach to the conventional "forward-mapping" analysis offered by top-down proponents.

As illustrated in Table 9.1, forward mapping is the typical way that legislatures design policies to address public problems. They identify a problem and then determine either logically or by political necessity which agency has traditionally handled the problem. Agency members then use the tools they have to implement policy. These tools include, but are not limited to, mandates, incentives (such as subsidies or loan guarantees), court suits, information provision, and grants. If given new tools to help them implement policy goals, they may or may not have the understanding, skill mix of professionals, or will to employ them.

These tools, in turn, are based on various assumptions that may or may not be valid for the policy goals being pursued, and they are affected by various situational factors. For instance, you may be employed in an agency having authority to create a market in pollution rights, but you may not know precisely what price is sufficient to alter an industry's fuel mix to reduce greenhouse gas emissions. Or an agency you work for may be armed with communication tools that are ineffective, because these types of tools assume that regulatory targets are in noncompliance due to lack of information on how to comply. In fact, they may know perfectly well what to do but simply do not comply. Alternatively, a federal drug agency you work for may require performance reports from state implementers. The latter may be pushing reports efficiently through the system but not actually

Table 9.1 Two Competing Models of Implementation Analysis

Backward Mapping	*Forward Mapping*
Target(s) (diversity)	Implementing Agency/Implementation Structure
↓	↓
Outcomes (behavioral)	Implements
↓	↓
Choices (made by targets and agents)	Parameters
↓	↓
Parameters (what affects their choices)	Targets
↓	↓
Implements	Choices
↓	↓
Implementing Agency/Implementation Structure	Outcomes

reducing heroin use. Forward mapping also means that these tools may only affect certain targets of a policy (e.g., homeless persons who are temporarily without a job) and not others (e.g., homeless persons who are mentally unstable). Or agencies may engage in "creaming" of the target population—that is, focusing on the easiest rather than hardest cases because of the reward structure and measures used to assess their performance.

In contrast, proponents of backward mapping urge policy makers to turn forward mapping on its head. Rather than focus first on identifying which agency ought to be assigned responsibility for implementing a policy, backward mapping focuses first on the outcomes sought and the behavioral choices of citizens that policy makers and implementers need to affect to reach those outcomes. In the words of Richard Elmore, decision makers should focus on the "point at which public policy intersects private choices."[24] Were you contemplating a family leave policy that would only allow mothers to take uncompensated leave after a birth, for example, you would put yourself in the minds of businesspersons choosing between hiring a male or a female employee (this is the point at which "policy intersects private choice"). You would start from the rebuttable presumption that an employer would lean toward hiring a male applicant, because the company would not incur maternity leave costs. From this analysis, you would argue for a policy that applies equally to male and female employees.

Once the desired outcomes and behavioral choices that have to be positively affected by policy are identified, backward mapping counsels policy makers to discern which policy tools can most affect those choices and the constraints that limit their effectiveness. Then they discern who closest to those choices either have those tools or should be given them. Thus, unlike forward mapping, identifying the tools most effective for affecting critical behavioral choices comes *before* identifying the actors comprising the implementation structure, not afterward as an incidental choice. One then works backward through existing implementation structures to eliminate unnecessary tasks and responsibilities (because they do not or cannot effect key behavioral choices that have to changed). Then one concentrates resources and discretion where they are needed most (i.e., where they can affect behavioral choices the most).

More recently, however, Elmore has suggested combining forward and backward mapping, thus forging a "reversible logic" mindset in your agency.[25] The best way for you to understand reversible logic is to think of it as a decision tree from your decision analysis, quantitative management, or policy analysis courses. Working the decision tree of choices forward and then backward from the distinct starting and ending points depicted earlier in Table 9.1 can help you identify with whom to partner, the obstacles and facilitating factors involved in trying to do so, and the implementation games that may ensue. For your convenience, Table 9.2 leads you through the thought processes involved in reversible logic.

Thus, as a future public manager, backward mapping offers you a decidedly different way to approach and perhaps finesse a variety of obstacles to successful policy implementation. In particular, it offers you a way to anticipate obstacles to implementation that a forward-mapping approach may skim over in its efforts at control. And when combined with the legitimate insights offered by forward mapping in a reversible-logic approach to implementation analysis, it offers a significant way for you to anticipate when policy implementation is likely to be more difficult, what games might be played by supporters and opponents, and what strategies you might take for dealing with them. Before reviewing these, however, you need to appreciate how reconnecting with citizens in social media networks can be another important weapon in your implementation arsenal.

Table 9.2 Reversible Logic: Putting It All Together for Practice

Who are the targets of the policy, and what behavioral changes are you trying to affect?	What key choices have to be affected in order to get the behavioral choices you want?	What kinds of tools can best affect those choices to bring about the behavioral choices you want (for example, authority, information, capacity, hortatory, etc.)?	Wielded by which actors closest to the problem? (note: this becomes the implementation structure)
————→	————→	————→	————→
What situational factors might reduce the effectiveness of those tools wielded by the implementers (e.g., agency doesn't know how to use them, subsystem actors oppose implementation, decision rules of agency)?	What key choices do implementers have to make for the policy to be a success?	What factors might constrain implementers from making the desired choices (e.g., they lack capacity to take actions, the behavioral choices involved are too great, or their culture is not supportive of the policy)?	What games do you anticipate will be played by implementers?	How will you cope with these games and how will you measure success?
————→	————→	————→	————→	————→

Reconnecting with Citizens in Social Media Networks

As you have noticed repeatedly in this book, terms such as collaboration and collective puzzlement on behalf of society trip easily from the lips of many scholars and practitioners when they speak of networked governance. Those advocating or identifying a new governance paradigm have emphasized public administration's traditional "bridge-building" relationship with citizens by extending it to the work of public managers in networks. As we reviewed in chapter 5, public managers as bridge-builders would do no less than stop the "decline of sovereignty, the decreasing importance of jurisdictional borders, and a general institutional fragmentation" in America.[26] They would do so, because politicians tend not to be rewarded electorally for addressing cross-jurisdictional problems, while public managers see interdependency everywhere in their functional areas. As "pedestrian bridges," public managers alone "constitute a strong and capable network for coordination and cooperation."[27] Hence, the only real change in collaborative government involves horizontal networks replacing vertical networks of bureaucrats representing citizen needs.

Given the caveats regarding democratic administration expressed earlier in this book about the bridge-building model for public managers, all this adds urgency to the need for you to be aware of how your role in various implementation structures either advances or compromises citizen trust in government more broadly. Fortunately, your generation of public managers stands on the threshold of a technological revolution that could catalyze civic deliberation. As we covered in several chapters already, the evolution of the internet and social media from a passive medium to a rich, interactive communication platform has the potential to transform many areas of business, government, and society in general during both policy formulation and implementation.[28] Sparking these opportunities are wikis, blogs, and other social networking tools.[29]

To be sure, many governments have moved toward a new vision for serving citizens in a more personalized, citizen-centric manner through social media.[30] For example, the City of Boston, Massachusetts; the City of Raleigh, North Carolina; the City of Palo Alto, California; and the metropolitan government of Nashville and Davidson County, Tennessee, are collaborating in the Multi-City Innovation Campaign to support the building of interoperable data sets and both large and small iPhone apps that will allow them to ascertain, tap into, and share best practices for local service delivery.[31] Others are taking advantage of IBM's three cloud-based Smarter Cities management centers for transportation, water, and emergency management. From these centers, analytics are available for such things as improving traffic management, integrated water management, and emergency scenario planning that cut across departments and jurisdictions.[32] Also, some governments and supra-governmental bodies have strengthened the opportunities for citizens to participate in democratic decision-making.[33]

Still, as we reviewed in chapters 2 and 5, success in generating meaningful citizen involvement at all levels of government and stages of the policy process—including implementation—is disappointing to date.[34] So, how can you as a public manager measure your agency's progress toward linking citizens to government through social media? Unfortunately, our field still lacks a set of success metrics for these technologies linked to an overarching theory of effective democratic governance. Until we do, most promising are broad measures of success that incorporate Mark Moore's influential notion of public value.[35]

Public value can be understood as the value or importance citizens attach to the outcomes of government policies and their experience of public services.[36] For example, OMB director and former secretary of Housing and Urban Development Shaun Donovan points out that a move by the Federal Housing Administration to adopt electronic signatures for loan documents meant more to citizens than gaining greater efficiency for their tax dollars. It also meant giving citizens more time to read and understand their loan agreements, a major issue for financial reform in the wake of today's continuing housing crisis. Similarly helping to improve government transparency and agency efficiency would be a single standard for reporting government spending in machine-readable formats.[37]

In the most comprehensive approach we have today, Murray Scott, William DeLone, and Willie Golden offer a set of "net benefits" measures for implementation of information technology and social media applications in public agencies.[38] They define net benefits in terms of three broad objectives central to policy implementation and geared toward building common purpose infused with democratic constitutional values: efficiency, effectiveness, and improved citizen participation in agency deliberations. Table 9.3 summarizes the criteria you might use to develop questions to track the public value of your agency's information technology and social media efforts during policy implementation (and more generally).

Table 9.3   eGovernment Net Benefits

Measure	Definition	eGov Goal(s)	Source(s)
Cost	Cost saving to the user from using the online channel	More efficient services	(Gilbert et al. 2004)
Time	Time saved by using the online channel	More efficient services	(Gilbert et al. 2004; Kolsaker and Lee-Kelley 2008; Wang and Liao 2008)
Communication	Efficient method of communicating with local/central government	More efficient services	(Kolsaker and Lee-Kelley 2008)
Avoid personal interaction	To receive public services without having to interact with service staff	More effective services	(Gilbert et al. 2004)
Control	The ability to exert personal control over the service	More effective services	(Gilbert et al. 2004; Grimsley and Meehan 2007)
Convenience	The ability to receive the service how and when the individual wants	More effective services	(Gilbert et al. 2004)
Personalisation	The ability to tailor the service to the individual	More effective services	(Gilbert et al. 2004; Kolsaker and Lee-Kelley 2008)
Ease of information retrieval	Useful and helps the user understand about the service	More effective services	(Kolsaker and Lee-Kelley 2008)
Trust	Increase in trust and confidence in government	Improved participation	(Teo et al. 2008; Warkentin et al. 2002; Welch et al. 2005)
Well-informedness	Citizens better informed, knowledgeable about government policy	Improved participation	(Coleman 2004; Grimsley and Meehan 2007; Kolsaker and Lee-Kelley 2008; Thomas and Streib 2003)
Participate in decision-making	Citizens involved, exert influence in the democratic process	Improved participation	(Coleman 2004; Grimsley and Meehan 2007; Kolsaker and Lee-Kelley 2008)

Source: Adapted from M. Scott, W. DeLone, and W. Golden (under review) "Measuring eGovernment Success: A Public Value Approach," *European Journal of Information Systems.*

Reengaging Resources and Recapitalizing Personnel Assets

By now, it should be clear to you why resources have to be reengaged and personnel assets recapitalized from lower to higher-priority items. We have considered some ways—forward mapping, backward mapping, and reversible logic—for doing so within and across organizations. But prior research also offers a way for you to anticipate and design coping strategies to deal with resistance to these efforts, much as we reviewed for strategic planning efforts in chapter 4. However, a warning is in order before proceeding: for the reasons we have covered already regarding such things as the validity of causal and technical theories, implementation as learning what to prefer and mutual adaptation, and portfolio management, do not assume that resistance is necessarily misplaced. It may be, but that is an empirical determination you must make first.

From the hundreds of implementation studies conducted, three sets of factors stand out for you to consider when designing your own policy or creating policies to implement those of others (e.g., federal statutes or court decisions).[39] And each of these is relevant when implementation involves reengaging financial and personnel resources to new or reprioritized policy areas. As noted in Tables 9.4–9.6, the three sets of factors summarized by Daniel Mazmanian and Paul Sabatier are: the tractability of the problem; the ability of a statute to structure implementation; and the sociopolitical, economic, and technological environment of implementation.[40] You will do well when thinking about implementing policies requiring the reengaging of financial resources and the recapitalizing of personnel assets to think of these as hypotheses from which you can derive rebuttable expectations about implementation difficulty for any policy. From these, you can discern ways to navigate the implementation minefield that your analysis reveals.

Tractability of the Problem

The first set of factors deserving your attention involves the inherent difficulty of solving the problem—that is, its tractability—that the policy is addressing. The more intractable the problem, the more difficulty when reprioritizing or reengaging resources or when trying to recapitalize personnel assets for these purposes. What factors indicate a problem is intractable? Certainly, some problems are inherently intractable, meaning extremely

Table 9.4 Tractability of the Problem

- Technical difficulties (related to nature of the problem) – for example, do we understand the problem involved? Do we have accepted ways to deal with the problem? Is the problem so complex that we don't know where to begin?
  - Is there such a thing as a given/objective problem?
  - Is there a valid technical theory?
- Diversity of Target Group Behavior
  - Size
  - Percent of population
  - Positive or negative valence
  - Strength
  - Geographical dispersion
  - Order (of becoming target)
- Extent of Behavioral Change Required

---

hard to understand and deal with. Essentially, it means that the less widely understood the policy problem, the greater the diversity of the groups targeted for behavioral change, and the greater the amount of behavioral change involved, the more intractable the problem and the more likely you will experience implementation difficulty.

You will also recall from chapter 6 that the valencing of a target group (e.g., "deserving" versus "undeserving" poor) can contribute to the level of tractability of the group's problems. The more negative the valence, the more intractable are problems associated with that target group because of a lack of general concern about dealing with them. And the more intractable, the more resistance you can expect when trying to implement policies associated with them. What is more, negatively valenced groups (e.g., drug dealers and illegal immigrants) usually face harsher implementation tools (e.g., more mandates and more severe punishments for their behaviors), making them more resistant to implementation and increasing the tractability of the problems associated with them.

Statutory Design

The second set of variables that you can use as a guide to predicting implementation difficulties involves the way a statute frames the design of implementation. Table 9.5 lists some of the variables for you to pay special attention to in discerning the level of difficulty to anticipate. You can expect greater levels of resistance to reengaging financial resources or recapitalizing personnel assets whenever goals are ambiguous, controversial, unprioritized, or inconsistent. If goals are unclear, unranked in priority relative to other goals in a statute or in terms of existing agency goals, or are controversial, more room or "legitimacy" exists for opponents to challenge implementation efforts. Likewise, the adequacy of the causal and technical theories discussed in chapter 6 condition implementation difficulties. Emphasized in that chapter was treating all policies as hypotheses, as well as jettisoning or refining policies that lack valid theories. Often, however, policies

Table 9.5 Statutory Design

• Clear and Constant Goals and Objectives
  – Precise
  – Priority-based
  – Consistent
• Adequate Causal Theory
• Threshold Financial Resources
• Institutional Culture
• Hierarchical Integration
  – Veto points
  – Inducements/sanctions
  – Credibility
• Decision Rules of Implementing Agencies
• Dominant Coalition
• Recruitment of Supportive Implementation Officials
• Degree of Formal Accessibility to Outsiders
• Social Entropy

---

with invalid theories are enacted, and you will nonetheless have to help implement them. In these cases, you can expect high levels of implementation difficulty (both within your agency and among target groups)—especially in reengaging or allocating resources for them—because they lack legitimacy, are rife with controversy, and, thus, offer a wide range for challenge.

Yet another set of factors trains your attention on the specific actors in the implementation structure. You can anticipate greater implementation difficulty and resistance to reengaging resources or recapitalizing personnel assets for new purposes whenever the organizations involved in implementation have inadequate resources to carry out the jobs they already have to do. This occurs most especially if they have to reengage their own resources to do new tasks, because the statute does not afford additional resources to implementing agents.

You should also anticipate greater implementation difficulty and resistance if the organizational culture(s) of implementers assigned to carry out the policy are not supportive of it and if their decision rules (i.e., rules for making policy choices relating to existing policies) are inconsistent with the policy and cannot be changed to accommodate it. Implementation resistance is also more likely if implementers lack the personnel skills needed to carry out the policy and will not be given appropriate new hires, or if little predisposition exists to carry out the assigned policy because their other constituencies will resist it. As we noted in chapter 5, members of both winning and losing legislative coalitions try to assign responsibility for carrying out policies to hospitable or inhospitable environments, respectively. As such, the odds for successful policy implementation involving a reengagement or recapitalizing of assets are especially low when assigned to agencies with unsupportive cultures.

Likewise, your antenna as a manager should go up whenever legislation addresses policy change, resource reengagement, or recapitalizing personnel assets targeted for specific purposes or citizens. When the Johnson administration launched the idea of the now-defunct Model Cities program in the 1960s, for example, the US Department of Housing and Urban Development was to use 10 to 12 cities as models for showing how the public, private, and nonprofit sectors could collaborate to enhance urban living. Given the realities of putting together a winning coalition to enact the law, however, hundreds of cities were able to receive funding in return for political support without a commensurate increase in the budget. Likewise, although funding from Congress was originally targeted for grants for African American students attending historically black colleges, grants for other groups (e.g., Hispanics) have been added over the years without a commensurate increase in funding.

Equally as disruptive to reengaging resources and recapitalizing personnel assets successfully for new purposes is the number and nature of the relationships among actors involved in implementing the policy. As noted, one of the seminal findings of implementation research involves the complexity of joint action required by a policy or program.[41] You should expect that the greater the number of actors, and the more sequential or reciprocal the relationships involved, the more likely implementation difficulty. Consider, for instance, a policy requiring that gun permits not be issued before background checks are made in a federal database that, in turn, requires states to input data into those databases. This is a linear sequential process—one thing has to be done before the next step can take place—that can fall victim to the weakest link in this chain of activities. Moreover, the process becomes even more vulnerable to delay and potential failure when back-and-forth negotiations (a reciprocal relationship) between actors must take place over the amount, substance, and quality of the data collected and input, or over who is going to pay the costs of data collection and input.

Finally, you should realize that your agency's work will be cut out for it when policies create implementation structures that are vulnerable to what analysts call "social entropy." In the natural sciences, entropy refers to the tendency of all systems to run down into chaos. Policy analysts take this term and apply it to social systems. They expect that the more that policies require extraordinary people to produce high-quality work over long periods of time, the more likely implementation difficulties will arise and resistance to change will emerge as systems break down. There simply are not enough talented people to go around, vacancies in positions emerge over time to jeopardize implementation, and talented people either move up in the organization or move on to others. Moreover, once social entropy occurs, everyone in the implementation structure may suffer reputationally, politically, or financially.

Realizing all this means that strategic or tactical responses will be necessary on your part. Strategies might include eliminating resistant actors by shifting tasks to others (e.g., contractors), finding ways to bring them into the process (e.g., by giving side payments such as helping in another unrelated area that they will value), or gaming the building of support to create what scholars call "bandwagon effects." This last strategy takes into account the reality that some actors whose consent or contribution you need are more powerful than others, and the latter often take their cues from them. Thus, persuading a key actor to do what needs to be done to effect change or reengagement of resources means that others will follow suit.[42] Moreover, once reluctant actors see that something is going to happen, they are likely to get on board in order to influence what finally occurs.

The Changing Environment

The third set of variables begging your attention when trying to implement policies requiring reengagement and recapitalization of assets deals with the changing social, political, economic, and technological environment of implementation. As listed in Table 9.6, these environments "evolve" over time and across different policy areas and

Table 9.6 Changing Environmental Conditions

- Socioeconomic, Political, and Technological Conditions
  - National, state, regional, local (micro-implementation structure)
- Media Attention to Problems
  - Not just a given; strategic use of outside strategy
- Public Support
  - Depends on diffuseness, attention cycle, and issue framing
- Attitudes and Resources of Constituency Groups
  - For example, iron triangles, subsystems, issue networks
- Court Decisions
- Support from Sovereigns
  - Oversight committees
- Leadership Skills
  - Fixtures, eyes and ears, fire alarms, smoke detectors

levels of government. As such, they can advance incremental progress toward policy goals (cumulative implementation), "stall out" or reverse progress (discontinuous implementation), and kick start them again (rejuvenated implementation).

Certainly, as reviewed earlier in chapter 5, a sense for the strength, durability, and consensus of existing subsystems, issue networks, or advocacy coalitions surrounding programs you are designing or implementing is important for anticipating the level of difficulty you can expect at any point in time. Thus, again, stakeholder analysis is imperative for you as an implementer. Unsupportive or conflictual subsystems mean severe implementation difficulties. But, as we noted in chapters 4 and 6, never take political environments as "givens." You need to be proactive and figure out how you might advance a supportive coalition by linking together the problem, policy solution, and political streams we discussed in these chapters. Nor should you forget the importance of softening policies, looking for windows of opportunity, and engaging in skillful issue redefinition.

However, perhaps the most important lesson from prior research is that ensuring durable policy change, reengagement of resources, and the recapitalizing of personnel for new purposes means that you should prepare for the times when unsupportive environments exist. And sometimes "reframing" the environment in ways supporting implementation is not possible at any particular point in time. Supportive actors in agencies, on legislative committees, and in the mayor's, governor's, county executive's, and president's offices come and go over the years, as do opponents and agnostics.

As such, eventual implementation success depends on three things. First, it depends on recreating the winning legislative coalition for a policy throughout the implementation process. As we covered in chapter 5, the audience paying attention to a fight determines the balance of political forces surrounding it and, thus, who wins and/or loses during implementation. For example, advisory boards might be created at the local level consisting of representatives of environmental groups that supported reallocating funds and resources toward sustainable development projects.

Second, what scholars call "fixers" are needed to protect or nurture the policy or program. Fixers are those positioned on key oversight committees or other strategic locations (e.g., boards of nonprofits) who can serve as "eyes and ears" alerting policy supporters when something is going wrong during implementation. Alternatively, they may be in a position to correct administrative or political implementation bottlenecks or to alert others who can—for example, on legislative budget committees. Consider how many governors of both parties have been central in supporting the implementation of the Obama administration's once-widely embraced "Common Core" educational reform program (albeit often renaming it in their states!) in the face of subsequent attacks from liberals and conservatives.

Finally, benchmarks (or milestones) and performance metrics are needed to chart progress toward realizing policy aims. Again, this does not mean sticking to established procedures but, rather, adapting them based on learning and changing circumstances to realize policy aspirations. Measures may be quantitative or qualitative, or focused on outputs, outcomes, or process concerns. In terms of process measures, a series of milestones should be stipulated indicating whether critical actions are taken or partial results attained in a timely way. Relatedly, more subjective qualitative questions might be asked on a regular basis to determine if short-term actions taken by implementers are reasonably related to program goals. At the same time, prior research suggests that output and outcome metrics that you use should be SMART: simple, measurable, ambitious but reasonable, and time-specific (having deadlines). These, too, can bring the original winning coalition back into the fight by serving as fire alarms or smoke detectors to indicate a lack of timely implementation progress.

Conclusion

This chapter has offered you an overview of the factors to anticipate as a public manager in the compensatory state when it comes to designing or implementing public policy during your career. Major lessons you should have drawn from it are that policy is a hypothesis to be tested and refined, that implementation amounts to learning what to prefer as you go, that the aspirational goals (what you want to accomplish) matter more than the specific means for attaining them, that democratic administration is a must, and that policy implementation contexts evolve over time rather than remain static. As such, you need to take a "dirty-minded" perspective, asking what can go wrong and figuring out strategically and tactically how best to navigate the minefields identified. What remains for us now in chapter 10 is to address the sixth and final "R" in our framework—revitalizing a sense of common purpose informed by democratic constitutional values—in greater strategic, tactical, and normative depth than we have covered so far.

CHAPTER 10

Revitalizing a Sense of Common Purpose

As we reviewed in chapter 5, public administration scholars have identified many reasons for the decline of trust in government in the United States since the early 1970s. One among these, we noted, is administrative reformers' overwhelming focus on bureaucratic over democratic administration during the twentieth century.[1] Thus, whether you want to be or not, you will be more than a specialist or "technocrat" in public management during your career. Your decisions, actions, and values will affect citizens' perceptions of government, themselves, and their role in a democratic republic. They will, in essence, affect feelings of the legitimacy of government and of public service itself in today's compensatory state.

This also means that, during your career, you will either be part of revitalizing a sense of common purpose that is infused with democratic constitutional values or be part of further jeopardizing it. Consequently, you will be facing calls to reconceptualize drastically your agencies' and partners' purposes, redefine their administrative rationality, reconnect them with citizens, reengage their financial resources, and recapitalize their personnel assets. You will also have to do so while helping to preserve, protect, and advance the values that are integral to becoming what we aspire to be as a nation.

As Woodrow Wilson noted so long ago, if government is viewed as incompetent, ineffectual, or tone deaf by citizens, even despots will lose legitimacy. Arguably, helping to avoid this means your generation of public managers will be judged on how well you help revitalize a sense of common purpose that has been on the wane in America and how well you help enhance perceptions of government legitimacy. Doing so will require *thinking systemically*, *purposively*, *democratically*, and *institutionally* as you perform the public's business. This final chapter discusses what each of these elements means for you and the agencies in which you serve, some strategies for pursuing them, and the normative grounding essential to their pursuit.

Thinking Systemically

As the preceding chapters have collectively illustrated, taking a holistic perspective in the public service has proven a distinct challenge. Legislators and interest groups focus overwhelmingly on the "parts" of public organizations or on separate agencies, meaning a focus on programs and policies that affect their particular constituents or interests. Advocates for programs and policies, in turn, are pitted against each other for access, influence, and resources within and across public agencies. Employees are hired on the basis of functional expertise, are placed in functional offices that are subdivided into cubicles, and are rewarded on the basis of how well they meet discrete performance targets for their programs.

But with the challenges, choices, and opportunities you will face during your public service career, you need in your own mind to "put Humpty Dumpty back together again." So let us see how the individual parts of the public management puzzle we have been discussing fit together as a system geared toward accomplishment while staying true to democratic constitutional values. We have already seen in chapter 9 how forward-mapping, backward-mapping, and reversible-logic strategies can be used to build networks, to assess factors that hinder their building, and to anticipate implementation games you may encounter in building or functioning within them. Thus, let us focus now on diagnostic frameworks for thinking systemically—that is, in terms of how the parts relate to the whole—*within* public organizations.

Most frameworks for thinking systemically within an agency give you a compass for aligning their various components to maximize their effectiveness. Consider two examples of management frameworks that you may encounter in your coursework and that are applicable to any level of government or type of agency. The first, known as an "integrative model of leadership," offers an information-driven model for building common purpose and agency effectiveness.[2] Leadership in this model is not just about articulating a vision, gaining buy-in, and inspiring others, although these are all critical to success. It is also about aligning the operations of various administrative subsystems—financial management, capital investment management, human resources management, and information technology (IT) management—with desired results, such as improving air quality by 5 percent or reducing the number of homeless persons by 10 percent each year.

For example, strategic information resource management (SIRM) plays a vital role in this model. SIRM involves assessing the computer hardware/software needs of an organization in light of agency missions or changing circumstances, ranking those needs in terms of priorities and cost-effectiveness, and ensuring that users have the skills to use the technology effectively. These, among other things, involve linking IT purchases to mission needs, providing adequate IT support personnel, and buying appropriate software while ensuring that different software used in various programs can "talk to each other." Throughout, the aim of the leader must be to foster communications in a readily understandable format to get needed information to program managers, personnel specialists, and budgeters in time to inform their decisions, while protecting against cybersecurity breaches at the same time that transparency for citizens is maintained.

But this is not all leaders must do in this integrated model. They must also be sure that the SIRM plan is integrated with the agency's strategic plan, its performance-based budgeting plan, its strategic human capital plan, and its strategic capital management plan. This means designing and evaluating continuous improvement of processes across all administrative subsystems. Put more concretely, leaders must ensure that personnel, financial management, IT, and infrastructure investments reinforce each other and are linked to agency mission and goals. One challenge that you and your agency may confront, however, is resistance by agency leaders and various program directors to having representatives from these functional areas involved in strategic planning and management discussions. Anecdotal evidence exists, for example, that human resource managers still often lack a seat at the table when broader strategic planning exercises, such as those discussed in chapter 7, occur in public agencies. Still, what is advocated by the integrative model of leadership *has* been done, and you should familiarize yourself with how the best-in-class have been able to do it on such a broad scale.

The second model (see Figure 10.1) goes beyond administrative subsystems and illustrates the components and logic for thinking systemically that became popular in many US states during the 1990s. In this model, a strategic planning process sets the direction and priorities, including for administrative subsystems, a process we reviewed in chapter 4. As you can see, three core elements—customer focus, performance measurement, and accountability for results—are central to this approach to systemic thinking. So, too, is alignment of the different tasks associated with the "what," "who," "how," and "how much" considerations that inform its logic. Thus, as in the leadership model, if any element does not positively reinforce the others, the quest for effectiveness suffers.

If both of these models strike you as nothing more than an embrace of the "rationality project" that has driven administrative reform movements in government, you are correct. Still, knowing how and why proper alignment of subsystems can improve organizational effectiveness and performance can help you think systemically about the obstacles and constraints you are facing as a manager and offer ways for you to think about lessening their impact. Moreover, if the aggressive patience approach we covered in chapter 4 informs your use of these strategic leadership frameworks, an important sense of realpolitik will be added to your efforts.

But what we cannot overlook in both models when democratic constitutional values become central to our thinking as public managers is the focus on bureaucratic rather than democratic administration. You can certainly read into either model opportunities

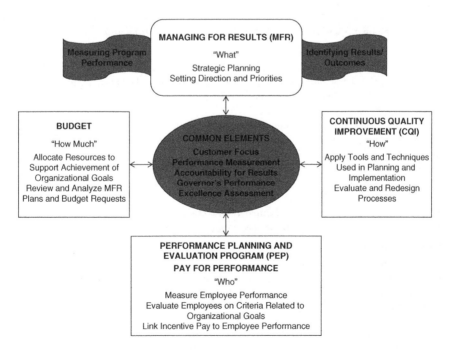

Figure 10.1 Maryland's Management Model

for advancing democratic constitutional values, and should. For example, involving citizens directly in developing such a plan or in basing performance measures at least partially on citizen preferences are important possibilities for action. Still, on their surface, each remains overwhelmingly management or instrumentally focused, so you will need to introduce democratic constitutional values more explicitly into them during your career.

Two approaches for doing so that you might find useful in this regard are offered by David Rosenbloom in what he calls "prescriptive democratic-constitutional impact statements" and "democratic-constitutional scorecards."[3] As illustrated in Table 10.1, the former are modeled on commonly used environmental impact statements and anticipate what the consequences of administrative reforms pursued under President Clinton's reinventing government (REGO) initiative might be on democratic constitutional values if adopted. Once these are identified, participants address ways to mitigate or eliminate these outcomes if they are too much of an assault on constitutional values.

Rosenbloom's proposal for a democratic-constitutional scorecard is based on the so-called "balanced scorecard" used in business but adapted for the unique responsibilities of public agencies.[4] The balanced scorecard looks at performance along four integrated dimensions: financial, customer service, internal business process, and learning and growth.[5] To illustrate how this scorecard might work, he applies a color-coded scheme to evaluate five components of the second Bush administration's management agenda. As Table 10.2 summarizes, assessed are their impact on individual rights, constitutional integrity, transparency, and rule of law. Afforded in the process by both models

Table 10.1 Example of a Democratic-Constitutional Impact Statement for the Clinton–Gore National Performance Review

---

Specific Components and Implications for Democratic-Constitutionalism

Steering, not Rowing (Outsourcing)
- Individual Rights: Reduction of constitutional and administrative law rights for individuals
- Transparency: Freedom of Information Act and Government in the Sunshine Act inapplicable; congressional oversight more difficult

Results Orientation
- Rule of Law: Loss of attention to non-mission-based values may compromise rule of law
- Transparency: Accountability for procedure may be weakened

Biennial Budgeting and Budget Rollovers
- Constitutional Integrity: Weakens congressional power of the purse
- Rule of Law: "No year money" reduces legal controls on agency spending

Internal Deregulation and Employee Empowerment
- Rule of Law: Enhances agency and employee discretion
- Constitutional Integrity: Weakens prospects for effective judicial review

Potential Mitigations

- Tailor overall prescriptions to specific programs
- Include protection of democratic-constitutional values in contracts, such as whistleblower protections, equal employment opportunity, and transparency requirements.

Source: D. H. Rosenbloom (2013) "Reinventing Administrative Prescriptions: The Case for Democratic-Constitutional Impact Statements and Scorecards," in R. F. Durant and J. R. S. Durant (eds.) *Debating Public Administration: Management Challenges, Choices, and Opportunities* (pp. 111–30) (Boca Raton, FL: CRC Press), p. 117.

Table 10.2 Example of a Democratic-Constitutional Scorecard Modeled on OMB's PMA Scorecard*

PMA Initiative	Individual Rights	Constitutional Integrity	Transparency	Rule of Law
Strategic Human Capital	Yellow Light: Reduction of due process	Yellow Light: Enhances executive authority	Yellow Light: Individualized financial arrangements	Yellow Light: Enhanced agency discretion
Competitive Sourcing	Red Light: Loss of constitutional and administrative law rights	Yellow Light: Legislative oversight more difficult	Red Light: Freedom of information, sunshine laws inapplicable	Yellow Light: Requires effective contract monitoring
Financial Performance	Green Light: No impact	Green Light: Enhanced financial accountability	Green Light: Enhanced financial reporting	Green Light: Enhanced control of spending
E-Gov	Green Light: Can inform public of legal rights	Yellow Light: Executive-centered control under OMB	Green Light: Enhances transparency	Green Light: Publicizes legal requirements
Budget and Performance Integration	Green Light: No impact	Yellow Light: Can weaken legislative role in budget decisions	Green Light: Greater information about agency performance	Yellow Light: Potential inattention to non-mission-based legal requirements

* In the PMA Scorecard, red indicates at least one serious flaw, yellow indicates success on some but not all criteria, and green indicates success on all criteria. Here, red means danger, yellow means caution, and green means positive or no impact.

Source: Rosenbloom, "Reinventing Administrative Prescriptions," p. 119.

are more systematic ways for you and your agency to ensure the consideration of values broader than economy and efficiency and to operationalize concern for democratic constitutional values that too easily get marginalized when reforms and policies are pursued or implemented by public agencies.

Thinking Purposively

Building a sense of common purpose also means you must be able to motivate actors within and outside your organization in today's networked state. French aristocrat, aviator, and author of the *Little Prince*, Antoine de Saint-Exupéry, put the power of purposiveness as a motivator of human beings this way: "If you want to build a [sailing] ship, don't drum up people to collect wood and don't assign them tasks and work, but rather teach them to long [first] for the endless immensity of the sea."[6] Modifying that logic a bit makes perfect sense as you think about the leadership role you may envision for yourself as a public manager. This is true whether or not you are applying motivation theory in a single organization or in today's networked compensatory state. For example, a 2014 workforce survey of human resource managers by the Center for State and Local Government Excellence found that staff development, succession planning, employee morale, and retaining staff for core services ranked higher as pressing concerns than compensation, health care, or retirement plan costs.[7] And each conveys a sense of agency purposiveness to government employees.

However, as we will review in this section, this logic has not always informed theories of motivation brought into public administration from other fields. More recently, however, a home-grown theory of motivation—public service motivation—is gaining momentum in public management research. The theories we will cover in this section are in no way indicative of the raft of motivation theories that exist today, but many of those not covered stem from, or are modifications of, some of the classics we will cover. The former include many you will learn more about in your studies, such as self-efficacy theory, equity theory, social learning theory, self-determination theory, goal-setting theory, needs theory, and behavior modification theory. Still, each of the theories we review in this section will help you get started in thinking about the basics of motivation theory and can help inform your approach to motivating others toward a sense of common purpose in your agency or network. But coupled with Saint-Exupéry's advice about motivating employees through "big picture" thinking, the two best pieces of advice to keep in mind from the motivation literature are that (1) the structure of a person's job affects their motivation, not just your interpersonal relationship with them; and (2) employees who do not believe you or your agency are treating or rewarding them fairly relative to "others" in the organization are less motivated, have lower commitment, and are far more likely to leave your agency.[8]

Motivation and Scientific Management

As you will recall from chapter 4, the idea that employees in organizations are largely passive, can be led by dangling material rewards in front of them, need to be closely supervised, and are interchangeable parts was ensconced in the work of early theorists such as Frederick Taylor. Nor have the principles of Taylor's scientific management approach disappeared today. Scientific management, for example, is manifested in operations research techniques that you may learn in your coursework and in the continuous process improvement focus of strategic planning that we just discussed. Indeed, it may inform the operations of some of your private sector partners, and it might be a quite effective means of motivation.

What you need to avoid as a public manager, however, is applying scientific management techniques to the wrong situations or assuming that existing processes are the correct ones for reaching your organizational goals. For example, scientific management techniques are less appropriate whenever the ends and means of what you are trying to accomplish are uncertain or controversial. By the same token, continually striving to make existing systems more efficient can be misguided if the processes themselves do not make sense for achieving your policy or program goals. Researchers call this "single-loop learning." Much better under these circumstances is what is called "double-loop learning."[9] Basically, you have to revisit the initial assumptions underlying policy or program ends to see if they are still valid and redesign processes to align with them better if they are not.[10] What is more, you would do well to ask those implementing these processes what is working and what is not, as well as their perceptions of how well the two are aligned; they are usually the ones who are best informed and from whom you might learn what to prefer.

Motivating through More Democratic Administration

Yet another, more democratically informed theory of motivation emerged in the late 1920s and early 1930s, one that placed motivation in a broader cultural context. It sought to develop in managers a democratic impulse or imperative that went beyond making a product efficiently. Proponents argued that "both private and public administration were in an important and far-reaching sense false to the ideal of democracy [in] their insistence that [it was] something peripheral to administration."[11]

Personnel specialist and industrial psychologist Ordway Tead was a major proponent of the "industrial democracy" movement in industry.[12] He defined industrial democracy as occurring when organizations "are guided and controlled in ways calculated to allow all members...an opportunity to help formulate its objectives and, also, to realize for themselves...a sense of personal growth, development, and realization."[13] Tead argued that industrial democracy was necessary at work lest democracy-at-large suffer. In the process, he claimed, even private organizations would become "training school[s] for more democracy."[14]

Tead is worth quoting at length given the estrangement of citizens from their government that was rife at the time he wrote, much like today. He argued that

the public sentiment as to the value of political democracy is, in certain quarters, increasingly skeptical and even cynical. Arguments are abroad which in conflicting fashion aver that political democracy is a failure, that good government is impossible under democratic control, that true political democracy has never been tried, that self-government is a ridiculous objective...[But] democracy is a process and a spirit and not a form...it is a dynamic experience of self-education...[whereby]...self-government is better than good government in the sense that the personal growth of citizens is more valuable than technical expertness in operation—this essentially spiritual and psychological outlook upon democracy has tended to be forgotten.[15]

But his position also had practical motivational implications for organizational effectiveness. As he put it in 1933, "The activities which people do well, faithfully, and persistently and which give them that vital sense of spontaneous generation from within are those prompted by a realization that they themselves are getting a sense of self-fulfillment from them."[16] Recall the early progressives' notion that experts applying scientific methods to motivate workers and improve industrial efficiency would cause a "rising economic tide that would lift all boats." Tead argued that the same would result if only a more democratic workplace were offered to employees.

In the end, however, industrial democracy never obtained sufficient traction in America in either private or public organizations to make a significant impact. But its logic for the workplace, at least, set the stage for putting people back into the picture as more than automatons. Indeed, his work presaged what your professors will call the "human relations" movement in motivational theory, so we will study its implications next.

The Human Relations Movement

Between 1927 and 1932, a group of industrial and social psychologists led by Elton Mayo and Fritz Roethlisberger of the Harvard Graduate School of Business conducted experiments at General Electric's Hawthorne Laboratories that would turn the world of motivation on its head. This is true despite repeated and serious criticisms ever since questioning the validity of the methodology used in the studies. You will at least read excerpts from these studies during your coursework. Although trying to discern what effect various alterations in the work environment would have on worker productivity—a traditional concern of scientific management—what they observed stunned them. No matter what they did to change the environment—dim the lights or increase the lights; give longer, shorter, or multiple rest breaks—they found that the productivity of workers increased.

Puzzled by this anomaly from conventional scientific management theory, researchers concluded that the workers were responding positively to the team's interest in them, their work, and their work conditions.[17] More precisely, they concluded that choosing one's coworkers, working as a team, being treated specially, and having a sympathetic supervisor were the real reasons for the productivity increase. For you, this means that people are not cogs-in-a-wheel or interchangeable parts in a bureaucratic machine. Nor are they robots who respond automatically to the material carrots-and-sticks that managers such as yourself might use to control them. They have their own aims, motives, needs for recognition, and desires, and you have to take these into consideration for efficiency to occur.

The Hawthorne experiments also revealed the importance to you as a manager of what is called the "informal organization." As opposed to formal authority relationships outlined on an organizational chart (the "formal" organization was most discussed in chapter 4), the Hawthorne experiments showed that coworkers—and the leaders among them—exert more control than those higher up in the chain of command over the pace, quality, and quantity of work produced. Thus, as a manager and leader, you need to learn who comprises the informal organizations in your agency, who its leaders are, and what motivates them in order for you to understand organizational behavior and then use these dynamics to advance your policy and program goals.

The Hawthorne findings were soon connected to leadership in organizations more generally by a titan of leadership studies: Chester Barnard. He wrote one of the most revered management books ever: *The Functions of the Executive*.[18] It is common today to view leadership as a two-way flow of authority between leaders and followers, but this was not so in Barnard's day. For him, however, authority had to be earned from employees.

Barnard advises us that workers will follow orders as long as they fall into what he called the employees' "zone of indifference." This does not mean that employees are actually indifferent to what they are being asked to do. Rather, they tend to comply with orders as long as you ask them to do things that (1) are consistent with their understanding of the terms of their employment, (2) involve skills that they already have or will be trained to do, (3) are not unreasonably difficult, (4) are perceived as linked to their organization's mission, and (5) are not illegal, unethical, or immoral. If an order is outside of an employee's zone of indifference (and is not immoral, unethical, or illegal), Barnard says managers have to induce their behavior by manipulating incentives to comply. Here, both material incentives—for example, pay raises—and nonmaterial incentives—such as recognition or a call to a higher purpose—are applicable and are tools you can use to motivate your colleagues.

You also need to be clear, however, that although Barnard alerted us to authority being a two-way relationship, he was not advocating participatory management, as Tead had done. For Barnard, the function of the executive is to identify a clear purpose for the organization. But setting purpose did *not* involve the participation of employees; only consultation with others at the top of the hierarchy was needed. Once discerned by those at the top, purpose had to be clearly communicated to subordinates with inducements to comply, if needed.

On these foundations was built the human relations movement. Perhaps most famous in this genre is the early work of Abraham Maslow in the 1940s.[19] Studying the factors associated with high-achieving individuals, Maslow's famous "hierarchy of needs" identifies physiology (food), safety (e.g., security and employment), and love or belonging (e.g., friendship) with what he called "lower-order needs." Meeting these needs had been the focus of the scientific management school. But to these he added three sets of higher-order needs associated with high achievers. These are esteem (e.g., need for achievement, recognition, and respect of and for others), cognitive needs (e.g., to explore and be creative), and self-actualization (reaching one's full potential). According to Maslow, persons had to satisfy lower-order needs first and move sequentially through each of the levels.

Not unlike criticisms of the scientific management movement and the Hawthorne experiments, and as noted, Maslow's work has been attacked on methodological grounds. And when subjected to testing, a variety of modifications had to be made. For example, individuals did not have to move sequentially from lower to higher needs, needs changed over time, and not all individuals aspired to self-actualize. But the intellectual power of Maslow's ideas informed future motivation theories, and they are a must read in whole or in part in your studies.

In 1960, Douglas McGregor leveled a devastating critique of the notion of top-down control as an effective organizational strategy, with his solution to the problem based on Maslow's higher-order needs.[20] In his book, *The Human Side of Enterprise*, McGregor "named" two different styles of leadership that he called Theory X (larger scientific management) and Theory Y (Maslow's higher-order needs). The former is an authoritarian style of control in which you closely supervise subordinates, because workers are basically lazy, uninterested in work, do not want responsibility, and avoid it as much as they can. In contrast, and the style he promoted as decidedly more effective than direct control, Theory Y posits that if employees exhibit these characteristics, it is because of the embrace in organizations of Theory X control techniques. The old adage, "Treat people like children and they will behave like children," comes to mind. His Theory Y advice: unleash the contributions of employees by appealing to Maslow's higher-order needs. But McGregor's typology also has not gone without criticism, perhaps for reasons that you were thinking about as you read its description. For instance, not everyone is a self-starter or wants more responsibility. Examples also exist of companies that have failed while using Theory Y precepts.[21]

None of the critiques leveled at Barnard, Maslow, or McGregor, however, stopped other researchers from joining them in questioning the validity of top-down authoritarian control. For example, Frederick Herzberg found that even if organizations allow employees to attain Maslow's lower-order needs—or what Herzberg called "hygiene" factors—workers *expected* those needs to be met.[22] Thus, they were not motivated by them to improve their performance. For this to occur, organizations—and you as a public manager—had to allow them to attain Maslow's higher-order needs—what Herzberg called "motivation" factors—meaning affording workers a path to self-actualization. Doing so includes giving employees recognition for work well done, as well as affording them important, meaningful jobs that give them a sense of worth and accomplishment when performed well. It is better, of course, if they internalize their own sense of motivation, as they are likely to do when Maslow's higher-order needs are fulfilled by doing the work.

Herzberg's "two-factor" (motivation-hygiene) theory of motivation was further refined for managers over the next two decades by a variety of so-called "contingency" perspectives. These sought to identify when different styles of management are more or less appropriate. Although not specifically motivated by Herzberg's theory, work by Paul Hersey and Kenneth Blanchard is illustrative.[23] In contrast to earlier human relations theorists, they identify general conditions where more authoritarian styles—what they call "task-oriented" approaches—are necessary, along with when more people-oriented styles are appropriate—what they call "relationship-oriented" approaches. Moreover, they advise you to adapt your style depending on the readiness of workers to assume self-direction and the level of their support for the policy; the higher your subordinates' readiness level, the more relationship rather than task-oriented you can be.

However, what you should be asking yourself at this point in thinking about contingency approaches is, "Can I really do that? Is it within me as a person to move from leadership style to leadership style and back again depending on the readiness level of those reporting to me?" Arguably, there is nothing worse than trying to use a style of leadership in which you do not believe or with which you are not personally comfortable. If, for instance, you basically do not trust people and revert quickly to a Theory X style of leadership at the first sign of difficulty, those reporting to you will become cynical—and vice versa. Certainly, some managers are adept at linking their style to the circumstances, and you may be one of them. All you are asked to do at this point is assess your ability to do so and decide how committed or skilled you will be in doing so.

Your adaptability to contingencies notwithstanding, recent research on what is called "emotional intelligence" (EI) suggests that you should definitely consider and develop strategies premised on your own emotions and those of others.[24] As you have seen throughout this book, the field of public administration has been dominated in many ways by the rationality project, a focus that typically categorizes emotions, sentiments, and feelings as irrational and too "soft" to be meaningful. How many times have you heard the following, for example: "Don't let your emotions get in the way of clear thinking." And if you are a woman, you are probably familiar and outraged with this term as a sexist putdown of your gender's qualifications to lead. Regardless of your gender, though, these sentiments should remind you of the plight of settlement women in the early Progressive Era, which we covered in chapter 1. Although they celebrated a public administration focused on community, nurturing, caring, and empathy, their efforts were framed derogatorily as "municipal housekeeping" and "public motherhood."

In contrast, proponents of EI theory posit that different kinds of intelligence exist besides means–ends rationality, including intelligence in emotions management and discernment. In addition to intuition, they contend that successful managers monitor their own and others' emotions; regulate their own emotions; and use that information, self-awareness, and emotional control to guide their own thinking and behavior when engaged in either task or relationship strategies. Despite ongoing controversies over EI, the commonsense "bottom line" is that your emotional temperament and empathy for those of others matters and are critical skills for your success in the public service. Knowing yourself and others is advice that cannot harm anyone in any situation! Consider how former US Treasury secretary Timothy Geithner reflects in his memoir that his "empathy mistakes" during the 2007–09 financial crisis were his major shortcoming in dealing with this otherwise most "wonkish" of all policy challenges.[25]

As you may read in your classes, the most explicit application of EI thinking to public management scholarship today is the concept of "emotional labor" (EL). As Mary Guy, Meredith Newman, and Sharon Mastracci develop and apply the term, EL reflects the reality that much of your public service career will involve person-to-person interactions.[26] In turn, this human dimension—with superiors, subordinates, and clients, among others—is the essence of the public service profession and requires managers to work "with feeling." In the process, EI can play a major role in determining how successful your interactions will be. As Guy and her associates put it, "The insight, anticipation, and tenor of the communication between persons prior to, during, and after the exchange requires energy, focus, and sensing—in other words, emotional labor."[27] These award-winning scholars also argue that EL has several organizational implications for you, depending on what types of agencies you work in during your career. After all, some types of organizations involve more EL than others and, thus, require different levels of EI. Those organizations—and different types of jobs within them—that are more relational than analytical or mechanical in nature require recruitment and retention policies that identify, train, nurture, and reward EI and not just technical or cognitive skills (e.g., 911 operators, caseworkers in social agencies, and police officers). Otherwise, you and your agency might expect that employees will focus only on the instrumental rather than the relational nature of their jobs. What is more, as a manager you might expect a host of pathologies that researchers have linked to EL. These include, but are not limited to, a variety of stress-related problems: loss of job satisfaction, absenteeism, reduced motivation, cynicism, and role alienation.

Toward Performance-Based Reward Systems

Since the early 1980s, governments at all levels in the United States have earnestly pursued yet another technique that has proven effective in the private sector when quality of work can be measured objectively: a pay-for-performance (PFP) model of motivation.

Efforts to reward government employees for high performance certainly are not new. As you will learn in your coursework, incentives for high performance were first instituted in the federal government in the Incentive Awards Act of 1954. The Salary Reform Act then authorized, among other things, a step-up-in-grade reward for high performance, defined as exceeding established levels of competence. Moreover, this system carried the day until the Civil Service Reform Act of 1978 expanded its scope and rewards—at least in theory—with PFP and bonuses.

Employees must see a direct link between their effort and their performance, they must believe that their supervisor can and will recognize good work by rewarding performance, and they must value that reward. Moreover, the relationship between the three is multiplicative, which means all three must be high for motivation to be high. If this reminds you a bit of early scientific management theorists' focus on material sources of motivation, you are to an extent correct. However, because rewards can be nonmaterial as well (e.g., recognition of meritorious accomplishment), it goes beyond Taylor's theory.

The common-sense nature of its theoretical underpinnings notwithstanding, researchers consistently find these efforts to be disappointing when introduced into the public sector.[28] To begin with, you might have already been thinking that some of the basic assumptions of expectancy theory are difficult to satisfy in public agencies. For example, faith in the fairness of the evaluation process itself is often compromised by perceptions of favoritism, while rewards have been less than promised as legislatures frequently cut back the expected size of awards. Diminished in the process is the perceived value of the reward. Likewise, the premise of awarding individuals rather than groups flies in the face of today's team-focused workplace, although if you have worked on a group project, you know how this can be abused as well by free-riders!

Also standing in the way of success, some argue, are public–private sector distinctions in implementation contexts. For starters, although salaries in the private sector are confidential, salaries in the public sector are open to everyone. Consequently, differences in merit pay are more visible to employees and external audiences and, thus, invite invidious and uninformed comparisons that can hurt morale. Likewise, budget and institutional constraints in the public sector often prompt financial rewards that many claim are too small to make a difference (although small rewards may also occur in the private sector). In contrast, expanding revenue streams can—but do not necessarily—combine with less transparency in the private sector to allow for higher merit pay and greater salary distinctions among employees. Moreover, because public and legislative oversight committees expect frugality in using taxpayer dollars, the political environment also places downward pressures on the size of rewards.[29] Equally problematic are public sector unions, for they have been quite successful in delaying and sometimes foiling PFP efforts (e.g., at the departments of Homeland Security and Defense).[30] Finally, evidence exists that PFP can have a disparate impact on African American employees, as well as on older workers.[31]

Reciting these shortcomings in no way should suggest to you that PFP systems will go away or that you should turn your back on them (although you may read other scholars in your coursework who would abandon PFP in the public sector). As noted, not everyone agrees with the idea of public–private distinctions diminishing the motivational power of PFP.[32] For example, although individual merit increases may be small, they accumulate and multiply over the years as they are built into an employee's base salary. Evidence also exists that it works better at lower rather than higher levels in an agency (as roles and tasks become more ambiguous), in distributive rather than regulatory agencies, and for programs with unambiguous goals and objectives. And, most important, politicians who press for performance-related pay see it as a mechanism to call bureaucrats to account, to punish them for noncompliance with politicians' preferences, and to make them conform to public and political expectations.[33] As such, efforts to refine PFP are likely to be on your plate during most of your career, and you may be among those who figure out when, where, and how this approach is effective.

Tapping into Public Service Motivation

The final and most recent iteration of motivation theory in the public sector that you may find useful is what is called "public service motivation" (PSM). Those engaged in the study of PSM start from the rebuttable premise that persons who aspire to work or are already employed in public agencies hold more public service-oriented values than those who work in private organizations.[34] Importantly, you should recognize, however, that this has not been tested empirically except with contemporaneous comparative surveys of public versus private sector employees. As J. Edward Kellough notes, to really test either premise, researchers would need to measure PSM for a group of subjects prior to their entry into a career (say, while they are undergraduates) and then follow up with them years later to see if they went into public service careers. Yet we still rely on those contemporaneous surveys of people in the public and private sectors. We see that those in the public sector have more PSM, but how do we know that this is not merely some type of rationalization on their part or whether they developed PSM after going to work in the public sector?[35]

This aside, and directly in contrast to the ideas underlying scientific management, human relations theory, contingency theories, and PFP, public employees are expected to be less motivated by elements you or your agency can manipulate than by their own intrinsic values. Specifically, public employees are said to be less motivated than their private sector counterparts by material rewards, to be more motivated by "doing good" for society, and to be more public interest-oriented. Even more significant, many proponents of PSM argue that those values can overcome other inadequate hygiene and motivation factors (such as lower pay scales, job insecurity, and unrecognized performance).

But is this really true? To date, research evidence is mixed. Studies using survey data suggest that older employees in public agencies, women, and the higher educated exhibit one or more of these PSM traits. Likewise, family background and religiosity matter. Employees raised in families stressing compassion, religious principles, and church attendance exhibit more of a public service commitment than others. Prior research also suggests that your agency can help increase the likelihood that employees and partnering organizations will harbor PSM values. For example, public employees who perceive lower levels of goal ambiguity and red tape, as well as employee-friendly policies, tend to exhibit these traits more than those who do not.[36] As such, they should be more motivated by normative appeals to a sense of public service value in their work.

Moreover, your agency can take further steps to nurture a sense of common purpose through PSM by applying what is called a "normative governance" model. This model is predicated on three critical processes, all designed to maintain the values of—or infuse values into—an agency's workforce (including democratic constitutional values). More precisely, your agency might select employees partly on the basis of their commitment to your agency's values, socialize new or existing employees by reinforcing these values, and evaluate them and agency partners partly in terms of their adherence to these values. At a minimum, however, the results of prior research are positive enough to suggest that you should be on the lookout as a public manager for such traits in agency personnel. Nor can it do any harm for you to include appeals to PSM in your arsenal of motivational tools. Importantly, although some claim that it cannot be combined with other motivational tools, especially performance-based pay, Edmund Stazyk, among others, has found in his research that PFP rewards are typically so small that they do not undermine appeals to PSM.[37]

A normative governance model incorporating PSM theory may also be an important component of motivating actors in various types of collaborative networks.[38] After all, a sense of common purpose grounded in PSM might have been the original reason for partnering with others. Moreover, a key component for you or your agency in building and sustaining any effective collaborative network in today's compensatory state is to identify the existing aspirations of potential partners or to raise and nurture the aspirational level of these actors if none exists. Certainly, looking for and framing appeals to PSM might play a significant motivational role in doing so.

Thinking Democratically

As you have read throughout this book, the values of bureaucratic administration have repeatedly trumped those of democratic administration in the public sector. Animated by a durable policy coalition of progressives, the corporate sector, and the social science professions, the political economy of administrative reform has propelled business rather than governance thinking to the forefront of our field. Citizens, at best, are often considered consumers of public services and, at worst, as meddlesome in affairs that experts should dominate. With the argumentative turn in the policy sciences that we covered extensively in chapter 6, however, a new impetus has been added to revive democratic administration in the twenty-first century.

Before reviewing the logic and prescriptions of the deliberative democracy movement, you need to appreciate its intellectual lineage in public administration. Since we have already covered the Progressive Era lineage during the first three decades of the twentieth century in the works of Jane Addams, William Allen, Mary Parker Follett, and Ordway Tead, our journey at this point starts in the 1940s. Writing in 1943, David Levitan called for abandoning the politics/policy–administration dichotomy covered in chapter 5, as well as the civil service system we reviewed in chapter 7. His rationale? Because policy is made at all levels of bureaucracy, "Democratic government means democracy in administration, as well as in the original legislation. It is of supreme importance that the administrative machinery established for the execution of legislation be permeated with democratic spirit and ideology" rather than the façade of neutrality.[39]

Although not sharing Levitan's animus toward the dichotomy or the civil service, David Lilienthal, then-chairman of the Board of Directors of the Tennessee Valley Authority, shared his embrace of democratic administration. Lilienthal portrayed the central problem of American governance as follows: "How can a democracy enjoy the advantages of a strong central government and escape the evils of remote, top-heavy central administration?"[40] His answer: "To achieve democracy [in America] citizen groups of all kinds must be brought into the administrative process and given the opportunity to state their interests and to help make and execute decisions affecting their lives."[41]

As we have covered in earlier chapters, the 1960s through the 1980s also saw in academia the aforementioned public choice, New Public Administration, and Blacksburg Manifesto initiatives—with their accompanying critiques. Although none of these pleas took enough root to upset the dominant instrumental focus of administrative reform movements, they totally lost traction in the 1990s and beyond as, first, REGO and, then, the New Public Management (NPM) dominated discourse and practice in the nation. But critics seeking meaningful citizen involvement in agency decision making did not remain silent during this era.

The most intellectually supple critique of REGO and the NPM—as well as the state of public administration—was offered by Louis Gawthrop in the late 1990s. The linkage is clear between Gawthrop's warning to us as public administration professionals and Levitan's arguments.[42] He wrote, "Many public administrators have sought to link their commitment of service to the amoral pretense of detached objectivity, neutral competence, and dispassionate rationality."[43] But public managers need to ask themselves not only "what do I do?" but "what should I do?" Moreover, addressing REGO and the NPM, Gawthrop argued that their focus on public managers as "entrepreneurs" undermined the spirit of public administration—unless the "value vision of democracy serve[d] as the lifeblood of [that] entrepreneurial spirit."[44]

But how can this democratic infusion take place today when it has so often been marginalized in administrative reform prescriptions—and, hence, in agencies—in the past? Is there something different today that makes a cultural shift toward democratic administration more likely to succeed? Proponents of what they call "practice-oriented" administration and policy analysis believe that the answer is yes—primarily because of the argumentative turn in public policy.

As we have stressed in prior chapters, your career as a public manager means living in a world where value pluralism—a range of competing values—predominates. It is a world where conflict is intense and prolonged in crowded policy and administrative spaces dealing with wicked problems. And it is a world where "solutions" are not so much objectively "right" or "wrong" but contingent and conditional, because their "meaning depends upon the setting in which they arise" and the values traded off.[45] Consequently, you will have to recognize that policy and administrative initiatives have to involve the collective puzzlement on behalf of society that we have covered in several chapters.

To gain a better sense of what this mental "revolution" entails for you or your agency trying to build a sense of common purpose infused with democratic constitutional values, it is worth quoting the following from Hendrik Wagenaar and Noam Cook:

Problem solving...is not manipulation of preconceived variables, but more the discovery of preferences, position, and identity; it is finding out where one stands in relation to the problem at hand...Success is not measured in terms of the one best solution, that is, in terms of a position on a set of hard, preferably quantitative, criteria, but rather...in terms of transitions. Is it possible, we need to ask, given a particular social problem, to move to a different situation that, although perhaps not optimal, is perceived by the parties involved as a gain in value and/or understanding, while the reverse does not hold?[46]

Dvora Yanow adds: "To understand the consequences of a policy [or administrative action or rule] for the broad range of people it will affect requires *local knowledge*—the very mundane, but still expert, understanding of and practical reasoning about local conditions derived from lived experience."[47] Grounded in the tradition of American pragmatism associated with philosopher John Dewey, this "logic of localism" and the wisdom of citizens turns traditional policy analysis and administration on its head. Echoing Deborah Stone, Yanow continues:

> Policy analysts have been trained since the 1970s largely in the technical tools of decision- and cost-benefit analysis. While these tools can be very useful in helping analysts think through their analyses more thoroughly and systematically, this training has…led to a dependence on the analytic expertise of the professional, concomitantly devaluing the typically non-quantitative expertise of policy clients/constituents which derives from their own intimate familiarity with the lived experience that the policy seeks somehow to alter.[48]

For you as a public manager, the consequences of these insights are profound. It means acknowledging that citizens have expertise—albeit of a different type than you have—that agencies badly need in today's compensatory state. In fact, citizens are a key component of it! It means not only being an intelligent consumer of the work that policy analysts present you but ensuring that those working with you also embrace the experiential "expertise" that citizens can bring to the policy and management "table." It also means occasionally convening what proponents of deliberative democracy call "communities of action" and taking advantage of new and evolving modes of conflict resolution. Finally, it means developing regimes of "joint responsibility" for building "shared problem definitions and…common paths of problem resolution."[49]

As such, this move toward democratic administration requires an expansion of your own and your agency's administrative toolkit as well. In addition to acquiring the conflict resolution tools that we reviewed in chapter 6, you or your agency should acquire skills in "meaning audits" and "meaning architectures." The former assess what meanings, for whom, and with what implications for implementation citizens hold, while the latter reveal the collective meanings of citizens in given locations. Also useful for you and your agency are skills in "frame analysis" and "category analysis." The former seeks to understand how diverse actors speak about things and how this effects policy and administration. The latter focuses on how people categorize things in ways that include or exclude policy options or target groups. Arguably, learning these techniques is no longer a luxury for you or your agency and will prove just as useful as all the econometric techniques in your toolkit for building a sense of common purpose informed by democratic constitutional values in an argumentative era.

Thinking Institutionally

To this point, this book has been all about alerting you to—and arming you for—the new challenges, choices, and opportunities facing public managers in the twenty-first century. As such, you can be excused for perhaps thinking that (1) change and innovation are the most important aspects of your job in the public service and (2) there is no redeeming value in the legacy you are inheriting from your predecessors. These, however, are the last things that this book wishes to convey to you! So, this concluding section builds the explicit case for you to make second nature the idea of "thinking institutionally" as your career in the public service unfolds in America's compensatory state.

What does this mean? Hugh Heclo describes institutional thinking as a mindset that embraces "faithful reception" of the past and the bountiful institutional inheritance bequeathed to you by your predecessors. However, it also means taking what you have inherited from your predecessors but adapting it to new and evolving challenges in order to ensure that the essence of that heritage is not lost. As Heclo puts it, "Innovation is not meant to change the [policy or administrative] game. Legitimate innovation is meant to realize, with greater skill and fidelity, the larger potential of what the game is"—in this case, helping to advance the original principles of a democratic republic.[50]

The example that Heclo uses is the game of basketball. As you may know, the game today is quite different from even 20 years ago, let alone when James Naismith invented it in the nineteenth century. What your father or mother might have considered "traveling" with the basketball is now overlooked, while the three-point jump shot has made it more exciting. But the game's ultimate aims, essence, and spirit remain the same. In the same way, writes Heclo, the astute public manager "seeks to understand what has been received in light of new circumstances...Without appropriate adaptations, the legacy cannot be preserved."[51]

Thinking institutionally also means weighing the long-term implications of your actions for your organization and society. This means thinking beyond the immediate instrumental focus of day-to-day operations and decisions to longer-term normative and ethical concerns about your organization's "soul" and your nation's well-being. An exclusive focus on instrumentalism, neutral competence, and the fiction of a politics/policy–administration dichotomy leads in both the short and long term to a mentality that says politics—decisions over who gets what, when, why, and how—are not your concern. More broadly, focusing solely on instrumentalism takes away the significance of the role played by public servants such as yourself and makes it tangential to the American experiment. It reduces you and other public managers to technicians whose only concern is the immediate objective. Lost in the process are the ennobling purposes those means, techniques, and expertise serve in helping to ensure a democratic republic.

A focus purely on instrumentalism also leads to a mindset that says, in effect, "as long as I didn't do anything wrong, I must have done right." Again, Gawthrop puts it best: public servants "become assiduous in ritualizing the moral life and, in the process...become expert in moralizing the ritual" of compliance.[52] He argues that this ethic of compliance results in a dysfunctional attitude of "tell me what is right, what is wrong, what is legal, what is not permissible...so that I can be judged an ethical public servant."[53] But history is replete with examples where what was legal was not ethical or even functional for our nation.

Nor is the "disinterestedness" we associate with and often laud as a part of neutral competence in the public service without its own negative side effects. Given a moment's pause to reflect, you would probably contend that disinterestedness has *not* characterized some of the most noted instances of advancing democratic constitutional values and meeting the needs of an American republic under stress in legally and ethically unassailable ways. As Gawthrop writes, at various times in American history, "career public servants have revealed an indomitable faith in the ethical-moral principles embedded in democracy" and put themselves at risk.[54] A recent study by Cheol Liu and John

Mikesell finds that high levels of corruption in states have substantive policy implications as well.[55] Analyzing political corruption convictions between 2007 and 2012, they found that more corrupt states spend more money on construction, highways, and police protection programs and less on health, education, and welfare. The former types of expenditures allow more opportunity to use public money for their own gain.

As Michael Spicer also contends, figuring out how best to ensure that policy and program goals and objectives are met is not the only responsibility of public managers in a democratic republic.[56] Stripped of the façade of a politics/policy–administration dichotomy, governance in America is partially but importantly about public managers facilitating enough comity among actors with sometimes irresolvable and incommensurable values to ensure that violence is avoided. It is about helping to run and preserve the legitimacy of the republic.

Yes, the American system of separation of powers, checks and balances, and federalism is a challenging context within which to pursue these aims. At some points during your public service career, you will wish that sufficient power was located somewhere in the Madisonian system to "do the right thing" without politics getting in the way. At other times, though, you might be relieved when the checks and balances afforded protect policies, programs, and values that you cherish from ill-advised or unreasonable assaults. Regardless, as Norton Long wrote in 1949, there remains no place in the Madisonian system where enough power is concentrated to split politics and policy from administration; agencies must be political actors and play the game well or else find themselves and the citizens they represent at a disadvantage for resources and influence.[57] Moreover, this is just as true in collaborative networks as in single agencies.

Thinking institutionally also means more than merely splitting the difference among competing interests and values or reacting to whatever pressures dominate. It also requires the courage to think about the constitutional implications of your actions, the precedents they set if they become general principles of behavior or decision making, and the ethical shortcomings that can harm your agency in both the short and long term. As Heclo puts it, a common thread exists today "in a great deal of the dysfunctional behavior we see.... people neglecting and dishonoring the longer-term values of the going concern of which they are a part."[58]

Keep in mind that reporting the shortcomings of your agency may not be an easy or pleasant process. A 2014 survey of federal employees by the US Merit Systems Protection Board, for example, finds that the overwhelming majority of respondents did not fear retaliation by their agency, supervisor, or coworkers for what is called "whistleblowing." However, nearly 30 percent thought that their organizational life would become "more difficult" for reporting inappropriate practices.[59] When asked whether they agreed or disagreed with a statement reading, "I can disclose a suspected violation of any law, rule or regulation without fear of reprisal," nearly 20 percent either disagreed or disagreed strongly. Forms of reprisal mentioned by whistleblowers "included firing, suspension, grade level downgrade, and transfers to different locations or to jobs with less desirable duties."[60] This, despite 11 percent of respondents saying that they had witnessed illegal or wasteful activities in their agency. Perhaps even more distressing, nearly 40 percent of respondents reported that "nothing happened" after misdeeds were reported. What was also clear, however, was that reprisals and non-responsiveness to reports differed across agencies, with some much more conducive to whistleblowing than others. Thus, as another part of thinking institutionally, it will be incumbent upon you as a manager to create a supportive environment for employees reporting wrongdoing in your agency and among your agency's partners.

Throughout this book, we have covered ways to help you evaluate how much weight tradition should be given in any instance. These include, but are not restricted to, basing your choices on the efficiency on which our field's founders focused and that contemporary proponents of the NPM embrace; on the social equity premises of representatives of the New Public Administration; on the agency perspective of proponents of the Blacksburg Manifesto; on the welfare economics of many policy analysts; and on the competing values framework offered by Rosenbloom in his democratic-constitutional scorecards and impact statements.

But thinking institutionally also involves what Philip Selznick calls defending the "institutional integrity" of your agency.[61] He saw organizations as more than the sum total of such things as their structures, procedures, informal organization, and standard operating procedures. At a certain point, he argued, they take on a life beyond the instrumental tasks they perform; those tasks and behaviors take on social meaning to everyone participating in them. They acquire a core competency—what they do best—and an organizational essence that goes beyond the sum total of their parts.

Upon this premise, Selznick argues that true leadership in an organization strives to protect its organizational essence from what he calls "opportunism." Rather than merely accept or reject outright proposed changes in policies, programs, and procedures, "administrative conservators" weigh whether they advance or threaten the organization's essence.[62] Much as Heclo suggests, this does not rule out changes to enhancing that essence but, rather, weighs whether or not they do so. If they do not, then change is too risky and likely unwise. In fact, change can produce more disastrous results than a failure to innovate.

Perhaps all this seems too heavy a load for any single individual such as yourself to tackle. If so, it might help to keep in mind the words of John Tyler, used as the epigraph to this book: "Good and able Men [and women] had better govern than be gover'd, since 'tis possible, indeed highly probable, that if the able and good withdraw themselves from Society, the venal and ignorant will succeed."[63] Moreover, as Martin Luther King so famously pointed out, "The arc of the Moral Universe is long, but It bends towards Justice."[64] To date, public managers have played critical roles in bending that arc of history toward—but also sometimes away from—justice. They have done so in both small and bold ways, and they will continue to do so in the future—hopefully, in a positive direction. Indeed, whether America ever completely lives up to its promise to be a "City on a Hill" for *all* the people will partially depend on the skills, temperaments, and values of its public managers at all levels of government.

At the conclusion of the Constitutional Convention in Philadelphia, Benjamin Franklin was asked what kind of government had been produced. "A republic," he responded, "if you can keep it."[65] Joining arms with others in the public service in a sense of common purpose infused with democratic constitutional values in the compensatory state, your will, commitment, and competence will provide the answer to this question. If you find that responsibility inspiring and see public service as a vocation rather than merely a job, the future of the American republic will rest in good hands.

Notes

Preface

1. H. Kaufman (1981) "Fear of Bureaucracy: A Raging Pandemic," *Public Administration Review*, 41(1), 1–9.
2. D. F. Morgan, R. T. Green, C. W. Shinn, and K. S. Robinson (2013) *Foundations of Public Service*, 2nd ed. (Armonk, NY: M. E. Sharpe); D. H. Rosenbloom (2013) "Reinventing Administrative Prescriptions: The Case for Democratic-Constitutional Impact Statements and Scorecards," in R. F. Durant and J. R. S. Durant (eds.) *Debating Public Administration: Management Challenges, Choices, and Opportunities* (pp. 111–30) (Boca Raton, FL: CRC Press).
3. C. Stivers (2000) *Bureau Men, Settlement Women: Constructing Public Administration in the Progressive Era* (Lawrence: University Press of Kansas), p. 14.

1 Engaging the Call to Public Service

1. D. H. Rosenbloom (1983) "Public Administrative Theory and the Separation of Powers," *Public Administration Review*, 43(3), 219–27.
2. Rather than repeat the inelegant phrase, "as a public manager in the career civil service at any level of government," the remainder of this book will largely use the more elegant phrase, "public manager." Moreover, because leadership can take place at any level of an organization—and since the pressures associated with the challenges, choices, and opportunities covered in this book involve leadership by public managers—you should understand that this is implied throughout the book when the phrase "public manager" is used.
3. P. F. Drucker (2001) *The Essential Drucker: Selection from the Management Works of Peter F. Drucker* (New York: HarperCollins), p. 81.
4. S. M. Lipset (1996) *American Exceptionalism: A Double-Edged Sword* (New York: W. W. Norton).
5. The phrase "administrative state" in this essay refers to a state managed by public administrators according to public administrative theories and principles. It is a state in which swaths of discretion are delegated by statutes to unelected career civil servants in agencies, who then interpret and operationalize statutory language that is often vague, contradictory, and even conflicting. As such, it raises questions of accountability in a democratic republic.
6. A. Jackson (1829) "First Annual Message to Congress," December 8, Washington, DC, http://www.presidency.ucsb.edu/ws/?pid=29471.

7. Jackson, "First Annual Message to Congress," emphasis added.

8. M. Nelson (2014) "A Short, Ironic History of American National Bureaucracy," in C. Jillson and D. B. Robertson (eds.) *Perspectives on American Government: Readings in Political Development and Institutional Change* (New York: Routledge), p. 380.

9. L. Marshall (1967) "The Strange Stillbirth of the Whig Party," *American Historical Review*, 72(2), 455–56.

10. These figures came from "Backgrounder on the Pendleton Act," *Basic Readings in U.S. Democracy*, http://usinfo.state.gov/usa/infousa/facts/democrac/28.htm, date accessed June 25, 2007. As of July 2010, available at http://usa.usembassy.de/etexts/democrac/28.htm.

11. M. Diamond (1959) "Democracy and the Federalist: A Reconsideration of the Framers' Intent," *American Political Science Review*, 53(1), 52–68.

12. D. Carpenter (2001) *The Forging of Bureaucratic Autonomy: Reputations, Networks, and Policy Innovation in Executive Agencies, 1862–1928* (Princeton: Princeton University Press).

13. W. Kennedy (2002) *Roscoe: A Novel* (New York: Viking), pp. 8–9.

14. C. Millard (2011) *Destiny of the Republic: A Tale of Madness, Medicine, and the Murder of a President* (New York: Anchor Books), p. 103.

15. Millard, *Destiny of the Republic*, p. 126.

16. Millard, *Destiny of the Republic*, p. 289.

17. Millard, *Destiny of the Republic*, p. 289.

18. T. Jones (2012) *More Powerful than Dynamite: Radicals, Plutocrats, Progressives, and New York's Year of Anarchy* (New York: Bloomsbury).

19. Millard, *Destiny of the Republic*, p. 241.

20. G. E. Roberts (2001) "A History of the Federal Civil Service: A Values-Based Perspective," in S. E. Condrey and R. Maranto (eds.) *Radical Reform of the Civil Service* (pp. 15–41) (Lanham, MD: Lexington Books).

21. American Federation of Government Employees (2011) Issue Papers, National Council of EPA Locals Council #238, February, http://thehill.com/sites/default/files/afge%20council%20238%20issue%20papers_0.pdf, p. 22; Roberts, "A History of the Federal Civil Service."

22. P. Van Riper (1958) *The History of the United States Civil Service* (Evanston, IL: Row, Peterson, and Company).

23. V. Ostrom (2008) *The Intellectual Crisis in American Public Administration*, 3rd ed. (Tuscaloosa: University of Alabama Press).

24. W. Wilson (1887) "The Study of Administration," *Political Science Quarterly*, 2(2), 197–222.

25. Wilson, "The Study of Administration," p. 200.

26. E. J. Eisenach (1994) *The Lost Promise of Progressivism* (Lawrence: University Press of Kansas); D. T. Rodgers (1998) *Atlantic Crossings: Social Politics in a Progressive Age* (Cambridge: Harvard University Press).

27. G. B. Adams and D. L. Balfour (2004) *Unmasking Administrative Evil*, rev. ed. (Armonk, NY: M. E. Sharpe); G. B. Adams and D. L. Balfour (2012) "The Prospects for Revitalizing Ethics in a New Governance Era," in R. F. Durant (ed.) *The Oxford Handbook of American Bureaucracy*, paperback ed. (pp. 766–85) (Oxford: Oxford University Press); G. Alchon (1985) *The Invisible Hand of Planning: Capitalism, Social Science, and the State in the 1920s* (Princeton: Princeton University Press); M. Lee (2008) *Bureaus of Efficiency: Reforming Local Government in the Progressive Era* (Milwaukee, WI: Marquette University Press).

28. J. H. Wilson (1992) *Herbert Hoover: Forgotten Progressive* (Long Grove, IL: Waveland Press).

29. K. A. Clements (1999) *Woodrow Wilson: World Statesman* (Chicago: Ivan R. Dee), pp. 6–7.

30. Clements, *Woodrow Wilson*, p. 101.
31. T. Throntveit (2013) "Philosophical Pragmatism and the Constitutional Watershed of 1912," *Political Science Quarterly*, 128(4), 617–51, esp. at 646–47.
32. L. L. Gould (2013) *Edith Kermit Roosevelt: Creating the Modern First Lady* (Lawrence: University Press of Kansas), p. 96.
33. C. Stivers (2000) *Bureau Men, Settlement Women: Constructing Public Administration in the Progressive Era* (Lawrence: University Press of Kansas), p. 9.
34. The seminal work on this topic is Stivers, *Bureau Men, Settlement Women*.
35. Stivers, *Bureau Men, Settlement Women*, pp. 11–12.
36. C. T. Goodsell (2005) "The Bureau as Unit of Governance," in P. du Gay (ed.) *The Values of Bureaucracy* (pp. 1–40) (Oxford: Oxford University Press), p. 33.
37. L. B. Bingham, T. Nabatchi, and R. O'Leary (2005) "The New Governance: Practices and Processes for Stakeholder and Citizen Participation in the Work of Government," *Public Administration Review*, 65(5), 547–58.
38. Clements, *Woodrow Wilson*, p. 26.
39. The discussion in this section relies heavily on F. C. Mosher (ed.) (1975) *American Public Administration: Past, Present, Future* (Birmingham: University of Alabama Press). Although about 80 percent of the graduates of these training programs went into government, other graduates later joined university programs.
40. Universities offering courses included Columbia University, New York University, Harvard University, Johns Hopkins University, Northwestern University, University of Chicago, University of Wisconsin, University of Minnesota, and Stanford University.
41. G. Alchon, *The Invisible Hand of Planning*.
42. The issue of uneven program quality reached its apex in 1967 with the publication of the *Honey Report to the Carnegie Corporation*. The report emphasized the overall weakness of most public administration programs in the United States. The field took steps to address this situation in ways that ensured top-quality programs for you today. In 1974, under the auspices of the National Association of Schools of Public Affairs and Administration (NASPAA), it established common program standards, and in 1986, NASPAA was approved as an accrediting body by the Council on Postsecondary Accreditation (COPA). It has since been renewed as an accrediting body by COPA's successor, the Council for Higher Education Accreditation. Since then, NASPAA's accrediting process has adapted to the changing needs of public affairs education and has become increasingly rigorous. By 2014, 285 graduate programs were accredited by NASPAA (now called the Network of Schools of Policy, Affairs, and Administration).
43. W. G. Scott (1992) *Chester I. Barnard and the Guardians of the Managerial State* (Lawrence: University Press of Kansas).
44. D. Waldo (1984) *The Administrative State: A Study of the Political Theory of American Public Administration*, 2nd ed. (New York: Holmes & Meier), p. 202.
45. Waldo, *The Administrative State*, p. 203.
46. Waldo, *The Administrative State*, p. 99.
47. R. A. Dahl (1947) "The Science of Public Administration: Three Problems," *Public Administration Review*, 7(1), 1–11.
48. F. X. Sutton (2006) "Nation Building in the Heyday of the Classic Development Ideology," in F. Fukuyama (ed.) *Nation-Building: Beyond Afghanistan and Iraq* (Baltimore: Johns Hopkins University Press), Chapter 2.
49. H. A. Simon (1997) *Administrative Behavior: Decision-Making Processes in Administrative Organizations*, 4th ed. (New York: Free Press).
50. N. E. Long (1954) "Public Policy and Administration: The Goals of Rationality and Responsibility," *Public Administration Review*, 14(1), 22–31.
51. Long, "Public Policy and Administration, p. 22.

52. N. E. Long (1949) "Power and Administration," *Public Administration Review*, 9(4) 257–64, at 257.
53. D. F. Kettl, P.W. Ingraham, R. P. Sanders, and C. Horner (1996) *Civil Service Reform: Building a Government that Works* (Washington, DC: Brookings Institution Press), p. 17.
54. D. B. Robertson (2012) *Federalism and the Making of America* (New York: Routledge), p. 11.
55. T. J. Lowi (1979) *The End of Liberalism: The Second Republic of the United States*, 2nd ed. (New York: W. W. Norton).
56. W. Lilley III and J. C. Miller III (1977) "The New 'Social Regulation,'" *Public Interest*, 47(Spring), 49–61.
57. F. Marini (ed.) (1971) *Toward a New Public Administration: The Minnowbrook Perspective* (Scranton, PA: Chandler Press).
58. E. Bardach (1977) *The Implementation Game: What Happens After a Bill Becomes a Law* (Cambridge: MIT Press).
59. See, for example, H. W. J. Rittel and M. M. Webber (1973) "Dilemmas in a General Theory of Planning," *Policy Sciences*, 4(2), 155–69.
60. J. Kooiman (1993) *Modern Governance: New Government–Society Interactions* (London: SAGE).
61. H. Heclo (1974) *Modern Social Politics in Britain and Sweden: From Relief to Income Maintenance* (New Haven: Yale University Press), p. 305.
62. Kettl, Ingraham, Sanders, and Horner, *Civil Service Reform*, p. 17.
63. For an insightful discussion of the impact of international factors on public administration within nations, see L. J. O'Toole Jr and K. Hanf (2002) "American Public Administration and Impacts of International Governance," *Public Administration Review*, 62(Special Issue), 158–67.
64. T. Benner, W. H. Reinicke, and J. M. Witte (2003) "Global Public Policy Networks: Lessons Learned and Challenges Ahead," *Brookings Review*, 21(2), 18–21.
65. H. B. Milward and K. G. Provan (2000) "Governing the Hollow State," *Journal of Public Administration Research and Theory*, 10(2), 359–80.
66. F. W. Scharpf (1993) *Games in Hierarchies and Networks: Analytical and Empirical Approaches to the Study of Governance Institutions* (Frankfurt am Main, Germany: Campus Verlag).
67. M. A. Hajer and H. Wagenaar (eds.) (2003) *Deliberative Policy Analysis: Understanding Governance in the Network Society* (Cambridge: Cambridge University Press), p. 19.
68. J. M. Gaus (1947) *Reflections on Public Administration* (Birmingham: University of Alabama Press).

2 Thinking Ecologically

1. J. M. Gaus (1947) *Reflections on Public Administration* (Birmingham: University of Alabama Press).
2. D. F. Morgan, R. T. Green, C. W. Shinn, and K. S. Robinson (2013) *Foundations of Public Service*, 2nd ed. (Armonk, NY: M. E. Sharpe); D. H. Rosenbloom (2013) "Reinventing Administrative Prescriptions: The Case for Democratic-Constitutional Impact Statements and Scorecards," in R. F. Durant and J. R. S. Durant (eds.) *Debating Public Administration: Management Challenges, Choices, and Opportunities* (pp. 111–30) (Boca Raton, FL: CRC Press).
3. United States Census Bureau (2001) *World Population Profile: 1998 Highlights*, 19 March, http://www.census.gov/ipc/www/wp98001.html.
4. D. H. Meadows, D. L. Meadows, J. Randers, and W. W. Behrens III (1972) *The Limits of Growth: A Report for the Club of Rome's Project on the Predicament of Mankind* (New York: Universe Books).
5. Poverty (2013) "Not Always With Us," *The Economist*, June 1–7, pp. 22–4.
6. U.S. Census Bureau, *World Population Profile: 1998 Highlights*.

7. N. C. Roberts (2013) "Spanning 'Bleeding' Boundaries: Humanitarianism, NGOs, and the Civilian-Military Nexus in the Post-Cold War Era," in Durant and Durant, *Debating Public Administration* (pp. 247–62).

8. M. T. Klare (2001) *Resource Wars: The New Landscape of Global Conflict* (New York: Metropolitan Books).

9. G. Hiscock (2012) *Earth Wars: The Battle for Global Resources* (Singapore: John Wiley, p. 15.

10. J. Parker (2013) "From Baby Boom to Bust: Crashing Fertility Will Transform the Asian Family," *The Economist (Special Edition: The World in 2014)*, November 18, p. 66.

11. Parker, "From Baby Boom to Bust."

12. Parker, "From Baby Boom to Bust."

13. N. Eberstadt (2001) "The Population Implosion," *Foreign Policy*, 123 (March/April), 42–53.

14. Population and Recession (2012) "Europe's Other Crisis," *The Economist*, June 30, p. 56.

15. R. F. Durant (2000) "Whither the Neoadministrative State? Toward a Polity-Centered Theory of Administrative Reform," *Journal of Public Administration Research and Theory*, 10(1), 79–109.

16. "Joint Efforts Needed to Fight HIV and TB, UN Health Agencies Say" (2001), *UN News Service*, March 23, http://www.un.org/News/dh/latest/page2.html#49.

17. "Joint Efforts Needed to Fight HIV and TB."

18. C. Howard (2012) "The World Is Fat," *The Economist (Special Edition, The World in 2013)*, November 8, p. 32.

19. The National Commission on Fiscal Responsibility and Reform (2010) "The Moment of Truth" (Washington, DC: The White House), December, p. 11.

20. Health-Spending Projections (2012) "Up, Up and Away," *The Economist*, June 16, http://www.economist.com/node/21556931, date accessed July 1, 2012.

21. L. M. Bartels (2008) *Unequal Democracy: The Political Economy of the New Gilded Age* (Princeton: Princeton University Press). This refers to the cut-throat excesses of corporate greed and corruption in the late nineteenth century that accompanied the industrial revolution and led to massive economic inequalities in America.

22. J. S. Hacker and P. Pierson (2012) "Presidents and the Political Economy: The Coalitional Foundations of Presidential Power," *Presidential Studies Quarterly*, 42(1), 101–31.

23. Hacker and Pierson, "Presidents and the Political Economy," p. 105.

24. Hacker and Pierson, "Presidents and the Political Economy," p. 109.

25. Statistics used in this paragraph are taken from Singletons (2012) "The Attraction of Solitude," *The Economist*, August 25–31, pp. 47–8, at 47.

26. S. Somashekhar and K. Tumulty (2013) "With New Year, Medicaid Takes On a Broader Health-Care Role," *Washington Post*, December 31, http://www.washingtonpost.com /national/health-science/with-new-year-medicaid-takes-on-a-broader-health-care -role/2013/12/31/83723810-6c07-11e3-b405-7e360f7e9fd2_story.html?hpid=z1.

27. Somashekhar and Tumulty, "With New Year, Medicaid Takes On a Broader Health-Care Role."

28. The following is taken from H. Pollack (2013) "The Complacency of the Meritocrats," *Washington Post*, June 21, http://www.washingtonpost.com/blogs/wonkblog/wp/2013 /06/21/the-complacency-of-the-meritocrats/.

29. A. P. Carnevale and S. J. Rose (2004) "Socioeconomic Status, Race/Ethnicity, and Selective College Admissions," in R. D. Kahlenberg (ed.) *America's Untapped Resource: Low-Income Students in Higher Education* (New York: Century Foundation Press).

30. D. F. Kettl (2009) *The Next Government of the United States: Why Our Institutions Fail Us and How to Fix Them* (New York: W. W. Norton).

31. J. A. Stever (2001) "Review: Values for Public Administration Renewal," *Public Administration Review*, 61(5), 625–29, at 625.

32. M. J. Sklar (1988) *The Corporate Reconstruction of American Capitalism, 1890–1916* (Cambridge: Cambridge University Press), p. 46.

33. A. Trachtenberg (2007) *The Incorporation of America: Culture and Society in the Gilded Age* (New York: Hill and Wang), pp. 88–9.

34. G. Alchon (1985) *The Invisible Hand of Planning: Capitalism, Social Science, and the State in the 1920s* (Princeton: Princeton University Press), pp. 8–9.

35. Alchon, *The Invisible Hand of Planning*.

36. R. H. Wiebe (1967) *The Search for Order, 1877–1920* (New York: Hill and Wang).

37. M. J. Sandel (1984) "The Procedural Republic and the Unencumbered Self," *Political Theory*, 12(1), 81–96.

38. M. J. Sandel (1996) *Democracy's Discontent: America in Search of a Public Philosophy* (Cambridge: Harvard University Press).

39. For a summary of this research, see C. Kerwin, S. Furlong, and W. West (2012) "Interest Groups, Rulemaking, and American Bureaucracy," in R. F. Durant (ed.) *The Oxford Handbook of American Bureaucracy*, paperback ed. (pp. 590–611) (Oxford: Oxford University Press).

40. R. Longley (2012) "Lifetime Earnings Soar with Education: Masters Degree Worth $2.5 Million Income Over a Lifetime," http://usgovinfo.about.com/od/moneymatters/a/edan-dearnings.htm, date accessed June 24, 2012.

41. G. S. Wood (2002) *The American Revolution: A History* (New York: Modern Library), p. 9.

42. J. Appleby (2000) *Inheriting the Revolution: The First Generation of Americans* (Cambridge: Harvard University Press); D. W. Howe (1979) *The Political Culture of the American Whigs* (Chicago: University of Chicago Press); R. V. Remini (2008) *A Short History of the United States* (New York: HarperCollins).

43. J. N. Neem (2010) "Civil Society and American Nationalism, 1776–1865," in E. S. Clemens and D. Guthrie (eds.) *Politics + Partnerships: The Role of Voluntary Associations in America's Political Past and Present* (pp. 29–53) (Chicago: University of Chicago Press), p. 39.

44. T. Skocpol, M. Ganz, and Z. Munson (2000) "A Nation of Organizers: The Institutional Origins of Civic Volunteerism in the United States," *American Political Science Review*, 94(3), 527–46; W. J. Novak (2001) "The American Law of Association: The Legal–Political Construction of Civil Society," *Studies in American Political Development*, 15(Fall), 163–88; P. Starr (2004) *The Creation of the Media: Political Origins of Modern Communications* (New York: Basic Books).

45. Neem, "Civil Society and American Nationalism," pp. 36–7; also see T. Skocpol, Z. Munson, A. Karch, and B. Camp (2002) "Patriotic Partnerships: Why Great Wars Nourished American Civic Voluntarism," in I. Katznelson and M. Shefter (eds.) *Shaped by War and Trade: International Influences on American Political Development* (pp. 134–80) (Princeton: Princeton University Press).

46. L. Peter, (2013) "Lampedusa Disaster: Europe's Migrant Dilemma," *BBC News*, October 4, http://www.bbc.com/news/world-europe-24396020, date accessed June 29, 2014.

47. J. Faux (1999) "Lost on the Third Way," *Dissent*, Spring, pp. 67–76, at 72.

48. J. S. Hacker and P. Pierson (2010) *Winner-Take-All Politics: How Washington Made the Rich Richer—And Turned Its Back on the Middle Class* (New York: Simon & Schuster).

49. L. Farmer (2014) "Economic Gardening is Growing, But What is It?" *Governing*, June 27, http://www.governing.com/topics/finance/gov-how-to-grow-businesses-that-grow-the-economy.html, date accessed June 29, 2014.

50. C. F. Epstein (1999) "The Part-Time Solution and the Part-Time Problem," *Dissent*, Spring, pp. 96–8.

51. Schumpeter (2012) "Fixing the Capitalist Machine: Some Sensible Ideas for Reviving American's Entrepreneurial Spirit," *The Economist*, September 29–October 5, p. 72.

52. T. L. Friedman (1999) *The Lexus and the Olive Tree* (New York: Farrar, Straus & Giroux).

53. W. Greider (1997) *One World, Ready or Not: The Manic Logic of Global Capitalism* (New York: Simon & Schuster).

54. K. P. Erb (2013) "Achtung Baby: Bono Defends U2 Tax Moves," *Forbes*, September 24, http://www.forbes.com/sites/kellyphillipserb/2013/09/24/achtung-baby-bono-defends-u2-tax-moves/, date accessed June 29, 2014.

55. R. F. Durant, J. M. Johnston, and A. M. Girth (2009) "American Exceptionalism, Human Resource Management, and the Contract State," *Review of Public Personnel Administration*, 29(3), 207–29; Kettl, *The Next Government of the United States*.

56. R. A. Dahl (1999) *On Democracy* (New Haven: Yale University Press); J. G. S. Koppell (2012) "Metaphors and the Development of American Bureaucracy," in Durant, *The Oxford Handbook of American Bureaucracy* (pp. 128–50).

57. E. Helleiner (2011) "Understanding the 2007–2008 Global Financial Crisis: Lessons for Scholars of International Political Economy," *Annual Review of Political Science*, 14(June), 67–87.

58. See, for example, Hacker and Pierson, *Winner-Take-All Politics*; A. Roberts (2010) *The Logic of Discipline: Global Capitalism and the Architecture of Government* (New York: Oxford University Press).

59. T. L. Friedman (2005) *The World Is Flat: A Brief History of the Twenty-First Century* (New York: Farrar, Straus & Giroux).

60. R. Florida (2002) *The Rise of the Creative Class: And How It's Transforming Work, Leisure, Community and Everyday Life* (New York: Basic Books), p. 283; see Durant, "Whither the Neoadministrative State."

61. Florida, *The Rise of the Creative Class.*

62. J. C. Morris and D. J. Watson (2013) "Commentary: Is the World 'Flat' or 'Spiky'? Rethinking the Governance Implications of Globalization for Economic Development," in Durant and Durant, *Debating Public Administration* (pp. 244–46).

63. K. L. Schlozman, S. Verba, and H. E. Brady (2012) *The Unheavenly Chorus: Unequal Political Voice and the Broken Promise of American Democracy* (Princeton: Princeton University Press), p. 5.

64. A. Haque (2001) "GIS, Public Service, and the Issue of Democratic Governance," *Public Administration Review*, 61(3), 259–65; J. Musso, C. Weare, T. Bryer, and T. L. Cooper (2013) "Toward 'Strong Democracy' in Global Cities? Social Capital Building, Theory-Driven Reform, and the Los Angeles Neighborhood Council Experience," in Durant and Durant, *Debating Public Administration* (pp. 89–109). But see T. L. Cooper (2011) "Citizen-Driven Administration: Civic Engagement in the United States," in D. C. Menzel and H. L. White (eds.) *The State of Public Administration: Issues, Challenges, and Opportunities* (pp. 238–56) (Armonk, NY: M. E. Sharpe).

65. L. A. Brainard and J. G. McNutt (2010) "Virtual Government–Citizen Relations: Informational, Transactional, or Collaborative?" *Administration & Society*, 42(7), 836–58; T. A. Bryer and S. Zavattaro (eds.) (2011) "Symposium on Social Media and Public Administration," *Administrative Theory & Praxis*, 33(3), 325–432.

66. J. Lanier (2013) *Who Owns the Future?* (New York: Simon & Schuster).

67. Lanier, *Who Owns the Future?* p. xxv.

68. Haque, "GIS, Public Service, and the Issue of Democratic Governance."

69. Lanier, *Who Owns the Future?*

70. A. L. Friedberg (2002) "American Antistatism and the Founding of the Cold War State," in I. Katznelson and M. Shefter (eds.) *Shaped by War: International Influences on American Political Development* (pp. 239–66) (Princeton: Princeton University Press), p. 240.

71. G. S. Wood (2008) *The Purpose of the Past: Reflections on the Uses of History* (New York: Penguin Press), p. 255.

72. S. M. Lipset (1996) *American Exceptionalism: A Double-Edged Sword* (New York: W. W. Norton).

73. M. A. Eisner (2000) *From Warfare State to Welfare State: World War I, Compensatory State Building, and the Limits of the Modern Order* (University Park: Pennsylvania State University Press).

74. B. Balogh (2009) *A Government Out of Sight: The Mystery of National Authority in Nineteenth-Century America* (Cambridge: Cambridge University Press).

75. Balogh, *A Government Out of Sight*, p. 24.

76. S. Skowronek (1982) *Building a New American State: The Expansion of National Administrative Capacities, 1877–1920* (Cambridge: Cambridge University Press).

77. D. M. Kennedy (2005) *Freedom from Fear: The American People in Depression and War, 1929–1945* (Oxford: Oxford University Press).

78. Eisner, *From Warfare State to Welfare State*, p. 12.

79. W. J. Novak (2008) "The Myth of the 'Weak' American State," *American Historical Review*, 119(3), 752–72, at 760.

80. R. Inglehart (1990) *Culture Shift in Advanced Industrial Society* (Princeton: Princeton University Press).

81. J. M. Berry (1999) *The New Liberalism: The Rising Power of Citizen Groups* (Washington, DC: Brookings Institution Press).

82. R. D. Putnam and D. E. Campbell (2012) *Amazing Grace: How Religion Divides and Unites Us* (New York: Simon & Schuster).

83. American Political Science Association (1950) "Toward a More Responsible Two-Party System: A Report of the Committee on Political Parties," *American Political Science Review*, 44(3), Part 2, Supplement.

84. American Political Science Association, "Toward a More Responsible Two-Party System," p. 1.

85. T. E. Mann and N. J. Ornstein (2012) *It's Even Worse than It Looks: How the American Constitutional System Collided With the New Politics of Extremism* (New York: Basic Books).

86. M. Davey (2014) "Twinned Cities Now Following Different Paths," *New York Times*, January 12, http://www.nytimes.com/2014/01/13/us/twinned-cities-now-following-different-paths.html?&action=click&contentCollection=U.S.&module=MostEmailed&version=Full&region=Marginalia&src=me&pgtype=article, accessed January 13, 2014.

3 Linking Problems, Policy, and Public Management

1. For the most obvious and now-classic exposition of this argument, see P. H. Appleby (1945) *Big Democracy* (New York: Knopf).

2. Appleby, *Big Democracy*, p. 118.

3. H. Wagenaar and S. D. N. Cook (2003) "Understanding Policy Practices: Action, Dialectic, and Deliberation in Policy Analysis," in M. A. Hajer and H. Wagenaar (eds.) *Deliberative Policy Analysis: Understanding Governance in the Network Society* (pp. 139–71) (Cambridge: Cambridge University Press), p. 170.

4. H. Heclo (1974) *Modern Social Politics in Britain and Sweden: From Relief to Income Maintenance* (New Haven: Yale University Press), p. 305.

5. F. R. Baumgartner, S. Brouard, E. Grossman, S. G. Lazardeux, and J. Moody (2014) "Divided Government, Legislative Productivity, and Policy Change in the USA and France," *Governance*, 27(3), 423–47.

6. Quoted in D. DeFusco (2014) "President Kerwin: Rule-Making Key to Shaping Public Policy," *SPA News*, May 30, http://www.american.edu/spa/news/kerwin-rule-making-shapes-policy-2014.cfm, date accessed June 1, 2014.

7. D. Waldo (1984) *The Administrative State: A Study of the Political Theory of American Public Administration*, 2nd ed. (New York: Holmes & Meier).

8. Statistics provided in this section on aging and associated chronic diseases rely heavily on S. Raymond (2003) "Foreign Assistance in an Aging World," *Foreign Affairs*, 82(2), 91–105.

9. For example, UN-designated high-fertility nations (where replacement rates will not be reached until 2045–50) comprise only 4.4 percent of the world's population and are expected to rise to only 5.2 percent by 2025. Moreover, for nations in Africa where the ravages of HIV are most dire and poignant, fertility rates are expected to fall anywhere from 23 percent to 39 percent by 2020.

10. N. Birdsall (2003) "Asymmetric Globalization: Global Markets Require Good Global Politics," *Brookings Review*, 21(2), 22–7, at 24.

11. Contraception and Development (2012) "Choice Not Chance," *The Economist*, July 14–20, pp. 53–4.

12. Contraception and Development, "Choice Not Chance."

13. D. A. Wolf and A. A. Amirkhanyan (2010) "Demographic Change and Its Public Sector Consequences," *Public Administration Review*, 70(S1), S12–23.

14. Wolf and Amirkhanyan, "Demographic Change and Its Public Section Consequences," p. S14.

15. Government Accountability Office (2012) *Opportunities to Reduce Duplication, Overlap and Fragmentation, Achieve Savings, and Enhance Revenue* (Washington, DC: GAO-12–342SP), February 28, http://www.gao.gov/products/GAO-12-342SP, date accessed July 7, 2012.

16. A. Haque (2001) "GIS, Public Service, and the Issue of Democratic Governance," *Public Administration Review*, 61(3), 259–65.

17. J. Galaskiewicz (1985) "Interorganizational Relations," *Annual Review of Sociology*, 11, 281–304; R. H. Hall (1999) *Organizations: Structures, Processes, and Outcomes* (Upper Saddle River, NJ: Prentice Hall); W. Powell (1998) "Learning From Collaboration: Knowledge and Networks in the Biotechnology and Pharmaceutical Industries," *California Management Review*, 40(3), 228–40.

18. S. S. Dawes, A. M. Cresswell, and T. A. Pardo (2013) "From 'Need to Know' to 'Need to Share': Tangled Problems, Information Boundaries, and the Building of Public Sector Knowledge Networks," in R. F. Durant and J. R. S. Durant (eds.) *Debating Public Administration: Management Challenges, Choices, and Opportunities* (pp. 67–88) (Boca Raton, FL: CRC Press).

19. This discussion relies heavily on statistics afforded in J. O. Lanjouw (2003) "Opening Doors to Research: A New Global Patent Regime for Pharmaceuticals," *Brookings Review*, 21(2), 13–17.

20. Raymond, "Foreign Assistance in an Aging World," p. 102.

21. Government Accountability Office (2012) *Progress Made to Deter Fraud, but More Could Be Done* (Washington, DC: GAO-12–801T), June 8, http://www.gao.gov/products/GAO-12-801T.

22. Government Accountability Office (2008) *Human Capital Planning Has Improved, but Strategic View of Contractor Workforce Is Needed* (Washington, DC: GAO-08–582), May 28, http://www.gao.gov/products/GAO-08-582, date accessed July 7, 2012.

23. J. Huang, C. Pray, and S. Rozelle (2002) "Enhancing the Crops to Feed the Poor," *Nature*, 418(August 8), 678–84, at 678.

24. J. A. Foley (2011) "Can We Feed the World and Sustain the Planet?" *Scientific American*, November, pp. 60–5, at 62.

25. See, for example, R. S. Hails (2002) "Assessing the Risks Associated with New Agricultural Practices," *Nature*, 418(August 8), 685–88; R. L. Paarlberg (2001) *The Politics of Precaution: Genetically Modified Crops in Developing Countries* (Baltimore: Johns Hopkins University Press).

26. For a summary of these issues and their consequences, see R. F. Durant with T. Boodphetcharat (2004) "The Precautionary Principle," in R. F. Durant, D. Fiorino, and R. O'Leary (eds.)

Environmental Governance Reconsidered: Challenges, Choices, and Opportunities (pp. 105–44) (Cambridge: MIT Press).

27. This discussion borrows heavily from R. L. Paarlberg (2003) "Reinvigorating Genetically Modified Crops," *Issues in Science & Technology*, Spring. Reprinted on List Serve of agbioreview@yahoo.com, date accessed April 24, 2003.

28. Government Accountability Office (2008) *Agencies Are Proposing Changes to Improve Oversight, but Could Take Additional Steps to Enhance Coordination and Monitoring* (Washington, DC: GAO-09-60), November 5, http://www.gao.gov/products/GAO-09-60, date accessed July 7, 2012.

29. J. M. Hollander (2003) *The Real Environmental Crisis: Why Poverty, Not Affluence, Is the Environment's Number One Enemy* (Berkeley: University of California Press).

30. Hollander, *The Real Environmental Crisis*, p. 40.

31. M. Kearns, R. Grove-White, P. Macnaghten, J. Wilsdon, and B. Wynne (2006) "From Bio to Nano: Learning Lessons from the UK Agricultural Biotechnology Controversy," *Science as Culture*, 15(4), 291–307.

32. R. F. Durant and J. S. Legge Jr (2005) "Public Opinion, Risk Perceptions, and Genetically Modified Food Regulatory Policy: Reassessing the Calculus of Dissent among European Citizens," *European Union Politics*, 6(2), 181–200; R. F. Durant and J. S. Legge Jr (2006) "'Wicked Problems,' Public Policy, and Administrative Theory: Lessons from the GM Food Regulatory Arena," *Administration & Society*, 38(3), 309–34; J. S. Legge Jr and R. F. Durant (2010) "Public Opinion, Risk Assessment, and Biotechnology: Lessons from Attitudes toward Genetically Modified Foods in the European Union," *Review of Policy Research*, 27(1), 59–76.

33. E. Montpetit (2003) *Misplaced Distrust: Policy Networks and the Environment in France, the United States, and Canada* (Vancouver: University of British Columbia Press).

34. Montpetit, *Misplaced Distrust*, p. 71.

35. The following examples are taken from Durant with Boodphetcharat, "The Precautionary Principle," pp. 134–35.

36. Genetically Modified Company (2002) "Sceptics Abound. Has Monsanto Learned Its Lesson Since Causing a Stir in the Late 1990s?" *The Economist*, August 15, www.agbioworld.com, date accessed August 18, 2002.

37. L. K. Caldwell (1990) *Between Two Worlds: Science, the Environmental Movement, and Policy Choice* (Cambridge: Cambridge University Press), p. xiii.

38. J. Lubchenco (2002) "State of the Planet 2002: Science and Sustainability," presented at the Earth Institute, Columbia University, May 13, www.earth.columbia.edu/sop2002/sopagenda.html, date accessed July 10, 2002.

39. R. Leakey and R. Lewin (1996) *The Sixth Extinction: Patterns of Life and the Future of Humankind* (New York: Anchor Books).

40. R. F. Durant (2004) "Reconceptualizing Purpose," in Durant, Fiorino, and O'Leary, *Environmental Governance Reconsidered* (pp. 29–34), p. 30.

41. J. Gillis (2013) "Climate Change Seen Posing Risk to Food Supplies," *New York Times*, November 1, http://www.nytimes.com/2013/11/02/science/earth/science-panel-warns-of-risks-to-food-supply-from-climate-change.html?_r=0.

42. A. Liptak (2013) "Supreme Court to Hear Challenge to E.P.A. Rules on Gas Emissions," *New York Times*, October 15, http://www.nytimes.com/2013/10/16/us/politics/supreme-court-to-hear-challenge-to-epa-emissions-rules.html?_r=0.

43. B. G. Rabe (2004) *Statehouse and Greenhouse: The Emerging Politics of American Climate Change Policy* (Washington, DC: Brookings Institution Press).

44. Data in this section on sustainable cities are taken from M. Bloomberg (2013) "Bloomberg: Why Sandy Forced Cities to Take Lead on Climate Change," *CNN*, August 26, http://www.cnn.com/2013/08/21/world/europe/bloomberg-why-sandy-force-cities/.

45. World Commission on Environment and Development (1987) *Our Common Future* (New York: Oxford University Press).

46. See, for example, R. C. Paehlke (2004) "Sustainability," in Durant, Fiorino, and O'Leary, *Environmental Governance Reconsidered* (pp. 35–68).

47. Quotations in this section are from V. Vaitheeswaran (2002) "Survey: The Global Environment," *The Economist*, July 4, www.economist.com/science/displayStory.cfm?storyid=1199867, date accessed July 9, 2002.

48. Also see D. J. Fiorino (2010) "Sustainability as a Conceptual Focus for Public Administration," *Public Administration Review*, 70(S1), S78–88.

49. W. D. Ruckelshaus (1995) "Stopping the Pendulum," *Environmental Forum*, 12(6), 25–9; D. J. Fiorino (1996) "Toward a New System of Environmental Regulation: The Case for an Industry Sector Approach," *Environmental Law*, 26, 457–88.

50. D. J. Fiorino (2006) *The New Environmental Regulation* (Cambridge: MIT Press).

51. Air Quality and Race (2014) "The Colour of Pollution: The Air is Getting Cleaner, but Less So for Non-Whites," *The Economist*, May 24–30, p. 29.

52. D. John (1994) *Civic Environmentalism: Alternatives to Regulation in States and Communities* (Washington, DC: Congressional Quarterly Press).

53. P. Murphy (2000) "Public Rails against Urban Traffic," *Environmental News Network*, March 14, http://www.enn.com/enn-features-archive/2000/03/03142000/ rails_9940.asp.

54. M. B. Gerrard (1994) *Whose Backyard, Whose Risk: Fear and Fairness in Toxic and Nuclear Waste Siting* (Cambridge: MIT Press).

55. J. Kahn (2001) "Energy Efficiency Programs Set for Bush Budget Cuts," *New York Times*, April 5, http://www.nytimes.com/2001/04/05/politics/05BUDG.html.

56. R. W. Cobb and C. D. Elder (1983) *Participation in American Politics: The Dynamics of Agenda-Building* (Baltimore: Johns Hopkins University Press).

57. See especially the 2001–03 *High Risk Series* of the US General Accounting Office.

58. General Accounting Office (2003) *Major Management Challenges and Program Risks: Environmental Protection Agency* (Washington, DC: GAO-03–112).

4 Aligning Structure and Strategy

1. For a robust set of essays defending bureaucracy, see P. du Gay (ed.) (2005) *The Values of Bureaucracy* (Oxford: Oxford University Press).

2. G. Berk, D. C. Galvan, and V. Hattam (eds.) (2013) *Political Creativity: Reconfiguring Institutional Order and Change* (Philadelphia: University of Pennsylvania Press).

3. C. Hood (1998) *The Art of the State: Culture, Rhetoric, and Public Management* (Oxford: Oxford University Press).

4. D. Osborne and T. Gaebler (1992) *Reinventing Government: How the Entrepreneurial Spirit Is Transforming the Public Sector* (New York: Penguin Books).

5. H. H. Gerth and C. W. Mills (1946) *From Max Weber: Essays in Sociology* (New York: Oxford University Press).

6. Gerth and Mills, *From Max Weber*.

7. D. Waldo (1948) *The Administrative State: A Study of the Political Theory of American Public Administration* (New York: Ronald Press).

8. F. W. Taylor (1947) *The Principles of Scientific Management* (New York: Harper and Brothers), originally published in 1911.

9. J. C. Tonn (2003) *Mary P. Follett: Creating Democracy, Transforming Management* (New Haven: Yale University Press).

10. H. L. Schachter (2012) "A Gendered Legacy? The Progressive Reform Era Revisited," in R. F. Durant (ed.) *The Oxford Handbook of American Bureaucracy*, paperback ed. (pp. 77–100) (Oxford: Oxford University Press), p. 83.

11. G. Alchon (1985) *The Invisible Hand of Planning: Capitalism, Social Science, and the State in the 1920s* (Princeton: Princeton University Press).

12. W. E. Nelson (1982) *The Roots of American Bureaucracy, 1830–1900* (Cambridge: Harvard University Press), p. 82.

13. H. W. J. Rittel and M. M. Webber (1973) "Dilemmas in a General Theory of Planning," *Policy Sciences*, 4(2), 155–69.

14. H. Seidman (1998) *Politics, Position, and Power: The Dynamics of Federal Organization*, 5th ed. (New York: Oxford University Press).

15. J. N. Clarke and D. C. McCool (1996) *Staking Out the Terrain: Power and Performance among Natural Resource Agencies*, 2nd ed. (Albany: State University of New York Press).

16. Clarke and McCool, *Staking Out the Terrain*.

17. T. H. Hammond and J. H. Knott (1996) "Who Controls the Bureaucracy? Presidential Power, Congressional Dominance, Legal Constraints, and Bureaucratic Autonomy in a Model of Multi-institutional Policy-Making," *Journal of Law, Economics, and Organization*, 12(1), 119–66; D. E. Lewis (2003) *Presidents and the Politics of Agency Design: Political Insulation in the United States Government Bureaucracy, 1946–1997* (Stanford: Stanford University Press); B. D. Wood and J. Bohte (2004) "Political Transaction Costs and the Politics of Administrative Design," *Journal of Politics*, 66(1), 176–202.

18. Lewis, *Presidents and the Politics of Agency Design*.

19. For a more thorough discussion of this problem, see S. Maynard-Moody and S. Portillo (2012) "Street-Level Bureaucracy Theory," in Durant, *The Oxford Handbook of American Bureaucracy* (pp. 252–77).

20. L. E. Lynn Jr, C. J. Heinrich, and C. J. Hill (2000) "Studying Governance and Public Management: Challenges and Prospects," *Journal of Public Administration Research and Theory*, 10(2), 233–62, at 238.

21. A. C. Rudalevige (2005) "The Structure of Leadership: Presidents, Hierarchies, and Information Flows," *Presidential Studies Quarterly*, 35(2), 333–60.

22. J. H. Knott and G. J. Miller (1987) *Reforming Bureaucracy: The Politics of Institutional Choice* (Upper Saddle River, NJ: Prentice Hall).

23. R. T. Golembiewski (1987) "Public Sector Organization: Why Theory and Practice Should Emphasize Purpose, and How to Do So?" in R. C. Chandler (ed.) *A Centennial History of the American Administrative State* (pp. 433–74) (New York: Free Press).

24. B. G. Peters (1996) *The Future of Governing: Four Emerging Models* (Lawrence: University Press of Kansas).

25. Osborne and Gaebler, *Reinventing Government*. Reinventing government was first popularized by a former city manager (Ted Gaebler) and a journalist (David Osborne).

26. Government Accountability Office (2006) *Highlights of a GAO Forum: Federal Acquisition Challenges and Opportunities in the 21st Century* (Washington, DC: GAO-07-45SP), October 6, p. 1.

27. L. D. Terry (2005) "The Thinning of Administrative Institutions in the Hollow State," *Administration & Society*, 37(4), 426–44.

28. Golembiewski, "Public Sector Organization"; G. W. Rainey (1990) "Implementation and Managerial Creativity," in D. J. Palumbo and D. Calista (eds.) *Implementation and the Policy Process* (pp. 89–105) (New York: Greenwood Press).

29. D. F. Kettl and J. J. DiIullio (eds.) (1995) *Cutting Government: A Report of the Brookings Institution's Center for Public Management* (Washington, DC: Brookings Institution Press); D. Osborne and P. Plastrik (1997) *Banishing Bureaucracy: The Five Strategies for Reinventing Government* (Reading, MA: Addison-Wesley); F. J. Thompson (ed.) (1993) *Revitalizing State and Local Public Service: Strengthening Performance, Accountability, and Citizen Confidence*, National Commission on the State and Local Public Service (San Francisco: Jossey-Bass).

30. Golembiewski, "Public Sector Organization"; Rainey, "Implementation and Managerial Creativity"; M. Hammer and J. Champy (1993) *Reengineering the Corporation: A Manifesto for Business Revolution* (New York: HarperBusiness).

31. Kettl and DiIullio, *Cutting Government*; P. C. Light (1995) *Thickening Government: Federal Hierarchy and the Diffusion of Accountability* (Washington, DC: Brookings Institution Press); Thompson, *Revitalizing State and Local Public Service*.

32. Light, *Thickening Government*.

33. See, for example, D. N. Ammons (ed.) (1995) *Accountability for Performance: Measurement and Monitoring in Local Government* (Washington, DC: International City/Council Management Association); D. N. Ammons (1995) "Overcoming the Inadequacies of Performance Measurement in Local Government: The Case of Libraries and Leisure Services," *Public Administration Review*, 55(1), 37–47; General Accounting Office (1995) *Managing for Results: Critical Actions for Measuring Performance* (Washington, DC: GAO/T-GGD/AIMD-95-187).

34. R. Agranoff (2007) *Managing within Networks: Adding Value to Public Organizations* (Washington, DC: Georgetown University Press).

35. J. S. Luke (1998) *Catalytic Leadership: Strategies for an Interconnected World* (San Francisco: Jossey-Bass).

36. W. Wilson (1887) "The Study of Administration," *Political Science Quarterly*, 2(2), 197–222.

37. Berk, Galvan, and Hattam, *Political Creativity*, p. 33.

38. J. P. Diggins (1996) *Max Weber: Politics and the Spirit of Tragedy* (New York: Basic Books), p. 84.

39. T. J. Lowi (1969) *The End of Liberalism: The Second Republic of the United States* (New York: W. W. Norton).

40. E. S. Redford (1969) *Democracy in the Administrative State* (New York: Oxford University Press).

41. H. G. Frederickson (1971) "Organization Theory and New Public Administration," in F. Marini (ed.) *Toward a New Public Administration: The Minnowbrook Perspective* (Scranton, PA: Chandler Press).

42. V. Ostrom (1973) *The Intellectual Crisis in American Public Administration* (Tuscaloosa: University of Alabama Press).

43. G. L. Wamsley, R. N. Bacher, C. T. Goodsell, P. S. Kronenberg, J. A. Rohr, C. M. Stivers, O. F. White, and J. F. Wolf (1990) *Refounding Public Administration* (Newbury Park, CA: SAGE).

44. K. J. Meier and L. J. O'Toole Jr (2006) *Bureaucracy in a Democratic State: A Governance Perspective* (Baltimore: Johns Hopkins University Press).

45. D. Schon (1983) *The Reflective Practitioner* (New York: Basic Books); R. P. Hummel and C. Stivers (2012) "Postmodernism, Bureaucracy, and Democracy," in Durant, *The Oxford Handbook of American Bureaucracy* (pp. 324–45).

46. R. Cooper and G. Burrell (1988) "Modernism, Postmodernism, and Organizational Analysis: An Introduction," *Organization Studies*, 9(1), 91–112, at 101.

47. Hummel and Stivers, "Postmodernism, Bureaucracy, and Democracy," p. 331.

48. H. Mintzberg (1994) "The Fall and Rise of Strategic Planning," *Harvard Business Review*, January–February, 110–14.

49. R. F. Durant and R. M. Marshak (working paper) "Rethinking Strategic Leadership in Public Agencies."

50. J. M. Bryson (2011) *Strategic Planning for Public and Nonprofit Organizations: A Guide to Strengthening and Sustaining Organizational Achievement*, 4th ed. (San Francisco: Jossey-Bass), p. 46.

51. D. A. Nadler (1998) *Champions of Change* (San Francisco: Jossey-Bass).

52. Z. Lan and H. G. Rainey (1992) "Goals, Rules, and Effectiveness in Public, Private, and Hybrid Organizations: More Evidence on Frequent Assertions about Differences," *Journal of Public Administration Research and Theory*, 2(1), 5–28; H. G. Rainey, S. K. Pandey, and B. Bozeman (1995) "Public and Private Managers' Perceptions of Red Tape," *Public Administration Review*, 55(6), 567–74.

53. Lan and Rainey, "Goals, Rules, and Effectiveness in Public, Private, and Hybrid Organizations"; H. G. Rainey (1983) "Public Agencies and Private Firms: Incentive Structures, Goals, and Individual Roles," *Administration & Society*, 15(2), 207–42; Rainey, Pandey, and Bozeman, "Public and Private Managers' Perceptions of Red Tape."

54. D. Stone (2011) *Policy Paradox: The Art of Political Decision Making*, 3rd ed. (New York: W. W. Norton).

55. Also see M. B. McCaskey (1974) "A Contingency Approach to Planning: Planning with Goals and Planning without Goals," *Academy of Management Journal*, 17(2), 281–91; H. Mintzberg, B. Ahlstrand, and J. Lampel (1998) *Strategy Safari: A Guided Tour through the Wilds of Strategic Management* (New York: Free Press).

56. Bryson, *Strategic Planning for Public and Nonprofit Organizations*, p. 26.

57. R. Pascale (1999) "Extract from Complexity and the Unconscious," in J. Henry (ed.) *Creativity, Innovation, and Change Media Book* (pp. 9–10) (Milton Keynes, UK: Open University Press).

58. United Nations Development Programme (2006) *Institutional Reform and Change Management: Managing Change in Public Sector Organizations* (New York: Capacity Building and Development Group, UNDP), p. 7.

59. J. P. Kotter (1995) "Leading Change: Why Transformation Efforts Fail," *Harvard Business Review*, 73(2), 59–67.

60. S. L. Brown and K. M. Eisenhardt (1997) "The Art of Continuous Change: Linking Complexity Theory and Time-Paced Evolution in Relentlessly Shifting Organizations," *Administrative Science Quarterly*, 42(1), 1–34, at 1.

61. G. L. Wamsley and M. N. Zald (1973) "The Political Economy of Public Organizations," *Public Administration Review*, 33(1), 62–73.

62. J. B. Quinn (1980) *Strategies for Change: Logical Incrementalism* (Homewood, IL: Richard D. Irwin).

63. E. Bardach (1977) *The Implementation Game: What Happens After a Bill Becomes a Law* (Cambridge: MIT Press).

64. E. R. Bowen (1982) "The Pressman-Wildavsky Paradox: Four Addenda or Why Models Based on Probability Theory Can Predict Implementation Success and Suggest Useful Tactical Advice for Implementers," *Journal of Public Policy*, 2(1), 1–21.

65. K. E. Weick (1984) "Small Wins: Redefining the Scale of Social Problems," *American Psychologist*, 39(1), 40–9. Also see J. M. Bryson (1988) "Strategic Planning: Big Wins and Small Wins," *Public Money and Management*, 8(3), 11–15; J. B. Quinn (1980) *Strategies for Change: Logical Incrementalism* (Homewood, IL: Richard D. Irwin).

66. See also Kotter, "Leading Change."

67. Weick, "Small Wins," p. 43.

68. Weick, "Small Wins," p. 43.

69. Weick, "Small Wins," p. 47.

70. Bryson, "Strategic Planning," p. 14; H. Mintzberg (1987) "Crafting Strategy," *Harvard Business Review*, 65 (July–August), 66–75; Quinn, *Strategies for Change*.

71. M. Barzelay and C. Campbell (2003) *Preparing for the Future: Strategic Planning in the U.S. Air Force* (Washington, DC: Brookings Institution Press).

72. For example, S. M. Teles (2007) "Conservative Mobilization against Entrenched Liberalism," in P. Pierson and T. Skocpol (eds.) *The Transformation of American Politics: Activist Government and the Rise of Conservatism* (pp. 160–88) (Princeton: Princeton University Press).

73. S. Fernandez and H. G. Rainey (2013) "Managing Successful Organizational Change in the Public Sector," in R. F. Durant and J. R. S. Durant (eds.) *Debating Public Administration: Management Challenges, Choices, and Opportunities* (pp. 7–26) (Boca Raton, FL: CRC Press).

5   Shooting the Political Rapids

1. N. Long (1949) "Power and Administration," *Public Administration Review*, 9(4), 257–64, at 257.
2. B. Webb, quoted in B. Crick (2006) "On Tap but Not on Top," *Times Higher Education*, September 8, http://www.timeshighereducation.co.uk/features/on-tap-but-not-on-top/205251.article.
3. W. Wilson (1887) "The Study of Administration," *Political Science Quarterly*, 2(2), 197–222.
4. M. A. Eisner (2000) *From Warfare State to Welfare State: World War I, Compensatory State Building, and the Limits of the Modern Order* (University Park: Pennsylvania State University Press), p. 38.
5. Eisner, *From Warfare State to Welfare State*, p. 38.
6. Eisner, *From Warfare State to Welfare State*, p. 39.
7. F. Goodnow (1916) *The American Conception of Liberty and Government* (Providence, RI: Stanford Printing Company), p. 41.
8. C. E. Merriam (2008) *American Political Ideas: 1865–1917* (New Brunswick, NJ: Transaction Publishers), originally published in 1920 by Macmillan, p. 101.
9. W. F. Willoughby (1919) *An Introduction to the Study of the Government of Modern States* (New York: Century Company), pp. 242, 250.
10. L. D. White (1933) *Trends in Public Administration* (New York: McGraw-Hill), p. 11.
11. See, for example, D. H. Rosenbloom (2008) "The Politics-Administration Dichotomy in U.S. Historical Context," *Public Administration Review*, 68(1), 57–60; M. Lee (2013) "Glimpsing an Alternate Construction of American Public Administration: The Later Life of William Allen, Cofounder of the New York Bureau of Municipal Research," *Administration & Society*, 45(5), 522–62.
12. A. Roberts (1994) "Demonstrating Neutrality: The Rockefeller Philanthropies and the Evolution of Public Administration, 1927–1936," *Public Administration Review*, 54(3), 221–28.
13. D. Waldo (1948) *The Administrative State: A Study of the Political Theory of American Public Administration* (New York: Ronald Press), p. 90.
14. W. E. Mosher (1939) "The Making of a Public Servant," *National Municipal Review*, 28(6), 416–37, at 416.
15. J. M. Pfiffner (1940) *Research Methods in Public Administration* (New York: The Ronald Press), p. 25.
16. D. Waldo, *The Administrative State*, p. 126.
17. E. P. Herring (1936) *Public Administration and the Public Interest* (New York: Russell & Russell).
18. The full name of the committee was the Senate Select Committee to Investigate Executive Agencies of the Government with a View to Co-ordination.
19. P. H. Appleby (1945) *Big Democracy* (New York: Knopf); R. A. Dahl (1947) "The Science of Public Administration: Three Problems," *Public Administration Review*, 7(1), 1–11; J. M. Gaus (1947) *Reflections on Public Administration* (Birmingham: University of Alabama Press); Long, "Power and Administration"; Waldo, *The Administrative State*.
20. J. L. Freeman (1965) *The Political Process: Executive Bureau-Legislative Committee Relations*, rev. ed. (New York: Random House); T. J. Lowi (1969) *The End of Liberalism: The Second*

Republic of the United States (New York: W. W. Norton); E. S. Redford (1969) *Democracy in the Administrative State* (New York: Oxford University Press).

21. H. Heclo (1977) *A Government of Strangers: Executive Politics in Washington* (Washington, DC: Brookings Institution Press).

22. H. Heclo (2013) "Issue Networks and the Executive Establishment," in S. Z. Theodoulou and M. A. Cahn (eds.) *Public Policy: The Essential Readings*, 2nd ed. (Chapter 9) (Boston: Pearson).

23. Heclo, "Issue Networks and the Executive Establishment," pp. 74–5.

24. M. Maciag (2014) "The Citizens Most Vocal in Local Government," *Governing*, July, http://www.governing.com/topics/politics/gov-national-survey-shows-citizens-most -vocal-active-in-local-government.html, date accessed July 2, 2014.

25. P. A. Sabatier and H. C. Jenkins-Smith (1993) *Policy Change and Learning: An Advocacy Coalition Approach* (Boulder: Westview Press).

26. T. Sanford (1967) *Storm Over the States* (New York: McGraw-Hill).

27. S. H. Beer (1978) "Federalism, Nationalism, and Democracy in America," *American Political Science Review*, 72(1), 9–21. Also see D. S. Wright (1990) "Federalism, Intergovernmental Relations, and Intergovernmental Management: Historical Reflections and Conceptual Comparisons," *Public Administration Review*, 50(2), 168–78.

28. L. Mainzer (1973) *Political Bureaucracy* (Glenview, IL: Scott Foresman), p. 71.

29. J. L. Brudney and D. S. Wright (2010) "The 'Revolt in Dullsville' Revisited: Lessons for Theory, Practice, and Research from the American State Administrators Project, 1964–2008," *Public Administration Review*, 70(1), 26–37.

30. See, for example, J. H. Svara (2008) "Beyond Dichotomy: Dwight Waldo and the Intertwined Politics–Administration Relationship," *Public Administration Review*, 68(1), 46–52; J. H. Svara (2006) "Introduction: Politicians and Administrators in the Political Process—A Review of Themes and Issues in the Literature," *International Journal of Public Administration*, 29(12), 953–76; J. H. Svara (2001) "The Myth of the Dichotomy: Complementarity of Politics and Administration in the Past and Future of Public Administration," *Public Administration Review*, 61(2), 176–83.

31. W. Churchill, http://www.todayinsci.com/C/Churchill_Winston/ChurchillWinston-Quotations.htm.

32. D. E. Lewis (2008) *The Politics of Presidential Appointees: Political Control and Bureaucratic Performance* (Princeton: Princeton University Press), p. 22, Figure 2.2.

33. R. Nathan (1983) *The Administrative Presidency* (New York: John Wiley); also see R. F. Durant (1992) *The Administrative Presidency Revisited: Public Lands, the BLM, and the Reagan Revolution* (Albany: State University of New York Press).

34. Also see Durant, *The Administrative Presidency Revisited*; W. G. Howell (2003) *Power without Persuasion: The Politics of Direct Presidential Action* (Princeton: Princeton University Press); E. Kagan (2001) "Presidential Administration," *Harvard Law Review*, 114(8), 2245–385; T. M. Moe (1989) "The Politics of Bureaucratic Structure," in J. E. Chubb and P. E. Peterson (eds.) *Can the Government Govern?* (pp. 267–329) (Washington, DC: Brookings Institution Press); T. M. Moe and W. G. Howell (1999) "The Presidential Power of Unilateral Action," *The Journal of Law, Economics, & Organization*, 15(1), 132–79; R. F. Durant and W. G. Resh (2012) "'Presidentializing' the Bureaucracy," in R. F. Durant (ed.) *The Oxford Handbook of American Bureaucracy*, paperback ed. (pp. 545–68) (Oxford: Oxford University Press).

35. D. E. Lewis (2008) *The Politics of Presidential Appointments: Political Control and Bureaucratic Performance* (Princeton: Princeton University Press).

36. A. C. Rudalevige (2002) *Managing the President's Program: Presidential Leadership and Legislative Policy Formulation* (Princeton: Princeton University Press).

37. W. F. West (2014) "The Administrative Presidency as Reactive Oversight: Implications for Descriptive and Prescriptive Theory," Unpublished working paper.

38. W. F. West (2006) "Presidential Leadership and Administrative Coordination: Examining the Theory of a Unified Executive," *Presidential Studies Quarterly*, 36(3), 433–56. Also see W. F. West (2005) "The Institutionalization of Regulatory Review: Organizational Stability and Responsive Competence at OIRA," *Presidential Studies Quarterly*, 35(1), 76–93.

39. West, "Presidential Leadership and Administrative Coordination," p. 445.

40. D. C. Menzel and H. L. White (eds.) (2011) *The State of Public Administration: Issues, Challenges, and Opportunities* (Armonk, NY: M. E. Sharpe), Chapter 15.

41. T. L. Cooper (2011) "Citizen-Driven Administration: Civic Engagement in the United States," in Menzel and White, *The State of Public Administration* (pp. 238–56), p. 242.

42. J. M. Berry, K. E. Portney, and K. Thompson (1993) *The Rebirth of Urban Democracy* (Washington, DC: Brookings Institution Press); J. C. Thomas (1986) *Between Citizen and City: Neighborhood Organizations and Urban Politics in Cincinnati* (Lawrence: University Press of Kansas).

43. C. S. King, K. M. Feltey, and B. O. Susel (1998) "The Question of Participation: Toward Authentic Public Participation in Public Administration," *Public Administration Review*, 58(4), 317–26, at 317. Also see P. deLeon (1992) "The Democratization of the Policy Sciences," *Public Administration Review*, 52(2), 125–29; F. Fischer (1993) "Citizen Participation and the Democratization of Policy Expertise: From Theoretical Inquiry to Practical Cases," *Policy Sciences*, 26(3), 165–87.

44. E. W. Hawley (1992) *The Great War and the Search for a Modern Order: A History of the American People and Their Institutions, 1917–1933* (Prospect Heights, IL: Waveland Press), p. 19.

45. Eisner, *From Warfare State to Welfare State*, p. 39.

46. W. G. Scott (1992) *Chester I. Barnard and the Guardians of the Managerial State* (Lawrence: University Press of Kansas). For an elaboration of this movement, see R. F. Durant and S. B. Ali (2013) "Repositioning American Public Administration? Citizen Estrangement, Administrative Reform, and the Disarticulated State," *Public Administration Review*, 73(2), 278–89.

47. Eisner, *From Warfare State to Welfare State*, p. 47.

48. Eisner, *From Warfare State to Welfare State*, p. 12.

49. Lowi, *The End of Liberalism*, p. 63.

50. R. B. Stewart (1988) "Regulation and the Crisis of Legalisation in the United States," in T. Daintith (ed.) *Law as an Instrument of Economic Policy: Comparative and Critical Approaches* (pp. 97–103) (Berlin: de Gruyter), p. 107.

51. Stewart, "Regulation and the Crisis of Legalisation in the United States," p. 108.

52. C. M. Klyza and D. Sousa (2008) *American Environmental Policy, 1990–2006: Beyond Gridlock* (Cambridge: MIT Press).

53. H. G. Frederickson and K. B. Smith (2003) *The Public Administration Theory Primer* (Boulder: Westview Press), p. 224.

54. Durant and Ali, "Repositioning American Public Administration."

55. M. Smith (2000) *American Business and Political Power: Public Opinion, Elections, and Democracy* (Chicago: University of Chicago Press).

56. D. Vogel (1984) "Why Businessmen Distrust Their State: The Political Consciousness of American Corporate Executives," *British Journal of Political Science*, 8(1), 45–78; D. Vogel (1989) *Fluctuating Fortunes: The Political Power of Business in America* (New York: Basic Books).

57. J. M. Berry (1999) *The New Liberalism: The Rising Power of Citizen Groups* (Washington, DC: Brookings Institution Press).

58. Berry, *The New Liberalism*.

59. T. Skocpol (2003) *Diminished Democracy: From Membership to Management in American Civic Life* (Norman: University of Oklahoma Press).

60. K. L. Schlozman, S. Verba, and H. E. Brady (2012) *The Unheavenly Chorus: Unequal Political Voice and the Broken Promise of American Democracy* (Princeton: Princeton University Press), quote from book description.

61. M. J. Sandel (1984) "The Procedural Republic and the Unencumbered Self," *Political Theory*, 12(1), 81–96.

62. C. M. Kerwin and S. R. Furlong (2010) *Rulemaking: How Government Agencies Write Law and Make Policy*, 4th ed. (Washington, DC: Congressional Quarterly Press), p. 114.

63. S. R. Furlong and C. M. Kerwin (2005) "Interest Group Participation in Rule Making: A Decade of Change," *Journal of Public Administration Research and Theory*, 15(3), 353–70; M. M. Golden (1998) "Interest Groups in the Rule-Making Process: Who Participates? Whose Voices Get Heard?" *Journal of Public Administration Research and Theory*, 8(2), 245–70; J. W. Yackee and S. W. Yackee (2006) "A Bias Towards Business? Assessing Interest Group Influence on the U.S. Bureaucracy," *Journal of Politics*, 68(1), 128–39.

64. M. E. Kraft and S. Kamieniecki (eds.) (2007) *Business and Environmental Policy: Corporate Interests in the American Political System* (Cambridge: MIT Press).

65. T. E. Mann and N. J. Ornstein (2012) *It's Even Worse Than it Looks: How the American Constitutional System Collided With the New Politics of Extremism* (New York: Basic Books); J. S. Nye Jr, P. D. Zelikow, and D. C. King (1997) *Why People Don't Trust Government* (Cambridge: Harvard University Press).

66. J. G. March and J. P. Olsen (1989) *Rediscovering Institutions: The Organizational Basis of Politics* (New York: Free Press), p. 16.

67. H. Ingram and S. R. Smith (1993) *Public Policy for Democracy* (Washington, DC: Brookings Institution Press); H. Ingram, A. L. Schneider, and P. deLeon (2007) "Social Construction and Policy Design," in P. A. Sabatier (ed.) *Theories of the Policy Process*, 2nd ed. (pp. 93–126) (Boulder: Westview Press); S. Mettler (1998) *Dividing Citizens: Gender and Federalism in New Deal Public Policy* (Ithaca: Cornell University Press); S. Mettler (2011) *The Submerged State: How Invisible Government Policies Undermine Democracy* (Chicago: University of Chicago Press); P. Pierson (2004) *Time and Politics: History, Institutions, and Social Analysis* (Princeton: Princeton University Press); J. Soss and S. F. Schram (2006) "Welfare Reform as a Failed Political Strategy: Evidence and Explanations for the Stability of Public Opinion," *Focus*, 24(3), 17–23; D. Stone (2011) *Policy Paradox: The Art of Political Decision Making*, 3rd ed. (New York: W. W. Norton).

68. A. L. Campbell (2003) *How Policies Make Citizens: Senior Political Activism and the Welfare State* (Princeton: Princeton University Press).

69. I. Shapiro, S. Skowronek, and D. Galvin (eds.) (2006) *Rethinking Political Institutions: The Art of the State* (New York: New York University Press), Chapter 8; P. Pierson and T. Skocpol (eds.) (2007) *The Transformation of American Politics: Activist Government and the Rise of Conservatism* (Princeton: Princeton University Press), Chapter 7.

70. Mettler, *The Submerged State*.

71. Mettler, *The Submerged State*.

72. J. S. Hacker and P. Pierson (2010) *Winner-Take-All Politics: How Washington Made the Rich Richer—And Turned Its Back on the Middle Class* (New York: Simon & Schuster); J. S. Hacker and P. Pierson (2012) "Presidents and the Political Economy: The Coalitional Foundations of Presidential Power," *Presidential Studies Quarterly*, 42(1), 101–31, at 103; Mettler, *The Submerged State*.

73. Maciag, "The Citizens Most Vocal in Government."

74. A. Haque (2001) "GIS, Public Service, and the Issue of Democratic Governance," *Public Administration Review*, 61(3), 259–65; J. Musso, C. Weare, T. Bryer, and T. L. Cooper (2013) "Toward 'Strong Democracy' in Global Cities? Social Capital Building, Theory-Driven Reform, and the Los Angeles Neighborhood Council Experience," in R. F. Durant and J. R. S. Durant (eds.) *Debating Public Administration: Management Challenges, Choices,*

and Opportunities (pp. 89–109) (Boca Raton, FL: CRC Press). For more positive experiences, see Cooper, "Citizen-Driven Administration."

75. J. E. Fountain (2001) *Building the Virtual State: Information Technology and Institutional Change* (Washington, DC: Brookings Institution Press), p. 98.

76. J. Walters (2014) "Governments Struggling to Get Social Media Right," *Governing*, July, http://www.governing.com/topics/mgmt/gov-government-social-media.html.

77. Walters, "Governments Struggling to Get Social Media Right."

78. Walters, "Governments Struggling to Get Social Media Right."

79. Entitlement programs are said to be "untouchable" because of the political costs elected officials fear they will pay in cutting them. Technically, they can be cut or their rates of increase lowered (for example, by adjusting the formula for cost-of-living benefit increases or gradually raising the retirement age, as was done in 1983), if Congress is willing to change their authorizing legislation.

80. S. Losey (2013) "Federal Workforce Dips 20 Percent Since May 2010 Peak," *Federal Times*, June 10, http://www.federaltimes.com/article/20130610/PERSONNEL/306100007 /Federal-workforce-dips-20-percent-since-May-2010-peak.

81. R. J. Samuelson (2013) "The Luxury of Muddling Through," *Washington Post*, December 15, http://www.washingtonpost.com/opinions/robert-samuelson-the-luxury-of-muddling -through/2013/12/15/9de8f1e8-641e-11e3-a373-0f9f2d1c2b61_story.html, date accessed December 18, 2013.

82. J. Hicks (2013) "Federal Workers' Job Satisfaction Falls, with Homeland Security Dept. Ranking Lowest Again," *Washington Post*, December 18, http://www.washingtonpost .com/politics/federal_government/homeland-security-ranks-lowest-amid-declining- job-satisfaction-among-feds/2013/12/18/9e87d7c4-6444-11e3-a373-0f9f2d1c2b61 _story.html?hpid=z1.

83. Center for State and Local Government Excellence (2012) "State and Local Government Workforce: 2012 Trends," April 17, http://slge.org/publications/state-and -local-government-workforce2012-trends.

84. C-A Chen (2009) "Antecedents of Contracting-Back-In: A View Beyond the Academic Paradigm," *Administration & Society*, 41(1), 101–26.

85. See D. P. Carpenter (2001) *The Forging of Bureaucratic Autonomy: Reputations, Networks, and Policy Innovation in Executive Agencies, 1862–1928* (Princeton: Princeton University Press).

86. Government Accountability Office (2013) *High-Risk Series: An Update* (Washington, DC: GAO-13-283), p. 97.

87. S. C. Selden (2009) *Human Capital: Tools and Strategies for the Public Sector* (Washington, DC: Congressional Quarterly Press).

88. S. E. Condrey and R. P. Battaglio (2007) "A Return to Spoils? Revisiting Radical Civil Service Reform in the United States," *Public Administration Review*, 67(3), 425–36; B. Tulgan (1997) *The Manager's Pocket Guide to Generation X* (Amherst, MA: HRD Press); J. P. West (2005) "Managing an Aging Workforce: Trends, Issues, and Strategies," in S. E. Condrey (ed.) *Handbook of Human Resources Management in Government*, 2nd ed. (pp. 164–88) (San Francisco: Jossey-Bass).

89. M. Fischetti (2014) "The Right Skill Sets for Contracting," *Federal Times*, July 2, http://www.federaltimes.com/article/20140702/BLG06/307020007/The-right-skill -sets-contracting.

90. Summarized by T. Fox (2014) "Tips from Federal Agencies with Happy Employees," *Washington Post*, January 2, http://www.washingtonpost.com/blogs/on-leadership/wp /2014/01/02/tips-from-federal-agencies-with-happy-employees/?tid=hpModule _308f7142-9199-11e2-bdea-e32ad90da239&hpid=z13.

6 Informing Policy Decisions

1. D. Stone (2011) *Policy Paradox: The Art of Political Decision Making*, 3rd ed. (New York: W. W. Norton).
2. Stone, *Policy Paradox*, pp. 9–10.
3. B. A. Radin (2000) *Beyond Machiavelli: Policy Analysis Comes of Age* (Washington, DC: Georgetown University Press).
4. Stone, *Policy Paradox*, p. 10.
5. G. Majone (1989) *Evidence, Argument, & Persuasion in the Policy Process* (New Haven: Yale University Press).
6. M. Minogue (1983) "Theory and Practice in Public Policy and Administration," *Policy and Politics*, 11(1), 63–85, at 76.
7. B. W. Hogwood and L. A. Gunn (1984) *Policy Analysis for the Real World* (New York: Oxford University Press), pp. 50–1.
8. K. Thelen (1999) "Historical Institutionalism and Comparative Politics," *Annual Review of Political Science*, 2, 369–404.
9. H. J. Aaron (1978) *Politics and the Professors: The Great Society in Perspective* (Washington, DC: Brookings Institution Press), p. 156.
10. Aaron, *Politics and the Professors*, p. 156.
11. F. Fischer (2007) "Deliberative Policy Analysis as Practical Reason: Integrating Empirical and Normative Arguments," in F. Fischer, G. J. Miller, and M. S. Sidney (eds.) *Handbook of Public Policy Analysis: Theory, Politics, and Methods* (pp. 223–36) (Boca Raton, FL: CRC Press), p. 230.
12. Fischer, "Deliberative Policy Analysis as Practical Reason," p. 230.
13. D. A. Rochefort and R. W. Cobb (eds.) (1994) *The Politics of Problem Definition: Shaping the Policy Agenda* (Lawrence: University Press of Kansas).
14. A. O. Hirschman (1991) *The Rhetoric of Reaction: Perversity, Futility, and Jeopardy* (Cambridge: Harvard University Press).
15. D. Schultz (2011) "The Crisis of Public Administration Theory in a Postglobal World," in D. C. Menzel and H. L. White (eds.) *The State of Public Administration: Issues, Challenges, and Opportunities* (pp. 453–63) (Armonk, NY: M. E. Sharpe).
16. P. A. Sabatier (2007) *Theories of the Policy Process*, 2nd ed. (Boulder: Westview Press).
17. E. E. Schattschneider (1960) *The Semisovereign People* (New York: Holt, Rinehart & Winston), p. 2.
18. A. L. Schneider, and H. M. Ingram (eds.) (2005) *The Deserving and Entitled: Social Constructions and Public Policy* (Albany: State University of New York Press).
19. J. W. Kingdon (2002) *Agendas, Alternatives, and Public Policy*, 2nd ed. (New York: Longman).
20. For an excellent review of this logic, see Chapter 4 in C. Scott and K. Baehler (2010) *Adding Value to Policy Analysis and Advice* (Sydney, Australia: University of New South Wales Press).
21. C. Kardish (2014) "Oregon Medicaid Model Covers More but Costs Less," *Governing*, July 8, http://www.governing.com/topics/health-human-services/gov-oregon-medicaid-approach.html.
22. C. W. Mills (1956) *The Power Elite* (New York: Oxford University Press), p. 5.
23. C. Crouch (2004) *Post-Democracy* (Cambridge: Polity Press).
24. R. A. Dahl (1999) *On Democracy* (New Haven: Yale University Press).
25. G. Stoker (1995) "Regime Theory and Urban Politics," in D. Judge, G. Stoker, and H. Wolman (eds.) *Theories of Urban Politics* (pp. 54–71) (London: SAGE).
26. Scott and Baehler, *Adding Value to Policy Analysis and Advice*, p. 63.
27. See J. M. Bryson (2011) *Strategic Planning for Public and Nonprofit Organizations: A Guide to Strengthening and Sustaining Organizational Achievement*, 4th ed. (San Francisco: Jossey-Bass).

28. This summary of findings is taken from G. A. Krause (2012) "Legislative Delegation of Authority to Bureaucratic Agencies," in R. F. Durant (ed.) *The Oxford Handbook of American Bureaucracy*, paperback ed. (pp. 521–44) (Oxford: Oxford University Press).

29. H. Ingram and A. Schneider (1990) "Improving Implementation through Framing Smarter Statutes," *Journal of Public Policy*, 10(1), 67–88.

30. Radin, *Beyond Machiavelli*.

31. This last phrase comes from A. Wildavsky (1979) *Speaking Truth to Power: The Art and Craft of Policy Analysis* (New Brunswick, NJ: Transaction Publishers).

32. Radin, *Beyond Machiavelli*, p. 34.

33. Radin, *Beyond Machiavelli*, p. 35.

34. C. H. Weiss (1989) "Congressional Committees as Users of Analysis," *Journal of Policy Analysis and Management*, 8(3), 411–31, at 411.

35. C. E. Lindblom (1959) "The Science of 'Muddling Through,'" *Public Administration Review*, 19(2), 79–88.

36. Lindblom, "The Science of 'Muddling Through.'"

37. O. A. Davis, M. A. H. Dempster, and A. Wildavsky (1966) "A Theory of the Budgetary Process," *American Political Science Review*, 60(3), 529–47; O. A. Davis, M. A. H. Dempster, and A. Wildavsky (1974) "Towards a Predictive Theory of Government Expenditure: US Domestic Appropriations," *British Journal of Political Science*, 4(4), 419–52.

38. S. Quehl (2014) "Operational Analytics: A Proactive Approach to Dealing with Shrinking Budgets," *Federal Times*, June 30, http://www.federaltimes.com/article/20140630/BLG05/306300004/Operational-Analytics-proactive-approach-dealing-shrinking-budgets.

39. A. Etzioni (1986) "Mixed Scanning Revisited," *Public Administration Review*, 46(1), 8–14.

40. M. D. Cohen, J. G. March, and J. P. Olsen (1972) "A Garbage Can Model of Organizational Choice," *Administrative Science Quarterly*, 17(1), 1–25.

41. Kingdon, *Agendas, Alternatives, and Public Policy*.

42. F. R. Baumgartner and B. D. Jones (2009) *Agendas and Instability in American Politics*, 2nd ed. (Chicago: University of Chicago Press).

43. J. L. True, B. D. Jones, and F. R. Baumgartner (2007) "Punctuated-Equilibrium Theory: Explaining Stability and Change in Public Policymaking," in P. A. Sabatier (ed.) *Theories of the Policy Process* (pp. 155–88) (Boulder: Westview Press), p. 165.

44. C. H. Weiss (1980) "Knowledge Creep and Decision Accretion," *Science Communication*, 1(3), 381–404.

45. Weiss, "Knowledge Creep and Decision Accretion," pp. 153–54.

46. B. Bozeman (2007) *Public Values and Public Interest: Counterbalancing Economic Individualism* (Washington, DC: Georgetown University Press).

47. H. W. J. Rittel and M. M. Webber (1973) "Dilemmas in a General Theory of Planning," *Policy Sciences*, 4(2), 155–69.

48. H. Heclo (1974) *Modern Social Politics in Britain and Sweden: From Relief to Income Maintenance* (New Haven: Yale University Press), p. 305.

49. M. Van Vliet (1993) "Environmental Regulation of Business: Options and Constraints for Communicative Governance," in J. Kooiman (ed.) *Modern Governance: New Government-Society Interactions* (pp. 105–18) (London: SAGE).

50. J. Meadowcroft (2004) "Deliberative Democracy," in R. F. Durant, D. J. Fiorino, and R. O'Leary (eds.) *Environmental Governance Reconsidered: Challenges, Choices, and Opportunities* (pp. 183–217) (Cambridge: MIT Press).

7 Linking People to Public Purposes

1. P. Whoriskey and D. Keating (2013) "How a Secretive Panel Uses Data that Distort Doctors' Pay," *Washington Post*, July 20.

2. Whoriskey and Keating, "How a Secretive Panel Uses Data that Distort Doctors' Pay."

3. D. F. Kettl (2009) *The Next Government of the United States: Why Our Institutions Fail Us and How to Fix Them* (New York: W. W. Norton), p. 10.

4. C. J. Friedrich (1940) "Public Policy and the Nature of Administrative Responsibility," in C. J. Friedrich and E. S. Mason (eds.) *Public Policy* (pp. 3–24) (Cambridge: Harvard University Press); H. Finer (1941) "Administrative Responsibility in Democratic Government," *Public Administration Review*, 1(4), 335–50.

5. Finer, "Administrative Responsibility in Democratic Government," p. 337.

6. F. C. Mosher (1982) *Democracy and the Public Service*, 2nd ed. (New York: Oxford University Press), p. 221.

7. National Commission on the State and Local Public Service (1993) *Hard Truths/Tough Choices: An Agenda for State and Local Reform* (Albany, NY: Rockefeller Institute of Government).

8. See N. M. Riccucci and K. C. Naff (2007) *Personnel Management in Government: Politics and Process*, 6th ed. (Boca Raton, FL: CRC Press).

9. Partnership for Public Service (2014) "Building the Enterprise: A New Civil Service Framework," April, https://www.ourpublicservice.org/OPS/, date accessed July 5, 2014.

10. As part of his efforts to politicize the bureaucracy, Nixon had his appointees pressure career civil servants in agencies to do things that the CSC should not have condoned—but did. After Watergate abuses were revealed, the CSC then engaged in its own cover-up by destroying evidence of its complicity.

11. G. E. Roberts (2001) "A History of the Federal Civil Service: A Values-Based Perspective," in S. E. Condrey and R. Maranto (eds.) *Radical Reform of the Civil Service* (pp. 15–41) (Lanham, MD: Lexington Books).

12. D. F. Kettl, P. W. Ingraham, R. P. Sanders, and C. Horner (1996) *Civil Service Reform: Building a Government That Works* (Washington, DC: Brookings Institution Press).

13. In 1939, Congress passed the Hatch Act to limit the use of career civil servants in political campaigns. More recently, President Obama signed the Hatch Act Modernization Act in 2012 to allow for disciplinary actions and not just the firing of federal employees engaged in electoral activities, and curtailed the prohibition on state and local government employees running for office, thus cutting back from original Hatch Act prohibitions.

14. Kettl, Ingraham, Sanders, and Horner, *Civil Service Reform*, back cover.

15. Kettl, Ingraham, Sanders, and Horner, *Civil Service Reform*, p. 17.

16. P. Ingraham and D. H. Rosenbloom (1990) "The State of Merit in the Federal Government," Occasional Paper, National Commission on the Public Service, Washington, DC, June.

17. Mosher, *Democracy and the Public Service*, p. 86.

18. N. Henry (2013) *Public Administration and Public Affairs*, 12th ed. (Boston: Pearson), p. 277.

19. Henry, *Public Administration and Public Affairs*, p. 318, fn 78.

20. Partnership for Public Service (2004) *Asking the Wrong Questions: A Look at How the Federal Government Assesses and Selects Its Workforce* (Washington, DC: Partnership for Public Service), p. 1.

21. Federal News Radio (2012) "Top 10 Agency Initiatives: Office of Personnel Management," September 13, http://www.federalnewsradio.com/1011/3035948/Top-10-Agency-Initiatives-Office-of-Personnel-Management.

22. E. Montalbano (2011) "USAJobs.com Website Problems Continue," October 24, http://www.informationweek.com/government/cloud-saas/usajobsgov-website-problems-continue/231901487.

23. Montalbano, "USAJobs.com Website Problems Continue."

24. E. Montalbano (2011) "USAJobs Site Glitches Point to Longtime IT Woes," November 16, http://www.informationweek.com/government/leadership/usajobs-site-glitches-point-to-longtime/231903159.

25. Henry, *Public Administration and Public Affairs*.

26. S. C. Selden (2009) *Human Capital: Tools and Strategies for the Public Sector* (Washington, DC: Congressional Quarterly Press), pp. 20–1.

27. Selden, *Human Capital*.

28. Selden, *Human Capital*, pp. 23–4.

29. J. Pfeffer and R. I. Sutton (2006) "Evidence-Based Management," *Harvard Business Review*, January, 1–13, at 3.

30. D. J. Kingsley (1944) *Representative Bureaucracy* (Yellow Springs, OH: Antioch Press); S. Krislov (1974) *Representative Bureaucracy* (Englewood Cliffs, NJ: Prentice-Hall); F. C. Mosher (1968) *Democracy and the Public Service* (Oxford: Oxford University Press).

31. The acronym LGB is used in this book, because the most research has been done on lesbians, gays, and bisexuals in private and public service. I do so without any intention of diminishing the importance of discrimination issues raised by transgender persons. I also do so recognizing that a great deal of controversy surrounds acronyms such as LGB. For example, some lesbians and gays do not like being lumped together, because their life and work experiences differ, while some others argue for including transgender and "queers" in the acronym to be as inclusive as possible (LGBTQ). As a public manager, you should be aware of these controversies, be sensitive to the desires of your employees and clientele, and respect those wishes as you try to be as inclusive and respectful as you can to all employees in your agency.

32. S. Krislov (1974) *Representative Bureaucracy*; S. Krislov (1967) *The Negro in Federal Employment: The Quest for Equal Opportunity* (Minneapolis: University of Minnesota Press).

33. G. B. Lewis (1997) "Lifting the Ban on Gays in the Civil Service: Federal Policy toward Gay and Lesbian Employees since the Cold War," *Public Administration Review*, 57(5), 387–95; G. B. Lewis (2001) "Barriers to Security Clearances for Gay Men and Lesbians: Fear of Blackmail or Fear of Homosexuals?" *Journal of Public Administration Research and Theory*, 11(4), 539–58; G. B. Lewis (2010) "Modeling Nonprofit Employment: Why Do So Many Lesbians and Gay Men Work for Nonprofit Organizations?" *Administration & Society*, 42(6), 720–48.

34. D. H. Rosenbloom (1977) *Federal Equal Employment Opportunity: Politics and Public Personnel Administration* (New York: Praeger).

35. This section relies on D. H. Rosenbloom, *Federal Equal Employment Opportunity*.

36. For a comprehensive review of affirmative action policy, see J. E. Kellough (2006) *Understanding Affirmative Action: Politics, Discrimination, and the Search for Justice* (Washington, DC: Georgetown University Press).

37. Henry, *Public Administration and Public Affairs*, p. 300.

38. *The Contractors Association of Eastern Pennsylvania v. The Secretary of Labor, George P. Shultz, et al.* (442 F.2d 159 [1971]).

39. P. N. Grabosky and D. H. Rosenbloom (1975) "Racial and Ethnic Integration in the Federal Service," *Social Science Quarterly*, 56, 71–84; D. Hellriegel and L. Short (1972) "Equal Employment Opportunity in the Federal Government: A Comparative Analysis," *Public Administrative Review*, 32(6), 851–58.

40. P. Page (1994) "African-Americans in Executive Branch Agencies," *Review of Public Personnel Administration*, 14(1), 24–51.

41. J. N. Baldwin (1996) "Female Promotions in the Male-Dominant Organizations: The Case of the United States Military," *Journal of Politics*, 58(4), 1184–197; N. C. Dometrius (1984) "Minorities and Women among State Agency Leaders," *Social Science Quarterly*, 65, 127–37; General Accounting Office (1991) *Federal Workforce: Continuing Need for Federal Affirmative Employment* (Washington, DC: GAO/GGD-92–27BR); V. Greene, S. C. Selden, and G. Brewer (2001) "Measuring Power and Presence: Bureaucratic Representation in the

American States," *Journal of Public Administration Research and Theory*, 11(3), 379–402; P. S. Kim (1993) "Racial Integration in the American Federal Government: With Special Reference to Asian-Americans," *Review of Public Personnel Administration*, 13(1), 52–66.

42. C. Burns, K. Barton, and S. Kerby (2012) "The State of Diversity in Today's Workforce: As Our Nation Becomes More Diverse So Too Does Our Workforce," The Center for American Progress, July 12, http://www.americanprogress.org/issues/labor/report/2012/07/12/11938/the-state-of-diversity-in-todays-workforce/.

43. Lewis, "Modeling Nonprofit Employment."

44. G. B. Lewis and D. W. Pitts (2011) "Representation of Lesbians and Gay Men in Federal, State, and Local Bureaucracies," *Journal of Public Administration Research and Theory*, 21(1), 159–80.

45. National Urban Fellows (2012) *Diversity Counts: Racial and Ethnic Diversity among Public Service Leadership* (New York: National Urban Fellows), http://www.nuf.org/sites/default/files/Documents/NUF_diversitycounts_V2FINAL.pdf.

46. D. H. Rosenbloom, *Federal Equal Employment Opportunity*, p. 56.

47. G. B. Lewis (1986) "Equal Employment Opportunity and the Early Career in Federal Employment," *Review of Public Personnel Administration*, 6(3), 1–18; G. B. Lewis (1986) "Gender and Promotions: Promotion Chances of White Men and Women in Federal White-Collar Employment," *Journal of Human Resources*, 21(3), 406–19; G. B. Lewis (1986) "Race, Sex, and Supervisory Authority in Federal White-Collar Employment," *Public Administration Review*, 46(1), 25–30; G. B. Lewis and K. Park (1989) "Turnover Rates in Federal White-Collar Employment: Are Women More Likely to Quit Than Men?" *American Review of Public Administration*, 19(1), 13–28; G. B. Lewis (1992) "Men and Women toward the Top: Backgrounds, Careers, and Potential of Federal Middle Managers," *Public Personnel Management*, 21(4), 473–92; G. B. Lewis (1994) "Women, Occupations, and Federal Agencies: Occupational Mix and Interagency Differences in Sexual Inequality in Federal White-Collar Employment," *Public Administration Review*, 54(3), 271–76.

48. J. Dolan (2000) "The Senior Executive Service: Gender, Attitudes, and Representative Bureaucracy," *Journal of Public Administration Research Theory*, 10(3), 513–30.

49. Lewis and Pitts, "Representation of Lesbians and Gay Men in Federal, State, and Local Bureaucracies."

50. M. Sledge (2012) "Women's Jobs Axed by State Austerity Policies," *Huff Post Politics*, April 13, http://www.huffingtonpost.com/2012/04/13/womens-jobs-state-austerity_n_1415276.html, date accessed December 28, 2013.

51. W. M. Rodgers III (2012) "The Great Recession's Impact on African American Public Sector Employment," National Poverty Center Working Paper Series, #12–01, January.

52. For example, J. J. Hindera (1993) "Representative Bureaucracy: Imprimis Evidence of Active Representation in the EEOC District Offices," *Social Science Quarterly*, 74, 95–108; J. J. Hindera (1993) "Representative Bureaucracy: Further Evidence of Active Representation in the EEOC District Offices," *Journal of Public Administration Research and Theory*, 3(4), 415–29; K. J. Meier (1993) "Latinos and Representative Bureaucracy: Testing the Thompson and Henderson Hypotheses," *Journal of Public Administration Research and Theory*, 3(4), 393–414; K. J. Meier and J. Stewart Jr (1992) "The Impact of Representative Bureaucracies: Educational Systems and Public Policies," *American Review of Public Administration*, 22(3), 157–71.

53. K. J. Meier and J. Nicholson-Crotty (2006) "Gender, Representative Bureaucracy, and Law Enforcement: The Case of Sexual Assault," *Public Administration Review*, 66(6), 850–60.

54. V. M. Wilkins and L. R. Keiser (2006) "Linking Passive and Active Representation by Gender: The Case of Child Support Agencies," *Journal of Public Administration Research and Theory*, 16(1), 87–102.

55. K. J. Meier, M. S. Pennington, and W. S. Eller (2005) "Race, Sex, and Clarence Thomas: Representation Change in the EEOC," *Public Administration Review*, 65(2), 171–79.

56. For example, R. Andrews, G. A. Boyne, K. J. Meier, L. J. O'Toole Jr, and R. M. Walker (2005) "Representative Bureaucracy, Organizational Strategy, and Public Service Performance: An Empirical Analysis of English Local Government," *Journal of Public Administration Research and Theory*, 15(4), 489–504; Hindera, "Representative Bureaucracy: Imprimis Evidence of Active Representation in the EEOC District Offices"; Hindera, "Representative Bureaucracy: Further Evidence of Active Representation in the EEOC District Offices"; J. J. Hindera and C. D. Young (1998) "Representative Bureaucracy: The Theoretical Implications of Statistical Interaction," *Political Research Quarterly*, 51(3), 655–71; Meier, "Latinos and Representative Bureaucracy"; Meier and Nicholson-Crotty, "Gender, Representative Bureaucracy, and Law Enforcement."

57. Meier, "Latinos and Representative Bureaucracy"; K. J. Meier and L. J. O'Toole Jr (2006) *Bureaucracy in a Democratic State: A Governance Perspective* (Baltimore: Johns Hopkins University Press); Meier and Stewart, "The Impact of Representative Bureaucracies"; K. J. Meier, J. Stewart Jr, and R. E. England (1989) *Race, Class, and Education: The Politics of Second-Generation Discrimination* (Madison: University of Wisconsin Press); D. W. Pitts (2005) "Diversity, Representation, and Performance: Evidence about Race and Ethnicity in Public Organizations," *Journal of Public Administration Research and Theory*, 15(4), 615–31.

58. J. L. Brudney, F. T. Hebert, and D. S. Wright (2000) "From Organizational Values to Organizational Roles: Examining Representative Bureaucracy in State Administration," *Journal of Public Administration Research and Theory*, 10(3), 491–512.

59. S. C. Selden, J. L. Brudney, and E. J. Kellough (1998) "Bureaucracy as a Representative Institution: Toward a Reconciliation of Bureaucratic Government and Democratic Theory," *American Journal of Political Science*, 42(3), 717–44.

60. Lewis and Pitts, "Representation of Lesbians and Gay Men in Federal, State, and Local Bureaucracies."

61. G. S. Thielemann and J. Stewart Jr (1996) "A Demand-Side Perspective on the Importance of Representative Bureaucracy: AIDS, Ethnicity, Gender, and Sexual Orientation," *Public Administration Review*, 56(2), 168–73.

62. D. P. Haider-Markel (2007) "Representation and Backlash: The Positive and Negative Influence of Descriptive Representation," *Legislative Studies Quarterly*, 32(1), 107–33; D. P. Haider-Markel, M. R. Joslyn, and C. J. Kniss (2000) "Minority Group Interests and Political Representation: Gay Elected Officials in the Policy Process," *Journal of Politics*, 6(2), 568–77; R. A. Smith, and D. P. Haider-Markel (2002) *Gay and Lesbian Americans and Political Participation: A Reference Handbook* (Santa Barbara, CA: ABC-CLIO).

63. D. W. Pitts and J. L. Weakley (2014) "Representation and Sexual Orientation in Higher Education," Working Paper, American University, Washington, DC.

64. You need to be clear that there is *no* affirmative action program per se for gays or lesbians, only equal protection under the law and a variety of federal, state, and local executive orders.

65. See, for example, N. M. Riccucci (2002) *Managing Diversity in Public Sector Workforces* (Boulder: Westview Press).

66. In both cases, Kellough (*Understanding Affirmative Action* and personal communication, May 30, 2014) notes that diversity was determined to be a sufficiently compelling interest to warrant preferential affirmative action. However, that was only one prong of the two-pronged test required by strict scrutiny under equal protection review. The other is narrow tailoring. The program in the *Grutter* case was found to be narrowly tailored, because the Law School individually reviewed each application and only considered race as a factor without any predetermined weight. The program in the *Gratz* case was found not to be

narrowly tailored, because undergraduate admission was based on a formula that awarded fixed points on the basis of race. Remember, also, that constitutional review only applies when the challenged program is operated by government (e.g., a state university). In addition, there are other forms of affirmative action besides preferential policies.

67. S. H. Mastracci (2013) "Commentary: A Solution in Search of a Problem? Discrimination, Affirmative Action, and the New Governance," in R. F. Durant and J. R. S. Durant (eds.) *Debating Public Administration: Management Challenges, Choices, and Opportunities* (pp. 218–19) (Boca Raton, FL: CRC Press).

68. A. Etzioni (1986) "Mixed Scanning Revisited," *Public Administration Review*, 46(1), 8–14.

69. Burns, Barton, and Kerby, "The State of Diversity in Today's Workforce." Other studies have suggested that the growth rate may be slowing, but it is still a formidable force for the future. See, for example, M. Toossi (2012) "Labor Force Projections to 2020: A More Slowly Growing Workforce," http://www.bls.gov/opub/mlr/2012/01/art3full.pdf, http://www.bls.gov/opub/mlr/2012/01/errata.pdf, date accessed June 13, 2014.

70. For a summary of various perspectives on at-will employment, see R. F. Durant (1998) "Rethinking the Unthinkable: A Cautionary Note," *Administration & Society*, 29(6), 643–52; C. T. Goodsell (1998) "A Radical Idea Welcomed—But with Some Buts," *Administration & Society*, 29(6), 653–59; J. H. Knott (1998) "A Return to Spoils: The Wrong Solution for the Right Problem," *Administration & Society*, 29(6), 660–69; R. Maranto (1998) "Thinking the Unthinkable in Public Administration: A Case for Spoils in the Federal Bureaucracy," *Administration & Society*, 29(6), 623–42; R. Maranto (1998) "Rethinking the Unthinkable: Reply to Durant, Goodsell, Knott, and Murray on 'A Case for Spoils' in Federal Personnel Management," *Administration & Society*, 30(1): 3–12; W. L. Murray (1998) "Rejoinder to Maranto: Been There, Done That," *Administration & Society*, 29(6), 670–76.

71. S. E. Condrey and R. P. Battaglio (2007) "A Return to Spoils? Revisiting Radical Civil Service Reform in the United States," *Public Administration Review*, 67(3), 425–36. Kellough (personal communication) writes: "One of the three pillars of traditional merit systems is relative security of tenure. This relative security takes the form of a promise to employees that they will be dismissed only for just causes. Once that promise is made, according to the U.S. Supreme Court, the employee has a 'property interest' in his or her job. Because the Constitution in the Fifth and Fourteenth amendments prohibits government from taking a person's property without due process, employees who have been promised that they will be terminated for just cause only may not be fired without due process. According to the Court, due process procedures in these instances require prior notice and a right for the employee to give his or her side of the story. This takes time, but it also fosters a sense of fairness within the organization. Nevertheless, when states have moved toward at-will employment, they have done so by removing from employees the promise that termination will be made for just cause only. Obviously, however, they don't sell the 'reform' in that manner."

72. K. S. Chi (2005) "State Civil Service Systems," in S. E. Condrey (ed.) *Handbook of Human Resource Management in Government*, 2nd ed. (pp. 76–94) (San Francisco: Jossey-Bass).

73. S. W. Hays and J. E. Sowa (2006) "A Broader Look at the 'Accountability' Movement: Some Grim Realities in State Civil Service Systems," *Review of Public Personnel Administration*, 26(2), 102–17.

74. F. J. Thompson (2008) "State and Local Governance Fifteen Years Later: Enduring and New Challenges," *Public Administration Review*, 68(S1), S8–19.

75. R. J. McGrath (2013) "The Rise and Fall of Radical Civil Service Reform in the U.S. States," *Public Administration Review*, 73(4), 638–49; J. E. Kellough and S. C. Selden (2003) "The Reinvention of Public Personnel Administration: An Analysis of the Diffusion of Personnel Reforms in the States," *Public Administration Review*, 63(2), 165–76.

76. Office of Program Policy Analysis and Government Accountability, Florida Legislature (2006) "While Improving, People First Still Lacks Intended Functionality, Limitations Increase State Agency Workload and Costs," Report No. 06–39, April, p. 2.

77. S. E. Condrey and R. P. Battaglio (2007) "A Return to Spoils? Revisiting Radical Civil Service Reform in the United States," *Public Administration Review*, 67(3), 425–36, at 428.

78. Condrey and Battaglio, "A Return to Spoils?" p. 428.

79. R. M. Sanders (2004) "GeorgiaGain or GeorgiaLoss? The Great Experiment in State Civil Service Reform," *Public Personnel Management*, 33(2), 151–64.

80. Sanders, "GeorgiaGain or GeorgiaLoss?"

81. J. S. Bowman and J. P. West (2006) "Ending Civil Service Protections in Florida Government: Experiences in State Agencies," *Review of Public Personnel Administration*, 26(2), 139–57, at 139.

82. J. D. Coggburn (2006) "At-Will Employment in Government: Insights from the State of Texas," *Review of Public Personnel Administration*, 26(2), 158–77, at 166.

83. R. C. Kearney with D. G. Carnevale (2001) *Labor Relations in the Public Sector*, 3rd ed. (New York: Marcel Dekker); D. H. Rosenbloom (1988) "The Public Employment Relationship and the Supreme Court in the 1980s," *Review of Public Personnel Administration*, 8(2), 49–65.

84. Kearney with Carnevale, *Labor Relations in the Public Sector*. You should know, however, that there are states (such as Georgia) that have a collective-bargaining statute, but, still, no collective bargaining is taking place.

85. See Kearney with Carnevale, *Labor Relations in the Public Sector*. Binding interest arbitration requires that once an impasse is reached at the bargaining table over contested items (e.g., pay and sick leave), a third, neutral party steps in to resolve the dispute.

86. Global Credit Research (2013) "Moody's: New State Adjusted Pension Liabilities Show Wide Range of Obligations; Effect of New Discount Rates Highlighted," June 27, https://www.moodys.com/research/Moodys-New-state-adjusted-pension-liabilities-show-wide-range-of--PR_276663.

87. P. W. Ingraham (2005) "'Are You Talking to Me?' Accountability and the Modern Public Service," *PS: Political Science and Politics*, 38(1), 17–21.

88. J. M. Johnston and B. S. Romzek (2012) "The Promises, Performance, and Pitfalls of Government Contracting," in R. F. Durant (ed.) *The Oxford Handbook of American Bureaucracy*, paperback ed. (pp. 396–420) (Oxford: Oxford University Press).

89. In the Public Interest (2013) "Backgrounder Brief: Insourcing," May, http://www.inthepublicinterest.org/sites/default/files/Insourcing%20Backgrounder%20Brief_Template.pdf, p. 2.

90. M. Warner (2011) "The Pendulum Swings Again," *New York Times*, April 4, http://www.nytimes.com/roomfordebate/2011/04/03/is-privatization-a-bad-deal-for-cities-and-states/the-pendulum-swings-again.

91. D. F. Kettl (2002) *The Transformation of Governance: Public Administration for the 21st Century* (Baltimore: Johns Hopkins University Press).

92. A. A. Amirkhanyan, H. J. Kim, and K. T. Lambright (2013) "Going Beyond Service Delivery: Exploring the Prevalence of Citizen Participation in Government Contracting," presented at the 11th Public Management Research Conference, Madison, WI, June 20–22. The analysis reported here is based on an email from Amirkhanyan to the author on October 7, 2013 noting that the findings of this conference paper continue with an increase in the number of respondents.

93. T. L. Brown, M. Potoski, and D. M. Van Slyke (2013) "Managing Public Service Contracts: Aligning Values, Institutions, and Markets," in Durant and Durant, *Debating Public Administration* (pp. 155–75).

94. A. Cole (2013) "The Retirement Wave You Didn't See Coming," *Government Executive*, September 24, http://www.govexec.com/excellence/promising-practices/2013/09 /retirement-wave-you-didnt-see-coming/70786/.

95. J. Moore (2014) "Survey Reveals Gaps in Agency Planning for Next-Generation Workforce," *Federal News Radio*, May 28, http://www.federalnewsradio.com/145/3630823/Survey -finds-gaps-in-agency-planning-for-next-generation-workforce, date accessed May 29, 2014.

96. L. Rein (2013) "Wave of Retirements Hitting Federal Workforce," *Washington Post*, August 26, http://www.washingtonpost.com/politics/wave-of-retirements-hitting-federal-workforce/2013/08/26/97adacee-09b8-11e3-8974-f97ab3b3c677_print.html.

97. Henry, *Public Administration and Public Affairs*, p. 272.

98. R. Feintzeig (2014) "U.S. Struggles to Draw Young, Savvy Staff," *Wall Street Journal*, June 10, http://online.wsj.com/articles/u-s-government-struggles-to-attract-young -savvy-staff-members-1402445198?tesla=y&mg=reno64-wsj&url=http://online.wsj .com/article/SB10001424052702303789904579602510156372836.htm, date accessed June 13, 2014.

99. R. C. Bates, C. Eger, S. Mintier, J. P. Naylor, E. Reed, and D. Harvey (2013) "Growing the Next Generation of Local Government Professionals," *PA Times*, 36(4), 7.

100. Feintzeig, "U.S. Struggles to Draw Young, Savvy Staff," ref. 89.

101. S. Reilly (2013) "Phased Retirement: Employees Eager, Agencies Wary: HR Managers Want More Details," *Federal Times*, September 15, http://www.federaltimes.com /article/20130915/BENEFITS02/309150001/Phased-retirement-Employees-eager -agencies-wary.

102. Moore, "Survey Reveals Gaps in Agency Planning for Next-Generation Workforce."

103. Henry, *Public Administration and Public Affairs*, p. 273.

104. Office of Management and Budget (2002) *The President's Management Agenda* (Washington, DC: U.S. Office of Management and Budget), p. i.

105. Office of Management and Budget, *The President's Management Agenda*, p. i.

106. Office of Management and Budget, *The President's Management Agenda*, p. i.

107. E. Katz (2014) "The Federal Government Lost 40,000 More Employees Than It Gained Last Year," *Government Executive*, July 9, http://www.govexec.com/management/2014/07 /more-feds-left-government-last-year-than-joined/88267/?oref=top-story. The hiring of veterans comes as the result of an executive order by President Obama to increase their hiring.

108. National Academy of Public Administration (1995) *Modernizing Federal Classification: Operational Broadbanding Systems Alternatives* (Washington, DC: National Academy of Public Administration), p. 1.

109. Kellough, personal communication, June 15, 2014.

110. Office of Personnel Management (2002) *A Fresh Start for Federal Pay: The Case for Modernization* (Washington, DC: Office of Personnel Management), p. 14.

111. D. L. Ness (2013) "A Bitter Pill: New Census Data Show Gender-Based Wage Gap is Largely Unchanged since 2002," *Huff Post Politics*, September 19, http://www.huffingtonpost.com/ debra-l-ness/gender-based-wage-gap_b_3941580.html, date accessed December 28, 2013.

112. M. J. D'Agostino and H. Levine (2011) *Women in Public Administration: Theory and Practice* (Sudbury, MA: Jones & Bartlett).

113. R. Wilson (2013) "Gay Marriage Fight Shifts to Federal Courts, 2014 Set to Tipping-Point Year," *Washington Post*, December 24, http://www.washingtonpost. com/blogs/govbeat/wp/2013/12/24/gay-marriage-fight-shifts-to-federal-courts-2014-set-to-be-tipping-point-year/?tid=hpModule_ba0d4c2a-86a2-11e2-9d71 -f0feafdd1394&hpid=z8, date accessed December 25, 2013.

114. L. Keen (2013) "SUPREME VICTORY: Stunning Victories: DOMA, Prop 8 Struck," *Keen News Service*, June 26, http://www.keennewsservice.com/2013/06/26/supreme-court-stun-ning-double-victory/#sthash.6lhgeqKe.dpuf.

115. L. Keen (2013) "Interpreting DOMA Ruling: Under Obama, the Ruling is Achieving Maximum Impact," *Keen News Service*, September 4, http://www.keennewsservice.com/2013/09/04/interpreting-doma-ruling-under-obama-the-ruling-is-achieving-maximum-impact/#sthash.l7lkrZVq.dpuf.
116. Keen, "Interpreting DOMA Ruling," paragraph 3.
117. Keen, "Interpreting DOMA Ruling."
118. E. Katz (2013) "OPM Proposes Extending Fed Health Benefits to Same Sex Partners," *Government Executive*, April 11, http://www.govexec.com/pay-benefits/2013/04/opm-proposes-extending-federal-health-benefits-same-sex-partners/62439/, date accessed December 22, 2013.
119. Pub. L. 110–233, 122 Stat. 881, enacted May 21, 2008.

8 Stewarding a Nation's Treasure

1. S. Steinmo (2010) *The Evolution of Modern States: Sweden, Japan, and the United States* (Cambridge: Cambridge University Press).
2. D. R. Mullins and J. L. Mikesell (2012) "Innovations in Budgeting and Financial Management," in R. F. Durant (ed.) *The Oxford Handbook of American Bureaucracy*, paperback ed. (pp. 738–65) (Oxford: Oxford University Press).
3. R. J. Samuelson (2013) "The Luxury of Muddling Through," *Washington Post*, December 15, http://www.washingtonpost.com/opinions/robert-samuelson-the-luxury-of-muddling-through/2013/12/15/9de8f1e8-641e-11e3-a373-0f9f2d1c2b61_story.html, date accessed December 18, 2013.
4. The standard method of determining the degree to which burdens are being inappropriately shifted to a future generation is to employ an appropriately structured capital budget. However, the federal government (unlike states and local governments) does not specifically define capital elements (that is, expenditures that convey long-term benefits). Therefore, it is difficult to determine how much of the $17 trillion legitimately places a burden on a generation which will reap the future benefits of current and past investment and how much represents a transfer of costs from the present to the future.
5. In your coursework, you will learn that these more macro dimensions are normally categorized as government "allocations" (spending across functions), "stabilization" (economic growth, full employment, and price stability), and "distribution" (redistributing effective demand between individuals and family spending units).
6. This, after President Andrew Jackson killed the Second National Bank of the United States in 1833.
7. You are likely to learn in your coursework that the highest marginal rate was 90 percent in 1969, 70 percent until 1981, then 50 percent with enactment of the Economic Recovery Tax Act of 1981. It then dropped to 28 percent with the 1986 tax reform and is now at 39.6 percent.
8. Granted, working with the Congress, the administration did take some pressure off the Social Security Trust Fund by gradually increasing the retirement age for baby boomers from 65 to 66. But costs for Medicare services continued to rise faster than inflation.
9. If these provisions were eliminated, we would not gain $1 trillion in revenue, as resources would be shifted to other shelters.
10. The Tax Reform Act of 1986 treated both capital gains and dividends as normal income and applied the 28 percent tax rate to them. It is true that marginal rates were reduced, but long-term capital gains were no longer given a 50 percent exemption from taxation.
11. TreasuryDirect, "Historical Debt Outstanding—Annual 1950–1999," http://www.treasurydirect.gov/govt/reports/pd/histdebt/histdebt_histo4.htm.

12. A. Wildavsky (1979) *The Politics of the Budgetary Process*, 3rd ed. (Boston: Little, Brown), p. 5.

13. A. Schick (1966) "The Road to PPB: The Stages of Budget Reform," *Public Administration Review*, 26(4), 243–58.

14. Schick, "The Road to PPB," p. 244. As Schick defines them, program budgets are the "process by which managers assure that resources are obtained and used effectively and efficiently in the accomplishment of the organization's objectives."

15. National Advisory Council on State and Local Budgeting (1998) *Recommended Budget Practices: A Framework for Improved State and Local Government Budgeting* (Chicago: Government Finance Officers Association), p. viii.

16. ZBB was actually first proposed by Verne Lewis in 1952. There has never been any implementation that started from scratch. This was a misconception reinforced by President Carter's failure to understand the actual process being used. It was always based on decision packages (for example, -10 percent, -5 percent, flat, +5 percent, +10 percent) and a package priority ordering. Personal correspondence with Dan Mullins, February 17, 2014.

17. Public budgeting expert Thomas P. Lauth argues that, in practice, ZBB actually institutionalized incrementalism. Personal correspondence, February 21, 2014.

18. The distinction between mandatory and discretionary budget items exempted over half of the federal budget from annual scrutiny. Other mandatory programs included means-tested entitlements, such as Medicaid, Aid to Families with Dependent Children, the Earned Income Tax Credit, child nutrition programs, federal pensions, and interest payments.

19. B. A. Radin (1998) "The Government Performance and Results Act (GPRA): Hydra-Headed Monster or Flexible Management Tool?" *Public Administration Review*, 58(4), 307–16.

20. Radin, "The Government Performance and Results Act," p. 307.

21. B. A. Radin (2011) "Does Performance Measurement Actually Improve Accountability?" in M. J. Dubnick and H. G. Frederickson (eds.) *Accountable Governance: Problems and Promises* (pp. 98–110) (Armonk, NY: M. E. Sharpe), p. 103.

22. Radin, "Does Performance Measurement Actually Improve Accountability?" p. 103.

23. T. Temin and E. Kopp (2014) Interview with Jitinder Kohli, Director in Public Sector Practice, Deloitte, *Federal News Radio*, http://www.federalnewsradio.com/?nid=1269&sid=3651948, date accessed July 6, 2014.

24. S. Watkins (2014) "OMB Launches Strategic Review," *Federal Times*, June 23, http://www.federaltimes.com/article/20140623/MGMT02/306230012/OMB-launches-strategic-reviews, date accessed July 3, 2014.

25. D. P. Moynihan (2008) *The Dynamics of Performance Measurement: Constructing Information and Reform* (Washington, DC: Georgetown University Press).

26. C. E. Lindblom (1959) "The Science of 'Muddling Through,'" *Public Administration Review*, 19(2), 79–88; A. Wildavsky (1992) *The New Politics of the Budgetary Process*, 2nd ed. (New York: HarperCollins).

27. The following discussion is taken from B. J. Cohn Berman (2012) *When Governments Listen: Moving Toward Publicly Engaged Governing* (New York: The National Center for Civic Innovation).

28. S. Maynard-Moody and S. Portillo (2012) "Street-Level Bureaucracy Theory," in Durant, *The Oxford Handbook of American Bureaucracy* (pp. 252–77). For a much more positive assessment of these features, see C. T. Goodsell (2004) *The Case for Bureaucracy: A Public Administration Polemic*, 4th ed. (Washington, DC: Congressional Quarterly Press).

29. V. Rometty (2013) "Business: The Year of the Smarter Enterprise," *The Economist*, November 18, http://www.economist.com/news/21589108-new-model-firm-its-way-says-virginia-rometty-chief-executive-ibm-year.

30. Rometty, "The Year of the Smarter Enterprise."

31. Rometty, "The Year of the Smarter Enterprise."
32. The federal revenue tables miss "offsetting receipts." As public budgeting and finance expert Daniel Mullins summarizes, "these are primarily resources from fees and charges, and they are substantial. The off-setting receipts were made off-budget due to the 1990 Budget Enforcement Act. The deal was that these resources could be used to allow spending above the budget spending caps and would not be counted as spending toward the cap. This provided a number of problematic incentives to enact fees (such as for parking via private concessionaire contracts for 'free' access national monuments, such as Mt. Rushmore) distorting public policy objectives. If you include excluded off-setting receipts (of $635 billion), personal income taxes were 33.4%, SSCI was 31.3%, and off-setting receipts were 22.7%." Personal correspondence, February 17, 2014.
33. Figure 8.4 also does not include offsetting receipts and thus distorts to an extent the breakdowns as per footnote 32. To make this point, one could also go back much further than the 1950s. In the 1950s (and consistent with this graph), taxes on wages, salaries, and income (personal taxes) were significantly greater than corporate taxes. As you will learn in your coursework, one also has to be a bit careful in subscribing all revenue from personal income taxes as coming from individuals; unincorporated businesses (sole proprietorships, for example) also pay under the personal income tax.
34. Government Accountability Office (2004) *Unfunded Mandates: Analysis of Reform Act Coverage* (Washington, DC: GAO-04–637).
35. Congressional Budget Office (2007) *The Long-Term Budget Outlook* (Washington, DC: Congress of the United States), December.
36. Mullins and Mikesell, "Innovations in Budgeting and Financial Management."
37. Utilities, trusts, and liquor stores are generally not considered part of general government spending but, rather, part of total spending. For descriptive purposes, general spending is usually used, because the latter includes commercial operations and the holding of trusts for others (which is not really government resources or spending).
38. E. D. Kleinbard (2008) "Rethinking Tax Expenditures," address to Chicago-Kent College of Law Federal Tax Institute, May 1, http://www.house.gov/jct/Rethinking_Tax_Expenditures.pdf.
39. As you will learn in your program, we also often include tax or expenditure provisions temporarily in the budget. For example, reenactment of an expiring tax increase is scored as a revenue increase. Extending an existing tax cut is scored as a revenue decrease. Likewise, reauthorizing and sunsetting a program is an expenditure increase, reinstating a temporary expenditure reduction as a new reduction to the base.
40. A. Levinson (1998) "Balanced Budgets and Business Cycles: Evidence from the States," *National Tax Journal*, 51(4), 715–32; J. M. Poterba (1995) "Balanced Budget Rules and Fiscal Policy: Evidence from the States," *National Tax Journal*, 48(3), 329–36.
41. J. L. True, B. D. Jones, and F. R. Baumgartner (2007) "Punctuated-Equilibrium Theory: Explaining Stability and Change in Public Policymaking," in P. Sabatier (ed.) *Theories of the Policy Process* (pp. 155–87) (Boulder: Westview Press), p. 165.
42. E. Burke (1796) Letters on a Regicide Peace, http://www.brainyquote.com/quotes/quotes/e/edmundburk136336.html.

9 Networking in the Shadow of Hierarchy

1. M. Maciag (2014) "State and Local Government Retirements are on the Rise," *Governing*, May 20, http://www.governing.com/topics/mgmt/gov-survey-finds-increase-state-and-local-government-employee-retirements-hiring.html, date accessed June 3, 2014.
2. The mandate came in the wake of soaring executive bonuses in those financial institutions that had received bailouts during the financial collapse of 2007–09.

3. M. Hill and P. Hupe (2009) *Implementing Public Policy: Governance in Theory and Practice*, 2nd ed. (Thousand Oaks, CA: SAGE).

4. E. Burke, http://www.quotationspage.com/quotes/Edmund_Burke/.

5. S. Satkunanandan (2014) "Max Weber and the Ethos of Politics beyond Calculation," *American Political Science Review*, 108(1), 169–81, at 173.

6. For additional definitions of policy implementation, see Hill and Hupe, *Implementing Public Policy*.

7. G. Majone and A. Wildavsky (1984) "Implementation as Evolution," in J. L. Pressman and A. Wildavsky *Implementation: How Great Expectations in Washington Are Dashed in Oakland; Or, Why It's Amazing that Federal Programs Work at All, This Being a Saga of the Economic Development Administration as Told by Two Sympathetic Observers Who Seek to Build Morals on a Foundation of Ruined Hopes*, 3rd ed. (pp. 163–80) (Berkeley: University of California Press), p. 180.

8. J. E. Anderson (1975) *Public Policy-Making* (New York: Praeger), p. 79.

9. H. G. Frederickson (1999) "The Repositioning of American Public Administration," *PS: Political Science & Politics*, 32(4), 701–11.

10. F. W. Scharpf (1993) *Games in Hierarchies and Networks: Analytical and Empirical Approaches to the Study of Governance Institutions* (Frankfurt am Main, Germany: Campus Verlag).

11. For an excellent summary of this literature plus its evolution over the years, see Hill and Hupe, *Implementing Public Policy*.

12. H. Ingram (1977) Policy Implementation through Bargaining: The Case of Federal Grants-in-Aid," *Public Policy*, 25(4), 499–526.

13. E. Bardach (1977) *The Implementation Game: What Happens after a Bill Becomes a Law* (Cambridge: MIT Press).

14. R. F. Elmore (1978) "Organizational Models of Social Program Implementation," *Public Policy*, 26(2), 185–228; R. F. Elmore (1979–80) "Backward Mapping: Implementation Research and Policy Decisions," *Political Science Quarterly*, 94(4), 601–16. Also see D. J. Fiorino (1997) "Strategies for Regulatory Reform: Forward Compared to Backward Mapping," *Policy Studies Journal*, 25(2), 249–65.

15. C. J. Fox and H. T. Miller (1996) *Postmodern Public Administration: Toward Discourse* (Thousand Oaks, CA: SAGE).

16. Ingram, "Policy Implementation through Bargaining."

17. M. Rein and F. Rabinovitz (1978) "Implementation: A Theoretical Perspective," in W. D. Burnham and M. W. Weinberg (eds.) *American Politics and Public Policy* (pp. 307–35) (Cambridge: MIT Press).

18. A. Browne and A. Wildavsky (1984) "Implementation as Mutual Adaptation," in Pressman and Wildavsky, *Implementation* (pp. 206–31).

19. R. E. Matland (1995) "Synthesizing the Implementation Literature: The Ambiguity-Conflict Model of Policy Implementation," *Journal of Public Administration Research and Theory*, 5(2), 145–74.

20. H. W. J. Rittel and M. M. Webber (1973) "Dilemmas in a General Theory of Planning," *Policy Sciences*, 4(2), 155–69.

21. J. L. Brudney and D. S. Wright (2010) "The 'Revolt in Dullsville' Revisited: Lessons for Theory, Practice, and Research from the American State Administrators Project, 1964–2008," *Public Administration Review*, 70(1), 26–37.

22. M. Grodzins (1960) "The Federal System," in the U. S. President's Commission on National Goals (eds.) *Goals for Americans: The Report of the President's Commission on National Goals* (pp. 265–84) (Upper Saddle River, NJ: Prentice Hall).

23. R. Agranoff and M. McGuire (2012) "Networking in the Shadow of Bureaucracy," in R. F. Durant (ed.) *The Oxford Handbook of American Bureaucracy*, paperback ed. (pp. 372–95) (Oxford: Oxford University Press).

24. Elmore, "Backward Mapping," p. 614.
25. R. F. Elmore (1985) "Forward and Backward Mapping: Reversible Logic in the Analysis of Public Policy," in K. Hanf and T. A. J. Toonen (eds.) *Policy Implementation in Federal and Unitary Systems: Questions of Analysis and Design* (pp. 33–70) (Dordrecht: Martinus Nijhoff).
26. H. G. Frederickson, K. B. Smith, C. W. Larimer, and M. J. Licari (2012) *The Public Administration Theory Primer*, 2nd ed. (Boulder: Westview Press), p. 235.
27. Frederickson, Smith, Larimer, and Licari, *The Public Administration Theory Primer*, p. 237.
28. D. J. Kim, K.-B. Yue, S. P. Hall, and S. Gates (2009) "Global Diffusion of the Internet XV: Web 2.0 Technologies, Principles, and Applications: A Conceptual Framework from Technology Push and Demand Pull Perspective," *Communications of the Association for Information Systems*, 24(1), 657–72.
29. M. Parameswaran and A. B. Whinston (2007) "Research Issues in Social Computing," *Journal of the Association for Information Systems*, 8(6), 336–50; Kim, Yue, Hall, and Gates, "Global Diffusion of the Internet XV"; A. P. McAfee (2006) "Enterprise 2.0: The Dawn of Emergent Collaboration," *MIT Sloan Management Review*, 47(3), 21–8. Also see V. Peristeras, G. Mentzas, K. A. Tarabanis, and A. Abecker (2009) "Transforming E-Government and E-Participation through IT," *Intelligent Systems, IEEE*, 24(5), 14–19.
30. Accenture (2006) "E-government Leadership: Building the Trust," Accenture, Dublin; Capgemini (2007) "The User Challenge Benchmarking the Supply of Online Public Services," https://www.google.com/url?sa=t&rct=j&q=&esrc=s&source=web&cd=1&ved =0CCwQFjAA&url=http%3A%2F%2Fwww.060.es%2F060%2FGetFile%3Furl%3D056 451&ei=zjqOUoPEEunNsQTf04LYDw&usg=AFQjCNHjE2tnmULR63n3AY1FFy3ioY T8Ug&sig2=hEIRaF9L_OZ4F8G7dkdg7g&bvm=bv.56988011,d.cWc.
31. J. Moore (2014) "Big Data in Raleigh: Opening Up and Reaching Out," *GCN: Technology, Tools, and Tactics for Public Sector IT*, June 3, http://gcn.com/articles/2014 /06/03/raleigh-big-data.aspx, date accessed June 4, 2014.
32. GNC Staff (2014) "Big Data Solutions for City Management," *GNC: Technology, Tools, and Tactics for Public Sector IT*, May 30, http://gcn.com/articles/2014/05/30 /ibm-smarter-cities.aspx?admgarea=TC_STATELOCA, date accessed June 4, 2014.
33. Commission of the European Communities (2006) "eGovernment i2010 Action Plan: Accelerating eGovernment in Europe for the Benefit of All," Commission of the European Communities, Brussels.
34. A. Haque (2001) "GIS, Public Service, and the Issue of Democratic Governance," *Public Administration Review*, 61(3), 259–65; J. Musso, C. Weare, T. Bryer, and T. L. Cooper (2013) "Toward 'Strong Democracy' in Global Cities? Social Capital Building, Theory-Driven Reform, and the Los Angeles Neighborhood Council Experience," in R. F. Durant and J. R. S. Durant (eds.) *Debating Public Administration: Management Challenges, Choices, and Opportunities* (pp. 89–109) (Boca Raton, FL: CRC Press). But see, for more positive experiences, T. L. Cooper (2011) "Citizen-Driven Administration: Civic Engagement in the United States," in D. C. Menzel and H. L. White (eds.) *The State of Public Administration: Issues, Challenges, and Opportunities* (pp. 238–56) (Armonk, NY: M. E. Sharpe).
35. M. H. Moore (1994) "Public Value as the Focus of Strategy," *Australian Journal of Public Administration*, 53(3), 296–303; M. H. Moore (1995) *Creating Public Value: Strategic Management in Government* (Cambridge: Harvard University Press); S. Petter, D. Straub, and A. Rai (2007) "Specifying Formative Constructs in Information Systems Research," *MIS Quarterly*, 31(4), 623–56; S. Petter, W. DeLone, and E. McLean (2008) "Measuring Information Systems Success: Models, Dimensions, Measures, and Interrelationships," *European Journal of Information Systems*, 17(3), 236–63; P. B. Seddon, S. Staples, R. Patnayakuni, and M. Bowtell (1999) "Dimensions of Information Systems Success," *Communications of the Association for Information Systems*, 2(20), 1–39.

36. Moore, "Public Value as the Focus of Strategy."
37. A. Mazmanian (2014) "Donovan Talks Up Management in OMB Confirmation Hearing," *FCW: The Business of Federal Technology*, June 11, http://fcw.com/articles /2014/06/11/sean-donovan-hearing.aspx?admgarea=TC_Management, date accessed June 16, 2014.
38. M. Scott, W. DeLone, and W. Golden (under review) "Measuring eGovernment Success: A Public Value Approach," *European Journal of Information Systems*.
39. D. A. Mazmanian and P. A. Sabatier (1989) *Implementation and Public Policy* (Lanham, MD: University Press of America).
40. Mazmanian and Sabatier, *Implementation and Public Policy*.
41. Pressman and Wildavsky, *Implementation*.
42. E. R. Bowen (1982) "The Pressman–Wildavsky Paradox: Four Addenda or Why Models Based on Probability Theory Can Predict Implementation Success and Suggest Useful Tactical Advice for Implementers," *Journal of Public Policy*, 2(1), 1–21.

10 Revitalizing a Sense of Common Purpose

1. R. F. Durant (2014) "Progressivism, Corporate Capitalism, and the Social Sciences: Confronting the Paradox of Federal Administrative Reform in America," *Administration & Society*, 46(6), 599–631; R. F. Durant and S. B. Ali (2013) "Repositioning American Public Administration? Citizen Estrangement, Administrative Reform, and the Disarticulated State," *Public Administration Review*, 73(2), 278–89; T. Nabatchi (2010) "Addressing the Citizenship and Democratic Deficits: The Potential of Deliberative Democracy for Public Administration," *American Review of Public Administration*, 40(4), 376–99; J. A. Stever (2001) "Review: Values for Public Administration Renewal," *Public Administration Review*, 61(5), 625–29; W. F. West (2011) *Program Budgeting and the Performance Movement: The Elusive Quest for Efficiency in Government* (Washington, DC: Georgetown University Press). For major exceptions in recommendations to reformers in the mainstream scholarly literature, see R. C. Box (2004) *Public Administration and Society: Critical Issues in American Governance* (Armonk, NY: M. E. Sharpe); H. G. Frederickson (1997) *The Spirit of Public Administration* (San Francisco: Jossey-Bass); C. S. King, C. Stivers, and Collaborators (1998) *Government Is Us: Public Administration in an Anti-Government Era* (Thousand Oaks, CA: SAGE); G. D. Wamsley, R. N. Bacher, C. T. Goodsell, P. S. Kronenberg, J. A. Rohr, C. M. Stivers, O. F. White, and J. F. Wolf (1990) *Refounding Public Administration* (Newbury Park, CA: SAGE).
2. D. P. Moynihan and P. W. Ingraham (2004) "Integrative Leadership in the Public Sector: A Model of Performance-Information Use," *Administration & Society*, 36(4), 427–53.
3. D. H. Rosenbloom (2013) "Reinventing Administrative Prescriptions: The Case for Democratic-Constitutional Impact Statements and Scorecards," in R. F. Durant and J. R. S. Durant (eds.) *Debating Public Administration: Management Challenges, Choices, and Opportunities* (pp. 111–30) (Boca Raton, FL: CRC Press).
4. R. S. Kaplan and D. P. Norton (1996) *The Balanced Scorecard: Translating Strategy into Action* (Boston: Harvard Business School Press).
5. Kaplan and Norton, *The Balanced Scorecard*; P. R. Niven (2008) *Balanced Scorecard: Step-by-Step for Government and Nonprofit Agencies*, 2nd ed. (Hoboken, NJ: John Wiley).
6. A. de Saint-Exupéry, http://www.brainyquote.com/quotes/authors/a/antoine_de_saintexu-pery.html.
7. E. K. Keller (2014) "The Challenge of Building the Workforce Government Needs," *Governing*, July 8, http://www.governing.com/columns/smart-mgmt/col-challenge-build-ing-workforce-government-needs.html, date accessed July 10, 2014.

8. The second point is best summarized in terms of "equity theory." See J. S. Adams (1963) "Toward an Understanding of Inequity," *Journal of Abnormal and Social Psychology*, 67(5), 422–36.

9. C. Argyris (1976) "Single-Loop and Double-Loop Models in Research on Decision Making," *Administrative Science Quarterly*, 21(3), 363–75.

10. Arturo.romeroper.eda.afs.org (2012) "Single-Loop and Double-Loop Learning," November 13, AFS Intercultural Programs, http://www.afs.org/blog/icl/?p=2653.

11. D. Waldo (1952) "Development of a Theory of Democratic Administration," *American Political Science Review*, 46(1), 81–103, at 87.

12. O. Tead (1933) *Human Nature and Management: The Applications of Psychology to Executive Leadership*, 2nd ed. (New York: McGraw-Hill).

13. Tead, *Human Nature and Management*, pp. 291–92.

14. Tead, *Human Nature and Management*, p. 292.

15. Tead, *Human Nature and Management*, pp. 284–85.

16. Tead, *Human Nature and Management*, p. 6.

17. B. R. Fry and J. C. N. Raadschelders (2008) *Mastering Public Administration: From Max Weber to Dwight Waldo* (Washington, DC: Congressional Quarterly Press), Chapter 5.

18. C. I. Barnard (1938) *The Functions of the Executive* (Cambridge: Harvard University Press).

19. A. H. Maslow (1943) "A Theory of Human Motivation," *Psychological Review*, 50(4), 370–96.

20. D. M. McGregor (1960) *The Human Side of Enterprise* (New York: McGraw Hill); C. Argyris (1973) "Some Limits of Rational Man Organizational Theory," *Public Administration Review*, 33(3), 253–67.

21. Guru (2008) "Douglas McGregor," *The Economist*, October 3, http://www.economist.com/node/12366698.

22. F. Herzberg (1964) "The Motivation-Hygiene Concept and Problems of Manpower," *Personnel Administration*, 27, 3–7.

23. P. Hersey and K. H. Blanchard (1988) *Management of Organizational Behavior: Utilizing Human Resources*, 5th ed. (Englewood Cliffs, NJ: Prentice-Hall).

24. Although prior research exists that refers to EI, the book that popularized the idea was written by D. Goleman (1996) *Emotional Intelligence: Why It Can Matter More than IQ* (New York: Bantam Books).

25. T. Geithner (2014) *Stress Test: Reflections on Financial Crises* (New York: Random House).

26. M. E. Guy, M. A. Newman, and S. H. Mastracci (2008) *Emotional Labor: Putting the Service in Public Service* (New York: M. E. Sharpe).

27. Guy, Newman, and Mastracci, *Emotional Labor*, p. 176.

28. See, for example, J. L. Perry (1986) "Merit Pay in the Public Sector: The Case for a Failure of Theory," *Review of Public Personnel Administration*, 7(1), 57–69; J. L. Perry (1991) "Linking Pay to Performance: The Controversy Continues," in C. Ban and N. M. Riccucci (eds.) *Public Personnel Management: Current Concerns, Future Challenges* (pp. 73–86) (White Plains, NY: Longman Press); S. W. Hays (2004) "Trends and Best Practices in State and Local Human Resource Management: Lessons to Be Learned?" *Review of Public Personnel Administration*, 24(3), 256–75; J. E. Kellough and L. G. Nigro (2002) "Pay for Performance in Georgia State Government: Employee Perspectives on GeorgiaGain After 5 Years," *Review of Public Personnel Administration*, 22(2), 146–66; J. Underhill and R. A. Oman (2007) "A Critical Review of the Sweeping Federal Civil Service Changes: The Case of the Departments of Homeland Security and Defense," *Review of Public Personnel Administration*, 27(4), 401–20.

29. J. L. Perry, T. A. Engbers, and S. Y. Jun (2013) "Back to the Future? Performance-Related Pay, Empirical Research, and the Perils of Persistence," in Durant and Durant, *Debating Public Administration* (pp. 27–65).

30. See, for example, *National Treasury Employees Union (NTEU) et al. v. Chertoff*, 452 F.3d 839 (D.C. Cir. 2006); B. Ballenstedt (2008) "Freedom to Manage," *Government Executive*, January 1, http://www.govexec.com/features/0108-01/0108-01s1.htm.

31. A. Rosenberg (2008) "Fair Pay, Fair Play," *Government Executive*, February 7, http://www.govexec.com/dailyfed/0208/020708pb.htm.

32. H. Risher (2013) "Commentary: Back to the Future? Performance-Related Pay, Empirical Research, and the Perils of Persistence," in Durant and Durant, *Debating Public Administration* (pp. 44–46).

33. J. E. Kellough and H. Lu (1993) "The Paradox of Merit Pay in the Public Sector: Persistence of a Problematic Procedure," *Review of Public Personnel Administration*, 13(2), 45–64; J. G. March and J. P. Olsen (1983) "Organizing Political Life: What Administrative Reorganization Tells Us About Government," *American Political Science Review*, 77(2), 281–96; J. L. Perry (1988) "Making Policy by Trial and Error: Merit Pay in the Federal Service," *Policy Studies Journal*, 17(2), 389–405.

34. J. L. Perry (1996) "Measuring Public Service Motivation: An Assessment of Construct Reliability and Validity," *Journal of Public Administration Research and Theory*, 6(1), 5–22; J. L. Perry (1997) "Antecedents of Public Service Motivation," *Journal of Public Administration Research and Theory*, 7(2), 181–97; J. L. Perry and L. R. Wise (1990) "The Motivational Bases of Public Service," *Public Administration Review*, 50(3), 367–73.

35. Personal correspondence with J. E. Kellough, July 7, 2014.

36. For a summary of these findings, see S. K. Pandey and E. C. Stazyk (2008) "Antecedents and Correlates of Public Service Motivation," in J. L. Perry and A. Hondeghem (eds.) *Motivation in Public Management: The Call of Public Service* (pp. 101–17) (New York: Oxford University Press).

37. E. C. Stazyk (2013) "Crowding Out Public Service Motivation? Comparing Theoretical Expectations with Empirical Findings on the Influence of Performance-Related Pay," *Review of Public Personnel Administration*, 33(3), 252–74.

38. See, for example, E. C. Stazyk, R. S. Davis, P. Sanabria, and S. Pettijohn (2014) "Working in the Hollow State: Exploring the Link between Public Service Motivation and Interlocal Collaboration," in Y. K. Dwivedi, M. A. Shareef, S. K. Pandey, and V. Kumar (eds.) *Public Administration Reformation: Market Demand from Public Organizations* (pp. 124–43) (New York: Routledge).

39. D. M. Levitan (1943) "Political Ends and Administrative Means," *Public Administration Review*, 3(4), 353–59, at 357.

40. D. Waldo (1984) *The Administrative State: A Study of the Political Theory of American Public Administration*, 2nd ed. (New York: Holmes & Meier), p. 150.

41. Waldo, "Development of a Theory of Democratic Administration," p. 92.

42. L. C. Gawthrop (1998) *Public Service and Democracy: Ethical Imperatives for the 21st Century* (New York: Chatham House).

43. Gawthrop, *Public Service and Democracy*, p. 41.

44. Gawthrop, *Public Service and Democracy*, p. xii.

45. H. Wagenaar and S. D. N. Cook (2003) "Understanding Policy Practices: Action, Dialectic, and Deliberation in Policy Analysis," in M. A. Hajer and H. Wagenaar (eds.) *Deliberative Policy Analysis: Understanding Governance in the Network Society* (pp. 139–71) (Cambridge: Cambridge University Press), p. 170.

46. Wagenaar and Cook, "Understanding Policy Practices," p. 170.

47. D. Yanow (2003) "Accessing Local Knowledge," in Hajer and Wagenaar, *Deliberative Policy Analysis* (pp. 228–46), p. 236.

48. Yanow, "Accessing Local Knowledge," p. 236.

49. Hajer and Wagenaar, *Deliberative Policy Analysis*, p. 11.

50. H. Heclo (2008) *On Thinking Institutionally* (Boulder: Paradigm Publishers), p. 99.

51. Heclo, *On Thinking Institutionally*, pp. 99–100.
52. Gawthrop, *Public Service and Democracy*, p. 153.
53. Gawthrop, *Public Service and Democracy*, p. 153.
54. Gawthrop, *Public Service and Democracy*, p. 99.
55. C. Liu and J. L. Mikesell (2014) "The Impact of Public Officials' Corruption on the Size and Allocation of U.S. State Spending," *Public Administration Review*, 74(3), 346–59.
56. M. W. Spicer (1995) *The Founders, the Constitution, and Public Administration: A Conflict in World Views* (Washington, DC: Georgetown University Press).
57. N. Long (1949) "Power and Administration," *Public Administration Review*, 9(4), 257–64.
58. Heclo, *On Thinking Institutionally*, p. 7.
59. E. Yoder (2014) "The Data on Federal Whistleblowing and Its Consequences," *Washington Post*, June 17, http://www.washingtonpost.com/blogs/federal-eye/wp/2014/06/17/the-data-on-federal-whistleblowing-and-its-consequences/, date accessed June 18, 2014.
60. Yoder, "The Data on Federal Whistleblowing and Its Consequences."
61. P. Selznick (1957) *Leadership in Administration: A Sociological Interpretation* (Evanston, IL: Row, Peterson).
62. L. D. Terry (2002) *Leadership of Public Bureaucracies: The Administrator as Conservator*, 2nd ed. (Armonk, NY: M. E. Sharpe).
63. G. May (2008) *John Tyler* (New York: Holt, Henry & Company), p. 14.
64. M. L. King Jr (1967) "Where Do We Go From Here?" Southern Christian Leadership Conference, August.
65. B. Franklin (1787) http://www.bartleby.com/73/1593.html.

Bibliography

Aaron, H. J. (1978) *Politics and the Professors: The Great Society in Perspective* (Washington, DC: Brookings Institution Press).

Adams, G. B., and D. L. Balfour (2004) *Unmasking Administrative Evil*, rev. ed. (Armonk, NY: M. E. Sharpe).

Adams, G. B., and D. L. Balfour (2012) "The Prospects for Revitalizing Ethics in a New Governance Era," in R. F. Durant (ed.) *The Oxford Handbook of American Bureaucracy*, paperback ed. (pp. 766–85) (Oxford: Oxford University Press).

Adams, J. S. (1963) "Toward an Understanding of Inequity," *Journal of Abnormal and Social Psychology*, 67(5), 422–36.

Agranoff, R. (2007) *Managing within Networks: Adding Value to Public Organizations* (Washington, DC: Georgetown University Press).

Agranoff, R., and M. McGuire (2012) "Networking in the Shadow of Bureaucracy," in R. F. Durant (ed.) *The Oxford Handbook of American Bureaucracy*, paperback ed. (pp. 372–95) (Oxford: Oxford University Press).

Alchon, G. (1985) *The Invisible Hand of Planning: Capitalism, Social Science, and the State in the 1920s* (Princeton: Princeton University Press).

American Political Science Association (1950) "Toward a More Responsible Two-Party System: A Report of the Committee on Political Parties," *American Political Science Review*, 44(3), Part 2, Supplement.

Amirkhanyan, A. A., H. J. Kim, and K. T. Lambright (2013) "Going Beyond Service Delivery: Exploring the Prevalence of Citizen Participation in Government Contracting," paper presented at the 11th Public Management Research Conference, Madison, WI, 20–22 June.

Ammons, D. N. (ed.) (1995) *Accountability for Performance: Measurement and Monitoring in Local Government* (Washington, DC: International City/Council Management Association).

Ammons, D. N. (1995) "Overcoming the Inadequacies of Performance Measurement in Local Government: The Case of Libraries and Leisure Services," *Public Administration Review*, 55(1), 37–47.

Anderson, J. E. (1975) *Public Policy-Making* (New York: Praeger).

Andrews, R., G. A. Boyne, K. J. Meier, L. J. O'Toole Jr, and R. M. Walker (2005) "Representative Bureaucracy, Organizational Strategy, and Public Service Performance: An Empirical Analysis of English Local Government," *Journal of Public Administration Research and Theory*, 15(4), 489–504.

Appleby, J. (2000) *Inheriting the Revolution: The First Generation of Americans* (Cambridge: Harvard University Press).

Appleby, P. H. (1945) *Big Democracy* (New York: Knopf).

Argyris, C. (1973) "Some Limits of Rational Man Organizational Theory," *Public Administration Review*, 33(3), 253–67.

Argyris, C. (1976) "Single-Loop and Double-Loop Models in Research on Decision Making," *Administrative Science Quarterly*, 21(3), 363–75.

Baldwin, J. N. (1996) "Female Promotions in the Male-Dominant Organizations: The Case of the United States Military," *Journal of Politics*, 58(4), 1184–197.

Balogh, B. (2009) *A Government Out of Sight: The Mystery of National Authority in Nineteenth-Century America* (Cambridge: Cambridge University Press).

Bardach, E. (1977) *The Implementation Game: What Happens after a Bill Becomes a Law* (Cambridge: MIT Press).

Barnard, C. I. (1938) *The Functions of the Executive* (Cambridge: Harvard University Press).

Bartels, L. M. (2008) *Unequal Democracy: The Political Economy of the New Gilded Age* (Princeton: Princeton University Press).

Barzelay, M., and C. Campbell (2003) *Preparing for the Future: Strategic Planning in the U.S. Air Force* (Washington, DC: Brookings Institution Press).

Bates, R. C., C. Eger, S. Mintier, J. P. Naylor, E. Reed, and D. Harvey (2013) "Growing the Next Generation of Local Government Professionals," *PA Times*, 36(4), 7.

Baumgartner, F. R., and B. D. Jones (2009) *Agendas and Instability in American Politics*, 2nd ed. (Chicago: University of Chicago Press).

Baumgartner, F. R., S. Brouard, E. Grossman, S. G. Lazardeux, and J. Moody (2014) "Divided Government, Legislative Productivity, and Policy Change in the USA and France," *Governance*, 27(3), 423–47.

Beer, S. H. (1978) "Federalism, Nationalism, and Democracy in America," *American Political Science Review*, 72(1), 9–21.

Benner, T., W. H. Reinicke, and J. M. Witte (2003) "Global Public Policy Networks: Lessons Learned and Challenges Ahead," *Brookings Review*, 21(2), 18–21.

Berk, G., D. C. Galvan, and V. Hattam (eds.) (2013) *Political Creativity: Reconfiguring Institutional Order and Change* (Philadelphia: University of Pennsylvania Press).

Berry, J. M. (1999) *The New Liberalism: The Rising Power of Citizen Groups* (Washington, DC: Brookings Institution Press).

Berry, J. M., K. E. Portney, and K. Thompson (1993) *The Rebirth of Urban Democracy* (Washington, DC: Brookings Institution Press).

Bingham, L. B., T. Nabatchi, and R. O'Leary (2005) "The New Governance: Practices and Processes for Stakeholder and Citizen Participation in the Work of Government," *Public Administration Review*, 65(5), 547–58.

Birdsall, N. (2003) "Asymmetric Globalization: Global Markets Require Good Global Politics," *Brookings Review*, 21(2), 22–7.

Bowen, E. R. (1982) "The Pressman-Wildavsky Paradox: Four Addenda or Why Models Based on Probability Theory Can Predict Implementation Success and Suggest Useful Tactical Advice for Implementers," *Journal of Public Policy*, 2(1), 1–21.

Bowman, J. S., and J. P. West (2006) "Ending Civil Service Protections in Florida Government: Experiences in State Agencies," *Review of Public Personnel Administration*, 26(2), 139–57.

Box, R. C. (2004) *Public Administration and Society: Critical Issues in American Governance* (Armonk, NY: M. E. Sharpe).

Bozeman, B. (2007) *Public Values and Public Interest: Counterbalancing Economic Individualism* (Washington, DC: Georgetown University Press).

Brainard, L. A., and J. G. McNutt (2010) "Virtual Government–Citizen Relations: Informational, Transactional, or Collaborative?" *Administration & Society*, 42(7), 836–58.

Brown, S. L., and K. M. Eisenhardt (1997) "The Art of Continuous Change: Linking Complexity Theory and Time-Paced Evolution in Relentlessly Shifting Organizations," *Administrative Science Quarterly*, 42(1), 1–34.

Brown, T. L., M. Potoski, and D. M. Van Slyke (2013) "Managing Public Service Contracts: Aligning Values, Institutions, and Markets," in R. F. Durant and J. R. S. Durant (eds.) *Debating Public Administration: Management Challenges, Choices, and Opportunities* (pp. 155–75) (Boca Raton, FL: CRC Press).

Browne, A., and A. Wildavsky (1984) "Implementation as Mutual Adaptation," in J. L. Pressman and A. Wildavsky *Implementation: How Great Expectations in Washington Are Dashed in Oakland; Or, Why It's Amazing that Federal Programs Work at All, This Being a Saga of the Economic Development Administration as Told by Two Sympathetic Observers Who Seek to Build Morals on a Foundation of Ruined Hopes*, 3rd ed. (pp. 206–31) (Berkeley: University of California Press).

Brudney, J. L., and D. S. Wright (2010) "The 'Revolt in Dullsville' Revisited: Lessons for Theory, Practice, and Research from the American State Administrators Project, 1964–2008," *Public Administration Review*, 70(1), 26–37.

Brudney, J. L., F. T. Hebert, and D. S. Wright (2000) "From Organizational Values to Organizational Roles: Examining Representative Bureaucracy in State Administration," *Journal of Public Administration Research and Theory*, 10(3), 491–512.

Bryer, T. A., and S. Zavattaro (eds.) (2011) "Symposium on Social Media and Public Administration," *Administrative Theory & Praxis*, 33(3), 325–432.

Bryson, J. M. (1988) "Strategic Planning: Big Wins and Small Wins," *Public Money and Management*, 8(3), 11–15.

Bryson, J. M. (2011) *Strategic Planning for Public and Nonprofit Organizations: A Guide to Strengthening and Sustaining Organizational Achievement*, 4th ed. (San Francisco: Jossey-Bass).

Caldwell, L. K. (1990) *Between Two Worlds: Science, the Environmental Movement, and Policy Choice* (Cambridge: Cambridge University Press).

Campbell, A. L. (2003) *How Policies Make Citizens: Senior Political Activism and the Welfare State* (Princeton: Princeton University Press).

Carnevale, A. P., and S. J. Rose (2004) "Socioeconomic Status, Race/Ethnicity, and Selective College Admissions," in R. D. Kahlenberg (ed.) *America's Untapped Resource: Low-Income Students in Higher Education* (New York: Century Foundation Press).

Carpenter, D. P. (2001) *The Forging of Bureaucratic Autonomy: Reputations, Networks, and Policy Innovation in Executive Agencies, 1862–1928* (Princeton: Princeton University Press).

Chen, C-A (2009) "Antecedents of Contracting-Back-In: A View beyond the Academic Paradigm," *Administration & Society*, 41(1), 101–26.

Chi, K. S. (2005) "State Civil Service Systems," in S. E. Condrey (ed.) *Handbook of Human Resource Management in Government*, 2nd ed. (pp. 76–94) (San Francisco: Jossey-Bass).

Clarke, J. N., and D. C. McCool (1996) *Staking Out the Terrain: Power and Performance among Natural Resource Agencies*, 2nd ed. (Albany: State University of New York Press).

Clements, K. A. (1999) *Woodrow Wilson: World Statesman* (Chicago: Ivan R. Dee).

Cobb, R. W., and C. D. Elder (1983) *Participation in American Politics: The Dynamics of Agenda-Building* (Baltimore: Johns Hopkins University Press).

Coggburn, J. D. (2006) "At-Will Employment in Government: Insights from the State of Texas," *Review of Public Personnel Administration*, 26(2), 158–77.

Cohen, M. D., J. G. March, and J. P. Olsen (1972) "A Garbage Can Model of Organizational Choice," *Administrative Science Quarterly*, 17(1), 1–25.

Cohn Berman, B. J. (2012) *When Governments Listen: Moving Toward Publicly Engaged Governing* (New York: The National Center for Civic Innovation).

Condrey, S. E., and R. P. Battaglio (2007) "A Return to Spoils? Revisiting Radical Civil Service Reform in the United States," *Public Administration Review*, 67(3), 425–36.

Cooper, R., and G. Burrell (1988) "Modernism, Postmodernism, and Organizational Analysis: An Introduction," *Organization Studies*, 9(1), 91–112.

Cooper, T. L. (2011) "Citizen-Driven Administration: Civic Engagement in the United States," in D. C. Menzel and H. L. White (eds.) *The State of Public Administration: Issues, Challenges, and Opportunities* (pp. 238–56) (Armonk, NY: M. E. Sharpe).

Crouch, C. (2004) *Post-Democracy* (Cambridge: Polity Press).

D'Agostino, M. J., and H. Levine (2011) *Women in Public Administration: Theory and Practice* (Sudbury, MA: Jones & Bartlett).

Dahl, R. A. (1947) "The Science of Public Administration: Three Problems," *Public Administration Review*, 7(1), 1–11.

Dahl, R. A. (1999) *On Democracy* (New Haven: Yale University Press).

Davis, O. A., M. A. H. Dempster, and A. Wildavsky (1966) "A Theory of the Budgetary Process," *American Political Science Review*, 60(3), 529–47.

Davis, O. A., M. A. H. Dempster, and A. Wildavsky (1974) "Towards a Predictive Theory of Government Expenditure: US Domestic Appropriations," *British Journal of Political Science*, 4(4), 419–52.

Dawes, S. S., A. M. Cresswell, and T. A. Pardo (2013) "From 'Need to Know' to 'Need to Share': Tangled Problems, Information Boundaries, and the Building of Public Sector Knowledge Networks," in R. F. Durant and J. R. S. Durant (eds.) *Debating Public Administration: Management Challenges, Choices, and Opportunities* (pp. 67–88) (Boca Raton, FL: CRC Press).

deLeon, P. (1992) "The Democratization of the Policy Sciences," *Public Administration Review*, 52(2), 125–29.

Diamond, M. (1959) "Democracy and the Federalist: A Reconsideration of the Framers' Intent," *American Political Science Review*, 53(1), 52–68.

Diggins, J. P. (1996) *Max Weber: Politics and the Spirit of Tragedy* (New York: Basic Books).

Dolan, J. (2000) "The Senior Executive Service: Gender, Attitudes, and Representative Bureaucracy," *Journal of Public Administration Research Theory*, 10(3), 513–30.

Dometrius, N. C. (1984) "Minorities and Women among State Agency Leaders," *Social Science Quarterly*, 65, 127–37.

Drucker, P. F. (2001) *The Essential Drucker: Selection from the Management Works of Peter F. Drucker* (New York: HarperCollins).

du Gay, P. (ed.) (2005) *The Values of Bureaucracy* (Oxford: Oxford University Press).

Durant, R. F. (1992) *The Administrative Presidency Revisited: Public Lands, the BLM, and the Reagan Revolution* (Albany: State University of New York Press).

Durant, R. F. (1998) "Rethinking the Unthinkable: A Cautionary Note," *Administration & Society*, 29(6), 643–52.

Durant, R. F. (2000) "Whither the Neoadministrative State? Toward a Polity-Centered Theory of Administrative Reform," *Journal of Public Administration Research and Theory*, 10(1), 79–109.

Durant, R. F. (2004) "Reconceptualizing Purpose," in R. F. Durant, D. Fiorino, and R. O'Leary (eds.) *Environmental Governance Reconsidered: Challenges, Choices, and Opportunities* (pp. 29–34) (Cambridge: MIT Press).

Durant, R. F. (2014) "Progressivism, Corporate Capitalism, and the Social Sciences: Confronting the Paradox of Federal Administrative Reform in America," *Administration & Society*, 46(6), 599–631.

Durant, R. F., and S. B. Ali (2013) "Repositioning American Public Administration? Citizen Estrangement, Administrative Reform, and the Disarticulated State," *Public Administration Review*, 73(2), 278–89.

Durant, R. F., with T. Boodphetcharat (2004) "The Precautionary Principle," in R. F. Durant, D. Fiorino, and R. O'Leary (eds.) *Environmental Governance Reconsidered: Challenges, Choices, and Opportunities* (pp. 105–44) (Cambridge: MIT Press).

Durant, R. F., and J. S. Legge Jr (2005) "Public Opinion, Risk Perceptions, and Genetically Modified Food Regulatory Policy: Reassessing the Calculus of Dissent among European Citizens," *European Union Politics*, 6(2), 181–200.

Durant, R. F., and J. S. Legge Jr (2006) "'Wicked Problems,' Public Policy, and Administrative Theory: Lessons from the GM Food Regulatory Arena," *Administration & Society*, 38(3), 309–34.

Durant, R. F., and R. M. Marshak (working paper) "Rethinking Strategic Leadership in Public Agencies."

Durant, R. F., and W. G. Resh (2012) "'Presidentializing' the Bureaucracy," in R. F. Durant (ed.) *The Oxford Handbook of American Bureaucracy*, paperback ed. (pp. 545–68) (Oxford: Oxford University Press).

Durant, R. F., J. M. Johnston, and A. M. Girth (2009) "American Exceptionalism, Human Resource Management, and the Contract State," *Review of Public Personnel Administration*, 29(3), 207–29.

Eberstadt, N. (2001) "The Population Implosion," *Foreign Policy*, 123(March/April), 42–53.

Eisenach, E. J. (1994) *The Lost Promise of Progressivism* (Lawrence: University Press of Kansas).

Eisner, M. A. (2000) *From Warfare State to Welfare State: World War I, Compensatory State Building, and the Limits of the Modern Order* (University Park: Pennsylvania State University Press).

Elmore, R. F. (1978) "Organizational Models of Social Program Implementation," *Public Policy*, 26(2), 185–228.

Elmore, R. F. (1979–80) "Backward Mapping: Implementation Research and Policy Decisions," *Political Science Quarterly*, 94(4), 601–16.

Elmore, R. F. (1985) "Forward and Backward Mapping: Reversible Logic in the Analysis of Public Policy," in K. Hanf and T. A. J. Toonen (eds.) *Policy Implementation in Federal and Unitary Systems: Questions of Analysis and Design* (pp. 33–70) (Dordrecht: Martinus Nijhoff).

Epstein, C. F. (1999) "The Part-Time Solution and the Part-Time Problem," *Dissent*, Spring, pp. 96–8.

Etzioni, A. (1986) "Mixed Scanning Revisited," *Public Administration Review*, 46(1), 8–14.

Faux, J. (1999) "Lost on the Third Way," *Dissent*, Spring, pp. 67–76.

Fernandez, S., and H. G. Rainey (2013) "Managing Successful Organizational Change in the Public Sector," in R. F. Durant and J. R. S. Durant (eds.) *Debating Public Administration: Management Challenges, Choices, and Opportunities* (pp. 7–26) (Boca Raton, FL: CRC Press).

Finer, H. (1941) "Administrative Responsibility in Democratic Government," *Public Administration Review*, 1(4), 335–50.

Fiorino, D. J. (1996) "Toward a New System of Environmental Regulation: The Case for an Industry Sector Approach," *Environmental Law*, 26, 457–88.

Fiorino, D. J. (1997) "Strategies for Regulatory Reform: Forward Compared to Backward Mapping," *Policy Studies Journal*, 25(2), 249–65.

Fiorino, D. J. (2006) *The New Environmental Regulation* (Cambridge: MIT Press).

Fiorino, D. J. (2010) "Sustainability as a Conceptual Focus for Public Administration," *Public Administration Review*, 70(S1), S78–88.

Fischer, F. (1993) "Citizen Participation and the Democratization of Policy Expertise: From Theoretical Inquiry to Practical Cases," *Policy Sciences*, 26(3), 165–87.

Fischer, F. (2007) "Deliberative Policy Analysis as Practical Reason: Integrating Empirical and Normative Arguments," in F. Fischer, G. J. Miller, and M. S. Sidney (eds.) *Handbook of Public Policy Analysis: Theory, Politics, and Methods* (pp. 223–36) (Boca Raton, FL: CRC Press).

Florida, R. (2002) *The Rise of the Creative Class: And How It's Transforming Work, Leisure, Community and Everyday Life* (New York: Basic Books).

Fountain, J. E. (2001) *Building the Virtual State: Information Technology and Institutional Change* (Washington, DC: Brookings Institution Press).

Fox, C. J., and H. T. Miller (1996) *Postmodern Public Administration: Toward Discourse* (Thousand Oaks, CA: SAGE).

Frederickson, H. G. (1971) "Organization Theory and New Public Administration," in F. Marini (ed.) *Toward a New Public Administration: The Minnowbrook Perspective* (Scranton, PA: Chandler Press).

Frederickson, H. G. (1997) *The Spirit of Public Administration* (San Francisco: Jossey-Bass).

Frederickson, H. G. (1999) "The Repositioning of American Public Administration," *PS: Political Science & Politics*, 32(4), 701–11.

Frederickson, H. G., and K. B. Smith (2003) *The Public Administration Theory Primer* (Boulder: Westview Press).

Frederickson, H. G., K. B. Smith, C. W. Larimer, and M. J. Licari (2012) *The Public Administration Theory Primer*, 2nd ed. (Boulder: Westview Press).

Freeman, J. L. (1965) *The Political Process: Executive Bureau-Legislative Committee Relations*, rev. ed. (New York: Random House).

Friedberg, A. L. (2002) "American Antistatism and the Founding of the Cold War State," in I. Katznelson and M. Shefter (eds.) *Shaped by War: International Influences on American Political Development* (pp. 239–66) (Princeton: Princeton University Press).

Friedman, T. L. (1999) *The Lexus and the Olive Tree* (New York: Farrar, Straus & Giroux).

Friedman, T. L. (2005) *The World Is Flat: A Brief History of the Twenty-First Century* (New York: Farrar, Straus & Giroux).

Friedrich, C. J. (1940) "Public Policy and the Nature of Administrative Responsibility," in C. J. Friedrich and E. S. Mason (eds.) *Public Policy* (pp. 3–24) (Cambridge: Harvard University Press)

Fry, B. R., and J. C. N. Raadschelders (2008) *Mastering Public Administration: From Max Weber to Dwight Waldo* (Washington, DC: Congressional Quarterly Press).

Furlong, S. R., and C. M. Kerwin (2005) "Interest Group Participation in Rule Making: A Decade of Change," *Journal of Public Administration Research and Theory*, 15(3), 353–70.

Galaskiewicz, J. (1985) "Interorganizational Relations," *Annual Review of Sociology*, 11, 281–304.

Gaus, J. M. (1947) *Reflections on Public Administration* (Birmingham: University of Alabama Press).

Gawthrop, L. C. (1998) *Public Service and Democracy: Ethical Imperatives for the 21st Century* (New York: Chatham House).

Geithner, T. (2014) *Stress Test: Reflections on Financial Crises* (New York: Random House).

General Accounting Office (1991) *Federal Workforce: Continuing Need for Federal Affirmative Employment* (Washington, DC: GAO/GGD-92-27BR).

General Accounting Office (1995) *Managing for Results: Critical Actions for Measuring Performance* (Washington, DC: GAO/T-GGD/AIMD-95-187).

General Accounting Office (2003) *Major Management Challenges and Program Risks: Environmental Protection Agency* (Washington, DC: GAO-03-112).

Gerrard, M. B. (1994) *Whose Backyard, Whose Risk: Fear and Fairness in Toxic and Nuclear Waste Siting* (Cambridge: MIT Press).

Gerth, H. H., and C. W. Mills (1946) *From Max Weber: Essays in Sociology* (New York: Oxford University Press).

Golden, M. M. (1998) "Interest Groups in the Rule-Making Process: Who Participates? Whose Voices Get Heard?" *Journal of Public Administration Research and Theory*, 8(2), 245–70.

Goleman, D. (1996) *Emotional Intelligence: Why It Can Matter More than IQ* (New York: Bantam Books).

Golembiewski, R. T. (1987) "Public Sector Organization: Why Theory and Practice Should Emphasize Purpose, and How to Do So?" in R. C. Chandler (ed.) *A Centennial History of the American Administrative State* (pp. 433–74) (New York: Free Press).

Goodnow, F. (1916) *The American Conception of Liberty and Government* (Providence, RI: Stanford Printing Company).

Goodsell, C. T. (1998) "A Radical Idea Welcomed—But with Some Buts," *Administration & Society*, 29(6), 653–59.

Goodsell, C. T. (2004) *The Case for Bureaucracy: A Public Administration Polemic*, 4th ed. (Washington, DC: Congressional Quarterly Press).

Goodsell, C. T. (2005) "The Bureau as Unit of Governance," in P. du Gay (ed.) *The Values of Bureaucracy* (pp. 1–40) (Oxford: Oxford University Press).

Gould, L. L. (2013) *Edith Kermit Roosevelt: Creating the Modern First Lady* (Lawrence: University Press of Kansas).

Government Accountability Office (2004) *Unfunded Mandates: Analysis of Reform Act Coverage* (Washington, DC: GAO-04–637).

Government Accountability Office (2006) *Highlights of a GAO Forum: Federal Acquisition Challenges and Opportunities in the 21st Century* (Washington, DC: GAO-07–45SP), October 6.

Government Accountability Office (2008) *Agencies Are Proposing Changes to Improve Oversight, but Could Take Additional Steps to Enhance Coordination and Monitoring* (Washington, DC: GAO-09–60).

Government Accountability Office (2008) *Human Capital Planning Has Improved, but Strategic View of Contractor Workforce Is Needed* (Washington, DC: GAO-08–582).

Government Accountability Office (2012) *Opportunities to Reduce Duplication, Overlap and Fragmentation, Achieve Savings, and Enhance Revenue* (Washington DC: GAO-12–342SP).

Government Accountability Office (2012) *Progress Made to Deter Fraud, but More Could Be Done* (Washington, DC: GAO-12–801T).

Government Accountability Office (2013) *High-Risk Series: An Update* (Washington, DC: GAO-13–283).

Grabosky, P. N., and D. H. Rosenbloom (1975) "Racial and Ethnic Integration in the Federal Service," *Social Science Quarterly*, 56, 71–84.

Greene, V., S. C. Selden, and G. Brewer (2001) "Measuring Power and Presence: Bureaucratic Representation in the American States," *Journal of Public Administration Research and Theory*, 11(3), 379–402.

Greider, W. (1997) *One World, Ready or Not: The Manic Logic of Global Capitalism* (New York: Simon & Schuster).

Grodzins, M. (1960) "The Federal System," in the U. S. President's Commission on National Goals, *Goals for Americans: The Report of the President's Commission on National Goals* (pp. 265–84) (Upper Saddle River, NJ: Prentice Hall).

Guy, M. E., M. A. Newman, and S. H. Mastracci (2008) *Emotional Labor: Putting the Service in Public Service* (New York: M. E. Sharpe).

Hacker, J. S., and P. Pierson (2010) *Winner-Take-All Politics: How Washington Made the Rich Richer—and Turned Its Back on the Middle Class* (New York: Simon & Schuster).

Hacker, J. S., and P. Pierson (2012) "Presidents and the Political Economy: The Coalitional Foundations of Presidential Power," *Presidential Studies Quarterly*, 42(1), 101–31.

Haider-Markel, D. P. (2007) "Representation and Backlash: The Positive and Negative Influence of Descriptive Representation," *Legislative Studies Quarterly*, 32(1), 107–33.

Haider-Markel, D. P., M. R. Joslyn, and C. J. Kniss (2000) "Minority Group Interests and Political Representation: Gay Elected Officials in the Policy Process," *Journal of Politics*, 6(2), 568–77.

Hails, R. S. (2002) "Assessing the Risks Associated with New Agricultural Practices," *Nature*, 418(August 8), 685–88.

Hajer, M. A., and H. Wagenaar (eds.) (2003) *Deliberative Policy Analysis: Understanding Governance in the Network Society* (Cambridge: Cambridge University Press).

Hall, R. H. (1999) *Organizations: Structures, Processes, and Outcomes* (Upper Saddle River, NJ: Prentice Hall).

Hammer, M., and J. Champy (1993) *Reengineering the Corporation: A Manifesto for Business Revolution* (New York: HarperBusiness).

Hammond, T. H., and J. H. Knott (1996) "Who Controls the Bureaucracy? Presidential Power, Congressional Dominance, Legal Constraints, and Bureaucratic Autonomy in a Model of Multi-institutional Policy-Making," *Journal of Law, Economics, and Organization*, 12(1), 119–66.

Haque, A. (2001) "GIS, Public Service, and the Issue of Democratic Governance," *Public Administration Review*, 61(3), 259–65.

Hawley, E. W. (1992) *The Great War and the Search for a Modern Order: A History of the American People and Their Institutions, 1917–1933* (Prospect Heights, IL: Waveland Press).

Hays, S. W. (2004) "Trends and Best Practices in State and Local Human Resource Management: Lessons to Be Learned?" *Review of Public Personnel Administration*, 24(3), 256–75.

Hays, S. W., and J. E. Sowa (2006) "A Broader Look at the 'Accountability' Movement: Some Grim Realities in State Civil Service Systems," *Review of Public Personnel Administration*, 26(2), 102–17.

Heclo, H. (1974) *Modern Social Politics in Britain and Sweden: From Relief to Income Maintenance* (New Haven: Yale University Press).

Heclo, H. (1977) *A Government of Strangers: Executive Politics in Washington* (Washington, DC: Brookings Institution Press).

Heclo, H. (2008) *On Thinking Institutionally* (Boulder: Paradigm Publishers).

Heclo, H. (2013) "Issue Networks and the Executive Establishment," in S. Z. Theodoulou and M. A. Cahn (eds.) *Public Policy: The Essential Readings*, 2nd ed. (Chapter 9) (Boston: Pearson).

Helleiner, E. (2011) "Understanding the 2007–2008 Global Financial Crisis: Lessons for Scholars of International Political Economy," *Annual Review of Political Science*, 14(June), 67–87.

Hellriegel, D., and L. Short (1972) "Equal Employment Opportunity in the Federal Government: A Comparative Analysis," *Public Administrative Review*, 32(6), 851–58.

Henry, N. (2013) *Public Administration and Public Affairs*, 12th ed. (Boston: Pearson).

Herring, E. P. (1936) *Public Administration and the Public Interest* (New York: Russell & Russell).

Hersey, P., and K. H. Blanchard (1988) *Management of Organizational Behavior: Utilizing Human Resources*, 5th ed. (Englewood Cliffs, NJ: Prentice-Hall).

Herzberg, F. (1964) "The Motivation-Hygiene Concept and Problems of Manpower," *Personnel Administration*, 27, 3–7.

Hill, M., and P. Hupe (2009) *Implementing Public Policy: Governance in Theory and Practice*, 2nd ed. (Thousand Oaks, CA: SAGE).

Hindera, J. J. (1993) "Representative Bureaucracy: Further Evidence of Active Representation in the EEOC District Offices," *Journal of Public Administration Research and Theory*, 3(4), 415–29.

Hindera, J. J. (1993) "Representative Bureaucracy: Imprimis Evidence of Active Representation in the EEOC District Offices," *Social Science Quarterly*, 74, 95–108.

Hindera, J. J., and C. D. Young (1998) "Representative Bureaucracy: The Theoretical Implications of Statistical Interaction," *Political Research Quarterly*, 51(3), 655–71.

Hirschman, A. O. (1991) *The Rhetoric of Reaction: Perversity, Futility, and Jeopardy* (Cambridge: Harvard University Press).

Hiscock, G. (2012) *Earth Wars: The Battle for Global Resources* (Singapore: John Wiley).

Hogwood, B. W., and L. A. Gunn (1984) *Policy Analysis for the Real World* (New York: Oxford University Press).

Hollander, J. M. (2003) *The Real Environmental Crisis: Why Poverty, Not Affluence, Is the Environment's Number One Enemy* (Berkeley: University of California Press).

Hood, C. (1998) *The Art of the State: Culture, Rhetoric, and Public Management* (Oxford: Oxford University Press).

Howe, D. W. (1979) *The Political Culture of the American Whigs* (Chicago: University of Chicago Press).

Howell, W. G. (2003) *Power without Persuasion: The Politics of Direct Presidential Action* (Princeton: Princeton University Press).

Huang, J., C. Pray, and S. Rozelle (2002) "Enhancing the Crops to Feed the Poor," *Nature*, 418(August 8), 678–84.

Hummel, R. P., and C. Stivers (2012) "Postmodernism, Bureaucracy, and Democracy," in R. F. Durant (ed.) *The Oxford Handbook of American Bureaucracy*, paperback ed. (pp. 324–45) (Oxford: Oxford University Press).

Inglehart, R. (1990) *Culture Shift in Advanced Industrial Society* (Princeton: Princeton University Press).

Ingraham, P. W. (2005) "'Are You Talking to Me?' Accountability and the Modern Public Service," *PS: Political Science and Politics*, 38(1), 17–21.

Ingraham, P., and D. H. Rosenbloom (1990) "The State of Merit in the Federal Government," Occasional Paper, National Commission on the Public Service, Washington, DC, June.

Ingram, H. (1977) Policy Implementation through Bargaining: The Case of Federal Grants-in-Aid," *Public Policy*, 25(4), 499–526.

Ingram, H., and A. Schneider (1990) "Improving Implementation through Framing Smarter Statutes," *Journal of Public Policy*, 10(1), 67–88.

Ingram, H., and S. R. Smith (1993) *Public Policy for Democracy* (Washington, DC: Brookings Institution Press).

Ingram, H., A. L. Schneider, and P. deLeon (2007) "Social Construction and Policy Design," in P. A. Sabatier (ed.) *Theories of the Policy Process*, 2nd ed. (pp. 93–126) (Boulder: Westview Press).

John, D. (1994) *Civic Environmentalism: Alternatives to Regulation in States and Communities* (Washington, DC: Congressional Quarterly Press).

Johnston, J. M., and B. S. Romzek (2012) "The Promises, Performance, and Pitfalls of Government Contracting," in R. F. Durant (ed.) *The Oxford Handbook of American Bureaucracy*, paperback ed. (pp. 396–420) (Oxford: Oxford University Press).

Jones, T. (2012) *More Powerful than Dynamite: Radicals, Plutocrats, Progressives, and New York's Year of Anarchy* (New York: Bloomsbury).

Kagan, E. (2001) "Presidential Administration," *Harvard Law Review*, 114(8), 2245–385.

Kaplan, R. S., and D. P. Norton (1996) *The Balanced Scorecard: Translating Strategy into Action* (Boston: Harvard Business School Press).

Kaufman, H. (1981) "Fear of Bureaucracy: A Raging Pandemic," *Public Administration Review*, 41(1), 1–9.

Kearney, R. C., with D. G. Carnevale (2001) *Labor Relations in the Public Sector*, 3rd ed. (New York: Marcel Dekker).

Kearns, M., R. Grove-White, P. Macnaghten, J. Wilsdon, and B. Wynne (2006) "From Bio to Nano: Learning Lessons from the UK Agricultural Biotechnology Controversy," *Science as Culture*, 15(4), 291–307.

Kellough, J. E. (2006) *Understanding Affirmative Action: Politics, Discrimination, and the Search for Justice* (Washington, DC: Georgetown University Press).

Kellough, J. E., and H. Lu (1993) "The Paradox of Merit Pay in the Public Sector: Persistence of a Problematic Procedure," *Review of Public Personnel Administration*, 13(2), 45–64.

Kellough, J. E., and L. G. Nigro (2002) "Pay for Performance in Georgia State Government: Employee Perspectives on GeorgiaGain After 5 Years," *Review of Public Personnel Administration*, 22(2), 146–66.

Kellough, J. E., and S. C. Selden (2003) "The Reinvention of Public Personnel Administration: An Analysis of the Diffusion of Personnel Reforms in the States," *Public Administration Review*, 63(2), 165–76.

Kennedy, D. M. (2005) *Freedom from Fear: The American People in Depression and War, 1929–1945* (Oxford: Oxford University Press).

Kennedy, W. (2002) *Roscoe: A Novel* (New York: Viking).

Kerwin, C. M., and S. R. Furlong (2010) *Rulemaking: How Government Agencies Write Law and Make Policy*, 4th ed. (Washington, DC: Congressional Quarterly Press).

Kerwin, C., S. Furlong, and W. West (2012) "Interest Groups, Rulemaking, and American Bureaucracy," in R. F. Durant (ed.) *The Oxford Handbook of American Bureaucracy*, paperback ed. (pp. 590–611) (Oxford: Oxford University Press).

Kettl, D. F. (2002) *The Transformation of Governance: Public Administration for the 21st Century* (Baltimore: Johns Hopkins University Press).

Kettl, D. F. (2009) *The Next Government of the United States: Why Our Institutions Fail Us and How to Fix Them* (New York: W. W. Norton).

Kettl, D. F., and J. J. DiIullio (eds.) (1995) *Cutting Government: A Report of the Brookings Institution's Center for Public Management* (Washington, DC: Brookings Institution Press).

Kettl, D. F., P. W. Ingraham, R. P. Sanders, and C. Horner (1996) *Civil Service Reform: Building a Government that Works* (Washington, DC: Brookings Institution Press).

Kim, D. J., K.-B. Yue, S. P. Hall, and S. Gates (2009) "Global Diffusion of the Internet XV: Web 2.0 Technologies, Principles, and Applications: A Conceptual Framework from Technology Push and Demand Pull Perspective," *Communications of the Association for Information Systems*, 24(1), 657–72.

Kim, P. S. (1993) "Racial Integration in the American Federal Government: With Special Reference to Asian-Americans," *Review of Public Personnel Administration*, 13(1), 52–66.

King, C. S., K. M. Feltey, and B. O. Susel (1998) "The Question of Participation: Toward Authentic Public Participation in Public Administration," *Public Administration Review*, 58(4), 317–26.

King, C. S., C. Stivers, and Collaborators (1998) *Government Is Us: Public Administration in an Anti-Government Era* (Thousand Oaks, CA: SAGE).

Kingdon, J. W. (2002) *Agendas, Alternatives, and Public Policy*, 2nd ed. (New York: Longman).

Kingsley, D. J. (1944) *Representative Bureaucracy* (Yellow Springs, OH: Antioch Press).

Klare, M. T. (2001) *Resource Wars: The New Landscape of Global Conflict* (New York: Metropolitan Books).

Klyza, C. M., and D. Sousa (2008) *American Environmental Policy, 1990–2006: Beyond Gridlock* (Cambridge: MIT Press).

Knott, J. H. (1998) "A Return to Spoils: The Wrong Solution for the Right Problem," *Administration & Society*, 29(6), 660–69.

Knott, J. H., and G. J. Miller (1987) *Reforming Bureaucracy: The Politics of Institutional Choice* (Upper Saddle River, NJ: Prentice Hall).

Kooiman, J. (1993) *Modern Governance: New Government–Society Interactions* (London: SAGE).

Koppell, J. G. S. (2012) "Metaphors and the Development of American Bureaucracy," in R. F. Durant (ed.) *The Oxford Handbook of American Bureaucracy*, paperback ed. (pp. 128–50) (Oxford: Oxford University Press).

Kotter, J. P. (1995) "Leading Change: Why Transformation Efforts Fail," *Harvard Business Review*, 73(2), 59–67.

Kraft, M. E., and S. Kamieniecki (eds.) (2007) *Business and Environmental Policy: Corporate Interests in the American Political System* (Cambridge: MIT Press).

Krause, G. A. (2012) "Legislative Delegation of Authority to Bureaucratic Agencies," in R. F. Durant (ed.) *The Oxford Handbook of American Bureaucracy*, paperback ed. (pp. 521–44) (Oxford: Oxford University Press).

Krislov, S. (1967) *The Negro in Federal Employment: The Quest for Equal Opportunity* (Minneapolis: University of Minnesota Press).

Krislov, S. (1974) *Representative Bureaucracy* (Englewood Cliffs, NJ: Prentice-Hall).

Lan, Z., and H. G. Rainey (1992) "Goals, Rules, and Effectiveness in Public, Private, and Hybrid Organizations: More Evidence on Frequent Assertions about Differences," *Journal of Public Administration Research and Theory*, 2(1), 5–28.

Lanier, J. (2013) *Who Owns the Future?* (New York: Simon & Schuster).

Lanjouw, J. O. (2003) "Opening Doors to Research: A New Global Patent Regime for Pharmaceuticals," *Brookings Review*, 21(2), 13–17.

Leakey, R., and R. Lewin (1996) *The Sixth Extinction: Patterns of Life and the Future of Humankind* (New York: Anchor Books).

Lee, M. (2008) *Bureaus of Efficiency: Reforming Local Government in the Progressive Era* (Milwaukee, WI: Marquette University Press).

Lee, M. (2013) "Glimpsing an Alternate Construction of American Public Administration: The Later Life of William Allen, Cofounder of the New York Bureau of Municipal Research," *Administration & Society*, 45(5), 522–62.

Legge Jr, J. S., and R. F. Durant (2010) "Public Opinion, Risk Assessment, and Biotechnology: Lessons from Attitudes toward Genetically Modified Foods in the European Union," *Review of Policy Research*, 27(1), 59–76.

Levinson, A. (1998) "Balanced Budgets and Business Cycles: Evidence from the States," *National Tax Journal*, 51(4), 715–32.

Levitan, D. M. (1943) "Political Ends and Administrative Means," *Public Administration Review*, 3(4), 353–59.

Lewis, D. E. (2003) *Presidents and the Politics of Agency Design: Political Insulation in the United States Government Bureaucracy, 1946–1997* (Stanford: Stanford University Press).

Lewis, D. E. (2008) *The Politics of Presidential Appointments: Political Control and Bureaucratic Performance* (Princeton: Princeton University Press).

Lewis, G. B. (1986) "Equal Employment Opportunity and the Early Career in Federal Employment," *Review of Public Personnel Administration*, 6(3), 1–18.

Lewis, G. B. (1986) "Gender and Promotions: Promotion Chances of White Men and Women in Federal White-Collar Employment," *Journal of Human Resources*, 21(3), 406–19.

Lewis, G. B. (1986) "Race, Sex, and Supervisory Authority in Federal White-Collar Employment," *Public Administration Review*, 46(1), 25–30.

Lewis, G. B. (1992) "Men and Women toward the Top: Backgrounds, Careers, and Potential of Federal Middle Managers," *Public Personnel Management*, 21(4), 473–92.

Lewis, G. B. (1994) "Women, Occupations, and Federal Agencies: Occupational Mix and Interagency Differences in Sexual Inequality in Federal White-Collar Employment," *Public Administration Review*, 54(3), 271–76.

Lewis, G. B. (1997) "Lifting the Ban on Gays in the Civil Service: Federal Policy toward Gay and Lesbian Employees since the Cold War," *Public Administration Review*, 57(5), 387–95.

Lewis, G. B. (2001) "Barriers to Security Clearances for Gay Men and Lesbians: Fear of Blackmail or Fear of Homosexuals?" *Journal of Public Administration Research and Theory*, 11(4), 539–58.

Lewis, G. B. (2010) "Modeling Nonprofit Employment: Why Do So Many Lesbians and Gay Men Work for Nonprofit Organizations?" *Administration & Society*, 42(6), 720–48.

Lewis, G. B., and K. Park (1989) "Turnover Rates in Federal White-Collar Employment: Are Women More Likely to Quit Than Men?" *American Review of Public Administration*, 19(1), 13–28.

Lewis, G. B., and D. W. Pitts (2011) "Representation of Lesbians and Gay Men in Federal, State, and Local Bureaucracies," *Journal of Public Administration Research and Theory*, 21(1), 159–80.

Light, P. C. (1995) *Thickening Government: Federal Hierarchy and the Diffusion of Accountability* (Washington, DC: Brookings Institution Press).

Lilley III, W., and J. C. Miller III (1977) "The New 'Social Regulation,'" *Public Interest*, 47(Spring), 49–61.

Lindblom, C. E. (1959) "The Science of 'Muddling Through,'" *Public Administration Review*, 19(2), 79–88.

Lipset, S. M. (1996) *American Exceptionalism: A Double-Edged Sword* (New York: W. W. Norton).

Liu, C., and J. L. Mikesell (2014) "The Impact of Public Officials' Corruption on the Size and Allocation of U.S. State Spending," *Public Administration Review*, 74(3), 346–59.

Long, N. E. (1949) "Power and Administration," *Public Administration Review*, 9(4) 257–64.

Long, N. E. (1954) "Public Policy and Administration: The Goals of Rationality and Responsibility," *Public Administration Review*, 14(1), 22–31.

Lowi, T. J. (1969) *The End of Liberalism: The Second Republic of the United States* (New York: W. W. Norton).

Lowi, T. J. (1979) *The End of Liberalism: The Second Republic of the United States*, 2nd ed. (New York: W. W. Norton).

Luke, J. S. (1998) *Catalytic Leadership: Strategies for an Interconnected World* (San Francisco: Jossey-Bass).

Lynn Jr, L. E., C. J. Heinrich, and C. J. Hill (2000) "Studying Governance and Public Management: Challenges and Prospects," *Journal of Public Administration Research and Theory*, 10(2), 233–62.

Mainzer, L. (1973) *Political Bureaucracy* (Glenview, IL: Scott Foresman).

Majone, G. (1989) *Evidence, Argument, & Persuasion in the Policy Process* (New Haven: Yale University Press).

Majone, G., and A. Wildavsky (1984) "Implementation as Evolution," in J. L. Pressman and A. Wildavsky *Implementation: How Great Expectations in Washington Are Dashed in Oakland; Or, Why It's Amazing that Federal Programs Work at All, This Being a Saga of the Economic Development Administration as Told by Two Sympathetic Observers Who Seek to Build Morals on a Foundation of Ruined Hopes*, 3rd ed. (pp. 163–80) (Berkeley: University of California Press).

Mann, T. E., and N. J. Ornstein (2012) *It's Even Worse Than It Looks: How the American Constitutional System Collided with the New Politics of Extremism* (New York: Basic Books).

Maranto, R. (1998) "Rethinking the Unthinkable: Reply to Durant, Goodsell, Knott, and Murray on 'A Case for Spoils' in Federal Personnel Management," *Administration & Society*, 30(1), 3–12.

Maranto, R. (1998) "Thinking the Unthinkable in Public Administration: A Case for Spoils in the Federal Bureaucracy," *Administration & Society*, 29(6), 623–42.

March, J. G., and J. P. Olsen (1983) "Organizing Political Life: What Administrative Reorganization Tells Us about Government," *American Political Science Review*, 77(2), 281–96.

March, J. G., and J. P. Olsen (1989) *Rediscovering Institutions: The Organizational Basis of Politics* (New York: Free Press).

Marini, F. (ed.) (1971) *Toward a New Public Administration: The Minnowbrook Perspective* (Scranton, PA: Chandler Press).

Marshall, L. (1967) "The Strange Stillbirth of the Whig Party," *American Historical Review*, 72(2), 455–56.

Maslow, A. H. (1943) "A Theory of Human Motivation," *Psychological Review*, 50(4), 370–96.

Mastracci, S. H. (2013) "Commentary: A Solution in Search of a Problem? Discrimination, Affirmative Action, and the New Governance," in R. F. Durant and J. R. S. Durant (eds.) *Debating Public Administration: Management Challenges, Choices, and Opportunities* (pp. 218–19) (Boca Raton, FL: CRC Press).

Matland, R. E. (1995) "Synthesizing the Implementation Literature: The Ambiguity-Conflict Model of Policy Implementation," *Journal of Public Administration Research and Theory*, 5(2), 145–74.

May, G. (2008) *John Tyler* (New York: Henry Holt).

Maynard-Moody, S., and S. Portillo (2012) "Street-Level Bureaucracy Theory," in R. F. Durant (ed.) *The Oxford Handbook of American Bureaucracy*, paperback ed. (pp. 252–77) (Oxford: Oxford University Press).

Mazmanian, D. A., and P. A. Sabatier (1989) *Implementation and Public Policy* (Lanham, MD: University Press of America).

McAfee, A. P. (2006) "Enterprise 2.0: The Dawn of Emergent Collaboration," *MIT Sloan Management Review*, 47(3), 21–8.

McCaskey, M. B. (1974) "A Contingency Approach to Planning: Planning with Goals and Planning without Goals," *Academy of Management Journal*, 17(2), 281–91.

McGrath, R. J. (2013) "The Rise and Fall of Radical Civil Service Reform in the U.S. States," *Public Administration Review*, 73(4), 638–49.

McGregor, D. M. (1960) *The Human Side of Enterprise* (New York: McGraw Hill).

Meadowcroft, J. (2004) "Deliberative Democracy," in R. F. Durant, D. J. Fiorino, and R. O'Leary (eds.) *Environmental Governance Reconsidered: Challenges, Choices, and Opportunities* (pp. 183–217) (Cambridge: MIT Press).

Meadows, D. H., D. L. Meadows, J. Randers, and W. W. Behrens III (1972) *The Limits of Growth: A Report for the Club of Rome's Project on the Predicament of Mankind* (New York: Universe Books).

Meier, K. J. (1993) "Latinos and Representative Bureaucracy: Testing the Thompson and Henderson Hypotheses," *Journal of Public Administration Research and Theory*, 3(4), 393–414.

Meier, K. J., and J. Nicholson-Crotty (2006) "Gender, Representative Bureaucracy, and Law Enforcement: The Case of Sexual Assault," *Public Administration Review*, 66(6), 850–60.

Meier, K. J., and L. J. O'Toole Jr (2006) *Bureaucracy in a Democratic State: A Governance Perspective* (Baltimore: Johns Hopkins University Press).

Meier, K. J., and J. Stewart Jr (1992) "The Impact of Representative Bureaucracies: Educational Systems and Public Policies," *American Review of Public Administration*, 22(3), 157–71.

Meier, K. J., M. S. Pennington, and W. S. Eller (2005) "Race, Sex, and Clarence Thomas: Representation Change in the EEOC," *Public Administration Review*, 65(2), 171–79.

Meier, K. J., J. Stewart Jr, and R. E. England (1989) *Race, Class, and Education: The Politics of Second-Generation Discrimination* (Madison: University of Wisconsin Press).

Menzel, D. C., and H. L. White (eds.) (2011) *The State of Public Administration: Issues, Challenges, and Opportunities* (Armonk, NY: M. E. Sharpe).

Merriam, C. E. (2008) *American Political Ideas: 1865–1917* (New Brunswick, NJ: Transaction Publishers), originally published in 1920 by Macmillan.

Mettler, S. (1998) *Dividing Citizens: Gender and Federalism in New Deal Public Policy* (Ithaca: Cornell University Press).

Mettler, S. (2011) *The Submerged State: How Invisible Government Policies Undermine Democracy* (Chicago: University of Chicago Press).

Millard, C. (2011) *Destiny of the Republic: A Tale of Madness, Medicine, and the Murder of a President* (New York: Anchor Books).

Mills, C. W. (1956) *The Power Elite* (New York: Oxford University Press).

Milward, H. B., and K. G. Provan (2000) "Governing the Hollow State," *Journal of Public Administration Research and Theory*, 10(2), 359–80.

Minogue, M. (1983) "Theory and Practice in Public Policy and Administration," *Policy and Politics*, 11(1), 63–85.

Mintzberg, H. (1987) "Crafting Strategy," *Harvard Business Review*, 65(July–August), 66–75.

Mintzberg, H. (1994) "The Fall and Rise of Strategic Planning," *Harvard Business Review*, January–February, 110–14.

Mintzberg, H., B. Ahlstrand, and J. Lampel (1998) *Strategy Safari: A Guided Tour through the Wilds of Strategic Management* (New York: Free Press).

Moe, T. M. (1989) "The Politics of Bureaucratic Structure," in J. E. Chubb and P. E. Peterson (eds.) *Can the Government Govern?* (pp. 267–329) (Washington, DC: Brookings Institution Press).

Moe, T. M., and W. G. Howell (1999) "The Presidential Power of Unilateral Action," *The Journal of Law, Economics, & Organization*, 15(1), 132–79.

Montpetit, E. (2003) *Misplaced Distrust: Policy Networks and the Environment in France, the United States, and Canada* (Vancouver: University of British Columbia Press).

Moore, M. H. (1994) "Public Value as the Focus of Strategy," *Australian Journal of Public Administration*, 53(3), 296–303.

Moore, M. H. (1995) *Creating Public Value: Strategic Management in Government* (Cambridge: Harvard University Press).

Morgan, D. F., R. T. Green, C. W. Shinn, and K. S. Robinson (2013) *Foundations of Public Service*, 2nd ed. (Armonk, NY: M. E. Sharpe).

Morris, J. C., and D. J. Watson (2013) "Commentary: Is the World 'Flat' or 'Spiky'? Rethinking the Governance Implications of Globalization for Economic Development," in R. F. Durant and J. R. S. Durant (eds.) *Debating Public Administration: Management Challenges, Choices, and Opportunities* (pp. 244–46) (Boca Raton, FL: CRC Press).

Mosher, F. C. (1968) *Democracy and the Public Service* (Oxford: Oxford University Press).

Mosher, F. C. (ed.) (1975) *American Public Administration: Past, Present, Future* (Birmingham: University of Alabama Press).

Mosher, F. C. (1982) *Democracy and the Public Service*, 2nd ed. (New York: Oxford University Press).

Mosher, W. E. (1939) "The Making of a Public Servant," *National Municipal Review*, 28(6), 416–37.

Moynihan, D. P. (2008) *The Dynamics of Performance Measurement: Constructing Information and Reform* (Washington, DC: Georgetown University Press).

Moynihan, D. P., and P. W. Ingraham (2004) "Integrative Leadership in the Public Sector: A Model of Performance-Information Use," *Administration & Society*, 36(4), 427–53.

Mullins, D. R., and J. L. Mikesell (2012) "Innovations in Budgeting and Financial Management," in R. F. Durant (ed.) *The Oxford Handbook of American Bureaucracy*, paperback ed. (pp. 738–65) (Oxford: Oxford University Press).

Murray, W. L. (1998) "Rejoinder to Maranto: Been There, Done That," *Administration & Society*, 29(6), 670–76.

Musso, J., C. Weare, T. Bryer, and T. L. Cooper (2013) "Toward 'Strong Democracy' in Global Cities? Social Capital Building, Theory-Driven Reform, and the Los Angeles Neighborhood Council Experience," in R. F. Durant and J. R. S. Durant (eds.) *Debating Public Administration: Management Challenges, Choices, and Opportunities* (pp. 89–109) (Boca Raton, FL: CRC Press).

Nabatchi, T. (2010) "Addressing the Citizenship and Democratic Deficits: The Potential of Deliberative Democracy for Public Administration," *American Review of Public Administration*, 40(4), 376–99.

Nadler, D. A. (1998) *Champions of Change* (San Francisco: Jossey-Bass).

Nathan, R. (1983) *The Administrative Presidency* (New York: John Wiley).

National Advisory Council on State and Local Budgeting (1998) *Recommended Budget Practices: A Framework for Improved State and Local Government Budgeting* (Chicago: Government Finance Officers Association).

National Urban Fellows (2012) *Diversity Counts: Racial and Ethnic Diversity among Public Service Leadership* (New York: National Urban Fellows).

National Academy of Public Administration (1995) *Modernizing Federal Classification: Operational Broadbanding Systems Alternatives* (Washington, DC: National Academy of Public Administration).

National Commission on the State and Local Public Service (1993) *Hard Truths/Tough Choices: An Agenda for State and Local Reform* (Albany, NY: Rockefeller Institute of Government).

Neem, J. N. (2010) "Civil Society and American Nationalism, 1776–1865," in E. S. Clemens and D. Guthrie (eds.) *Politics + Partnerships: The Role of Voluntary Associations in America's Political Past and Present* (pp. 29–53) (Chicago: University of Chicago Press).

Nelson, M. (2014) "A Short, Ironic History of American National Bureaucracy," in C. Jillson and D. B. Robertson (eds.) *Perspectives on American Government: Readings in Political Development and Institutional Change* (New York: Routledge).

Nelson, W. E. (1982) *The Roots of American Bureaucracy, 1830–1900* (Cambridge: Harvard University Press).

Niven, P. R. (2008) *Balanced Scorecard: Step-by-Step for Government and Nonprofit Agencies*, 2nd ed. (Hoboken, NJ: John Wiley).

Novak, W. J. (2001) "The American Law of Association: The Legal–Political Construction of Civil Society," *Studies in American Political Development*, 15(Fall), 163–88.

Novak, W. J. (2008) "The Myth of the 'Weak' American State," *American Historical Review*, 119(3), 752–72.

Nye Jr, J. S., P. D. Zelikow, and D. C. King (1997) *Why People Don't Trust Government* (Cambridge: Harvard University Press).

Office of Management and Budget (2002) *The President's Management Agenda* (Washington, DC: Office of Management and Budget).

Office of Personnel Management (2002) *A Fresh Start for Federal Pay: The Case for Modernization* (Washington, DC: Office of Personnel Management).

Osborne, D., and T. Gaebler (1992) *Reinventing Government: How the Entrepreneurial Spirit Is Transforming the Public Sector* (New York: Penguin Books).

Osborne, D., and P. Plastrik (1997) *Banishing Bureaucracy: The Five Strategies for Reinventing Government* (Reading, MA: Addison-Wesley).

Ostrom, V. (1973) *The Intellectual Crisis in American Public Administration* (Tuscaloosa: University of Alabama Press).

Ostrom, V. (2008) *The Intellectual Crisis in American Public Administration*, 3rd ed. (Tuscaloosa: University of Alabama Press).

O'Toole Jr, L. J., and K. Hanf (2002) "American Public Administration and Impacts of International Governance," *Public Administration Review*, 62(Special Issue), 158–67.

Paarlberg, R. L. (2001) *The Politics of Precaution: Genetically Modified Crops in Developing Countries* (Baltimore: Johns Hopkins University Press).

Paarlberg, R. L. (2003) "Reinvigorating Genetically Modified Crops," *Issues in Science & Technology*, Spring. Reprinted on List Serve of agbioreview@yahoo.com, date accessed April 24, 2003.

Paehlke, R. C. (2004) "Sustainability," in R. F. Durant, D. Fiorino, and R. O'Leary (eds.) *Environmental Governance Reconsidered: Challenges, Choices, and Opportunities* (pp. 35–68) (Cambridge: MIT Press).

Page, P. (1994) "African-Americans in Executive Branch Agencies," *Review of Public Personnel Administration*, 14(1), 24–51.

Pandey, S. K., and E. C. Stazyk (2008) "Antecedents and Correlates of Public Service Motivation," in J. L. Perry and A. Hondeghem (eds.) *Motivation in Public Management: The Call of Public Service* (pp. 101–17) (New York: Oxford University Press).

Parameswaran, M., and A. B. Whinston (2007) "Research Issues in Social Computing," *Journal of the Association for Information Systems*, 8(6), 336–50.

Partnership for Public Service (2004) *Asking the Wrong Questions: A Look at How the Federal Government Assesses and Selects Its Workforce* (Washington, DC: Partnership for Public Service).

Pascale, R. (1999) "Extract from Complexity and the Unconscious," in J. Henry (ed.) *Creativity, Innovation, and Change Media Book* (pp. 9–10) (Milton Keynes, UK: Open University Press).

Peristeras, V., G. Mentzas, K. A. Tarabanis, and A. Abecker (2009) "Transforming E-government and E-participation through IT," *Intelligent Systems, IEEE*, 24(5), 14–19.

Perry, J. L. (1986) "Merit Pay in the Public Sector: The Case for a Failure of Theory," *Review of Public Personnel Administration*, 7(1), 57–69.

Perry, J. L. (1988) "Making Policy by Trial and Error: Merit Pay in the Federal Service," *Policy Studies Journal*, 17(2), 389–405.

Perry, J. L. (1991) "Linking Pay to Performance: The Controversy Continues," in C. Ban and N. M. Riccucci (eds.) *Public Personnel Management: Current Concerns, Future Challenges* (pp. 73–86) (White Plains, NY: Longman Press).

Perry, J. L. (1996) "Measuring Public Service Motivation: An Assessment of Construct Reliability and Validity," *Journal of Public Administration Research and Theory*, 6(1), 5–22.

Perry, J. L. (1997) "Antecedents of Public Service Motivation," *Journal of Public Administration Research and Theory*, 7(2), 181–97.

Perry, J. L., and L. R. Wise (1990) "The Motivational Bases of Public Service," *Public Administration Review*, 50(3), 367–73.

Perry, J. L., T. A. Engbers, and S. Y. Jun (2013) "Back to the Future? Performance-Related Pay, Empirical Research, and the Perils of Persistence," in R. F. Durant and J. R. S. Durant (eds.) *Debating Public Administration: Management Challenges, Choices, and Opportunities* (pp. 27–65) (Boca Raton, FL: CRC Press).

Peters, B. G. (1996) *The Future of Governing: Four Emerging Models* (Lawrence: University Press of Kansas).

Petter, S., W. DeLone, and E. McLean (2008) "Measuring Information Systems Success: Models, Dimensions, Measures, and Interrelationships," *European Journal of Information Systems*, 17(3), 236–63.

Petter, S., D. Straub, and A. Rai (2007) "Specifying Formative Constructs in Information Systems Research," *MIS Quarterly*, 31(4), 623–56.

Pfeffer, J., and R. I. Sutton (2006) "Evidence-Based Management," *Harvard Business Review*, January, 1–13.

Pfiffner, J. M. (1940) *Research Methods in Public Administration* (New York: Ronald Press).

Pierson, P. (2004) *Time and Politics: History, Institutions, and Social Analysis* (Princeton: Princeton University Press).

Pierson, P., and T. Skocpol (eds.) (2007) *The Transformation of American Politics: Activist Government and the Rise of Conservatism* (Princeton: Princeton University Press).

Pitts, D. W. (2005) "Diversity, Representation, and Performance: Evidence about Race and Ethnicity in Public Organizations," *Journal of Public Administration Research and Theory*, 15(4), 615–31.

Pitts, D. W., and J. L. Weakley (2014) "Representation and Sexual Orientation in Higher Education," Working Paper, American University, Washington, DC.

Poterba, J. M. (1995) "Balanced Budget Rules and Fiscal Policy: Evidence from the States," *National Tax Journal*, 48(3), 329–36.

Powell, W. (1998) "Learning From Collaboration: Knowledge and Networks in the Biotechnology and Pharmaceutical Industries," *California Management Review*, 40(3), 228–40.

Putnam, R. D., and D. E. Campbell (2012) *Amazing Grace: How Religion Divides and Unites Us* (New York: Simon & Schuster).

Quinn, J. B. (1980) *Strategies for Change: Logical Incrementalism* (Homewood, IL: Richard D. Irwin).

Rabe, B. G. (2004) *Statehouse and Greenhouse: The Emerging Politics of American Climate Change Policy* (Washington, DC: Brookings Institution Press).

Radin, B. A. (1998) "The Government Performance and Results Act (GPRA): Hydra-Headed Monster or Flexible Management Tool?" *Public Administration Review*, 58(4), 307–16.

Radin, B. A. (2000) *Beyond Machiavelli: Policy Analysis Comes of Age* (Washington, DC: Georgetown University Press).

Radin, B. A. (2011) "Does Performance Measurement Actually Improve Accountability?" in M. J. Dubnick and H. G. Frederickson (eds.) *Accountable Governance: Problems and Promises* (pp. 98–110) (Armonk, NY: M. E. Sharpe).

Rainey, G. W. (1990) "Implementation and Managerial Creativity," in D. J. Palumbo and D. Calista (eds.) *Implementation and the Policy Process* (pp. 89–105) (New York: Greenwood Press).

Rainey, H. G. (1983) "Public Agencies and Private Firms: Incentive Structures, Goals, and Individual Roles," *Administration & Society*, 15(2), 207–42.

Rainey, H. G., S. K. Pandey, and B. Bozeman (1995) "Public and Private Managers' Perceptions of Red Tape," *Public Administration Review*, 55(6), 567–74.

Raymond, S. (2003) "Foreign Assistance in an Aging World," *Foreign Affairs*, 82(2), 91–105.

Redford, E. S. (1969) *Democracy in the Administrative State* (New York: Oxford University Press).

Rein, M., and F. Rabinovitz (1978) "Implementation: A Theoretical Perspective," in W. D. Burnham and M. W. Weinberg (eds.) *American Politics and Public Policy* (pp. 307–35) (Cambridge: MIT Press).

Remini, R. V. (2008) *A Short History of the United States* (New York: HarperCollins).

Riccucci, N. M. (2002) *Managing Diversity in Public Sector Workforces* (Boulder: Westview Press).

Riccucci, N. M., and K. C. Naff (2007) *Personnel Management in Government: Politics and Process*, 6th ed. (Boca Raton, FL: CRC Press).

Risher, H. (2013) "Commentary: Back to the Future? Performance-Related Pay, Empirical Research, and the Perils of Persistence," in R. F. Durant and J. R. S. Durant (eds.) *Debating Public Administration: Management Challenges, Choices, and Opportunities* (pp. 44–6) (Boca Raton, FL: CRC Press).

Rittel, H. W. J., and M. M. Webber (1973) "Dilemmas in a General Theory of Planning," *Policy Sciences*, 4(2), 155–69.

Roberts, A. (1994) "Demonstrating Neutrality: The Rockefeller Philanthropies and the Evolution of Public Administration, 1927–1936," *Public Administration Review*, 54(3), 221–28.

Roberts, A. (2010) *The Logic of Discipline: Global Capitalism and the Architecture of Government* (New York: Oxford University Press).

Roberts, G. E. (2001) "A History of the Federal Civil Service: A Values-Based Perspective," in S. E. Condrey and R. Maranto (eds.) *Radical Reform of the Civil Service* (pp. 15–41) (Lanham, MD: Lexington Books).

Roberts, N. C. (2013) "Spanning 'Bleeding' Boundaries: Humanitarianism, NGOs, and the Civilian-Military Nexus in the Post–Cold War Era," in R. F. Durant and J. R. S. Durant (eds.) *Debating Public Administration: Management Challenges, Choices, and Opportunities* (pp. 247–62) (Boca Raton, FL: CRC Press).

Robertson, D. B. (2012) *Federalism and the Making of America* (New York: Routledge).

Rochefort, D. A., and R. W. Cobb (eds.) (1994) *The Politics of Problem Definition: Shaping the Policy Agenda* (Lawrence: University Press of Kansas).

Rodgers, D. T. (1998) *Atlantic Crossings: Social Politics in a Progressive Age* (Cambridge: Harvard University Press).

Rosenbloom, D. H. (1977) *Federal Equal Employment Opportunity: Politics and Public Personnel Administration* (New York: Praeger).

Rosenbloom, D. H. (1983) "Public Administrative Theory and the Separation of Powers," *Public Administration Review*, 43(3), 219–27.

Rosenbloom, D. H. (1988) "The Public Employment Relationship and the Supreme Court in the 1980s," *Review of Public Personnel Administration*, 8(2), 49–65.

Rosenbloom, D. H. (2008) "The Politics-Administration Dichotomy in U.S. Historical Context," *Public Administration Review*, 68(1), 57–60.

Rosenbloom, D. H. (2013) "Reinventing Administrative Prescriptions: The Case for Democratic-Constitutional Impact Statements and Scorecards," in R. F. Durant and J. R. S. Durant (eds.) *Debating Public Administration: Management Challenges, Choices, and Opportunities* (pp. 111–30) (Boca Raton, FL: CRC Press).

Ruckelshaus, W. D. (1995) "Stopping the Pendulum," *Environmental Forum*, 12(6), 25–9.

Rudalevige, A. C. (2002) *Managing the President's Program: Presidential Leadership and Legislative Policy Formulation* (Princeton: Princeton University Press).

Rudalevige, A. C. (2005) "The Structure of Leadership: Presidents, Hierarchies, and Information Flows," *Presidential Studies Quarterly*, 35(2), 333–60.

Sabatier, P. A. (2007) *Theories of the Policy Process*, 2nd ed. (Boulder, CO: Westview Press).

Sabatier, P. A., and H. C. Jenkins-Smith (1993) *Policy Change and Learning: An Advocacy Coalition Approach* (Boulder: Westview Press).

Sandel, M. J. (1984) "The Procedural Republic and the Unencumbered Self," *Political Theory*, 12(1), 81–96.

Sandel, M. J. (1996) *Democracy's Discontent: America in Search of a Public Philosophy* (Cambridge: Harvard University Press).

Sanders, R. M. (2004) "GeorgiaGain or GeorgiaLoss? The Great Experiment in State Civil Service Reform," *Public Personnel Management*, 33(2), 151–64.

Sanford, T. (1967) *Storm Over the States* (New York: McGraw-Hill).

Satkunanandan, S. (2014) "Max Weber and the Ethos of Politics beyond Calculation," *American Political Science Review*, 108(1), 169–81.

Schachter, H. L. (2012) "A Gendered Legacy? The Progressive Reform Era Revisited," in R. F. Durant (ed.) *The Oxford Handbook of American Bureaucracy*, paperback ed. (pp. 77–100) (Oxford: Oxford University Press).

Scharpf, F. W. (1993) *Games in Hierarchies and Networks: Analytical and Empirical Approaches to the Study of Governance Institutions* (Frankfurt am Main, Germany: Campus Verlag).

Schattschneider, E. E. (1960) *The Semisovereign People* (New York: Holt, Rinehart & Winston).

Schick, A. (1966) "The Road to PPB: The Stages of Budget Reform," *Public Administration Review*, 26(4), 243–58.

Schlozman, K. L., S. Verba, and H. E. Brady (2012) *The Unheavenly Chorus: Unequal Political Voice and the Broken Promise of American Democracy* (Princeton: Princeton University Press).

Schneider, A. L., and H. M. Ingram (eds.) (2005) *The Deserving and Entitled: Social Constructions and Public Policy* (Albany: State University of New York Press).

Schon, D. (1983) *The Reflective Practitioner* (New York: Basic Books).

Schultz, D. (2011) "The Crisis of Public Administration Theory in a Postglobal World," in D. C. Menzel and H. L. White (eds.) *The State of Public Administration: Issues, Challenges, and Opportunities* (pp. 453–63) (Armonk, NY: M. E. Sharpe).

Scott, C., and K. Baehler (2010) *Adding Value to Policy Analysis and Advice* (Sydney, Australia: University of New South Wales Press).

Scott, M., W. DeLone, and W. Golden (under review) "Measuring eGovernment Success: A Public Value Approach," *European Journal of Information Systems*.

Scott, W. G. (1992) *Chester I. Barnard and the Guardians of the Managerial State* (Lawrence: University Press of Kansas).

Seddon, P. B., S. Staples, R. Patnayakuni, and M. Bowtell (1999) "Dimensions of Information Systems Success," *Communications of the Association for Information Systems*, 2(20), 1–39.

Seidman, H. (1998) *Politics, Position, and Power: The Dynamics of Federal Organization*, 5th ed. (New York: Oxford University Press).

Selden, S. C. (2009) *Human Capital: Tools and Strategies for the Public Sector* (Washington, DC: Congressional Quarterly Press).

Selden, S. C., J. L. Brudney, and E. J. Kellough (1998) "Bureaucracy as a Representative Institution: Toward a Reconciliation of Bureaucratic Government and Democratic Theory," *American Journal of Political Science*, 42(3), 717–44.

Selznick, P. (1957) *Leadership in Administration: A Sociological Interpretation* (Evanston, IL: Row, Peterson).

Shapiro, I., S. Skowronek, and D. Galvin (eds.) (2006) *Rethinking Political Institutions: The Art of the State* (New York: New York University Press).

Simon, H. A. (1997) *Administrative Behavior: Decision-Making Processes in Administrative Organizations*, 4th ed. (New York: Free Press).

Sklar, M. J. (1988) *The Corporate Reconstruction of American Capitalism, 1890–1916* (Cambridge: Cambridge University Press).

Skocpol, T. (2003) *Diminished Democracy: From Membership to Management in American Civic Life* (Norman: University of Oklahoma Press).

Skocpol, T., M. Ganz, and Z. Munson (2000) "A Nation of Organizers: The Institutional Origins of Civic Volunteerism in the United States," *American Political Science Review*, 94(3), 527–46.

Skocpol, T., Z. Munson, A. Karch, and B. Camp (2002) "Patriotic Partnerships: Why Great Wars Nourished American Civic Voluntarism," in I. Katznelson and M. Shefter (eds.) *Shaped by War and Trade: International Influences on American Political Development* (pp. 134–80) (Princeton: Princeton University Press).

Skowronek, S. (1982) *Building a New American State: The Expansion of National Administrative Capacities, 1877–1920* (Cambridge: Cambridge University Press).

Smith, M. (2000) *American Business and Political Power: Public Opinion, Elections, and Democracy* (Chicago: University of Chicago Press).

Smith, R. A., and D. P. Haider-Markel (2002) *Gay and Lesbian Americans and Political Participation: A Reference Handbook* (Santa Barbara, CA: ABC-CLIO).

Soss, J., and S. F. Schram (2006) "Welfare Reform as a Failed Political Strategy: Evidence and Explanations for the Stability of Public Opinion," *Focus*, 24(3), 17–23.

Spicer, M. W. (1995) *The Founders, the Constitution, and Public Administration: A Conflict in World Views* (Washington, DC: Georgetown University Press).

Starr, P. (2004) *The Creation of the Media: Political Origins of Modern Communications* (New York: Basic Books).

Stazyk, E. C. (2013) "Crowding Out Public Service Motivation? Comparing Theoretical Expectations with Empirical Findings on the Influence of Performance-Related Pay," *Review of Public Personnel Administration*, 33(3), 252–74.

Stazyk, E. C., R. S. Davis, P. Sanabria, and S. Pettijohn (2014) "Working in the Hollow State: Exploring the Link between Public Service Motivation and Interlocal Collaboration," in Y. K. Dwivedi, M. A. Shareef, S. K. Pandey, and V. Kumar (eds.) *Public Administration Reformation: Market Demand from Public Organizations* (pp. 124–43) (New York: Routledge).

Steinmo, S. (2010) *The Evolution of Modern States: Sweden, Japan, and the United States* (Cambridge: Cambridge University Press).

Stever, J. A. (2001) "Review: Values for Public Administration Renewal," *Public Administration Review*, 61(5), 625–29.

Stewart, R. B. (1988) "Regulation and the Crisis of Legalisation in the United States," in T. Daintith (ed.) *Law as an Instrument of Economic Policy: Comparative and Critical Approaches* (pp. 97–103) (Berlin: de Gruyter).

Stivers, C. (2000) *Bureau Men, Settlement Women: Constructing Public Administration in the Progressive Era* (Lawrence: University Press of Kansas).

Stoker, G. (1995) "Regime Theory and Urban Politics," in D. Judge, G. Stoker, and H. Wolman (eds.) *Theories of Urban Politics* (pp. 54–71) (London: SAGE).

Stone, D. (2011) *Policy Paradox: The Art of Political Decision Making*, 3rd ed. (New York: W. W. Norton).

Sutton, F. X. (2006) "Nation Building in the Heyday of the Classic Development Ideology," in F. Fukuyama (ed.) *Nation-Building: Beyond Afghanistan and Iraq* (Baltimore: Johns Hopkins University Press).

Svara, J. H. (2001) "The Myth of the Dichotomy: Complementarity of Politics and Administration in the Past and Future of Public Administration," *Public Administration Review*, 61(2), 176–83.

Svara, J. H. (2006) "Introduction: Politicians and Administrators in the Political Process—A Review of Themes and Issues in the Literature," *International Journal of Public Administration*, 29(12), 953–76.

Svara, J. H. (2008) "Beyond Dichotomy: Dwight Waldo and the Intertwined Politics–Administration Relationship," *Public Administration Review*, 68(1): 46–52.

Taylor, F. W. (1947) *The Principles of Scientific Management* (New York: Harper and Brothers), originally published in 1911.

Tead, O. (1933) *Human Nature and Management: The Applications of Psychology to Executive Leadership*, 2nd ed. (New York: McGraw-Hill).

Teles, S. M. (2007) "Conservative Mobilization against Entrenched Liberalism," in P. Pierson and T. Skocpol (eds.) *The Transformation of American Politics: Activist Government and the Rise of Conservatism* (pp. 160–88) (Princeton: Princeton University Press).

Terry, L. D. (2002) *Leadership of Public Bureaucracies: The Administrator as Conservator*, 2nd ed. (Armonk, NY: M. E. Sharpe).

Terry, L. D. (2005) "The Thinning of Administrative Institutions in the Hollow State," *Administration & Society*, 37(4), 426–44.

The National Commission on Fiscal Responsibility and Reform (2010) "The Moment of Truth" (Washington, DC: The White House), December.

Thelen, K. (1999) "Historical Institutionalism and Comparative Politics," *Annual Review of Political Science*, 2, 369–404.

Thielemann, G. S., and J. Stewart Jr (1996) "A Demand-Side Perspective on the Importance of Representative Bureaucracy: AIDS, Ethnicity, Gender, and Sexual Orientation," *Public Administration Review*, 56(2), 168–73.

Thomas, J. C. (1986) *Between Citizen and City: Neighborhood Organizations and Urban Politics in Cincinnati* (Lawrence: University Press of Kansas).

Thompson, F. J. (ed.) (1993) *Revitalizing State and Local Public Service: Strengthening Performance, Accountability, and Citizen Confidence*, National Commission on the State and Local Public Service (San Francisco: Jossey-Bass).

Thompson, F. J. (2008) "State and Local Governance Fifteen Years Later: Enduring and New Challenges," *Public Administration Review*, 68(S1), S8–19.

Throntveit, T. (2013) "Philosophical Pragmatism and the Constitutional Watershed of 1912," *Political Science Quarterly*, 128(4), 617–51.

Tonn, J. C. (2003) *Mary P. Follett: Creating Democracy, Transforming Management* (New Haven: Yale University Press).

Trachtenberg, A. (2007) *The Incorporation of America: Culture and Society in the Gilded Age* (New York: Hill and Wang).

True, J. L., B. D. Jones, and F. R. Baumgartner (2007) "Punctuated-Equilibrium Theory: Explaining Stability and Change in Public Policymaking," in P. A. Sabatier (ed.) *Theories of the Policy Process* (pp. 155–88) (Boulder: Westview Press).

Tulgan, B. (1997) *The Manager's Pocket Guide to Generation X* (Amherst, MA: HRD Press).

Underhill, J., and R. A. Oman (2007) "A Critical Review of the Sweeping Federal Civil Service Changes: The Case of the Departments of Homeland Security and Defense," *Review of Public Personnel Administration*, 27(4), 401–20.

United Nations Development Programme (2006) *Institutional Reform and Change Management: Managing Change in Public Sector Organizations* (New York: Capacity Building and Development Group, UNDP).

Van Riper, P. (1958) *The History of the United States Civil Service* (Evanston, IL: Row, Peterson).

Van Vliet, M. (1993) "Environmental Regulation of Business: Options and Constraints for Communicative Governance," in J. Kooiman (ed.) *Modern Governance: New Government-Society Interactions* (pp. 105–18) (London: SAGE).

Vogel, D. (1984) "Why Businessmen Distrust Their State: The Political Consciousness of American Corporate Executives," *British Journal of Political Science*, 8(1), 45–78.

Vogel, D. (1989) *Fluctuating Fortunes: The Political Power of Business in America* (New York: Basic Books).

Wagenaar, H., and S. D. N. Cook (2003) "Understanding Policy Practices: Action, Dialectic, and Deliberation in Policy Analysis," in M. A. Hajer and H. Wagenaar (eds.) *Deliberative*

Policy Analysis: Understanding Governance in the Network Society (pp. 139–71) (Cambridge: Cambridge University Press).

Waldo, D. (1948) *The Administrative State: A Study of the Political Theory of American Public Administration* (New York: Ronald Press).

Waldo, D. (1952) "Development of a Theory of Democratic Administration," *American Political Science Review*, 46(1), 81–103.

Waldo, D. (1984) *The Administrative State: A Study of the Political Theory of American Public Administration*, 2nd ed. (New York: Holmes & Meier).

Wamsley, G. L., and M. N. Zald (1973) "The Political Economy of Public Organizations," *Public Administration Review*, 33(1), 62–73.

Wamsley, G. L., R. N. Bacher, C. T. Goodsell, P. S. Kronenberg, J. A. Rohr, C. M. Stivers, O. F. White, and J. F. Wolf (1990) *Refounding Public Administration* (Newbury Park, CA: SAGE).

Weick, K. E. (1984) "Small Wins: Redefining the Scale of Social Problems," *American Psychologist*, 39(1), 40–9.

Weiss, C. H. (1980) "Knowledge Creep and Decision Accretion," *Science Communication*, 1(3), 381–404.

Weiss, C. H. (1989) "Congressional Committees as Users of Analysis," *Journal of Policy Analysis and Management*, 8(3), 411–31.

West, J. P. (2005) "Managing an Aging Workforce: Trends, Issues, and Strategies," in S. E. Condrey (ed.) *Handbook of Human Resources Management in Government*, 2nd ed. (pp. 164–88) (San Francisco: Jossey-Bass).

West, W. F. (2005) "The Institutionalization of Regulatory Review: Organizational Stability and Responsive Competence at OIRA," *Presidential Studies Quarterly*, 35(1), 76–93.

West, W. F. (2006) "Presidential Leadership and Administrative Coordination: Examining the Theory of a Unified Executive," *Presidential Studies Quarterly*, 36(3), 433–56.

West, W. F. (2011) *Program Budgeting and the Performance Movement: The Elusive Quest for Efficiency in Government* (Washington, DC: Georgetown University Press).

White, L. D. (1933) *Trends in Public Administration* (New York: McGraw-Hill).

Wiebe, R. H. (1967) *The Search for Order, 1877–1920* (New York: Hill and Wang).

Wildavsky, A. (1979) *Speaking Truth to Power: The Art and Craft of Policy Analysis* (New Brunswick, NJ: Transaction Publishers).

Wildavsky, A. (1979) *The Politics of the Budgetary Process*, 3rd ed. (Boston: Little, Brown).

Wildavsky, A. (1992) *The New Politics of the Budgetary Process*, 2nd ed. (New York: HarperCollins).

Wilkins, V. M., and L. R. Keiser (2006) "Linking Passive and Active Representation by Gender: The Case of Child Support Agencies," *Journal of Public Administration Research and Theory*, 16(1), 87–102.

Willoughby, W. F. (1919) *An Introduction to the Study of the Government of Modern States* (New York: Century).

Wilson, J. H. (1992) *Herbert Hoover: Forgotten Progressive* (Long Grove, IL: Waveland Press).

Wilson, W. (1887) "The Study of Administration," *Political Science Quarterly*, 2(2), 197–222.

Wolf, D. A., and A. A. Amirkhanyan (2010) "Demographic Change and Its Public Sector Consequences," *Public Administration Review*, 70(S1), S12–23.

Wood, B. D., and J. Bohte (2004) "Political Transaction Costs and the Politics of Administrative Design," *Journal of Politics*, 66(1), 176–202.

Wood, G. S. (2002) *The American Revolution: A History* (New York: Modern Library).

Wood, G. S. (2008) *The Purpose of the Past: Reflections on the Uses of History* (New York: Penguin Press).

World Commission on Environment and Development (1987) *Our Common Future* (New York: Oxford University Press).

Wright, D. S. (1990) "Federalism, Intergovernmental Relations, and Intergovernmental Management: Historical Reflections and Conceptual Comparisons," *Public Administration Review*, 50(2), 168–78.

Yackee, J. W., and S. W. Yackee (2006) "A Bias towards Business? Assessing Interest Group Influence on the U.S. Bureaucracy," *Journal of Politics*, 68(1), 128–39.

Yanow, D. (2003) "Accessing Local Knowledge," in M. A. Hajer and H. Wagenaar (eds.) *Deliberative Policy Analysis: Understanding Governance in the Network Society* (pp. 228–46) (Cambridge: Cambridge University Press).

Index

Made in the USA
Columbia, SC
17 August 2019